THE LIFE AND TEACHINGS
OF THE
NEW TESTAMENT APOSTLES

Also edited by Richard Neitzel Holzapfel and Thomas A. Wayment

THE LIFE AND TEACHINGS OF JESUS CHRIST

Volume 1

From Bethlehem through the Sermon on the Mount

Volume 2

From the Transfiguration through the Triumphal Entry

Volume 3

*From the Last Supper through the Resurrection:
The Savior's Final Hours*

THE LIFE AND TEACHINGS
OF THE
NEW TESTAMENT APOSTLES

FROM THE DAY OF PENTECOST THROUGH THE APOCALYPSE

EDITED BY
RICHARD NEITZEL HOLZAPFEL
& THOMAS A. WAYMENT

DESERET BOOK

Salt Lake City, Utah

For Margaret McConkie Pope, my religion teacher at Brigham Young University in 1973—the right person at the right time in the right place

—*Richard Neitzel Holzapfel*

To Cathryne Ivory Wayment, for your pure heart and open arms

—*Thomas A. Wayment*

© 2010 Richard Neitzel Holzapfel and Thomas A. Wayment

All rights reserved. No part of this book may be reproduced in any form or by any means without permission in writing from the publisher, Deseret Book Company, P. O. Box 30178, Salt Lake City, Utah 84130. This work is not an official publication of The Church of Jesus Christ of Latter-day Saints. The views expressed herein are the responsibility of the authors and do not necessarily represent the position of the Church or of Deseret Book Company.

Deseret Book is a registered trademark of Deseret Book Company.

Visit us at DeseretBook.com

Library of Congress Cataloging-in-Publication Data
The life and teachings of the New Testament apostles : from the day of Pentecost through the Apocalypse / edited by Richard Neitzel Holzapfel and Thomas A. Wayment.
    p. cm.
  Includes bibliographical references and index.
  ISBN 978-1-60641-824-6 (hardbound : alk. paper)
  1. Bible. N.T.—Criticism, interpretation, etc. 2. Apostles. 3. Church history—Primitive and early church, ca. 30–600.   I. Holzapfel, Richard Neitzel. II. Wayment, Thomas A.
  BS2361.3.L55 2010
  225.6—dc22
                                                                                    2010019363

Printed in the United States of America
Publishers Printing, Salt Lake City, UT

10 9 8 7 6 5 4 3 2 1

CONTENTS

Acknowledgments   vii
Key to Abbreviations   ix

Introduction: A Distant and Foreign Land: Acts through Revelation   1
Richard Neitzel Holzapfel and Thomas A. Wayment

1. From Jesus to the Written Gospels: The Oral Origins of the Gospel   11
Thomas A. Wayment

2. The Church of the First Century   35
Gaye Strathearn and Joshua M. Sears

3. Unto the Uttermost Part of the Earth   63
Richard Neitzel Holzapfel and Thomas A. Wayment

4. The Impact of Gentile Conversions in the Greco-Roman World   80
Eric D. Huntsman

5. The Roman World outside Judea   97
Eric D. Huntsman

6. From Temple and Synagogue to House-Church   117
Richard Neitzel Holzapfel

CONTENTS

7. The Continuing Influence of the Family of Jesus
   in Early Christianity — 134
   Thomas A. Wayment

8. The Epistle of James: Anti-Pauline Rhetoric
   or a New Emphasis? — 157
   Brian M. Hauglid

9. James, First and Second Peter, and Jude:
   Epistles of Persecution — 171
   John Gee

10. John's Later Ministry and His Banishment
    to Patmos: The Background to Revelation — 191
    Richard D. Draper

11. Imperial Cult and the Beasts of Revelation — 221
    Eric D. Huntsman and Cecilia M. Peek

12. The End of the Early Church — 250
    Kent P. Jackson

13. *Sōma Sēma:* The Influence of "The Body Is a Tomb"
    in Early Christian Debates and the New Testament — 276
    Gaye Strathearn

14. The Creeds and Councils — 299
    Jennifer C. Lane

    Conclusion: Profound Effects of the Second
    Half of the New Testament on the Gospel — 330
    Richard Neitzel Holzapfel and Thomas A. Wayment

    Contributors — 343
    Scripture Index — 345
    Subject Index — 351

ACKNOWLEDGMENTS

We thank our colleagues at Brigham Young University and BYU–Hawaii who have contributed to this volume and to its companion three-volume series, The Life and Teachings of Jesus Christ. It has been a tremendous experience to work with such articulate and skilled scholars and teachers. These volumes have been made much stronger through the collaboration.

Additionally, we thank Deseret Book Company for publishing a book that is both scholarly and faithful in its approach. Cory Maxwell has been especially encouraging over the years, trusting us to provide a work that is accessible and meaningful. He and Suzanne Brady, Richard Erickson, and Rachael Ward have helped us get our ideas into a publishable shape.

Again, as with two previous volumes, we thank Walter Rane for providing the cover art. His willingness to join us is much appreciated.

We likewise appreciate the help of our dedicated student research assistants, including Emily Broadbent, Nick Brown, Alan Taylor Farnes, Berit Green, and Christopher Keneipp.

Finally, we thank our many readers over the years who have encouraged us to continue writing and pushing ourselves to look at the stories of the second half of the New Testament with fresh eyes.

KEY TO ABBREVIATIONS

BOOKS

ABD David Noel Freedman, ed., *The Anchor Bible Dictionary*, 6 vols. (New York: Doubleday, 1992).

AJ Josephus, *Antiquities of the Jews,* trans. Ralph Marcus, Loeb Classical Library (Cambridge, Massachusetts: Harvard University Press, 1943).

GEL William F. Arndt and F. Wilbur Gingrich, *A Greek-English Lexicon of the New Testament and Other Early Christian Literature,* ed. Frederick W. Danker, 3d ed. (Chicago: University of Chicago Press, 2000).

JW Josephus, *The Jewish War,* trans. H. St. J. Thackeray, Loeb Classical Library (Cambridge, Massachusetts: Harvard University Press, 1927–28).

TDNT Gerhard Kittel and Gerhard Friedrich, eds., *Theological Dictionary of the New Testament,* ed. and trans. Geoffrey W. Bromiley, 10 vols. (Grand Rapids, Michigan: Eerdmans, 1964–99).

TPJS Joseph Smith, *Teachings of the Prophet Joseph Smith,* sel. Joseph Fielding Smith (Salt Lake City: Deseret Book, 1976).

KEY TO ABBREVIATIONS

BIBLE VERSIONS AND STUDY AIDS

ESV   English Standard Version.
JST   Joseph Smith Translation.
KJV   King James Version.
LXX   Septuagint.
NIV   New International Version.
NJB   New Jerusalem Bible.
NRSV New Revised Standard Version.
RSV   Revised Standard Version.

INTRODUCTION

A DISTANT AND FOREIGN LAND: ACTS THROUGH REVELATION

RICHARD NEITZEL HOLZAPFEL AND THOMAS A. WAYMENT

Visiting the past is like visiting a foreign country, and as a result we find ourselves in a completely foreign place when we read Acts through Revelation, the second half of the New Testament. There we encounter personal names that do not fall from our lips naturally, such as Tryphena and Tryphosa (two fellow laborers of the Apostle Paul), Dionysius the Areopagite (one of Paul's converts in Athens), and Nymphas (leader of a local house-church somewhere in Asia). We are often challenged by unfamiliar geographical place-names not easily placed on our mental maps of the New Testament world, such as Hierapolis (a city where missionaries established a congregation of Saints), Amphipolis and Apollonia (two towns Paul passed through in Macedonia), and Cenchrea (a port city of Corinth and the home of Phebe, one of Paul's fellow laborers).

Additionally, we are less familiar with the timeline of the twenty-three books in the second half of the New Testament than we are with the timeline of the Gospels. The stories in the Gospels are generally well-known to us. The Nativity story and the accounts of the Savior's Atonement, Crucifixion, and Resurrection are retold often, particularly during the Christmas and Easter seasons. There are no similar holidays or special seasons that provide an opportunity to tell and retell the stories of the second half of the New Testament. Latter-day Saints, like many Christians, do not celebrate the Jewish holy days (holidays) that were familiar to Peter, James, Mary, Paul, and other first-century Jewish-Christians. We have few calendar dates on which to hang the stories when we read the second half of the New Testament.

Virtually all New Testament artists depict scenes from the life of Jesus; few depict the events and stories of Acts through Revelation. An exception to this is Walter Rane's depiction of the stoning of Stephen, entitled *I Saw the Son of Man Standing on the Right Hand of God* (which appears on the cover of this volume), an event that serves to introduce the reader to the man who became the Apostle Paul. Many may have visited the sites in the Holy Land associated with Jesus' ministry recounted in the Gospels. Far fewer have visited the sites mentioned in the second half of the New Testament, except a few famous tourist destinations such as Ephesus and Athens. Significant New Testament sites such as Damascus (in Syria), Tarsus (in modern southeast Turkey), Philippi (in modern northern Greece), Melita (modern Malta), and Puteoli (north of modern Naples) are difficult to get to and are generally not on a typical travel itinerary.

Furthermore, unlike the four Gospels, the remainder of the New Testament contains only one text with a storyline at all: the book of Acts. The remaining books are mostly letters (Hebrews and Revelation are exceptions in some ways), which by their very nature do not provide any historical context—hence, no story. And if the archaic King James English sometimes presents a roadblock to negotiate the nuances of Matthew, Mark, Luke, and John, it is perhaps doubly so with Paul's letters.

Finally, the focus of the second half of the New Testament is different from that of the Gospels. Jesus dominates almost every verse in the Gospels. Even in those passages where He is physically absent (for example, Matthew 26:14–16), the stories still focus on Jesus through people who came to know Him or knew of Him. In the second half of the New Testament, others take center stage. To be sure, they preach in Jesus' name, and once in a while they quote Him or mention some historic moment in His life (see, for example, Acts 20:35; 1 Corinthians 11:23–25). Nevertheless, the story centers on what they did and what they said as His witnesses.

The Coming of Paul

We believe that Jesus is the fulfillment of the long history of the people of Israel in the Old Testament, and He is the central focus of the Gospels. We also believe that the voice of Jesus permeates the second half of the New Testament. Nevertheless, we recognize that another person dominates the second half of the New Testament. His name is Paul, the second most frequently mentioned figure in the New Testament. Of the twenty-seven New Testament books, fourteen are associated with Paul as author, and one (the book of Acts) focuses principally on parts of his life and ministry.

We are grateful beyond measure that Luke recorded what he knew about Paul. Through the book of Acts we know Paul first as Saul, a persecutor of the disciples of Jesus (see Acts 8:1–3); then as an ardent disciple of Jesus after he met the risen Lord on the road to Damascus (see Acts 9:1–20); and finally as a great missionary who eventually made his way to the very heart of the Roman Empire, the imperial capital where the story of Acts ends (Acts 28:16–31). Paul's efforts to spread the gospel provide some of the most exciting and descriptive travel narratives from antiquity as he journeyed through much of the Mediterranean basin. His profound effect on history, however, is not so much in the miles he traveled as in the cultural frontier he crossed as the Lord's instrument to take the "good news" to the Gentiles. All this was not easy, nor was it without a price (see 2 Corinthians 11:22–28). Yet many of Paul's contemporaries did not appreciate his message. The book of Acts and Paul's own letters offer strong clues that his mission and message faced opposition not only from Gentiles and Jews but also from other Christians (see Galatians 2:4).

Luke and Paul

As we begin our journey to a faraway land in a time when Roman emperors ruled the Mediterranean basin; when philosophers, Jews, and Christians challenged and confronted the gods of Mount Olympus; and when a small group of Jews began to proclaim the crucified Jesus as Messiah and Lord, "unto the Jews a stumbling-block, and unto the Greeks foolishness" (1 Corinthians 1:23), we need to discuss the relationship between Luke and Paul—the two authors who provide most of the texts on which we will base our discussions in this volume.

Their writings are essential. Without Luke and Paul, we would know very little about the events following Jesus' death, Resurrection, and Ascension. We would know virtually nothing about the first decades of the Church, including the events of Pentecost (about A.D. 30) and the Jerusalem Conference (about A.D. 49). We certainly would know nothing about Paul's early career and his call by Jesus (about A.D. 33). The earliest accounts of the Last Supper and Jesus' suffering, death, burial, and Resurrection would be those found in the Gospels themselves instead of Paul's accounts of those events written at least a decade earlier than Matthew, Mark, Luke, and John (see 1 Corinthians 11:23–26).

In the writings of both Luke and Paul, we have the basis for reconstructing the early history of the Church and Paul's own life. Certainly we would appreciate more information that would help us piece together this story more accurately because there are significant gaps. Who has not wished that Luke had provided a third installment of his story? We would like to know what happened

INTRODUCTION: A DISTANT AND FOREIGN LAND

to Paul after his two-year imprisonment in Rome. Who has not wished that additional letters of Paul could have survived the ravages of time (see 1 Corinthians 5:9) or that he had written more letters explaining what he knew, felt, and experienced. Given the difficulties and expense in preparing a text in the ancient world, however, it is quite remarkable that we have as much as we do. Given that others prepared alternative interpretations of the story and fanciful accounts of Jesus' early life, we are fortunate that the early Church preserved an excellent collection of documents. Not one of them is a forgery or uninspired—this is a miracle.

Although Paul's letters provide us the most reliable clues to his life, mission, and message, another source is Luke's account, the book of Acts. Some scholars question whether Acts can provide anything reliable about Paul. However, there is no reason to doubt the added historical information about Paul found in Acts, especially if it does not contradict data provided by Paul in his own letters.

Luke was likely the traveling companion of Paul at times, if the famous "we" passages are to be taken seriously (see Acts 16:10; 20:14; 21:1–18; 27:1–28:31). The book of Acts also suggests Luke knew stories about Paul from fellow laborers whom Luke met along the way. Because the prologue to the Gospel of Luke indicates that eyewitness accounts were delivered to him, Luke may have even interviewed these eyewitnesses himself (Luke 1:1–3).

The Gospel of Luke and the Book of Acts

Luke is identified as the author of two books in the New Testament—the Gospel of Luke and the Acts of the Apostles. The prologues of both Luke and Acts encourage the reader to see the two books as part of one work, perhaps deserving the designation "Luke–Acts" (see Luke 1:1–4; Acts 1:1–3).

One tragic and likely unintended consequence of how the New Testament finally took shape is the separation between Luke's writings when the Gospel of John was placed between them. Luke most likely intended and imagined that his books would be read and heard together. As a result, certain themes are maintained in both, and an assumption is made that those who read his text would see the interconnection between the vocabulary as well as the stories and themes as they build upon each other. For example, we might miss the fact that the "women" mentioned in Acts 1 have already been identified previously in the Gospel (see Luke 8:1–3) and that their significance is already known (see Luke 23:49, 55).

Another example of the connection between the Gospel of Luke and the book of Acts is illustrated by the mention of two men. In Luke we read of Jesus, Peter, James, and John ascending a mountain: "And it came to pass about an eight days after these sayings, he took Peter and John and James, and went up into a mountain to pray" (Luke 9:28). On the mount, Luke says, "As [Jesus] prayed, the fashion of his countenance was altered, and his raiment was white and glistering. And, behold, there talked with him two men, which were Moses and Elias [the Greek form of Elijah]: who appeared in glory, and spake of his decease [departure, "exodus"] which he should accomplish at Jerusalem" (Luke 9:29–31). Later, at the end of the Gospel of Luke, we read a story of the empty tomb: "Now upon the first day of the week, very early in the morning, they came unto the sepulchre, bringing the spices which they had prepared, and certain others with them. And they found the stone rolled away from the sepulchre. And they entered in, and found not the body of the Lord Jesus. And it came to pass, as they were much perplexed thereabout, behold, two men stood by them in shining garments" (Luke 24:1–4).

Luke had previously identified the women in this story, as noted above (see Luke 8:1–3; cf. 23:49, 55). But what may be overlooked is that he did the same for the two men (see Luke 9:30); they are most likely Moses and Elias (Elijah). In this case he describes the men in the same terms he used earlier—appearing in glory with shining garments. Finally, at the beginning of Acts, we read of Jesus' Ascension: "And when he had spoken these things, while they beheld, he was taken up; and a cloud received him out of their sight. And while they looked steadfastly toward heaven as he went up, behold, two men stood by them in white apparel" (Acts 1:9–10). Again, Luke highlights the presence of two men (Moses and Elijah), who this time appear in "white apparel."

Only after we identify the common thread of two heavenly beings present on three occasions do we ask why Luke tells us these interconnected stories in the first place. In this case, Luke's purpose in relating these three stories is most likely to emphasize that both the Law, represented by Moses, and the Prophets, represented by Elijah—two major divisions of Jewish scripture—witness all three significant events of Jesus' ministry. First, they witness the prophecies of His departure; second, they witness that He rose and left the tomb empty; and third, they witness that He ascended to heaven. In other words, just as Jesus said: "These are the words which I spake unto you, while I was yet with you, that *all things must be fulfilled, which were written in the law of Moses, and in the prophets, and in the psalms, concerning me.* Then opened he their understanding, that they might understand the scriptures, and said unto them, Thus it is written, and thus it behooved Christ to suffer, and to rise from the dead the third day" (Luke 24:44–46; emphasis added).

Many more examples demonstrate how important it is to read the book of Acts in the context of the Gospel of Luke. Only by carefully reading them together is it possible to see connections between seemingly separate stories or incidents that Luke likely intended. As we read Acts in the context of the Gospel of Luke, we will notice subtle connections that make his writings some of the most sophisticated literary texts in the New Testament.

Jesus and Paul

Before we begin our journey to the world of the second half of the New Testament, we should briefly talk about Jesus and Paul. In so many ways they were different, living mostly in different worlds. Jesus was, of course, a Jew living among pockets of Gentiles in the Holy Land when the Roman eagle was planted firmly in Judean soil. Paul, in contrast, was a citizen of at least three worlds: Jewish, Roman, and Christian.

According to Luke, Paul was born outside the Holy Land. Unlike Jesus, Paul sat at the feet of one of the great Jewish scholars of the period, Gamaliel (Acts 22:3). Paul was likely fluent in both Aramaic and Greek and had some knowledge of Latin. Jesus, on the other hand, spoke Aramaic and little Greek (this point is vigorously debated, but thus far it is indeterminable given the lack of direct evidence). Paul wrote letters and traveled widely throughout the Mediterranean basin. Jesus, on the other hand, wrote nothing that we know of and limited His travels to a rather confined area of Galilee and Judea.

Jesus' missionary strategy was basically limited to Jews living in hamlets, villages, and small towns, most lacking the features of Greco-Roman town planning or construction, such as symmetrical streets, red-tiled roofs, monumental public buildings, and ornamented fountains and pools. Jesus deliberately avoided the large cities, except Jerusalem, where the temple was. The second largest city (Sepphoris, located only a few miles from His home in Nazareth) is not even mentioned in the Gospels, and Tiberias, Herod Antipas's new capital, is mentioned only once in John (see John 6:23) and not at all by the other Gospel authors. Paul, on the other hand, limited his efforts to the large cities of the Roman Empire and expanded his audience well beyond his countrymen, the Jews. He traveled to Damascus, Antioch, Philippi, among other cities, and finally to Rome.

Jesus' audience was the poor: the least, the last, and the lost. Paul certainly preached among the poor, but they were the urban poor, a completely different group within the first century's rigid hierarchical society. Paul, however, often reached to higher social strata of the society—including more well-to-do individuals who could accommodate small congregations in their homes—and established house-churches that became important in the process of moving from synagogue to church (see, for example, Acts 16:14–15).

Because a Roman client-king ruled even the Galileans, Jesus was a member of a subject people. Paul, according to Luke, was a Roman citizen who was provided the benefits only a favored few enjoyed. Even after being sentenced to death, he was apparently spared the agony of crucifixion. According to tradition, Paul was beheaded—a quick, less painful, and less demeaning form of execution.

Finally, Jesus came "preaching the gospel of the kingdom of God, and saying, The time is fulfilled, and the kingdom of God is at hand: repent ye, and believe the gospel" (Mark 1:14–15). Paul, on the other hand, said, "But we preach Christ crucified" (1 Corinthians 1:23). In other words, the one who taught the "good news" was now Himself the good news. Certainly one was the Master and the other His "slave" (Romans 1:1; KJV "servant").

Even though Jesus and Paul lived about the same time, they lived in different worlds separated by social, economic, and political barriers difficult to imagine in today's pluralistic, democratic societies. Nevertheless, as Paul said, "For as many of you as have been baptized into Christ have put on Christ. There is neither Jew nor Greek, there is neither bond nor free, there is neither male nor female: for ye are all one in Christ Jesus. And if ye be Christ's, then are ye Abraham's seed, and heirs according to the promise" (Galatians 3:27–29).

The Beginning of the End

Although Luke and Paul both tell the story of a growing and vibrant Church, one with triumphs and setbacks, the later authors of the New Testament tell the story of a Church in decline, beset by inner dissension and mutiny (Greek, *apostasia*). The problems faced by Peter, John, and Jude were not unique, but the fact that persecution and trial so fully color their writings does reveal the beginning of a breakdown in authority. The New Testament itself omits telling us whether any new Apostles were ordained after the middle of the first century, and indeed, 1–2 Peter, 1–3 John, Jude, and Revelation were all written in the last two or three decades of the first century and are thus from a time when the absence of Apostles was beginning to have an effect upon the fledgling Church.

The beginning of the Apostasy, which is documented in the later writings of the New Testament, is told through letters and not in narrative form. In essence, we are forced to reconstruct the events of the Apostasy through prophetic warnings and inspired counsel. We cannot know how the members responded to Peter's warning that fiery trials were coming or John's counsel to excommunicate the troublesome Diotrephes (3 John 1:9–10). We cannot even convincingly state that the majority of Christians fell away or disregarded counsel. It may very well be that the falling away of a minority of Christians (powerful and influential teachers and leaders) inflicted a catastrophe upon the majority.

Witnessing this increasingly hostile environment to faith, John recorded a significant revelation that he received concerning his day and the latter days, in which catastrophe, apostasy, restoration, and revelation would again find a balance. Harmony and free worship of the Lamb of God came only with a price; they would be the final result of a cataclysmic upheaval that would embroil all nations in war against God's people. This viewpoint may indeed parallel the feelings of the early Saints who felt at war with all nations: Jews, Gentiles, and even the Roman Empire. They were too few in number to win the battle, but John promised them that they would be sealed up, thus overcoming the fear of death and its temporary sting (see, for example, Revelation 7:13–17; 22:1–7).

I.

FROM JESUS TO THE WRITTEN GOSPELS: THE ORAL ORIGINS OF THE GOSPEL

THOMAS A. WAYMENT

But these are written, that ye might believe that Jesus is the Christ, the Son of God; and that believing ye might have life through his name.

JOHN 20:31

For nearly two centuries the form and content of the earliest Christian gospel has been the subject of heated scholarly debate. In fact, accepting the gospel stories at face value has most recently been considered naïve and historically uncritical. It is not enough to accept the truth that the Bible has not always been translated or transmitted correctly; instead, scholars question the very foundation of the message, whether Jesus' death was originally understood as a vicarious sacrifice, and whether Christianity itself is a colossal myth foisted upon the unsuspecting.[1]

Certainly these views seem extreme to many, but they dominate many scholarly discussions today. Nevertheless, this extreme

---

[1] Perhaps the most extreme form of this view is expressed by Burton L. Mack, *A Myth of Innocence: Mark and Christian Origins* (Philadelphia: Fortress Press, 1988).

view notwithstanding, it is possible to bring to bear careful scholarship, language training, and historical acumen to see the same evidence in a different light. In fact, the earliest documents in the New Testament—the preserved Christian hymns, Peter's discourse at Pentecost, and the letters of Paul and James—tell of a fascinatingly rich history, when believers in Christ faced setbacks and internal disputes yet also remained focused on a saving gospel message, a message of hope and salvation.

This chapter will not approach the question of the earliest Christian gospel through a discussion of the canonical process and which books were written first and which ones contain the earliest materials, although that would certainly be an interesting way to look at the issue.[2] Rather, it will look first at Peter's speech on the day of Pentecost and then at the earliest Christian hymns for traces of the earliest Christian teaching. It will then examine the structure of early Christian meetings and the content of the gospel message taught in them. Moving beyond those meetings, we will discuss Paul's presentation of the gospel as it is recorded shortly after the hymns were composed. In that early formative period before the fall of Jerusalem, when a Roman army destroyed the temple and occupied the city in A.D. 70, the missionary effort was dominated by a give-and-take relationship between Jewish-Christians in Judea and Gentile-Christians in Asia, Greece, and Rome. With the fall of Jerusalem and the flight of Christians to Pella, the center of the Church moved west, and with it the Church became almost uniquely Gentile. The fall of Jerusalem provided the impetus for writing the Gospels, and indeed some Gospel authors reached back to the Jews and some looked forward to the Gentiles. Finally, this

---

[2] For a collection of excellent studies on the formation of the canon and how the words of Jesus were preserved and shaped over time, see Kent P. Jackson and Frank F. Judd Jr., eds., *How the New Testament Came to Be* (Salt Lake City and Provo: Deseret Book and the Religious Studies Center, 2006).

chapter will consider the issue of Peter's authority, which lies behind the Gospel of Mark, and how the gospel message itself remained unchanged as questions of authority arose in the late first century during the postapostolic era.

Peter's Discourse on the Day of Pentecost

It is no mistake that one of the first things that Luke recounted in the book of Acts was Peter's discourse on the Day of Pentecost, which occurred roughly fifty days after Jesus' death during the Passover celebration. In Jesus' lifetime one of the central issues of the struggle between Jesus and His opponents was the issue of whether Jesus was the promised Messiah.[3] Certainly many other issues also divided the followers of Jesus and the Pharisees and Sadducees. The question is not simply a matter of whether Jesus was the Messiah but also of what it meant to be the Messiah. For Jews living at the time of Jesus, the Messiah was not a divine figure, and indeed the idea of a deliverer is more akin to what they expected.

The Old Testament provided the basis for this thinking when it applied the title to Cyrus. In Isaiah 45:1 the prophet refers to Cyrus, the Persian king, as a messiah: "Thus saith the Lord to his anointed [messiah], to Cyrus, whose right hand I have holden, to subdue nations before him; and I will loose the loins of kings, to open before him the two leaved gates; and the gates shall not be shut." Other passages from the Old Testament established the expectation that the Messiah would be a political, perhaps priestly leader (Numbers 24:17–19; 1 Kings 13:1–2; Ezekiel 37:22–26), whereas Jesus taught that He was the unanticipated Messiah who

---

[3] For a discussion of the evidence, see Jennifer C. Lane, "From Opposition to Hostility: Changing Reactions during Jesus' Ministry," in Richard Neitzel Holzapfel and Thomas A. Wayment, eds., *From the Transfiguration through the Triumphal Entry*, vol. 2 of The Life and Teachings of Jesus Christ (Salt Lake City: Deseret Book, 2006), 125–51.

would suffer (Matthew 16:21–22). The Gospel of John made the Messiah debate a central issue in the confrontations between Jesus and His opponents: "If thou be the Christ [Messiah], tell us plainly" (John 10:24).

Even though Peter's speech on the Day of Pentecost was written in Acts many years after the event took place, the speech may have been preserved primarily because it definitively answered the question of the Messiah's identity. It also addressed the challenges of the divide between Jewish-Christian and Gentile-Christian, which originated in the middle of the first century A.D. The speech is remarkable for several reasons, but the one that is particularly important in this discussion—namely the declaration *"that God hath made that same Jesus, whom ye have crucified, both Lord and Christ* [Messiah]" (Acts 2:36; emphasis added)—is perhaps one of the most profound declarations of the New Testament.

Peter established what later became a Christian practice of laying the foundation for the Lord's ministry through Old Testament prophecy. In this particular speech, Peter drew upon Joel 2:28–32 and Psalm 16:8–11; 110:1, with allusions to Psalm 132:11 and 2 Samuel 7:12–13. It is important to note that this speech, which was heavily influenced by the Old Testament and followed very closely the wording of the Greek translation of that book (the Septuagint or LXX), would have been comprehensible primarily to Diaspora Jews who had traveled to Jerusalem for the Feast of Pentecost and who were intimately familiar with the Old Testament prophecies.

Drawing in his audience using an idea that all Jews would agree to, namely that salvation could be obtained through calling upon the name of the Lord—"And it shall come to pass, that whosoever shall call on the name of the Lord shall be saved" (Acts 2:21)—Peter alluded to the traditional idea that Jehovah saves. Through prophetic reference, Peter was able to reach out to fellow Jews, but the surprise came when he declared that Jesus is the Lord who saves (see Acts 2:36). Such a testimony would certainly have been shocking to many and probably blasphemous to some. However, Luke carefully laid a foundation demonstrating that Jesus' name genuinely saves, "that by the name of Jesus Christ of Nazareth . . . doth this man stand here before you whole" (Acts 4:10; see also Acts 2:38; 3:6; 16:18).

Peter's re-contextualization of the identity of Jehovah is not surprising inasmuch as the process of laying an Old Testament foundation for understanding Jesus' ministry had probably already begun in His lifetime. However, a Jewish audience would not have missed the dramatic conclusion, the declaration of Jesus as "Lord and Christ" (Greek, *kyrion . . . kai Christon*). The title "Christ" hearkens back to the debates which raged during His mortal ministry, but the declaration of Jesus as "Lord" unequivocally announced that Jesus is God, the "LORD" of the Old Testament.[4] Such a declaration of Jesus' divine status leaves no room for equivocation, and Luke placed it firmly at the beginning of the book of Acts before relating any apostolic or other missions. It is also important to note that Luke established this teaching as an apostolic witness, "whereof we are all witnesses" (Acts 2:32), thus anticipating Paul, "For I delivered unto you first of all that which I also received" (1 Corinthians 15:3).

The Earliest Christian Hymns

A number of early Christian hymn fragments have been preserved in the Epistles and Gospels, and although they were at times only paraphrased, these early hymns consistently taught the exaltation of Jesus Christ as Lord, thus confirming Peter's testimony in Acts 2:32.[5] Because this chapter focuses on the content of the

---

[4] Arndt and Gingrich, *GEL*, "*kyrios*."

[5] Some scholars have seen a number of other hymns in the New Testament Epistles and Gospels. See, for example, F. Forrester Church and Terrence J. Mulry, *The*

earliest gospel message, it cannot digress to discuss the early hymns at length. These hymns are typically established through the poetic parallelism of the Greek New Testament text and their divergence in structure from the context in which they were recorded. And even though these early hymns come from different decades and authors who may not even have known one another, they still show a remarkable degree of similarity of language and thought.

Perhaps the most profound statement of any of the hymns comes from the author of the Philippian hymn, whom Paul quoted freely and without interpolation: "Who, being in the form of God, thought it not robbery *to be equal with God:* But made himself of no reputation, and took upon him the form of a servant, and was made in the likeness of men: And being found in fashion as a man, he humbled himself, and became obedient unto death, even the death of the cross. Wherefore *God also hath highly exalted him,* and given him a name which is above every name: That at the name of Jesus every knee should bow, of things in heaven, and things in earth, and things under the earth; *and that every tongue should confess that Jesus Christ is Lord,* to the glory of God the Father" (Philippians 2:6–11; emphasis added). The last sentence in particular preserved an early Christian declaration of faith, that as Peter declared, Jesus Christ is "LORD" (Greek, *kyrios*). Additionally, the hymn showed that the exaltation of Christ was the central component of early Christian teaching and that the cross of Christ was also a key doctrine. This hymn predated the writings of Paul—the earliest author in the New Testament—thus pushing the date for its composition into the two decades after Jesus' death.

Writing many decades later, the author of the Gospel of John again made the exaltation of Jesus the central theme of his Gospel

---

Macmillan Book of Earliest Christian Hymns (New York and London: Macmillan and Collier, 1988). For a critical study of the hymns, see Daniel Liderbach, *Christ in the Early Christian Hymns* (New York: Paulist Press, 1998).

through the quotation of an earlier hymn, sometimes referred to as the Logos Hymn: "In the beginning was the Word, and the Word was with God, *and the Word was God*" (John 1:1; emphasis added). The word translated as "Word" (Greek, *logos*) denotes "divine reason," "an account," or perhaps even "God's saving declaration" in Jesus. This hymn, written before the Gospel of John, declares the Word to be the Creator— "All things were made by him; and without him was not any thing made that was made" (John 1:3)— and thus again testifies that He is the "Lord." In this respect the hymn recorded in Colossians is very similar to the Logos Hymn: "For by him were all things created, that are in heaven, and that are in earth, visible and invisible, whether they be thrones, or dominions, or principalities, or powers: all things were created by him, and for him: And he is before all things, and by him all things consist" (Colossians 1:16–17). The uniformity in the message seems to be no coincidence, and it speaks to the very core of the Christian message: Jesus Christ is both Lord and Savior (see Colossians 1:15–20; 2 Timothy 2:11–13; Hebrews 1:1–4).

From these hymns, which preserve the earliest Christian writings that have survived the ravages of decay and neglect, it is apparent that, in its earliest form, the gospel message was in part a conversation with Jews who perhaps struggled with the idea that Jesus could be Lord. It is not a stretch of the imagination to envision Jews accepting Jesus as a great teacher or even being intrigued by His charismatic personality, but generating the faith necessary to leave behind a national identity, a deeply religious past in the law of Moses, and a uniquely Jewish way of life took more than a great teacher or an enigmatic persona. To Greeks this may have been enough, but to Jews it would have required the belief that

Jesus was indeed Lord and Christ.[6] It is no wonder then that the earliest declarations of faith made this the central issue.

Early Christian Meetings

In his *First Apology,* written between A.D. 147 and 161, Justin Martyr preserved one of the earliest descriptions of a Christian sacrament meeting, where both the ordinance of the bread and water were described. He also presented an important account of the content of their teaching. He wrote:

"And on the day called Sunday, all who live in cities or in the country gather together to one place, and the memoirs of the apostles or the writings of the prophets are read, as long as time permits; then, when the reader has ceased, the president verbally instructs, and exhorts to the imitation of these good things. Then we all rise together and pray, and, as we before said, when our prayer is ended, bread and wine and water[7] are brought, and the president in like manner offers prayers and thanksgivings, according to his ability, and the people assent, saying Amen; and there is a distribution to each, and a participation of that over which thanks have been given, and to those who are absent a portion is sent by the deacons."[8]

There is no historic reason to suppose that a radical change in meeting practice took place between the Apostles' era and the middle of the second century when Justin wrote his apology of the Christian faith. In fact, there is evidence in Paul's writings that

---

[6] Larry W. Hurtado, *Lord Jesus Christ: Devotion to Jesus in Earliest Christianity* (Grand Rapids, Mich.: Eerdmans, 2003), 29–52.

[7] The reference to bread and wine and water actually describes bread and wine being used for the sacrament, where the wine was mixed with water, as was the custom of the day.

[8] "The First Apology of Justin: Chapter LXVII.—Weekly Worship of the Christians," in *Ante-Nicene Fathers,* vol. 2, eds. Alexander Roberts, D.D. and James Donaldson, LL.D. (Peabody, Mass.: Hendrickson, 1999).

first-century meetings were very similar to what Justin described, if not identical to it: "How is it then, brethren? when ye come together, every one of you hath a psalm, hath a doctrine, hath a tongue, hath a revelation, hath an interpretation. Let all things be done unto edifying" (1 Corinthians 14:26). Justin's description specifically mentioned the content of what was taught in the meetings, while Paul's reference broadly described them. In those meetings, the Saints read "the memoirs of the apostles or the writings of the prophets," which indicates that already by the middle of the second century the Saints were focused not on the letters of Paul, which certainly would be described not as memoirs but as epistles, but they focused rather on the Gospels. They may have had other gospels written by Apostles (we now have two), but it is certain that this central core was the focus of their meetings. Moreover, the Saints *also* read the words of the Old Testament prophets, probably in their effort to demonstrate through earlier writings the prophetic anticipation and foundation of the atoning sacrifice and the promise of a Messiah.

Justin's note omitted any reference to reading from the Torah or reading from the Psalms or other books of the Old Testament precisely because Jesus Christ's atoning sacrifice was the center of those meetings and not the law of Moses, in which the Torah would have been the central focus. It was the gospel, or the good news, they proclaimed.

Paul's first letter to the Corinthians established his core message, which in many respects appears to have the tenor of a declaration of what was to be taught. It also followed the pattern of using the Old Testament to teach the truthfulness of the Lord's atoning sacrifice: "Moreover, brethren, I declare unto you the gospel which I preached unto you, which also ye have received, and wherein ye stand; by which also ye are saved, if ye keep in memory what I preached unto you, unless ye have believed in vain. For I delivered unto you first of all that which I also received, how that

Christ died for our sins according to the scriptures; and that he was buried, and that he arose again the third day according to the scriptures" (1 Corinthians 15:1–4).

In a more succinct form, Paul declared the essence of the gospel message in a threefold way: first, "Christ died for our sins"; second, "he was buried"; and third "he arose again the third day."[9] Each of these truths was demonstrated by reference to scripture ("according to the scriptures"), which certainly refers to the writings of the Old Testament, a practice continued in the days of Justin. The practice of reading the scriptures together as a branch and traditionally comparing the ministry of the Lord to the canonical scriptures (the Old Testament) went back to their days in the synagogue when the very same practice was observed; except in those instances the Old Testament was read, and those in attendance provided commentary as they sought answers to challenges of their day. In fact, Jesus participated in one such occurrence when the text in question spoke of His ministry and many in the crowd suspected that Jesus would make a declaration of its literal fulfillment in His ministry (Luke 4:16–30, which paraphrases Isaiah 61:1–2). Because Christianity found its most fertile ground in Diaspora synagogues (see, for example, Acts 18:26), it is no surprise then that the original proclamation would focus on the life of Jesus as confirmed through the prophets. The Old Testament was the foundation of

---

[9] This core gospel message is remarkably similar to Jesus' own definition of what the gospel entails in 3 Nephi 27:13–15: "Behold I have given unto you my gospel, and this is the gospel which I have given unto you—that I came into the world to do the will of my Father, because my Father sent me. And my Father sent me that I might be lifted up upon the cross; and after that I had been lifted up upon the cross, that I might draw all men unto me, that as I have been lifted up by men even so should men be lifted up by the Father, to stand before me, to be judged of their works, whether they be good or whether they be evil—and for this cause have I been lifted up; therefore, according to the power of the Father I will draw all men unto me, that they may be judged according to their works."

their original faith, and it is natural that they would look to it for the foundation of their new faith.

Another important point of emphasis in Paul's teaching is found in the following verses where he maintained that the gospel message is also apostolic in nature: "And that he was seen of Cephas, then of the twelve: After that, he was seen of above five hundred brethren at once; of whom the greater part remain unto this present, but some are fallen asleep. After that, he was seen of James; then of all the apostles. And last of all he was seen of me also, as of one born out of due time" (1 Corinthians 15:5–8). This list of appearances was not simply generated for historical interest, in which case Mary Magdalene should head the list. On the contrary, the Apostles and subapostolic witnesses were given in 1 Corinthians 15 specifically to confirm the authenticity of the gospel Paul preached. In this respect the Apostles stood alongside the prophets of the Old Testament, testifying and confirming the truth of the threefold gospel message.

Other important elements of Paul's message can be found in 1 Corinthians 11:23–25: "For I have received of the Lord that which also I delivered unto you, That the Lord Jesus the same night in which he was betrayed took bread: and when he had given thanks, he brake it, and said, Take, eat: this is my body, which is broken for you: this do in remembrance of me. After the same manner also he took the cup, when he had supped, saying, This cup is the new testament in my blood: this do ye, as oft as ye drink it, in remembrance of me." Here, Paul testified that in addition to the threefold gospel he taught, he also taught that the sacrament administered on the night of the Last Supper was a "new testament" or new covenant that they should observe in remembrance of Jesus' death.

The language that Paul used in each of these references indicates that he had received the message from others, or in other words, he passed on the gospel in the same way that he received it. Specifically, Paul "received" (Greek, *parelabon*) or "learned, accepted, or passed on" (1 Corinthians 11:23) the teachings that he had delivered to the Saints, and his concern in emphasizing this point is particularly important because it shows solidarity with the brethren and Apostles of the Lord. Later in the epistle, Paul reminded the Saints that they had also received the gospel, using the same verb that he had used when speaking of his own instruction in the things of the Lord (1 Corinthians 15:1). Luke, who was probably influenced by Paul, used precisely the same language, "*Even as they delivered them unto us,* which from the beginning were eyewitnesses, and ministers of the word" (Luke 1:2; emphasis added). The verb used in each of these instances (Greek, *paralambanō*) conveys the idea that the thing received was preserved intact. It contains no hint that the message was received and then altered, adapted, or massaged. For both Paul and Luke, the gospel they taught is the same gospel that the Apostles and eyewitnesses taught to them. It is also important to note that Paul frequently offered his own opinion when he felt the need to apply the threefold gospel to challenging situations, but the gospel itself remained unchanged (see, for example, 1 Corinthians 7:12).

In his Epistle to the Galatians, Paul cursed those who preached a false or altered gospel. In addition, Paul was careful to note that his testimony of the Lord was received through revelation. Some critics have attempted to discredit Paul because his witness—as expressed to the Galatian Saints—was simply derived from those who had known the Lord personally, thus making Paul's testimony hearsay: "I marvel that ye are so soon removed from him that called you into the grace of Christ unto another gospel: Which is not another; but there be some that trouble you, and would pervert the gospel of Christ" (Galatians 1:6–7). This reference to "another gospel" clearly indicates that the gospel of Jesus Christ was so fully articulated that it could be completely differentiated from a false gospel. Interestingly, this reference in Galatians is preserved in one of the earliest writings in the New Testament before the canonical Gospels were written. Even though the letter to the Galatians does not expressly state the fulness of the gospel he taught, Paul reminded the Saints that they had received the gospel from him: "If any man preach any other gospel unto you than that ye have received, let him be accursed" (Galatians 1:9). Paul trusted that the Saints would know the gospel well enough that they would be able to reject a spurious gospel, underlining his trust that they had heard the threefold gospel many times.

One key element of Paul's speech, however, may be taken to mean that he, in fact, did not receive the gospel from others, but rather that it was revealed to him, thus opening the door to critics who wish to see Paul as the creator of the Christian religion rather than Paul the missionary of the apostolic faith: "But I certify you, brethren, that the gospel which was preached of me is not after man. For I neither received it of man, neither was I taught it, but by the revelation of Jesus Christ" (Galatians 1:11–12). This would seem to imply that, contrary to his later statements, the gospel Paul taught was not passed on to him from others.

The question at hand in Galatians is whether Paul received *any* revelation or whether the gospel he taught was acquired in the same way that one learns an academic subject: "For ye have heard of my conversation in time past in the Jews' religion. . . . And profited in the Jews' religion above many my equals in mine own nation, being more exceedingly zealous of the traditions of my fathers" (Galatians 1:13–14). This describes Paul's academic training or the way in which he learned other subjects, but his Christian training was inherently different; it was a prophetic call: "It pleased God, who separated me from my mother's womb, and called me by his grace, to reveal his Son in me" (Galatians 1:15–16). Paul intentionally contrasted two methods of learning truth: the academic route and revelation. For Paul, the two experiences were fundamentally different. Judaism was a scholastic experience, and Christianity was revelatory, although he was careful to add that later he sought out a knowledge of the history of Jesus and the Apostles and other matters (see Galatians 1:18–19).

What is confusing at times is that Paul's letters confronted many other issues, such as Christians going to court against other Christians, customs of hair, questions of unclean foods, donations to the poor, spiritual gifts, and many other challenging issues. In fact, the letters of Paul were filled with questions but were frequently devoid of doctrinal discussion. This silence has led many commentators to assume that there was no consistent gospel message early on and that the gospel of Jesus developed over time to meet the needs of the Church. But this view misses the fact that what Paul taught prior to the letters constitutes the gospel he received from others and the testimony he received through revelation and that the letters represent application of the gospel with Jesus as the central focus.

In many ways it was a difficult time, as Christians transitioned from the synagogue to house-churches. Paul's practice, "And he reasoned in the synagogue every sabbath, and persuaded the Jews and the Greeks" (Acts 18:4), brought in converts but also established the eventual need to make a clean break with the synagogue at some point in time. When Christians left the synagogue, or, as Jesus prophesied, they were thrown out—"They shall put you out of the synagogues" (John 16:2)—they brought with them the practice of reasoning from the scriptures.[10] In its earliest form, the gospel of Jesus Christ was transmitted orally alongside a written proof of that message. The Torah and the prophets were thus used to testify of Jesus Christ.

---

[10] The Gospel of John twice records that the effort to expel Christians from the synagogue was already underway during Jesus' ministry. Whether this practice was also in effect in the synagogues of the Diaspora shortly after Christ's death is unlikely. The expulsion of Christians from the synagogues in Asia and Greece likely accompanied the visits of Christian missionaries to those cities.

The Fall of Jerusalem and Its Effect on the Oral Gospel

One of the most challenging questions of New Testament scholarship is why the evangelists waited so long to record their testimonies of Jesus when the need to do so seems apparent from the moment the first Christian mission was begun. Jesus died ca. A.D. 30, and yet the earliest gospel accounts are traditionally assigned to ca. A.D. 65, and the two apostolic gospels were not written until as late as A.D. 70 (Matthew) or ca. A.D. 90 (John). There may have been many reasons for writing so late in life, after decades had passed and memories had dimmed, but one of the most significant reasons may be tied to the fall of Jerusalem in A.D. 70.

In the roughly forty years between Jesus' death and the fall of the temple and the city of Jerusalem itself, Christianity was almost exclusively a Jewish phenomenon with a Gentile veneer. During Jesus' ministry He gathered enormous crowds in Galilee, numbering sometimes four to five thousand, although that represents only the adult males in attendance (Mark 6:44; 8:9). These crowds openly believed in Jesus, and in the triumphal entry they again proclaimed Jesus as Lord and Messiah. Perhaps the crowds were smaller on that day than those who were fed in Galilee, but it is no stretch of the imagination to suggest that the number of Saints may actually have grown over the course of the ministry. Just because Jesus was crucified does not mean that those believing followers of the mortal ministry simply faded away as the Church moved into Greek-speaking communities.

Luke reported that the center of the Church was in Jerusalem prior to the Jerusalem Conference (ca. A.D. 49), and it probably continued there for some time afterward. Luke never explained why or how the Church left Jerusalem but only gives the faintest details of the thriving community in the city. What can be gleaned from Acts is that the members of the Church in Jerusalem at one time practiced the law of consecration (Acts 4:34–37), they cared for the widows (Acts 6:1–4), and thousands were baptized into the branch (Acts 2:41; 4:4). Luke also indicated that the Saints looked to Jerusalem when dissension arose: "When therefore Paul and Barnabas had no small dissension and disputation with them, they determined that Paul and Barnabas, and certain other of them, *should go up to Jerusalem unto the apostles and elders about this question*" (Acts 15:2; emphasis added). This is, of course, not unexpected because the Apostles and elders were in the city. But as long as the center of the Church remained in Jerusalem, hundreds, if not thousands, could orally report the sayings of the Lord ("he was seen of above five hundred brethren at once"; 1 Corinthians 15:6). For the earliest community of Saints, the oral transmission was sufficient because the oral gospel was built upon the written word and the testimony of the living Apostles.

Even Paul, who led the effort to bring the gospel to the Gentiles (see Galatians 2:9), always returned to Jerusalem at the end of each mission. Jerusalem was the place where questions received answers and where problems were resolved (Acts 15:1–11). But the first thirty years of Christianity did not fully anticipate the next thirty years, when Christians were no longer welcome in the synagogues and when an Old Testament structuring of the message no longer made sense to a purely Gentile audience. As long as the Church remained centered in Jerusalem and in the synagogues, or the gospel was taught to Gentiles who had already partially accepted the law of Moses (see Acts 10:1–2), there was no significant need for a re-contextualization of the message for a new audience. The declaration that Jesus was Lord and Messiah was sufficient.

Eusebius recorded that before the Romans destroyed Jerusalem, faithful Christians were warned to flee to a city in the Decapolis known as Pella, located northeast of Jerusalem in what is modern Jordan: "Furthermore, the members of the Jerusalem church, by means of an oracle given by revelation to acceptable persons there, were ordered to leave the City before the war began and settle in a town in Peraea called Pella. To Pella those who believed in Christ migrated from Jerusalem."[11] The knowledge of the Pella prophecy was likely taken from the writings of Hegesippus or Ariston, who wrote in the second century A.D.[12] The flight of Christian Jews from the city of Jerusalem initiated the need to document the testimonies of the eyewitness generation, who were forty years removed from the time of Jesus' death at the time of the Pella flight. Mark, who may have begun writing around A.D. 60, may have started writing his Gospel because his source (Peter) was growing old or even facing death.[13]

Because Paul wrote prior to the fall of Jerusalem, his letters alone represent the transitional period between the early Judean ministry and the Gentile mission when the Apostles still resided almost exclusively in Jerusalem. Their early message was centered on Jesus as Lord and Messiah, but those same truths after the fall of Jerusalem needed to be restated in a way that would be more inclusive of Gentile interests. In other words, after A.D. 70, it was necessary to present the gospel of Jesus Christ in a way that answered Gentile questions as well as solidified the eyewitness and oral traditions.

The Synoptic Gospels (Matthew, Mark, and Luke)

The synoptic Gospels, which have roughly 90 percent shared material, had different aims and purposes. As a new frontier opened in the west and as Jerusalem no longer offered a safe haven for Christians and Jews, the authors of the Gospels wrote to

---

[11] Eusebius, *The History of the Church from Christ to Constantine,* trans. G. A. Williamson, rev. and ed. by Andrew Louth (New York: Penguin Books, 1965), 3.5. Hereafter cited as *Ecclesiastical History.*

[12] Craig Koester, "The Origin and Significance of the Flight to Pella Tradition," *Catholic Biblical Quarterly* 51 (1989): 92; see also John A. T. Robinson, *Redating the New Testament* (London: SCM Press, 1976), 16.

[13] Eusebius, *Ecclesiastical History,* 3.39.

specific audiences. It is frequently said that the Gospel of Matthew was written to Jews, while the Gospel of Luke was written to Gentiles, and the Gospel of Mark was written for the Church in Rome.[14] Of course the Gospels do not carry any ascriptions that would permit us to make such conclusions. Instead, the authors left slight hints that must be weighed carefully in consideration of their concerns in the era after A.D. 70.

But important for this discussion are not the specifics of the evangelists' aims but rather a powerful emphasis that emerges as the synoptic Gospels turn to the Gospel of Mark as a source. Luke's assertion that his Gospel was reliant upon eyewitness sources—"as they delivered them unto us, which from the beginning were eyewitnesses" (Luke 1:2)—makes reliance upon the Gospel of Mark readily understandable, even though one might initially assume that Luke would gravitate to the known apostolic Gospels (Matthew and John). But what is intriguing is the Gospel of Matthew—its author traditionally connected with the Apostle Matthew (see Matthew 9:9). If indeed Matthew drew upon the Gospel of Mark, whose author was not a known eyewitness, then there must have been a powerful reason for doing so. Certainly, the simplest academic solution would be to suggest that the Gospel of Matthew was not written by the Apostle Matthew, and therefore its author, a later disciple, drew upon Mark because the latter had a greater claim to authority. Such a solution is a commonplace assertion in many introductions to the Gospels.[15]

---

[14] See Martin Hengel, *The Four Gospels and the One Gospel of Jesus Christ: An Investigation of the Collection and Origin of the Canonical Gospels*, trans. John Bowden (Harrisburg, Pa.: Trinity Press, 2000), 78–105.

[15] John S. Kloppenborg Verbin, *Excavating Q: The History and Setting of the Sayings Gospel* (Minneapolis: Fortress Press, 2000), 11–54; Mark Goodacre, *The Case Against Q: Studies in Markan Priority and the Synoptic Problem* (Harrisburg, Pa.: Trinity Press, 2002), 1–18; Thomas A. Wayment, "A Viewpoint on the Supposedly Lost Gospel Q," *Religious Educator* 5, no. 3 (2004): 105–15.

Eusebius, who wrote at the beginning of the fourth century A.D. but cited Papias's late first-century or early second-century history of the early Church, may provide a more reasonable solution as to why Matthew might have relied on Mark for much of his information, even though he himself had eyewitness information. "So brightly shone the light of true religion on the minds of Peter's hearers that, not satisfied with a single hearing or with the oral teaching of the divine message, they resorted to appeals of every kind to induce Mark (whose gospel we have), as he was a follower of Peter, to leave them in writing a summary of the instruction they had received by word of mouth, nor did they let him go till they had persuaded him, and thus became responsible for the writing of what is known as the Gospel according to Mark. It is said that, on learning by revelation of the spirit what had happened, the apostle was delighted at their enthusiasm and authorized the reading of the book in the churches."[16]

Later in the same book, Eusebius cited another tradition tying the canonical Gospel of Mark with the authority of the Apostle Peter. In this instance the tradition was passed on by the presbyter John, a figure that some scholars associate with the author of the three epistles of John (see 2 John 1:1; 3 John 1:1).[17] According to John the elder (presbyter), "Mark, who had been Peter's interpreter, wrote down carefully, but not in order, all that he remembered of the Lord's sayings and doings. For he had not heard the Lord or been one of His followers, but later, as I said, one of Peter's. Peter used to adapt his teachings to the occasion, without making a systematic arrangement of the Lord's sayings, so that Mark was quite justified in writing down some things just as he remembered them.

---

[16] Eusebius, *Ecclesiastical History*, 2.15.
[17] Robert Kysar, "John, Epistles of" in Freedman, *ABD*, 3:901–12.

For he had one purpose only—to leave out nothing that he had heard, and to make no misstatement about it."[18]

Without corroborating evidence, these assertions would remain tantalizing suggestions, but probably nothing more than that. Fortunately, the synoptic Gospels do contain information that Matthew and Luke borrowed heavily from the Gospel of Mark in the era after the fall of Jerusalem. Their borrowing was not, however, wholesale. Matthew and Luke freely adapted the order of the sayings that they borrowed as well as changed the context for certain stories when other historical information available indicated that Mark had placed an event or saying of Jesus out of order.

A few examples will bear out this phenomenon. First, Matthew's main thrust was to take the sayings of Jesus found in Mark and gather them into five substantial discourses: the Sermon on the Mount (Matthew 5–7), the Mission Discourse (Matthew 10–11:1), the Parables (Matthew 13), the Church Discourse (Matthew 18–19:1), and the Olivet Discourse (Matthew 24–25). A quick glance at the Bible Dictionary entry "Gospels, Harmony of" reveals that Matthew and Mark shared much of the same order, but Matthew added a significant amount of material to his outline.[19] At times, the order of events was substantially altered (compare Matthew 9:1–8 with Mark 2:1–12), but for the most part they followed a very similar order. Also, Matthew left the words of Jesus nearly intact in most instances, as demonstrated by a quick comparison of similar sayings between the two (compare Matthew 8:23–27 and Mark 4:35–41).

With Luke the situation is somewhat more complicated. Luke informed the reader at the beginning of his Gospel that he desired

---

[18] Eusebius, *Ecclesiastical History*, 3.39.

[19] The 1979 LDS Bible Dictionary entry "Gospels, Harmony of" follows the order of the Gospel of Matthew almost exclusively with only a few minor deviations (see Matthew 14:3–5). Although not stated in the entry, the reason for doing so is probably pragmatic rather than an intentional statement on historical order.

to present the story of Jesus in its correct historical order: "It seemed good to me also, having had perfect understanding of all things from the very first, to write unto thee in order" (Luke 1:3). The phrase "to write unto thee in order" means to set the story in correct order or sequence (Greek, *akribōs kathezēs*) in comparison to another report that is not in order or sequence. A comparison of almost any two sayings between the Gospel of Mark and Luke bears out the very divergent order of events. Additionally, the Gospel of Luke also structured the story with a greater focus on Jesus' trip to Jerusalem and His lifelong effort toward His own sacrificial death in Jerusalem (sometimes called the central section in Luke; see Luke 9:51–18:14). While Luke was careful to preserve in his Gospel the sayings of Jesus as they were recorded in the Gospel of Mark, Luke felt free to change the order of events and place them in different contexts and settings.

This comparison of the three accounts is immensely important. In the post A.D. 70 era of the Church, when the Apostles and leaders had fled Jerusalem and the Judean Saints were under threat of expulsion or even extermination, the leaders initially fled to Pella. Then, over the next few decades they migrated west, thus shifting the balance of power from Jerusalem to Pella and eventually to Rome. With that shift in power came an enduring change in the population of the Church from being a Judean phenomenon with a Gentile veneer to being a Gentile church with some remaining Jewish members. In the course of that shift, when it was possible for the gospel message to become corrupted, and when there were likely vacancies in leadership positions, the Gospels of Matthew and Luke show that the words of Jesus remained sacred. Although there are instances when Matthew and Luke changed the words of Jesus as received from Mark, they left the vast majority of sayings intact and unaltered.

Moreover, the context of those sayings was open to critique. From Matthew, that critique likely came in the form of eyewitness understanding; therefore, he subtly restored Jesus' sayings into their original context. Luke, on the other hand, altered the order of events from a historian's standpoint, believing that his sources were credible enough to warrant a rewriting of the sequence of events. But both authors showed respect for the authority behind the Gospel of Mark, namely Peter's.

This continuity from Peter to Mark and then to both Matthew and Luke shows that there was still a unified gospel message in the era after the fall of Jerusalem in A.D. 70 and that while there was flexibility in that period for changes to be made, the core message remained safe and protected. The aims of the different evangelists also may have contributed to the way they structured their Gospels and the way that they freely changed the order of events. If the standard attributions are correct that Matthew was written for Jews, Luke for Gentiles, and Mark for the Saints in Rome, then the order of events may have been shaped or altered to emphasize those concerns. A much longer study would be required to align the needs of post A.D. 70 Christianity with the varying points of emphasis found in the synoptic Gospels.

Conclusion

The earliest form of the gospel of Jesus Christ was both profound and decisive for what it declared and implied. Our earliest writers, many of them anonymous, declared Jesus to be more than the Messiah of Jewish expectation. This declaration has strong verbal parallels to the Shema, the prayer that was repeated morning and evening in Jerusalem. The Shema declares, "Hear, O Israel: The Lord our God is one Lord" (Deuteronomy 6:4). Christians similarly declared Jesus to be "Lord and Christ" (Acts 2:36). The testimony is unequivocal and would certainly clarify the nagging question of the mortal ministry: was Jesus the Messiah? He was, in fact, more.

Early Christians were deeply moved by this testimony and it

led several now-unknown authors to write hymns praising Jesus as Lord, Savior, and God. Those hymns are likely the oldest Christian writings to have come down to us. Paul and other authors picked up those hymns and included them in their letters as a way of conveying their own thoughts and testimony, and this emerging gospel of Jesus Christ quickly became the central focus of apostolic teaching. Paul and others added a discussion of key events from Jesus' lifetime: His betrayal, the Last Supper with His disciples, and His atoning sacrifice, but the message always remained centered on Jesus. Both Luke, the author of Acts, and Paul associated these teachings with apostolic authority, and they connected the message as they taught it with what the Apostles taught.

As long as the eyewitness generation thrived, a written gospel was likely an unnecessary luxury because of a strong institutional identity in the Church and the availability of hundreds, if not thousands, of individuals who could repeat the words of Jesus as they had heard them. Certainly as those stories were retold in the oral age of the Church, they began to take shape into collections, such as the Sermon on the Mount or the sayings associated with Jesus' last week of life. As soon as the Jerusalem branch lost its footing in Judea and the Saints fled the city at the threat of Roman annihilation, the old ways would no longer suffice and a written gospel was needed to supplant the oral memory of the eyewitnesses. Another critical shift took place as well. Previous to the fall of Jerusalem, the words of Jesus circulated much like the words of a prophet, without a biographical sketch of the prophet's life. In other words, the biographical details of Jesus' life may have been seen largely as unnecessary to people who had few biographical details from the lives of the prophets. This may also help explain why so few details are known from the early years of Jesus' life.

As the gospel expanded into Gentile areas and the Church became increasingly Gentile in its makeup, the need for a written gospel grew. In Asia, Greece, and Rome, where Greek and Roman literature and thinking prevailed, a biographical description of Jesus' life would have been a more logical approach to conveying the gospel message. A biography would have been a more powerful tool, particularly for those who were largely unfamiliar with Jewish ways and customs and for those who were asked to embrace Christianity, originally a Judean phenomenon. The Gospels, which are a type of biography of the Lord, updated the Church to face the needs of the second-century Church. The gospel was still the same, but the packaging was slightly different from what it previously had been.

II.

THE CHURCH OF THE FIRST CENTURY

GAYE STRATHEARN AND JOSHUA M. SEARS

And God hath set some in the church, first apostles, secondarily prophets, thirdly teachers, after that miracles, then gifts of healings, helps, governments, diversities of tongues.

1 CORINTHIANS 12:28

In the well-known 1842 Wentworth letter, Joseph Smith included thirteen statements about the beliefs of The Church of Jesus Christ of Latter-day Saints, known today as the Articles of Faith. The sixth statement says: "We believe in the same organization that existed in the Primitive Church, namely, apostles, prophets, pastors, teachers, evangelists, and so forth" (Articles of Faith 1:6). Later, Elder James E. Talmage wrote: "In the dispensation of the meridian of time Jesus Christ established His Church upon the earth, appointing therein the officers necessary for the carrying out of the Father's purposes. Every person so appointed was divinely commissioned with authority to officiate in the ordinances of his calling; and, after Christ's ascension, the same organization was continued, those who had received authority ordaining others to the various offices in the Priesthood. In this way were given unto the Church, apostles, prophets, evangelists, pastors, high priests, seventies, elders, bishops, priests, teachers, and deacons."[1]

Both the ancient and modern Church grew from a rather small number of believers to a much larger community of believers, developing offices and structures to deal with its growth. For example, the restored Church in 1830 was led by the first and second elders with apostolic keys. Additionally, several men were ordained to various offices, including deacon, teacher, and priest. Later, additional offices were added, including bishop (1831), high priest (1831), patriarch (1833), and seventy (1835). By 1835, the First Presidency, Quorum of the Twelve, and the Quorum of the Seventy had been organized to help administer an expanding Church membership. A similar development had occurred in the first century. The early Church, moved by inspiration, revelations, and needs, expanded its organizational structure as membership increased and new situations called for expansion.

As we examine the development of the early Christian Church organization and government within the first century, two important questions emerge: Did Jesus organize a church during His mortal ministry? and How did the Church function after Jesus' Ascension? To help answer this latter question, we will specifically examine the function of Apostles and other titles and offices in the early Church, the administrative impact of a growing church, and Jesus' designation in Matthew 16:18 of the Church as "my church."

Did Jesus Organize a Church during His Mortal Ministry?

Is there evidence of a formal church existing during the mortal ministry of Jesus? The answer is difficult to determine and is

---

[1] James E. Talmage, *The Articles of Faith* (Salt Lake City: Deseret Book, 1984), 180.

dependent to some extent on how we define the word *church*. The Greek word for "church" used throughout the New Testament is *ekklēsia*. In its basic sense, it refers to a legislative body or assembly, but it can also refer to a casual gathering of people or a community of people with shared beliefs.[2] It is the last of these meanings that most closely reflects the New Testament concept of church, but we must remember that a community of people with shared beliefs can exist without a formal organization that includes initiatory rituals, priesthood, scripture, etc. Without doubt, the word eventually takes on all of these meanings, but the question is, when? One of the difficulties comes because the word *church* only appears three times in the four Gospels, and all of those occurrences are in just two verses in Matthew (Matthew 16:18; 18:17). By the time we reach Acts, however, we find a very different scenario. In Acts through Revelation, the word occurs more than one hundred times. Thus the distinct existence of an individually functioning Christian Church is much more significant or well-known *after* Jesus' mortal ministry.

Nevertheless, some indicators suggest that a basic organization did exist during Jesus' mortal ministry, at least a community with priesthood. First, there is one cryptic comment in John that indicates Jesus' disciples performed baptisms that seem to be independent of those performed by John the Baptist: "When therefore the Lord knew how the Pharisees had heard that Jesus made and baptized more disciples than John, (Though Jesus himself baptized not, but his disciples)" (John 4:1–2). The Joseph Smith Translation amends the parenthetical portion to read, "Now the Lord knew this, though he himself baptized not so many as his disciples; for he suffered them for an example, preferring one another" (JST, John 4:3–4). Unfortunately, neither the Johannine nor the Joseph

---

[2] Arndt and Gingrich, *GEL*, "*ekklēsia*," 240–41.

Smith Translation passage tells us about the purpose of this baptism. Was it like John the Baptist's—for the remission of sins—or was it an initiation into a formal church? The texts simply give no answer. The fact that they were baptizing, however, implies that they had at least the Aaronic Priesthood.

Second, some of the followers of Jesus were part of an inner circle, showing that there was at least some basic level of hierarchy within the community. All three synoptic Gospels record that Jesus called Apostles (Matthew 10:1–5; Mark 6:7–13; Luke 6:13–16).[3] The Greek word for *apostle* is *apostolos* and comes from the verb meaning to "send forth." When used in conjunction with people, *apostolos* indicates that they were sent forth with a specific purpose.[4] This definition fits well with the accounts in Matthew and Mark, but there is no indication at this point that the term *apostle* refers to a specific priesthood office, although, as we will suggest, it does at a later time in Jesus' ministry. Rather, according to Matthew, the Apostles are directed to heal (Matthew 10:8) and to "preach saying the kingdom of heaven is at hand" (Matthew 10:7). In the New Testament, there is little evidence that the Apostles engaged in either of these activities until after Jesus' Ascension in Acts 1. Prior to this time, the Gospels portray them as accompanying Jesus as He healed and preached.[5] Even within this inner circle

---

[3] John P. Meier, "The Circle of the Twelve: Did It Exist During Jesus' Public Ministry?" *Journal of Biblical Literature*, 116, no. 4 (1997): 637. The Gospel of John does not contain any specific reference to the calling of the Apostles, and it uses the word *apostolos* only once (John 13:16) but in a very general sense. John does, however, refer to the Twelve (John 6:67–70; 20:24). The synoptic Gospels also refer to the Twelve, but only twice do we find the phrase "twelve apostles" (Matthew 10:2; Luke 22:14).

[4] Arndt and Gingrich, *GEL*, "*apostolos*," 99. See also Eric D. Huntsman, "Galilee and the Call of the Twelve Apostles," in Richard Neitzel Holzapfel and Thomas A. Wayment, eds., *From Bethlehem through the Sermon on the Mount*, vol. 1 of The Life and Teachings of Jesus Christ (Salt Lake City: Deseret Book, 2005), 228–38.

[5] The one exception *may* be when the disciples failed to heal a boy who was possessed of a spirit. The text never calls them Apostles but the context, most clearly in

of Apostles, there is a further division with Peter, James, and John being privy to some events, such as the raising of Jairus's daughter, the events on the Mount of Transfiguration, and the invitation to come further into the Garden of Gethsemane than the other eight Apostles.

That the apostles (in a general sense) eventually became Apostles (in the sense of a priesthood office) during Jesus' mortal ministry is implied, rather than explicitly stated. At Caesarea Philippi, Peter receives the promise from Jesus, "I will build my church" (Matthew 16:18). Here the promise of a church is in the future tense. Immediately after this first promise, Jesus says, again in the future tense, "I will give unto thee [singular] the keys of the kingdom of heaven: and whatsoever thou [singular] shalt bind on earth shall be bound in heaven: and whatsoever thou shalt loose on earth shall be loosed in heaven" (Matthew 16:19). The promise of a church with priesthood keys given specifically to Peter strongly suggests a shift to an official church, rather than simply a collection of like-minded people. It must be remembered, however, that in this passage it is a promise, not a statement of fact—yet. Latter-day Saints understand that Jesus, Moses, and Elijah gave these promised keys to Peter, James, and John on the Mount of Transfiguration about a week after the events at Caesarea Philippi (Matthew 17:1–13; compare D&C 110:11, 13–16).[6]

It is therefore probably not happenstance that in Matthew 18, the chapter that immediately follows the events on the Mount of Transfiguration, Jesus delivers the Church Discourse. Here, the

---

Matthew, suggests they may have been the nine Apostles who did not go up into the mountain. The question is whether the disciples attempted to heal the boy through the power of the priesthood or simply through the power of faith. Jesus' response to the disciples' question, "Why could not we cast him out?" suggests that it may have been the latter. He says that they could not heal the boy "because of your unbelief" (Matthew 17:19–20).

[6] Smith, *TPJS*, 158.

word *church* is found twice in verse 17, in a context of establishing boundaries for participation in the Church and the use of the sealing power. Jesus teaches the process that should be followed if "thy brother shall trespass against thee." First, the injured party should go and discuss it with the offender. If that doesn't work, he or she should bring in witnesses. Finally, if reconciliation is still not achieved, "tell it unto the church: but if he neglect to hear the church, let him be unto thee as an heathen man and a publican" (i.e., he should be put out or excommunicated from the Church). "Verily I say unto you, Whatsoever ye [plural] shall bind on earth shall be bound in heaven: and whatsoever ye [plural] shall loose on earth shall be loosed in heaven" (Matthew 18:15–18). Here the Church is spoken of as a present reality, rather than as a future promise. In addition, the power to bind is now available, not just to Peter but to the disciples—presumably the Twelve.

In addition to the Twelve, Luke also mentions the calling of seventy.[7] Luke tells us that Jesus "sent them two and two before his face into every city and place, whither he himself would come" (Luke 10:1). Jesus instructed them, "Carry neither purse, nor scrip, nor shoes" (Luke 10:4). In Luke's sequence of events, these seventy were called after the events on the Mount of Transfiguration and the bestowal of the priesthood keys. Their responsibility is similar to that given to the Twelve in Luke 9:1–6. The specific mention that they go in pairs may reflect the rejection and hostility that Jesus experienced in Samaria (Luke 9:52–53).[8] Unfortunately we know very little about this group. Luke gives no account of their mission; he simply records that when they returned they rejoiced because "even the devils are subject unto us through thy name"

---

[7] A number of manuscripts say that Jesus called seventy-two, not seventy (e.g., Sinaiticus, ℵ; Alexandrinus, A; Ephraemi, C; Bezae, D; and Freer, W).

[8] Joel B. Green, *The Gospel of Luke*, The New International Commentary on the New Testament (Grand Rapids, Mich.: Eerdmans, 1997), 412–13.

(Luke 10:17). After Luke 10:20 they are never mentioned again.[9] Luke probably includes them because the number seventy represents the whole world—in the Table of Nations in Genesis 10, the world after the flood is divided into seventy nations—and even though this group seems to teach only among the Jews, they foreshadow the time when the gospel will be taught "in Jerusalem, and in all Judaea, and in Samaria, and unto the uttermost part of the earth" (Acts 1:8).

How Did the Church Function After Jesus' Ascension?

The limited information we have about Jesus' forty-day ministry tells us little about the Church and its organization. Robert J. Matthews suggests, "It is probable that it was during this period that the church was organized with quorums and various officers."[10] If this is indeed the case, then it helps us understand

---

[9] The fourth-century Church historian Eusebius claims that Matthias, who was called to fill the vacancy left in the Twelve by the death of Judas, had served among the Seventy, as had Barnabas and an otherwise unknown figure named Thaddaeus. He recounts that "after [Christ's] resurrection from the dead and ascent into heaven, Thomas, one of the twelve Apostles, was divinely moved to send Thaddaeus to Edessa, himself listed among the number of the Seventy disciples of Christ, as a herald and evangelist of the teaching about Christ" (*Ecclesiastical History*, 1:13). He also cites Clement of Alexandria, who wrote that after the resurrection the Apostles passed divine instruction on to the Seventy (*Ecclesiastical History*, 2:1). If these records have a historical basis, it would indicate that the Seventy continued as an organized body in the Christian Church beyond the Resurrection under Apostolic direction.

[10] Robert J. Matthews, *Unto All Nations: A Guide to the Book of Acts and the Writings of Paul* (Salt Lake City: Deseret Book, 1975), 1. Robert L. Millet suggests that the phrase "speaking of the things pertaining to the kingdom of God" (Acts 1:3) could indicate that it was at this time that Jesus "provided the more complex church organization" to the Apostles ("The Saga of the Early Christian Church," in Robert L. Millet, ed., *Acts to Revelation,* vol. 6 of Studies in Scripture [Salt Lake City: Deseret Book, 1987], 2). After surveying various interpretations of the forty-day ministry, Hugh Nibley concludes that Jesus' desire to better prepare the Twelve was "the argument most confidently put forth today" ("Evangelium Quadraginta Dierum: The Forty-day Mission of Christ—The Forgotten Heritage," in *Mormonism and Early Christianity,* vol. 4 of The Collected Works of Hugh Nibley [Salt Lake City: Deseret Book and FARMS, 1987], 12).

why in Acts, much more clearly than in the Gospels, we see the Apostles using the priesthood in the workings and organization of a church.

Ephesians includes two passages on Church organization that are particularly important for Latter-day Saints: "Now therefore ye are no more strangers and foreigners, but fellowcitizens with the saints, and of the household of God; and are built upon the foundation of the apostles and prophets, Jesus Christ himself being the chief corner stone" (Ephesians 2:19–20); "And he gave some, apostles; and some, prophets; and some, evangelists; and some, pastors and teachers; for the perfecting of the saints, for the work of the ministry, for the edifying of the body of Christ: Till we all come in the unity of the faith, and of the knowledge of the Son of God, unto a perfect man, unto the measure of the stature of the fulness of Christ: That we henceforth be no more children, tossed to and fro, and carried about with every wind of doctrine, by the sleight of men, and cunning craftiness, whereby they lie in wait to deceive" (Ephesians 4:11–14).

The emphasis on Christ is the bedrock of all teaching from the very beginning of Christian missionary work, but the list of offices included in Ephesians is neither exhaustive nor uniform in the New Testament. Ephesians does not mention, for example, the seven (Acts 6:3) or elders (Acts 15:4) nor bishops (1 Timothy 3:1) or deacons (1 Timothy 3:10). While mention of the importance of Apostles is very early and extensive, the New Testament descriptions of prophets, evangelists, pastors, and teachers are fragmentary.

The Apostles

Luke records the process of calling a new member of the Twelve in some detail, outlining a pattern which may be assumed later in his account when other Apostles are mentioned. The prerequisite for considering someone to become a member of the

Twelve was that they "have companied with us all the time that the Lord Jesus went in and out among us, beginning from the baptism of John, unto that same day that he was taken up from us, must one be ordained to be a witness with us of his resurrection" (Acts 1:21–22). The language of the KJV in this passage is a little misleading. There is no Greek word in the sentence that can be translated as "ordained." Instead, the Greek literally reads "one of these must *become* a witness (Greek, *martyra*) with us of his resurrection" (authors' translation). The language of this verse, then, does not require a priesthood ordination. Nevertheless, it is significant that the first thing Peter does after the Ascension is to fill the vacancy in the Twelve. This action indicates that, in Peter's mind, having a group of eleven was *not* the same as having a group of twelve and that the latter was important for the Church to move forward.

Luke records the Twelve doing the two things Jesus had assigned them to do in Matthew 10: perform miracles and teach the gospel. Peter and John now heal "in the name of Jesus Christ" (Acts 3:6). As a representative example of their healings, Luke recounts Peter's healing of a man "lame from his mother's womb" (Acts 3:1–11), but he also notes "by the hands of the apostles were many signs and wonders wrought among the people" (Acts 5:12; compare 2 Corinthians 12:12). The Apostles also teach the gospel, initially at and around the temple and later in Samaria and the rest of the known world. In addition, when Peter and John are in Samaria, Luke records that they laid "their hands on [the new converts], and they received the Holy Ghost" (Acts 8:17), giving evidence that they had the authority of the Melchizedek Priesthood.

We also see that the Twelve had administrative responsibility, both in Jerusalem and also in regional centers of the Church. Initially, when the members of the Church brought the money from the sale of their lands and possessions, they "laid them down at the apostles' feet: and distribution was made unto every man according as he had need" (Acts 4:35). When there was a problem with the Grecian widows being neglected, the issue was brought to the Twelve (Acts 6:1–4). When Paul and Barnabas and "certain men which came down from Judaea" disputed over whether Gentile converts needed to be circumcised, they agreed to take the question to "the apostles and elders" in Jerusalem (Acts 15:1–2).[11]

What is not evident is whether all of the Apostles in the early Church were members of the Twelve. Our earliest Christian text that mentions the Apostles, 1 Corinthians (written c. A.D. 55), seems to make a distinction between the Twelve and the Apostles. When discussing the Resurrection appearances, Paul mentions Jesus' appearance to the Twelve and then noted that afterward He appeared to all of the Apostles: "He was seen of Cephas, then of the twelve. . . . After that, he was seen of James; *then of all the apostles*" (1 Corinthians 15:5, 7; emphasis added).

This situation seems to be corroborated in other New Testament sources. We know that Herod Agrippa I killed James, the brother of John, at an early date (Acts 12:1–2). Unlike Acts 1, Luke does not give any details of the Twelve meeting to find a replacement for James. In chapter 14, when Paul and Barnabas are on their first missionary journey, Luke begins to identify them as Apostles (vv. 4, 14), which could mean that there were at least thirteen members of the Twelve. In addition, at the conclusion of Paul's letter to the Romans he mentions Andronicus and Junia (a female name) as Apostles (Romans 16:7). In 2 Corinthians, Paul mentions the "messengers [Greek, *apostoloi*] of the churches" (8:23) and, more specifically, in Philippians he refers to Epaphroditus as "my brother, and companion in labour, and fellowsoldier, but your messenger [Greek, *apostolos*], and he that ministered to my wants" (2:25). Here Epaphroditus is not an Apostle for the entire church

---

[11] For a detailed discussion of the Jerusalem Council, see Richard Neitzel Holzapfel and Thomas A. Wayment, "Unto the Uttermost Part of the Earth," in this volume.

but only an apostle for the Philippians—an envoy or representative for the Philippian branch of the Church. In these instances, we should probably understand *apostle* in a general sense, rather than as an office of the Melchizedek Priesthood.

In antiquity, there was some debate in the Church over Paul's status as an Apostle. Paul did not fit the requirements for being a member of the Twelve, as outlined in Acts 1; although he was witness of the Resurrection, he was not a disciple "beginning from the baptism of John, unto that same day that he was taken up from us" (Acts 1:22). This may be the reason that some in Corinth questioned his Apostolic status, especially in relation to Cephas (Peter) and the other Apostles (1 Corinthians 9:1–5). Paul declares, "If I be not an apostle unto others, yet doubtless I am to you: for the seal of mine apostleship are ye in the Lord" (1 Corinthians 9:2). Is he suggesting that he was only an Apostle for the Corinthians? Although Luke identifies him as an Apostle during his first missionary journey (Acts 14:4, 14), Paul does not seem to be one of the Apostles at the Jerusalem Council (Acts 15), and he does not call himself an Apostle in his earliest epistles to the Thessalonians written during his second missionary journey.[12]

In latter epistles, however, Paul begins each epistle with a reference to his being an Apostle. In Romans 1:1 and 1 Corinthians 1:1, he specifically says that he was "called to be an apostle." It is worth noting that there are three particular epistles where Paul has to justify his authority: Romans, 1 Corinthians, and Galatians. In Galatians, he calls himself an Apostle but does not say that he was "called to be an apostle," as he does in Romans 1:1 and 1 Corinthians 1:1. This suggests that when Paul wrote Galatians, his Apostolic status may have been as a missionary, not yet called

---

[12] Nor does Paul identify himself as an Apostle in Philippians 1:1; Titus 1:1; or Philemon 1:1. In these instances it may be because there is no question about his Apostolic status.

as a member of the Twelve (as was the case by the time he wrote Romans and 1 Corinthians).[13] Although Paul calls himself the "least of the apostles" (1 Corinthians 15:9), it is clear that he fights to be recognized along with the other Apostles.

Prophets

In addition to mention of the Apostles, we also find frequent reference to prophets. During the Apostolic ministry, a number of unnamed and named individuals are called prophets: a group of prophets traveling from Jerusalem to Antioch (Acts 11:27); Agabus (Acts 11:28; 21:10); Barnabas, Simeon, Lucius, Manaen, and Saul (Acts 13:1); and Judas and Silas (Acts 15:32). Prophecy as a spiritual gift within the early Church is mentioned on numerous occasions and is also featured prominently in John's Revelation.[14] With the exception of the Apostles, we have on record only the prophecies of Agabus, who first prophesied of a coming famine (Acts 11:27–28) and later of Paul's Roman incarceration (Acts 21:10–11).

What was the role of a prophet? Within the Israelite context from which Christianity grew, being a prophet (Hebrew, *nābî*) was not a description of an office but of an endowment of the gift of prophecy. When Eldad and Medad prophesied in the Israelite camp, Joshua was concerned by what he perceived to be a challenge to Moses' leadership. Moses, however, responded that he wished "that *all* the Lord's people were prophets, and that the Lord would put his spirit upon them!" (Numbers 11:29; emphasis added). To Moses, such prophesying did not in itself give one ecclesiastical authority and thus was not a challenge to his position.

---

[13] Thomas A. Wayment, *From Persecutor to Apostle: A Biography of Paul* (Salt Lake City: Deseret Book, 2006), 153.

[14] Acts 2:16–18; 19:6; 21:9; Romans 12:6; 1 Corinthians 11:4–5; 12:10; 13:2, 8–9; 14:1–6, 22–26, 31–32, 37, 39; 1 Thessalonians 5:20; 1 Timothy 1:18; 4:14; 2 Peter 1:19; Revelation 1:3; 10:11; 16:6; 18:20, 24; 19:10; 22:6–7, 9–10, 18–19.

This understanding prevailed throughout the Old Testament and continued into the New Testament world.[15] Although prophets are frequently mentioned in the New Testament, we never read of them being ordained in any sense. Thus to be a prophet meant that one possessed the gift of prophecy, but did not necessarily mean one held ecclesiastical office.

What was the relationship between Apostles and prophets? With the exception of Jesus' statement in Luke 11:49, Paul is the only writer ever to mention Apostles and prophets together, and whenever he does, Apostles are always listed first (1 Corinthians 12:28; Ephesians 2:20; 3:5; 4:11). The ordering in the sentences was most likely deliberate and perhaps suggests Paul's recognition that though the gift of prophecy was valuable, it was subject to those formally authorized to administer. Paul himself demonstrates this when, writing to the Saints at Corinth in his capacity as an Apostle (1 Corinthians 1:1), he gives instructions to help regulate the speaking and interpreting of prophecies among them (see 1 Corinthians 14:26–40). Within this same passage he also counsels them to "covet to prophesy" (v. 39), instruction that would certainly have created chaos had prophecy been thought of in itself as giving a right to leadership.

Prophets, then, were an important feature of the early Christian Church. The presence of prophets was evidence that "the manifestation of the Spirit [was being] given to every man to profit withal. For to one is given by the Spirit the word of wisdom; to another the word of knowledge by the same Spirit; to another faith by the same Spirit; to another the gifts of healing by the same Spirit; to another the working of miracles; to another prophecy"

---

[15] This explains why such women as Miriam (Exodus 15:20), Deborah (Judges 4:4), Huldah (2 Kings 22:14; 2 Chronicles 34:22), and Anna (Luke 2:36) could be considered prophetesses despite a gender-based priesthood restriction. See also Acts 2:16–17; 1 Corinthians 11:5.

(1 Corinthians 12:7–10). Being a prophet was not an office or position; rather, all Saints were encouraged to seek "the testimony of Jesus [which] is the spirit of prophecy" (Revelation 19:10).[16]

Evangelists

A rather enigmatic office is that of evangelist (Greek, *euangelistēs*). In addition to the Ephesians passage, the term is found only two other times in the New Testament to describe Philip (Acts 21:8) and Timothy (2 Timothy 4:5), but these passages give no indication of the meaning of the term. Linguistically the word refers to someone who declares the "good news" or gospel (Greek, *euangellos*). Although it is clear that Apostles were evangelists in the sense that they declared, not all evangelists were Apostles. Neither Philip nor Timothy were ever considered to be Apostles. Outside the New Testament, *euangelistēs* is found in an inscription from Rhodes where it describes "one who proclaims oracular sayings."[17] This definition fits well with the Prophet Joseph Smith's explanation that "an Evangelist is a Patriarch."[18]

Pastors

The term pastor (Greek, *poimenas*) refers to someone who looks after sheep, and so is used to refer to shepherds or leaders. Christ identified Himself as the Good Shepherd (John 10:14), and He instructed Peter three times to "feed my lambs/sheep" (John 21:15–17). Ephesians 4 is the only place in the New Testament

---

[16] Andrew T. Lincoln, *Ephesians,* vol. 42 of Word Biblical Commentary (Dallas: Word Books, 1990), 153.

[17] Kittel and Friedrich, eds., *TDNT, "euangelistēs,"* 2:736.

[18] Smith, *TPJS,* 151. John W. Welch has noted: "Today we cannot be certain of the origins of the New Testament term *euangelistēs*. But of all the meanings attributed to the word *evangelist* over the years, the Prophet Joseph Smith's identification of this office as that of a patriarch who gives spiritual and prophetic blessings to individuals still comes closest to the meaning of this term in its earliest known occurrence" ("Word Studies from the New Testament," *Ensign,* January 1995, 29).

where the word *pastor* is used in a technical sense of a Church office, but variations of the Greek stem are often found in conjunction with other Church offices such as elder and bishop (1 Peter 5:1–2; Acts 20:17–35) and may indicate "their initial synonymous use as designations for Christian leaders."[19]

Teachers

In the New Testament, *teacher* seems to be a descriptive term, rather than a priesthood office. Twice Paul identifies himself as an Apostle and "a teacher of the Gentiles" (1 Timothy 2:7; 2 Timothy 1:11). Likewise, Luke identifies prophets and teachers in the Church at Antioch such as Barnabas and Saul (Paul), whom we know about from other places, but others we do not: Simeon, Lucius of Cyrene, and Manaen (Acts 13:1). Paul also encourages women to be "teachers of good things" (Titus 2:3). But the New Testament also warns against those who desire to be teachers but who understand "neither what they say, nor whereof they affirm" (1 Timothy 1:7) and "false teachers among you, who privily shall bring in damnable heresies, even denying the Lord that bought them, and bring upon themselves swift destruction" (2 Peter 2:1).

Elders

In both the Greek Old and New Testaments, the term *elder* (Greek, *presbyteros*) is often used to refer to older men who were respected for their experience and wisdom.[20] In this context it appears frequently to denote the elders of the Jews, a group often in opposition to Jesus and His ministry. However, in a Christian

---

[19] John H. Elliott, "Elders As Leaders in 1 Peter and the Early Church," *Harvard Theological Studies* 64, no. 2 (2008): 687.

[20] In fact, "throughout the ancient world, both in Greco-Roman and Israelite circles, heads of households respected for their age and prestige were known as 'elders' (*zekanim, presbyteroi, gerontes, seniors*) and exercised the role of local leadership" (Elliott, "Elders As Leaders," 686).

context the term seems to refer to a specific office, received by appointment or ordination (Acts 14:23; Titus 1:5; Greek, *kathistēmi*). In Acts, elders work in close association with the Apostles (Acts 15:2, 4, 6, 22–23; 16:4). Peter even identifies himself as a "co-elder"[21] (see 1 Peter 5:1; Greek, *sympresbyteros*). Luke records that Paul and Barnabas, on their first missionary journey, "ordained [or appointed; Greek, *cheirotoneō*] them elders in every church" (Acts 14:23). Paul similarly instructs Titus to "ordain elders in *every* city, as I had appointed thee" (Titus 1:5; emphasis added).

The responsibilities of these elders were many and varied: they received and distributed welfare goods (Acts 11:29–30); helped settle doctrinal disputes (Acts 15:2, 4, 6, 22–23; 16:4); oversaw and fed the flocks of God (Acts 20:28; 1 Peter 5:1–3); received reports of missionary efforts (Acts 21:17–20); sought to correct misunderstandings among Church members (Acts 21:18–25); ordained others to the ministry (1 Timothy 4:14); ruled (1 Timothy 5:17); labored in "the word and doctrine" (1 Timothy 5:17); anointed and blessed the sick (James 5:14–15); and served as examples for the rest of God's flock (1 Peter 5:3).

Elders appear to have held a priesthood office on the local level and led the Saints in the absence of traveling Apostolic authorities like Paul. At the end of Paul's third mission, he went to Miletus and sent for the elders of the Church from Ephesus to come to him. Knowing that he would not return to the area (Acts 20:25), he directed them, "Take heed therefore unto yourselves, and to all the flock, over the which the Holy Ghost hath made you overseers [Greek, *episkopoi*], to feed the church of God" (Acts 20:28).

---

[21] Elliott, "Elders As Leaders," 685.

Bishops

The Greek word for bishops is *episkopoi* and refers to "overseers." The KJV is not always consistent in its translation of *episkopoi*. Sometimes it will translate it literally as "overseers" (Acts 20:28) and sometimes technically as bishops (Philippians 1:1; 1 Timothy 3:2; Titus 1:7). The only time we find the term *bishop* (Greek, *episkopos*) in the New Testament in a singular form is when Peter uses it to describe Christ (1 Peter 2:25). Again we are reminded of the fluid boundaries in the early Church between elders and bishops; both are described as overseers who shepherd their flocks. According to Paul's letters to Timothy and Titus, bishops were responsible to teach (1 Timothy 3:2); take care of the Church (1 Timothy 3:5); serve as stewards of God (Titus 1:7); and exhort and convince gainsayers (Titus 1:9). It is not until the early second century that we find concrete evidence, in the writings of Ignatius, bishop of Antioch, of a clear distinction between elders and bishops, with elders yielding to the bishop who is *the* representative of Christ and the leader of the congregation (*Ephesians,* 1:3; 4:1; *Magnesians,* 2:1; 3:1; *Trallians,* 1:1). In Ignatius's letters, the bishop is now the only one who is described as a shepherd or pastor (*Philadelphians,* 1–2; compare *Romans,* 9:1–2).[22]

Deacons

Paul writes to the Philippians, "Paul and Timotheus, the servants of Jesus Christ, to all the saints in Christ Jesus which are at Philippi, with the bishops [Greek, *episkopoi*] and deacons [Greek, *diakonoi*]" (1:1). Not only were bishops associated with elders, they were also associated with deacons. The difficulty again in understanding the many passages that use *diakonoi* is determining whether it is being used in the general sense of one who ministers,

---

[22] Elliott, "Elders As Leaders," 688.

or in the technical sense of the office of deacon.[23] For example, Paul describes himself and Apollos as "ministers [Greek, *diakonoi*] by whom ye believed" (1 Corinthians 3:5), yet at the beginning of the epistle he identifies himself as an Apostle (1:1). Is he, therefore, identifying himself as an Apostle who ministers to the Saints at Corinth, or is he indicating that he is a deacon in the Church? In another epistle, Paul commends to the Roman church a woman by the name of Phebe, whom he describes as "our sister, which is a servant [Greek, *diakonon*] of the church which is at Cenchrea" (Romans 16:1). In most cases in the New Testament the context suggests that *diakonoi* should be translated as "ministers," rather than "deacons." One exception to this may be 1 Timothy 3:8–13, which describes the qualifications for being a *diakonos*. The passage says nothing about the duties of a *diakonos* but indicates that he must be serious, not double-tongued, not addicted to wine or money, and must hold to the mystery of the faith with a clear conscience. Then Paul instructs Timothy that an individual must be tested and, if he is found blameless, let him serve as deacon (Greek, *diakoneitōsan*). In this context, it does not appear to be a general reference to ministering, because people who are not blameless can still effectively minister to others.

We have noted that on two occasions deacons are mentioned in conjunction with bishops. We see the same kind of pairing in *1 Clement*, 42:4, and the *Didache*, 15:1, Christian texts which date to around the turn of the first century. Ignatius encourages the Trallians: "Let everyone respect the deacons as Jesus Christ, just as they should respect the bishop" (3.1). However, it is clear that Ignatius does not consider deacons to enjoy equal status

---

[23] Other places where *diakonos* is translated as the generic "minister" include Matthew 20:26; 22:13; Mark 9:35; 10:43; John 2:5, 9; 12:26; Romans 13:4; 15:8; 16:1; 1 Corinthians 3:5; 2 Corinthians 3:6; 6:4; 11:15, 23; Galatians 2:17; Ephesians 3:7; 6:21; Philippians 1:1; Colossians 1:7, 23, 25; 4:7; 1 Thessalonians 3:2; 1 Timothy 3:8, 12; 4:6. This is clearly the predominant sense of the word.

with bishops; rather they are subject to the bishop and the elders (*Magnesians,* 2). He specifically describes "Philo, the deacon from Cilicia, a man with a good reputation, who even now assists me [Ignatius, who was a bishop] in the word of God" (*Philadelphians,* 11:1). Deacons, he writes to the Trallians, "are not merely 'deacons' of food and drink, but ministers of God's church. Therefore they must avoid criticism as though it were fire" (2:3). Thus it appears that the role of deacons was to aid the bishop by helping with the temporal welfare of the Church and by teaching the word, which, as we will see, corresponds remarkably with the seven who are called to minister in Acts 6.

The Administrative Effects of a Growing Church

Having examined the various groups in the early Church, we are now in a position to examine the ways it may have functioned. According to Acts, the Church began with very few members; only one hundred and twenty people were gathered with the Apostles and women when the vacancy in the Twelve was filled (Acts 1:15). But events that followed led to an exponential increase in Church membership. After Peter's teaching at Pentecost, "about three thousand souls" joined the Church (Acts 2:41). After Peter and John's teaching at the temple, "many of them which heard the word believed; and the number of the men was about five thousand" (Acts 4:4), although the number could have been much greater if it included women and children. As a result of the "many signs and wonders wrought among the people" by the Apostles, "believers were the more added to the Lord, multitudes both of men and women" (Acts 5:12, 14).

The rapid growth of the Church inevitably led to some administrative difficulties. Acts 6 records that "when the number of the disciples was multiplied, there arose a murmuring of the Grecians [Greek-speaking Jews] against the Hebrews [Aramaic-speaking Jews], because their widows were neglected in the daily ministration" (v. 1). During this time the Church members were consecrating their wealth (Acts 4:37; contrast 5:1–11),[24] but due to the administrative difficulty of keeping up with the Church's growth, some of the members—specifically the widows—were being neglected. This was a problem because they had given all to the Church and were relying on the Church for support.

When made aware of the situation, Peter realized that the Apostles did not have the time to take care of these matters. He declared, "It is not reason that we should leave the word of God, and serve tables. Wherefore, brethren, look ye out among you seven men of honest report, full of the Holy Ghost and wisdom, whom we may appoint over this business. But we will give ourselves continually to prayer, and to the ministry of the word" (Acts 6:2–4). As a result we have the first administrative expansion of the Church leadership. Acts does not tell us much about these seven men, though Peter does say that the Twelve would "appoint" them. The Greek word is *kathistēmi,* which means to "assign someone a position of authority."[25] Elsewhere in the KJV it is translated as "ordain" (Titus 1:5; Hebrews 5:1; 8:3), perhaps suggesting a formal priesthood role. The only information that we have about any of them, specifically Stephen and Philip, describes them out preaching the gospel (Acts 6:8–7:60; 8:5–40). At least in the case of Philip, they seem to be operating under the authority of the Aaronic Priesthood, rather than the Melchizedek, because while Philip baptized, it was Peter and John who came to Samaria and "prayed for them, that they might receive the Holy Ghost. . . . Then laid they their hands on them, and they received the Holy Ghost" (Acts 8:15, 17).

Beyond what specific duties the seven performed, the most

---

[24] There is no evidence that this practice was entered into by Church members outside Jerusalem.

[25] Arndt and Gingrich, *GEL,* "*kathistēmi.*"

important feature of this account is its demonstration of how the organizational structure of the Church was able to grow and adapt to meet new needs. Christ did not establish His Church, initially, in all its organizational potential. Initially there was simply no need for an extensive structure including bishops, welfare administrators, deacons, councils of elders, etc. Rather, He revealed the offices and organization of His Church gradually, line upon line, as the Church had need. Although the New Testament does not provide a record of how most Church offices developed, the calling of the seven serves as a potential model. First, there was a practical need for adaptation. Second, the Apostles considered the situation and—no doubt under inspiration—came to a solution. Third, they implemented an organizational change, and as a result, "the word of God increased" (Acts 6:7), and the Lord blessed the Church.

The rapid growth of the Church must have also caused difficulties for the Church members in finding places to worship. While they "continu[ed] daily with one accord in the temple" (Acts 2:46), they also needed places where they could meet together as followers of Christ. Houses seem to have been the gathering places of choice for members of the Church. Acts 1:13 says that the Church members met in an upper room of someone's home, possibly the same one where Jesus instituted the sacrament (see also Mark 14:15). Luke says, "Breaking bread from house to house, [they] did eat their meat with gladness and singleness of heart" (Acts 2:46). When Peter was delivered out of jail, "he came to the house of Mary the mother of John, whose surname was Mark; where many were gathered together praying" (Acts 12:12). Archaeologists have uncovered in Capernaum a house that seems to have been used as a Christian "place of meeting or worship as early as the end of the first century [A.D.]."[26]

---

[26] John J. Rousseau and Rami Arav, *Jesus and His World: An Archaeological and Cultural Dictionary* (Minneapolis, Minn.: Fortress Press, 1995), 40.

This practice of meeting in houses continued as missionary work expanded among the Gentiles and seems to have become the basic unit of the Church. Paul rarely speaks of the "whole church" (Romans 16:23; 1 Corinthians 14:23). Instead he usually speaks of the Church in somebody's house (Greek, *hē kat' oikon ekklēsia*). Thus Priscilla and Aquila, Paul's companions in Corinth and Ephesus, hosted a branch of the Church in their house (1 Corinthians 16:19; Romans 16:3–5). Likewise, Philemon hosted a branch in Colossae (Philemon 1:2), and Nymphas hosted a branch in Laodicea (Colossians 4:15). These house-churches "enabled the followers of Jesus to have a distinctively Christian worship and fellowship from the very first days of the apostolic age."[27] It is probable that in larger cities more than one house-church existed. This state may be reflected in the groupings of salutations Paul sends in Romans 16:14–15.[28] The patrons of these house-churches, some of which may have been women (e.g., Lydia and Chloe), were probably not only responsible for providing the space for the Christian gathering, they probably also provided the meal that was a part of the sacramental celebration.

House-churches were a natural outgrowth of the societal emphasis on the extended family in the first century. Cornelius was "a devout man, and one that feared God *with all his house*" (Acts 10:2; emphasis added). While he waited for Peter to come he "called together his kinsmen and near friends" to listen to Peter (Acts 10:24). This household and friends were the first Gentile converts. Likewise, when Paul taught in Philippi, he baptized Lydia "and her household" (Acts 16:15), and in Corinth he "baptized also the household of Stephanas" (1 Corinthians 1:16). A household could

---

[27] Floyd V. Filson, "The Significance of the Early House Churches," *Journal of Biblical Literature* 58 (1939): 109.

[28] Wayne A. Meeks, *The First Urban Christians: The Social World of the Apostle Paul* (New Haven: Yale University Press, 1983), 75.

consist of parents, children, grandparents, and other extended family members as well as servants and slaves. Not all members of the household, however, automatically joined the Church, as seen in the case of Onesimus who, as a slave, did not convert with his owner, Philemon (Philemon 1:1–2, 10).[29] It is possible that the early missionaries sought to baptize households that could become the nucleus of the Church in a new city.

While the Church was small, the house was a viable meeting place, where all of the membership could gather together, but the exponential growth must have eventually made it impossible to gather everyone into one place (see Acts 12:17). Therefore, in any one city there was probably more than one house-church. Given the huge distances between cities and the difficulty of communication in the first century, a centralized Church government was difficult to administer and maintain with house-churches, which probably existed with a fair amount of autonomy, except for the infrequent visits from the Apostles and the letters that they sent. It appears that the contention in Corinth may have resulted from conflicts between different house-churches that were established by different Christian missionaries (1 Corinthians 1:10–16). Likewise, 3 John may be describing a rogue leader of a house-church in its description of Diotrephes (3 John 1:9–10). Only in one instance is there a suggestion that one of these house-churches, the house of Stephanas, may have been viewed in a leadership capacity for other members of the Church (1 Corinthians 16:15–16).

"My Church"

When Jesus promised Peter at Caesarea Philippi that He would build a church, He specifically called it "my church" (Matthew 16:18). In 3 Nephi 27:8 Jesus identifies two qualifications for a

---

[29] Meeks, *First Urban Christians*, 76.

church to belong to Him: "And how be it my church save it be called in my name? For if a church be called in Moses' name then it be Moses' church; or if it be called in the name of a man then it be the church of a man; but if it be called in my name then it is my church, if it so be that they are built upon my gospel." Jesus then gives a definition of *gospel*. He encloses it within two bookends, so to speak. He begins this definition with "Behold I have given unto you my gospel, and this is the gospel which I have given unto you," and he closes with "Verily, verily, I say unto you, this is my gospel" (3 Nephi 27:13, 21). Within these two statements He teaches that the gospel, or good news, is that He came to do the will of the Father and to be lifted up on the cross that He might draw all men unto Him so that they can "stand before me, to be judged of their works, whether they be good or whether they be evil" (v. 14). But the good news is not just what *Jesus* has done; it also includes what *we* must do: repent, be baptized, remain faithful to the end, wash our garments in Christ's blood, and "be sanctified by the reception of the Holy Ghost" (v. 20). All of these principles and ordinances were taught and practiced in the New Testament. According to Jesus' definition, therefore, the New Testament contains a fulness of the gospel and the New Testament Church qualifies to be called "my church."

The New Testament, however, does not give us many indications of how the early Church members were identified, though in Acts we learn of two. In Acts 9:2 Paul seems to be calling them the "way." Before going to Damascus he went to the high priest, desiring letters to the synagogues in Damascus so that "if he found any of this way [Greek, *tēs hodou*], whether they were men or women, he might bring them bound unto Jerusalem" (Acts 9:2). Scholars have argued that the word *way* may be a term used to identify members of the Church.[30] And the Revised Standard Version contains the phrase "so if he found any belonging to the Way." Similar language is also found in Acts 19:23; 22:4; 24:14, 22. "The Way" may thus have been the earliest means to identify Church members who were still considered to be Jews but who were traveling a different path. Later, when Paul was arrested in Jerusalem, another name for the members of the Church was used when he was accused of being "a ringleader of the sect of the Nazarenes" (Acts 24:5).

But how did the earliest members of the Church identify themselves? The most frequent self-designation in the New Testament is "saints," from the Greek word *hagioi*, "dedicated to God" or "holy." This designation is used sixty times from Acts to Revelation, but only once in the four Gospels (Matthew 27:52). In Antioch, Ananias worries about "how much evil [Paul] hath done to thy saints at Jerusalem" (Acts 9:13). Twice Paul teaches about those who are "called to be saints" (1 Corinthians 1:2; Romans 1:7). Both of these references follow Paul's declaration that he was "called to be an apostle" (1 Corinthians 1:1; Romans 1:1), perhaps indicating that he saw membership in the Church as something more than an individual's decision to join. One of the principal reasons for a Church organization is for the "perfecting of the saints" (Ephesians 4:12).

But there is also another possible self-designation. Like the people who inhabited Qumran (4QpPs37 3.10; "the community of the poor"), they simply identified themselves as the poor. As we have noted, Acts makes it clear that the members of the Church donated their wealth to the Church, similar to the lifestyle practiced by those at Qumran. Twice Paul identifies the members of the Church in Jerusalem as *ho ptōchoi* ("the poor"). In Galatians,

---

[30] S. Vernon McCasland, "The Way," *Journal of Biblical Literature* (1958): 222–30.

Paul describes James, Cephas, and John's directions that as he and Barnabas preach to the Gentiles, "they would that we should remember the poor" (Galatians 2:10). Paul writes, "For it hath pleased them of Macedonia and Achaia to make a certain contribution for the poor saints which are at Jerusalem" (Romans 15:26). Both of these instances have reference to the collection Paul is making to take to the Jerusalem church and, on one level, may refer to their economic state after the famine prophesied by Agabus (Acts 11:27–28), but it may also refer to a life of consecration.[31]

The term *Christian* seems to have come later. In two of the three occasions in the New Testament, it is outsiders who use the term *Christian*. Acts 11:26 describes the period when Barnabas and Paul are teaching in the Church at Antioch: "And it came to pass, that a whole year they assembled themselves with the church, and taught much people." Then it records, "The disciples were called Christians first in Antioch." The passive voice in this verse suggests that outsiders, rather than insiders, coined this name.[32] In the second instance King Agrippa tells Paul, "Almost thou persuadest me to be a Christian" (Acts 26:28). Thus it seems that

---

[31] The early Church Fathers knew of an early group of Christians, whom they regarded as heretical, who lived the law of Moses (cf. Acts 21:20) and were called the Ebionites, from the Hebrew word for poor, *ebyônîm* (see Irenaeus, *Against Heresies*, 1.26.2; 3.11.7, 21.1; 4.33.4).

[32] For examples of outsiders using the term, see Josephus, *AJ*, 8.3.3, Pliny, *Letters*, 10.96, and Suetonius, *Claudius*, 25.13–15, where the word *Chrestus* is used. "'Christus' was often confused with 'Chrestus' by non-Christians, and sometimes even by Christians. This confusion arose from two sources, of meaning and sound. The Greek 'Christos' and its Latin equivalent 'Christus' would have suggested a strange meaning to most ancients, especially those unfamiliar with its Jewish background. Its primary Greek meaning in everyday life suggests the medical term 'anointer' or the construction term 'plasterer.' These meanings would not have the religious content that 'Christ' would have to someone on the inside of Christianity. These unusual meanings could have prompted this shift to a more recognizable, meaningful name. Due to a widespread phonetic feature of Greek, 'Christus' and 'Chrestus' were even closer in pronunciation than they appear to be today" (Robert E. Van Voorst, *Jesus outside the New Testament: An Introduction to the Ancient Evidence* [Grand Rapids, Mich.: Eerdmans, 2000], 34).

the term *Christian*, like the term *Mormon*, was originally coined by outsiders, although it eventually became a self-designation, as we see in 1 Peter 4:16: "Yet if any man suffer as a Christian, let him not be ashamed; but let him glorify God on this behalf." By the beginning of the second century, Ignatius frequently uses it as a self-designation (see his letters *Ephesians,* 11:2; *Magnesians,* 4; *Romans,* 3:2; and *Polycarp,* 7:3).

There is no doubt that the Church of the first century qualifies to be called Jesus' church on the basis of its teaching of judgment, atonement, repentance, baptism, enduring to the end, and sanctification. The case for its qualifying as His church because it was called in Jesus' name is more difficult to make in our present New Testament, although *Christian* did eventually become a self-designation.

Conclusion

From the information we have in the New Testament and early Christian literature, we see that the organization of Christ's Church on earth developed over a period of time, in a way similar to the organization of the Church in this dispensation. This development came as the fledgling Church grew and expanded both in numbers and geography. As we read the New Testament, it is important for us to understand that it gives us only the equivalent of snapshots of what the Church looked like at any one time. But the nature of the text, as it stands today, often does not join all of the pictures together into a movie of the Church in the first century. Oftentimes we have more questions than we have answers. What is true, however, is that the early Church was grounded on the teachings and Atonement of Jesus Christ, just as it is today; that it operated under the power and authority of the priesthood, just as it does today; and that the offices of the Church developed as the needs of the members and the administration dictated.

Joseph Smith did not carefully study the New Testament as

did other Christian Primitivists (Restorationists) in the nineteenth century who attempted to pattern their organizations after the church outlined in the book of Acts. The Church of Jesus Christ was organized as revealed to the Prophet by the Lord Jesus Christ. In this sense, "We believe in the same organization that existed in the Primitive Church" (Articles of Faith 1:6), that is, a church led by revelation and inspiration that adapts to the current needs of the times and to the growing membership of the Church spread across the earth.

III.

UNTO THE UTTERMOST PART OF THE EARTH

RICHARD NEITZEL HOLZAPFEL AND THOMAS A. WAYMENT

When therefore Paul and Barnabas had no small dissension and disputation with them, they determined that Paul and Barnabas, and certain other of them, should go up to Jerusalem unto the apostles and elders about this question.

Acts 15:2

Luke's Gospel account concludes with an appearance by the resurrected Lord to the disciples in an upper room in Jerusalem on the first Easter Sunday (Luke 24:33–36). During this gathering Jesus "opened . . . their understanding, that they might understand the scriptures" (Luke 24:45). He wanted them to know that the Messiah's mission included suffering, death, and resurrection so that "repentance and remission of sins should be *preached in his name among all nations,* beginning at Jerusalem" (Luke 24:47; emphasis added).

Luke does not inform his readers how the early disciples interpreted Jesus' teachings on this remarkable first Easter Sunday. Did they imagine that they had been commanded to take the gospel to all Jews living throughout the Mediterranean basin? Or did they think Jesus wanted them to preach to anyone who would be willing to listen, Jew or Gentile? Most likely, based on the religious and cultural context of Second Temple Judaism, many disciples, if not all, would not have considered that they had been commissioned to take the "good news" to both Jews and Gentiles in all the world. Probably, these disciples simply assumed that Jesus intended them to find and teach Jews living in the great Diaspora (the Jewish world).

Few Jews would have thought of themselves as "sinners" like "the Gentiles" (Galatians 2:15). Table fellowship, one of the primary ways Jews separated themselves from Gentiles, would have made it impossible for any type of meaningful social interaction between these two disparate groups because Jews would not eat in the presence of those who were considered unclean. Note the general Jewish attitude revealed by Peter when he visited at the home of a Gentile in Caesarea: "Ye know how that it is an unlawful thing for a man that is a Jew to keep company, or come unto one of another nation" (Acts 10:28). As a result, the early disciples most likely imagined that their mission among the lost sheep of Israel, which had been basically limited to Galilee and Judea, would eventually spread to the nations of the earth where scattered Israel was found (see Matthew 10:5–6).

This chapter will look at the ramifications that table fellowship had for the expansion of the Church into the Gentile world, and to a lesser extent how circumcision impeded the spread of the gospel. Additionally, this chapter will trace Luke's account of early conversions and visions to show that the book of Acts subtly teaches that a conversion of the heart was needed in order for the gospel to spread.

Pentecost

Fifty days after Passover, the disciples gathered in an upper room in Jerusalem when "suddenly there came a sound from heaven as of a rushing mighty wind, and it filled all the house where they were sitting. And there appeared unto them cloven tongues like as of fire, and it sat upon each of them. And they were all filled with the Holy Ghost, and began to speak with other tongues, as the Spirit gave them utterance" (Acts 2:2–4). Obviously, Luke believed this event fulfilled John the Baptist's prophecy (Luke 3:16; compare Acts 1:5) and Jesus' promise (Luke 24:49; Acts 1:8). Additionally, Luke most likely associated the endowment of the Spirit on Pentecost with Jesus' command to preach "in his name among all nations" (Luke 24:47) as he observed, "And there were dwelling at Jerusalem Jews, devout men, *out of every nation under heaven*" (Acts 2:5; emphasis added). Despite the obvious hyperbole, Luke reported that the good news was in fact preached to Jews from every nation at the very beginning (see Luke's list as recorded in Acts 2:9–11). Nevertheless, Luke realized that this was not the literal and complete fulfillment of Jesus' command.

Pentecost was a major event in the life of the early Church because it had "transformed and galvanized" those disciples who had earlier "doubted, deserted, and denied Jesus."[1] As a result, within a short time frame, the early Church moved from a rather small number of disciples, mainly Galileans (Acts 1:11; 2:7), living in Jerusalem to a rapidly expanding movement with three thousand being added on Pentecost (Acts 2:41) and another five thousand added shortly thereafter (Acts 4:4).[2]

What followed in the next few chapters of Acts prepared Luke's audience for the important steps in taking the gospel beyond Jerusalem as Jesus had commanded the disciples to do after the Resurrection (Luke 24:47). There were Greek-speaking Jewish disciples (KJV, "Grecians") present in Jerusalem (see Acts 6:1), although it appears that Aramaic-speaking Jewish disciples (KJV,

---

[1] Ben Witherington III, *New Testament History: A Narrative Account* (Grand Rapids, Mich.: Baker, 2001), 166, 170.

[2] See James D. G. Dunn, *Beginning from Jerusalem: Christianity in the Making*, (Grand Rapids, Mich.: Eerdmans, 2009), 2:178–80.

"Hebrews") numerically and socially dominated the early movement. However, to effectively expand the work, Greek-speaking disciples were needed if the Church was ever to expand into the Greek-speaking communities of the Diaspora. Additionally, the Twelve needed help looking after the temporal needs of the Church if they were ever going to take the gospel to the world. Faced with this somewhat sudden predicament, Luke noted that seven additional leaders, all with Greek names, supplemented the Twelve's leadership (Acts 6:2–6). Although the Twelve, apparently all Galilean and Aramaic-speaking at that time, continued their ministry, Luke turned his attention to the Greek-speaking disciples. In particular, Luke highlighted the ministries of Stephen and Philip (see Acts 6:8–15; 7:54–60; 8:5–13, 26–40).

Stephen's work was essential in preparing for the good news to spread beyond Jerusalem. He testified in a non-Aramaic-speaking synagogue in Jerusalem, known as the "synagogue of the Libertines [Freedmen]," which was composed of Jews who had formerly been slaves from Cyprus, Egypt, and Asia (see Acts 6:9), again highlighting the fact that Jews from around the Mediterranean basin were exposed to the preaching of the "good news" at a very early period.[3] Additionally, these people had connections to family and friends away from Jerusalem—a helpful situation for anyone who wished to travel and teach the gospel.

Luke highlighted another important element to the story. In the wake of intense persecution (Acts 8:1–4), Philip took the message to the Samaritans, the longtime Jewish antagonists (Acts 8:5–13).[4] James D. G. Dunn highlights the significance of this

---

[3] Luke is most likely referring to one synagogue here instead of several; see Ben Witherington III, *The Acts of the Apostles: A Socio-Rhetorical Commentary* (Grand Rapids, Mich.: Eerdmans, 1998), 253–57.

[4] Luke's access to these early stories is not difficult to accept because, if we take the "we" passages literally, he stayed with Philip in Caesarea many years later when he traveled to Jerusalem with Paul (see Acts 21:8).

particular mission, "The step of taking the proclamation of Jesus Messiah to them as well constituted a significant step across a major boundary. . . . A deliberate stepping across (Philip goes to a/ the city of Samaria), one of the boundaries by which Judaism had defined itself as Jew and not Samaritan!"[5] The Apostles sustained this mission beyond Jerusalem by sending Peter and John to follow in Philip's footsteps (Acts 8:14–25).

The First Gentile Convert

In the next scene, Luke preserved the story of Philip's boundary-crossing experience on the road from Jerusalem to Gaza when he taught a court official from Ethiopia (the region south of Egypt). The official was an overseer of the treasury of the Ethiopian queen Candace, and he was both wealthy and prominent himself.[6] He may have already been a Jewish convert as it appears he traveled a long distance to worship in Jerusalem (at the Temple) and that he had spent a significant amount of money in order to own a scroll of Isaiah (see Acts 8:27–28). Such an assumption would not have necessarily surprised anyone since there were numerous examples of well-known converts to Judaism during the first century. For example, Queen Helene of Adiabene, a minor kingdom in Mesopotamia (located in modern Iraq), converted about the same time, around A.D. 30. She eventually moved to Jerusalem and built a magnificent tomb complex where she and her family were eventually buried.[7]

However, Luke provided an important clue that is generally missed by the casual reader when he described him as "a man of

---

[5] Dunn, *Beginning from Jerusalem,* 280.

[6] F. Scott Spencer, "Ethiopian Eunuch," in David Noel Freedman et al., eds., *Eerdmans Dictionary of the Bible* (Grand Rapids, Mich.: Eerdmans, 2000), 433.

[7] See Jerome Murphy-O'Connor, *The Holy Land: An Oxford Archaeological Guide from Earliest Times to 1700,* 5th ed. (New York: Oxford University Press, 2008), 158–59.

Ethiopia, *an eunuch*" (Acts 8:27; emphasis added). A eunuch was unable to submit to circumcision and therefore could not be a proselyte (see Leviticus 21:18–21; Deuteronomy 23:1), and thus he could only remain a "God-Fearer" or one who admired, appreciated, and followed the Jewish law but always as an outsider. Behind this narrative is Isaiah's prophecy of the future day when eunuchs would be welcomed into the house of the Lord (Isaiah 56:3–8).

Underlying the story is the role of the "God-Fearers," Gentiles who attached themselves to the Jewish synagogue, without becoming full-fledged converts (see Acts 8:27). Luke highlighted how they had been prepared for the "good news" through their study of the Septuagint (LXX), fasting, prayer, and good works.

To emphasize the significance of the event, Luke bracketed the story between two miraculous events: first, the appearance of an angel, and second, Philip's departure through the medium of "the Spirit of the Lord" which transported him away to Azotus, ancient Ashdod, some twenty miles north of Gaza. The story's focus then follows the historical and geographical context Luke provided: "Then Philip opened his mouth, and began at the same scripture, and preached unto him Jesus. And as they went on their way, they came unto a certain water: and the eunuch said, See, here is water; what doth hinder me to be baptized? And Philip said, If thou believest with all thine heart, thou mayest. And he answered and said, I believe that Jesus Christ is the Son of God. And he commanded the chariot to stand still: and they went down both into the water, both Philip and the eunuch; and he baptized him" (Acts 8:35–38).

With the conversion and baptism of the first Gentile, the foundation is laid for the wider Gentile mission Jesus envisioned from the beginning. Luke's designation that the convert was from Ethiopia, a land considered by the Mediterranean people to be at the ends of civilization, most likely reminded his audience of Jesus' command to take the gospel to the "uttermost part of the earth" (Acts 1:8).

Luke, having prepared his readers for such a significant and bold move, then highlights three additional important conversions: first, Paul's conversion (Acts 9:1–20); second, Peter's conversion (Acts 10:1–48); and third, the Jerusalem Church leadership's conversion (Acts 11:1–18). In using the word *conversion* in these three instances, we should not think that Paul, Peter, or the leadership in Jerusalem had moved from a state of rebellion against the Lord to discipleship or that any of them had moved from one religion to another. These three episodes are better understood "as calls by God to new roles."[8] J. L. Houlden, highlighting Paul's conversion, noted that it "is in many ways comparable to such prophetic calls; indeed, 'call' (Greek, *kaleō*) is Paul's own most characteristic word for the summons of God both to himself and to others (1 Corinthians 1:1–2; 7:17–24)."[9]

The Ethiopian's baptism and Paul's, Peter's, and the Jerusalem leadership's call to a new role are the foundation to another important landmark in the story of the early Church—the Jerusalem Conference held in A.D. 49 (see Acts 15:1–34).

Paul's Conversion

Luke had already introduced his readers to Saul (Paul) at the time of Stephen's martyrdom (Acts 7:58; 8:1). He provided additional insights when he noted that Saul "made havock of the church, entering into every house, and hailing men and women committed them to prison" (Acts 8:3). Following Philip's mission to the Samaritans and the baptism of the Ethiopian eunuch, ironically facilitated by Saul's persecution, Luke then provided

---

[8] J. L. Houlden, "Conversion," in Bruce M. Metzger and Michael D. Coogan, eds., *The Oxford Companion to the Bible* (New York: Oxford University Press, 1993), 133.

[9] Houlden, "Conversion," 133.

a rather detailed story of how the persecutor had become the disciple.

Again highlighting Saul's persecution of the Church, Luke wrote that Saul was "breathing out threatenings and slaughter against the disciples of the Lord" (Acts 9:1). Although Luke does not specifically mention it, Saul could not legally kill Christians in Damascus or in Jerusalem, which may be hinted at with the verb "breathing" (Greek, *empneōn*). Moreover, Saul sought permission from the high priest in Jerusalem (probably Caiaphas) to harass Christians in Damascus. The KJV uses the term "bound" (Acts 9:2), but historically it seems unlikely that Paul would have had power to actually arrest and bind anyone. Rather, those Christians whom he found "of this way" (Acts 9:2) would have to willingly submit to their excommunication and any associated punishments.

But on his way to harass Christians, Saul received a vision that powerfully changed his direction in life, and Saul discovered that he must follow the Lord Jesus Christ: "And he fell to the earth, and heard a voice saying unto him, Saul, Saul, why persecutest thou me? And he said, Who art thou, Lord? And the Lord said, I am Jesus whom thou persecutest: it is hard for thee to kick against the pricks. And he trembling and astonished said, Lord, what wilt thou have me to do? And the Lord said unto him, Arise, and go into the city, and it shall be told thee what thou must do" (Acts 9:4–6).

Saul was taken to Damascus where he waited to receive further directions from one of the leaders of the Church, an otherwise unknown disciple identified as Ananias. Luke said that the Lord spoke to Ananias, commanding him, "Arise, and go into the street which is called Straight, and enquire in the house of Judas for one called Saul, of Tarsus: for, behold, he prayeth" (Acts 9:11). At first, Ananias questioned the Lord about the prudence to visit the one who had been sent to "bind all that call on thy name" (Acts 9:14). Ananias was then informed about Saul's important role: "But the Lord said unto him, Go thy way: for he is a chosen vessel unto me, to bear my name before the Gentiles, and kings, and the children of Israel: For I will shew him how great things he must suffer for my name's sake" (Acts 9:15–16). The persecutor would soon become the persecuted.

Eventually Saul, having been healed, baptized, and strengthened, "preached Christ in the synagogues, that he is the Son of God" (Acts 9:20). As he continued his ministry, "Saul increased the more in strength, and confounded the Jews which dwelt at Damascus, proving that this is very Christ" (Acts 9:22).

Underlying the story is the Lord's direct intervention in the history of the early Church. Jerome Murphy-O'Connor wrote, "Paul explicitly reports that Jesus took the initiative, 'Last of all, as to one untimely born, he appeared also to me' (1 Corinthians 15:8)."[10] The stage was set for the next important conversion narrative, that of Peter, the senior Apostle.

Peter's Conversion

Like Saul, Peter also experienced a complete turnaround in accepting Gentiles into the Church (Acts 10:28). The decisive moment came about only after a series of interconnected visions (Acts 10:3–6, 10–16), reminding the reader of the visions Saul and Ananias had experienced earlier that also signaled another decisive moment in the history of the early Church (Acts 9:3–6, 10–16). The visions, signaling a moment of change, came in the form of Peter's prompting by the Holy Spirit to visit Cornelius (Acts 10:19–20), and the unexpected and visible reception of the Holy Ghost by Cornelius and his household—most likely understood as a second Pentecost (Acts 10:44).

Peter's conversion began with the realization that the Lord's work was not constrained by traditional boundaries, whether

---

[10] Jerome Murphy-O'Connor, *Paul: His Story* (New York: Oxford University Press, 2004), 23.

geographical or social. Peter observed, "Of a truth I perceive that God is no respecter of persons: But in every nation he that feareth him, and worketh righteousness, is accepted with him" (Acts 10:34–35). In this way, Peter began to acknowledge that the Lord had accepted those he previously believed were unacceptable to the Lord. In other words, Peter learned that the gospel was for all people, and it was now the only way to salvation.

Yet Peter's vision of the unclean food, the heavenly voice commanding him to eat (Acts 10:11–16), and the recitation of the angelic visitation to Cornelius (Acts 10:22, 30–33) were still not enough to compel Peter to baptize the Roman soldier; that event would occur only after another heavenly intervention: "While Peter yet spake these words, the Holy Ghost fell on all them which heard the word. And they of the circumcision which believed were astonished, as many as came with Peter, because that on the Gentiles also was poured out the gift of the Holy Ghost. For they heard them speak with tongues, and magnify God. Then answered Peter, Can any man forbid water, that these should not be baptized, which have received the Holy Ghost as well as we? And he commanded them to be baptized in the name of the Lord" (Acts 10:44–48).

The Jerusalem Church Leaders' Conversion

The story of Peter and Cornelius is repeated in Acts 11, when the senior Apostle related his experience in Caesarea to Church leaders in Jerusalem. The story is more about accepting Peter's decision to eat with Gentiles (Acts 11:3), an act that crossed an important boundary that separated Jews and Gentiles in the first century, than accepting a Gentile into the Church, which may have been seen as a simple exception to Gentiles being perceived as being beyond salvation. The situation was resolved when Peter informed the Apostles and brethren in Jerusalem about his visions in Joppa (Acts 11:5–10); the prompting of the Holy Spirit to travel to

Caesarea (Acts 11:11–12), Cornelius's vision (Acts 11:13–14); and finally, how the Holy Ghost fell upon the uncircumcised Gentiles while he preached to them (Acts 11:15–17). Luke concluded by saying, "When they heard these things, they held their peace, and glorified God, saying, Then hath God also to the Gentiles granted repentance unto life" (Acts 11:18).

Nonetheless, the conversions of the Ethiopian eunuch, Paul, Peter, and the Church leaders in Jerusalem to the Lord's vision of inclusion still did not resolve the practical consideration of how Jewish-Christians and Gentile-Christians would interact. This issue is highlighted by the conflict and crisis that arose in Antioch.

Conflict and Crisis in Antioch

In his letter to the Galatians, dated between A.D. 48–49, Paul stated that he had worked in harmony with Church leaders in Jerusalem and noted he made an important second visit to Jerusalem to insure that his missionary strategy was accepted and supported by the Apostles and elders: "Then fourteen years after I went up again to Jerusalem with Barnabas, and took Titus with me also. And I went up by revelation, and communicated unto them that gospel which I preach among the Gentiles, but privately to them which were of reputation, lest by any means I should run, or had run, in vain. But neither Titus, who was with me, being a Greek, was compelled to be circumcised" (Galatians 2:1–3). Traditionally, many commentators have argued that this meeting is also described in Acts 15.[11] However, an increasing number of scholars argue that this meeting should be associated with the one mentioned in Acts 11:30.[12] In the end, the sequence is

---

[11] See, for example, John T. Squires, "Acts," in James D. G. Dunn and John W. Rogerson, eds., *Eerdmans Commentary on the Bible* (Grand Rapids, Mich.: Eerdmans, 2003), 1244.

[12] See, for example, Ben Witherington III, *Grace in Galatia: A Commentary on St. Paul's Letter to the Galatians* (Grand Rapids, Mich.: Eerdmans, 1998), 2–20.

less important than the result of the Jerusalem Conference itself.[13] Nevertheless, the second proposal places Paul back in Antioch (modern Antakya, Turkey), along with Barnabas and Peter, sometime before the famous Jerusalem Conference (see Acts 15), and thus helps clarify how Peter came to be in Antioch (Galatians 2:11–12).

While in Antioch, Peter ate with the Gentile converts, as did Barnabas and Paul. However, when a group of emissaries from Jerusalem appeared on the scene claiming to represent James, Peter waffled. These men from Jerusalem were probably the "false brethren" Paul identified "who came in privily to spy out our liberty which we have in Christ Jesus, that they might bring us into bondage" (Galatians 2:4–5).

Paul continued, "When they were come, [Peter] withdrew and separated himself, fearing them which were of the circumcision [party]" (Galatians 2:12). The other Jewish-Christians present, including Barnabas, followed Peter's example and withdrew from eating with the Gentile-Christians. This was all too much for Paul, so he confronted Peter in front of the entire group and "withstood [Peter]" face to face (see Galatians 2:11–12).

What was at stake was nothing more or less than one of the major boundary makers in first-century Judaism. Circumcision, another major boundary maker, was interconnected with table fellowship because it signified obedience to a covenant in a way that was similar to the acceptance to live the kosher requirements (the *Kashrut*). These two interrelated aspects were essential to Jewish self-understanding. Jerome Murphy-O'Connor noted, "In the ancient Near East a formal meal was the prime social event. To share food was to initiate or reinforce a social bonding which implied permanent commitment and deep ethical obligation."[14] He further

---

[13] Dunn, *Beginning from Jerusalem*, 447.
[14] Murphy-O'Connor, *Paul*, 42.

noted, "Nowhere was the significance of a meal more accentuated than in Judaism. . . . The vast majority would have observed the fundamental distinction between clean and unclean food. . . . It was a matter of principle for which their ancestors had died, and it was one of the most obvious identity markers of the Jewish religion."[15]

Luke provided another version of the crisis, emphasizing the root cause—circumcision: "And certain men which came down from Judaea taught the brethren, and said, Except ye be circumcised after the manner of Moses, ye cannot be saved. When therefore Paul and Barnabas had no small dissension and disputation with them, they determined that Paul and Barnabas, and certain other of them, should go up to Jerusalem unto the apostles and elders about this question" (Acts 15:1–2).

What may be surprising is that it took so long for the issue to come to the forefront. However, in the years following Jesus' Resurrection, a small trickle of Gentile converts joined the Church. Traditional Jewish-Christians may have accepted them in the same way that uncircumcised "God-Fearers" were accepted in the local synagogues as an anomaly, a minority among the sea of Jews and proselytes. Additionally, there may have been the hope they would continue their spiritual journey to become full-fledged converts. However, as the numbers of Gentile-Christians increased in the Church, especially in light of Paul's stunning successes (Acts 13–14), tensions naturally arose. Dunn emphasized, "It was only when the number of Gentile converts began to outnumber the believing Jews that alarm bells began to ring."[16]

By A.D. 49, the situation had come to a critical point as exemplified by Paul's experience in Antioch. In this setting, an important council, identified as the Jerusalem Conference, was held. The

---

[15] Ibid.

[16] Dunn, *Beginning from Jerusalem,* 446.

time between the crisis in Antioch and the Jerusalem Conference is undeterminable. However, we should not imagine a lengthy period between both events.

The Jerusalem Conference

Luke's report of the meeting in Jerusalem in A.D. 49 is important on several levels. First, the "attention Luke gives to *how* the Church makes the decision required of it is an intrinsic part of this narrative's message."[17] Although it was not Luke's intention to provide such details, in narrating the story he provides historical clues along the way that allow us to reconstruct to some extent how the Church operated. Second, and more importantly, the content of the report is theologically central to Luke's story.

From Luke we learn that some Jewish-Christians, identified as Pharisees "which believed," argued that Gentile-Christians needed to submit to circumcision (see Acts 15:5). Most likely, they had their own scriptural justifications to sustain their position (see, for example, Genesis 17:9–14).

As the Church gathered in the Holy City for this important meeting, Luke informed his readers that the major actors were all present: Barnabas, Paul, James, and Peter. In this section, Luke preserved three discourses delivered at the meeting. Peter delivered the first talk and reminded those attending what the Lord had revealed to him (Acts 15:7). He taught that God had already decided, since He knows the hearts of all men, that the Gentiles and the Jewish-Christians were on equal footing: "We believe that through the grace of the Lord Jesus Christ we shall be saved, even as they" (Acts 15:11). As a result, Peter asked, "Why tempt ye God?" (Acts 15:10). Luke's account seems to reach a conclusion at the end of Peter's declaration. However, that conclusion is interrupted by the

---

[17] Luke Timothy Johnson, *The Acts of the Apostles* (Collegeville, Minn.: Glazier, 1992), 271.

second discourse, a short summary report by Barnabas and Paul in which they reaffirmed that God was working among the Gentiles (Acts 15:12; compare Acts 14:27).

The final discourse, more extended than the first two, was made by James, the brother of Jesus and leader of the Jerusalem Church (Acts 15:13–21). James, like Peter, Barnabas, and Paul, referred to past events (Acts 15:14). Additionally he provided scriptural justification (Jeremiah 12:15) for rejecting the claim by "the Pharisees which believed" (Acts 15:5) that Gentile-Christians had to be circumcised. James concluded, like Peter, "we trouble not them" (Acts 15:19), and therefore did not require circumcision of male Gentile converts. This removed the most significant obstacle for future Gentile conversions. Obviously, for some present, this decision would have been very difficult to accept because Judaism was more than a religion: it also provided Jews with a national identity. Therefore, the line between tradition and law was almost impossible to determine in some instances. Recognizing the challenge the proposal faced, James added what may be considered a compromise. Based on scriptural justification also, he suggested, "We write unto them, that they abstain from pollutions of idols [Exodus 34:11–17; Leviticus 17:8–9], and from fornication [Leviticus 18:6–29], and from things strangled [Exodus 22:31; Leviticus 17:10–16], and from blood [Genesis 9:4; Deuteronomy 12:15–16, 23–25; Leviticus 17:11–14]" (Acts 15:19–20).

The Apostles, elders, and the Church sustained the decision, which is sometimes identified as the "Apostolic Decree" (Acts 15:22). Dunn reminds us, "We should not underestimate how astonishing a decision was here made: that Jews, leaders of a Jewish messianic sect, agreed in considered and formal terms that circumcision need no longer be required of Gentiles wishing to be counted full members of that sect—despite Genesis 17:9–14," which has rather strong scriptural pronouncements on the subject.¹⁸ He adds, "Clear scriptural teaching and historic tradition had been set aside and discounted in the light of events clearly perceived as the work of God."¹⁹

In keeping with first-century practice, the Apostles, elders, and Church sent representatives and letters outlining the decision, indicating that the "Holy Ghost" confirmed their decision (Acts 15:28). With the conclusion of this important gathering, Luke turned his attention to Paul's ministry, which would eventually take him to the heart of the empire: to Rome itself. And with this emphatic shift in focus, Peter completely disappears from the narrative.

Conclusion

Luke's purpose in preparing the book of Acts seems to have been an effort to show how Jesus' commands to the disciples were fulfilled. Specifically, Luke noted that Jesus told the Apostles, "But ye shall receive power, after that the Holy Ghost is come upon you: and ye shall be witnesses unto me both in Jerusalem, and in all Judaea, and in Samaria, and unto *the uttermost part of the earth*" (Acts 1:8; emphasis added).

The story of how the "good news" was preached beyond Jerusalem was not only about the geographical expansion of the work but also about a boundary-breaking ministry to those beyond the confines of Judaism. Dunn opined, "The events which transformed the new sect functioning primarily, even exclusively, in Jerusalem and its immediate environs into a powerful missionary movement reaching out beyond Palestine and Judaism."²⁰

The conversions of the Ethiopian eunuch, Paul, Peter, and the leaders of the Jerusalem Church were essential in bringing

---

[18] Dunn, *Beginning from Jerusalem*, 456.
[19] Ibid.
[20] Ibid., 294.

the Gentiles into the Church but did not completely resolve the practical issues related to relations between Jewish-Christians and Gentile-Christians. The Jerusalem Conference, outlined in Acts 15, aimed to do so. As one scholar noted, "It is no exaggeration to say that Acts 15 is the most critical chapter in the whole book."[21] It provides a window into the early Church's efforts to understand the new world Jesus inaugurated.

---

[21] Witherington, *New Testament History,* 243.

IV.

THE IMPACT OF GENTILE CONVERSIONS IN THE GRECO-ROMAN WORLD

ERIC D. HUNTSMAN

Ye know how that it is an unlawful thing for a man that is a Jew to keep company, or come unto one of another nation; but God hath shewed me that I should not call any man common or unclean.

Acts 10:28

Conversion to Christianity necessitated obvious changes in lifestyle, and, as noted by Paul, the most striking change in pagans who accepted Jesus manifested itself in their moral behavior: "Know ye not that the unrighteous shall not inherit the kingdom of God? Be not deceived: neither fornicators, nor idolaters, nor adulterers, nor effeminate, nor abusers of themselves with mankind, nor thieves, nor covetous, nor drunkards, nor revilers, nor extortioners, shall inherit the kingdom of God. And such were some of you: but ye are washed, but ye are sanctified, but ye are justified in the name of the Lord Jesus, and by the Spirit of our God" (1 Corinthians 6:9–11).

Such changes not only had spiritual, eternal consequences but also improved the quality of converts' earthly lives and relationships. Leaving their previous lifestyles, however, affected new

Christians in many ancillary ways, some of which separated them from the mainstream of Greek and Roman society, sometimes with negative—albeit temporal—implications. Outside of the spiritual realm, the consequences of Gentile conversions can primarily be seen in the familial, socioeconomic, and civic aspects of their lives. As a result, some Christians increasingly found themselves strangers in their own homes and communities and suffered everything from alienation to the early stages of persecution for their beliefs. Nevertheless, such Apostles as Paul and Peter assured them that their sufferings were worth the reward of eternal life.

Family Life

While Paul's list in 1 Corinthians 6:9–11 of sinful behaviors might leave modern readers with the impression that Greco-Roman society was degenerate, the reality was that there were many positive aspects to their social and family life. Indeed, rather than completely revising the way Christians looked at their family relations, Paul and Peter both began their teaching on this subject by using as a starting place what are often called Greek and Roman "household codes" (see, for example, Ephesians 5:21–6:9; cf. Colossians 3:18–24; Titus 2:1–10; 1 Peter 2:11–3:12).[1] Rather than defining the family in terms of the modern nuclear family, Greeks and Romans looked at them as households (Greek, *oikia;* Latin, *familia*) that consisted of everyone under the legal authority

---

[1] David C. Verner, *The Household of God: The Social World of the Pastoral Epistles,* SBL Dissertation Series 71 (Chico, Calif.: Scholars, 1983), 16–23, 83–91; F. F. Bruce, *The Epistles to the Colossians, to Philemon, and to the Ephesians,* a vol. in The New International Commentary on the New Testament (Grand Rapids, Mich.: Eerdmans, 1984), 160–70, 381–402; James D. G. Dunn, *The Epistles to the Colossians and to Philemon: A Commentary on the Greek Text* (Grand Rapids, Mich.: Eerdmans, 1996), 242–57; George W. Knight III, *The Pastoral Epistles: A Commentary on the Greek Text* (Grand Rapids, Mich.: Eerdmans, 1992), 316–18; Peter H. Davids, *The First Epistle of Peter: A Commentary on the Greek Text* (Grand Rapids, Mich.: Eerdmans, 1990), 94, 105–6, 114–16, 121–23.

of the oldest living male (Greek, *kyrios;* Latin, *pater familias*). This group included not only a wife and minor children but also frequently included grown children, slaves, former slaves, and other clients (these latter consisting of individuals who voluntarily submitted themselves to a patron and thereby came under his authority and became part of his household). By extension, households could also consist of stem families, including a lone grandparent or any unmarried female relatives living with the family. Strictly hierarchical, all these family relationships were largely asymmetrical with wives subject to husbands, children to parents, and slaves to masters.[2]

While this asymmetry may seem heavily gender- and class-biased today, the Apostles seem to have recognized that most of the core relationships—and even some of the roles—reflected lasting principles.[3] What Paul and Peter did for new Christians was emphasize responsibility and duty over rights and privileges, tempering Greek and Roman household codes with love and the example of Jesus Christ. For instance, Paul stressed that Christians should improve upon Greek and Roman precedents, writing "Husbands, love your wives, even as Christ also loved the church, and gave himself for it" and "Fathers, provoke not your children to wrath: but bring them up in the nurture and admonition of

---

[2] Classical works on the nature and management of the household include Xenophon, *Oeconomicus*; Aristotle, *Politics,* I.1253b.1–14; and Dionysius of Halicarnassus, *Roman Antiquities,* 2.25.4–26.4. See Beryl Rawson, "The Roman Family," in Beryl Rawson, ed., *The Family in Ancient Rome: New Perspectives* (Ithaca: Cornell University Press, 1986), 7–31; Verner, *Household of God,* 27–35, 64–71, 79–81; and Lin Foxhall and Keith R. Bradley, "Household," in Simon Hornblower and Antony Spawforth, eds., *The Oxford Classical Dictionary* (Oxford and New York: Oxford University Press, 1996), 729–30.

[3] Compare this to the Proclamation on the Family: "By divine design, fathers are to preside over their families in love and righteousness and are responsible to provide the necessities of life and protection for their families. Mothers are primarily responsible for the nurture of their children. . . . Extended families should lend support when needed" ("The Family: A Proclamation to the World," *Ensign,* November 1995, 102).

the Lord" (Ephesians 5:25; 6:4).[4] Christian conduct (KJV, "conversation"), not just in family life but in general, would then serve as an example for non-Christians: "Conduct yourselves honorably among the Gentiles, so that, though they malign you as evildoers, they may see your honorable deeds and glorify God when he comes to judge" (NRSV, 1 Peter 2:12).

Nevertheless, Christian conversion could be a divisive factor in family life, as Jesus Himself had prophesied (see Matthew 10:34–37). Paul addressed the issue more specifically when presented with the situation of only one spouse in a family being converted: "But to the rest speak I, not the Lord: If any brother hath a wife that believeth not, and she be pleased to dwell with him, let him not put her away. And the woman which hath an husband that believeth not, and if he be pleased to dwell with her, let her not leave him. . . . But if the unbelieving depart, let him depart. A brother or a sister is not under bondage in such cases: but God hath called us to peace" (1 Corinthians 7:12–13, 15).

In short, Christian belief supported existing families, and Christians need not find themselves in conflict with the basic aspects of household codes if the unbelieving partner was willing to allow the believer his or her spiritual freedom. The Christian's primary loyalty, however, would always be to God, and if a conflict on this issue arose, Paul hoped for amicable separation. Indeed, Christians should not be "unequally yoked together with unbelievers" (2 Corinthians 6:14), although this passage may well have applied to other relationships than just marriage. Nevertheless, Paul's belief was that the unbelieving spouse would be sanctified by the believer, perhaps because his or her example would lead to eventual conversion, a hope shared by Peter (see 1 Peter 3:1). Likewise the children would hopefully come under Christian influence if the

---

[4] Bruce, *Epistles to the Colossians,* 391–92.

marriage endured,[5] especially since under Roman law children remained with the father in the event of a divorce.[6]

Even if a mixed family was able to stay together, the believer could still find himself or herself alienated from many of the family's activities, both in the immediate household and in the extended clan. This was because paganism was not only a communal religious system, but also, above all, a family religion. The goddess of the hearth, *Hestia,* was primarily worshiped in the Greek home, and particular aspects of some well-known deities, such as Hera and Artemis, that dealt with such family issues as marriage and childbirth were also the focus of household cults. More particularly, dating from at least the fourth century B.C., Greek families venerated a tutelary or protective spirit known as *agathē tychē* ("good fortune") in order to invoke her blessing on the home and secure its prosperity, and the first libation of every meal was poured out to a mysterious figure known as *agathos daimōn* (or the "good divinity").[7] Greeks or other Hellenized believers might have found themselves isolated or left out of family worship, and consequently other family members might have viewed them suspiciously if misfortune befell the family. Furthermore, in Greece, families and clans shared ancestral cults known as the *patrōoi theoi,* or inherited gods. While these went by names such as *Apollōn Patroös* (the "ancestral Apollo") and *Zeus Herkeios* ("Zeus of the Courtyard"), there was the sense that each clan or tribe's Apollo and Zeus was specific to it.[8] In addition to not being able to participate in such rites

---

[5] See Eric D. Huntsman, "The Wisdom of Men," in Ray L. Huntington, Frank F. Judd, and David M. Whitchurch, eds., *Shedding Light on the New Testament: Acts–Revelation* (Provo, Utah: Religious Studies Center, 2009), 89–90.

[6] Rawson, "The Roman Family," 30, 35–36.

[7] Walter Burkert, *Greek Religion,* trans. John Raffan (Cambridge: Harvard University Press, 1985), 180; Robert C. T. Parker, "Agathos Daimon," in *Oxford Classical Dictionary,* 38.

[8] Burkert, *Greek Religion,* 130, 255–56; Robert Christopher Towneley Parker, "*patrōoi theoi,*" in *Oxford Classical Dictionary,* 1127.

at clan festivals and gatherings, Christians could have conceivably suffered civic disabilities because political rights in some communities were tied to clan membership and participation.[9]

Slightly more is known about the religious life of Roman families. Like Greek homes, the Roman home centered on the *focus* or "hearth," where the daughters of the family regularly offered sacred salt cakes to the goddess Vesta and where the family as a whole worshiped all of its domestic gods. The Lares and Penates, commonly interpreted as "the household gods," actually represented two different but important forces. The *Lar familiaris* was probably the spirit of the family's ancestral plot and thus represented the power of production and increase sought by the family, while the *di penates* were the divinities who guarded the house's storerooms. These household gods were honored on the so-called "named days" of each month (the *kalends, nones,* and *ides*) as well as on other days important to the family, when the *focus* was adorned with garlands and small sacrifices were made in the fire.[10] All-important in the household cult was the regular veneration of the *genius,* or tutelary spirit of the *pater familias* or "head of the family." Representing both his guardian spirit and his procreative and productive force, the *genius* was the regular focus of the household cult, particularly at the marriage of the *pater* and on his birthday.[11] The mother had a similar but less well-known or documented spiritual counterpart, known as the *iuno.*[12]

---

[9] Burkert, *Greek Religion,* 255.

[10] Celia E. Shultz, *Women's Religious Activity in the Roman Republic* (Chapel Hill: University of North Carolina Press, 2006), 123–24.

[11] W. Warde Fowler, *The Religious Experience of the Roman People: From the Earliest Times to the Age of Augustus* (London: Macmillan, 1911), 74–75; John Scheid, "genius," in *Oxford Classical Dictionary,* 630; Shultz, *Women's Religious Activity in the Roman Republic,* 124.

[12] Shultz, *Women's Religious Activity in the Roman Republic,* 124. Robert E. A. Palmer, *Roman Religion and Roman Empire: Five Essays* (Philadelphia: University of Pennsylvania Press, 1974), 118.

As with Greek families, Roman families also had religious cults specific to the extended family or clan, members of which all shared a common ancestor. Connected with this was a common form of ancestor worship focused on the mysterious *di manes.* Additionally, prominent noble families kept masks of their ancestors—the *imagines*—in the atrium or main room of the house, which may have been honored almost to the point of worship. A Christian in a mixed family would thus find himself or herself regularly left out of the *sacra,* or "sacred rites," as well as other central acts of worship in the home. Because these rites occurred daily in connection with meals and for the prosperity of the home and because they were performed frequently in connection with births, birthdays, coming-of-age ceremonies, anniversaries, and deaths, Christians often found themselves separated from their own families, even if they were able to continue to live with them.

Economic and Social Life

The pervasiveness of paganism extended to most aspects of life outside the home as well. Even if Christians no longer worshiped in Greek and Roman temples, for instance, they could not escape the ubiquitous presence of pagan altars, shrines, and precincts. Furthermore, large temples frequently served as banks, public records offices, and meeting places, complicating some routine business for Christians who would prefer to have nothing to do with their former religion.[13]

While some Christians might differentiate clearly in their own minds between religious and business activities in these locations, the distinction might have been blurry for others, helping provide context for Paul's discussion about offending a brother's conscience by one's behavior in the case of eating meat that was slaughtered as

---

[13] Richard Neitzel Holzapfel, Eric D. Huntsman, and Thomas A. Wayment, *Jesus Christ and the World of the New Testament* (Salt Lake City: Deseret Book, 2006), 226.

part of a sacrifice in pagan temples (1 Corinthians 8:1–13).[14] This was not simply a case of a Christian needing to decide whether he could participate in a public festival—effectively a community cookout—where sacrificial food was shared among those attending. Because meat was a luxury item and a rare part of most people's diets, there were not large-scale slaughter facilities, and much of the meat sold in the markets (KJV, "shambles") may have come from large temples. In this case Paul advised that Christians not concern themselves with where the meat had originally come from, since they had not been present at, and hence were not endorsing, the ceremony in which it had been offered to a pagan deity (1 Corinthians 10:25).[15]

Paul's subsequent discussion of options when meat was presented to a Christian at a private dinner party—he counseled that believers need not ask whether it came from a pagan temple but ought to decline eating it if informed by the host that it had (1 Corinthians 10:27–29)[16]—raises a larger issue of private social interactions. For example, feasts hosted in private homes regularly began with prayers and libations to the gods, perhaps discouraging new Christians from continuing some of their previous social interactions. This social disability would have particularly impacted Christians who came from the socioeconomic elite, because their economic and political lives were tied closely to their social networks. This no doubt led to increasing distance between believers and their former friends and neighbors, who might have seen

---

[14] Huntsman, "Wisdom of Men," 79–81.

[15] Hints in the correspondence of Pliny, Roman governor of Bithynia, to the emperor Trajan in A.D. 112 actually suggest that some of those who complained against the Christians in that province included guilds of butchers, who reported that sales of sacrificial meat had declined because Christians would not buy it: "Flesh of sacrificial victims is on sale everywhere, though up till recently scarcely anyone could be found to buy it" (Pliny, *Epistles*, 10.97. See Robert L. Wilken, *The Christians As the Romans Saw Them* (New Haven: Yale University Press, 1984), 15–16.

[16] Huntsman, "Wisdom of Men," 81–82.

Christians as antisocial or aloof. The need to counter this perception may have been an important reason why the Apostles regularly stressed the importance of setting a good example and positively engaging the outside world.

Conversion impacted another set of social networks common in Greek and Roman cities, where Christianity experienced most of its early growth. These networks consisted of voluntary associations known as *hetairiai* and in Latin as *collegia* (as well as by other terms, such as *sodales* or, based on the Greek term, *hetaeria*) and were made up of groups of people who shared a mutual interest—whether it was the devotion to a common god, economic activity, political objective, or other personal pursuit or hobby. While such clubs were increasingly regulated in the imperial period because of their potential for political activism, they were particularly popular among merchants or craftsmen, who did not have the same opportunities for social interaction that the upper classes did.[17] Because these groups often consisted of people engaged in similar lines of economic activity, they were somewhat analogous to the guilds of the medieval period. They were different than trade guilds or modern unions, however, in that their primary object was social. Meeting together on occasion for shared meals or to celebrate the accomplishments of their members, they were more comparable to fraternal organizations such as the Freemasons or social organizations such as modern Lions and Elks Clubs. However, because all of these associations had religious aspects to them, including religious rites and frequently a common divine patron, Christians would have found themselves uncomfortable with many of the clubs' activities, leading many of them to withdraw from their previous associations. Severing such ties doubtless had economic

---

[17] Wilken, *Christians As the Romans Saw Them*, 13, 32–40; Marcus Niehbur Todd, "Clubs, Greek," and George Hope Stevenson and Andrew William Lintott, "Clubs, Roman," in *Oxford Classical Dictionary*, 351–52.

as well as social implications, depriving some Christians of earlier networks that might have contributed to their business or other activities.

Perhaps as a result, Christians increasingly turned to each other for support and social interaction. As part of the house-church structure of the early New Testament Church, Christians already followed the pattern of gathering regularly in a member's home to partake of a communal meal, celebrate the Lord's Supper, and worship, but as is often the case with converts today, the Church also became the primary social network for new believers to socialize. The term Christians used for their congregations was *ekklēsiae*, which was actually a borrowed political term that meant "assembly," but the term that Roman sources used for these gatherings was *hetaeria* or "clubs." In many ways Christian practice seemed indistinguishable to pagans from associations formed to worship Isis, Mithras, Bacchus, or other particular deities outside official state cults.[18]

Furthermore, Christian congregations quickly began to assume another important function filled by Greek *hetairiai* and Roman *collegia,* namely that of service as a burial society. Whereas the wealthy could afford private tombs and could pay for lavish funerals commemorating their dead, the poor and working class often pooled their efforts and resources to see that their dead were properly cared for. Many clubs with other primary purposes also collected funds to insure the proper disposition of its members' bodies and the honoring of their memories, and some clubs were organized with this function solely in mind. No longer free to avail themselves of these services from clubs that included the worship of pagan deities, Christian congregations became their own burial societies. In fact, rather than being places of secret worship, the

---

[18] Wilken, *Christians As the Romans Saw Them,* 33.

famous Christian catacombs of Rome served the same function as the subterranean tomb complexes or *columbaria* of pagan burial societies and the communal tombs of the Jewish community in the capital.[19]

Some Gentile-Christians had already chosen to separate themselves to some extent from their pagan neighbors even before their conversion to Christianity. These were the so-called God-fearers, who had accepted YHWH and the Jewish scriptures and chose to worship along with Jews without formally converting. An inscription from Miletus indicates that some God-fearers chose to attend public events, such as the theater, with Jews rather than with Greeks.[20] However, pressure seems to have been growing to force Jewish-Christians and probably God-fearers out of the synagogue. Secure evidence of this, the so-called *birkhat ha-minim* or "curse on the heretics," does not date until after the destruction of Jerusalem and its temple in A.D. 70,[21] but references in the Gospels to being persecuted (see Matthew 10:17; Mark 13:9; Luke 21:12) and "put out of the synagogue" (Greek, *aposynagōgos;* John 9:22; 12:42) may suggest that this pressure began as early as Christ's ministry.[22] In

---

[19] See Ian A. Richmon et al., "catacombs," in *Oxford Classical Dictionary*, 302.

[20] J. B. Frey, ed., *Corpus Inscriptionum Judaicarum*, 2 vols. (Rome, 1936–52), no. 748. See Tessa Rajak, "Jews and Christians as Groups," in *"To See Ourselves As Others See Us": Christians, Jews, "Others" in Late Antiquity,* Jacob Neusner and Ernest S. Frerichs, eds. (Chico, Calif.: Scholars Press, 1985), 258–59; Holzapfel, Huntsman, and Wayment, *Jesus Christ and the World of the New Testament,* 162.

[21] For a translation of the Twelfth Benediction, see C. K. Barrett, ed., *The New Testament Background: Writings from Ancient Greece and the Roman Empire That Illuminate Christian Origins* (San Francisco: HarperCollins, 1989), no. 200, 211, and the discussion of James H. Charlesworth, "Christians and Jews in the First Six Centuries," in Hershel Shanks, ed., *Christianity and Rabbinic Judaism* (Washington, D.C.: Biblical Archaeological Society, 1992), 312.

[22] Much New Testament scholarship sees these references as having been written back into the teachings of Jesus from the experiences of the evangelists or the Gospels' final redactors, but this position is by no means conclusive. See Wayne A. Meeks, "Breaking Away: Three New Testament Pictures of Christianity's Separation from the Jewish Communities," in *"To See Ourselves As Others See Us,"* 93–115.

turn, Christian antipathy towards the synagogues seems to have grown as suggested by Revelation 2:3, 9 in the New Testament and from the writings of Ignatius in the immediate postapostolic period.[23] Thus Christians found themselves increasingly alienated from both pagan and Jewish society.

Civic and Political Life

The seats for the Jews and God-fearers at Miletus suggest that at least some Jews and later Christians may have felt comfortable attending pagan cultural events, even though all these activities would have included some degree of superficial pagan religious ceremony. Although Christians from elite backgrounds may have continued to be involved in local government and politics,[24] the religious performances often connected with office would have increasingly shut them out of civic affairs. In addition, major city and imperial festivals would have involved a degree of pagan practice that would have been unacceptable to both Christians and Jews of all classes. These included regular city festivals in honor of patron deities, such as Athena in Athens and Artemis (KJV, "Diana") in Ephesus, and celebrations in honor of the emperor and empire associated with the growing imperial cult. The latter was increasingly seen as an outward sign of loyalty and patriotism to the Roman Empire. While the evidence is unclear as to when adherence to the imperial cult became mandatory,[25] Christian abstention from imperial festivals no doubt made them suspect in the eyes of their friends and neighbors. As members of a recognized religion in the empire, Jews had long enjoyed a dispensation freeing them from

---

[23] Especially Ignatius, *Magnesians,* 8–9, and *Philadelphians,* 6.

[24] The example usually cited of this is that of the Erastus mentioned in Romans 16:23. Exactly who this was and what position he held is still debated (see Holzapfel, Huntsman, and Wayment, *Jesus Christ and the World of the New Testament,* 227).

[25] See Huntsman and Peek, "Imperial Cult and the Beasts of Revelation," in this volume.

obligation to the imperial cult, but with the separation between Church and synagogue, many Christians lost that protection.

Under both Hellenistic kings and Roman emperors, Jews had signaled their loyalty to the temporal order by sacrificing *for* (as opposed to *to*) the sovereign in the Jerusalem Temple and praying for him in their synagogues. Paul and Peter seem to have counseled a similar strategy, encouraging Christians to be good citizens and directing them to honor and pray for the emperor (1 Timothy 2:1–2; Titus 3:1–2; 1 Peter 2:13–17, where the KJV refers to the emperor as "king").[26] Nevertheless, whereas Jewish synagogues were legally recognized associations, Christian house-churches seem to have been increasingly viewed as illegal *collegia*. While clubs and guilds had been freely organized during the Hellenistic period and throughout most of the Roman Republic, the Roman government had some history of trying to regulate and, at times, even suppress such associations. The Senate, for instance, vigorously suppressed a group that sponsored an ecstatic form of worship of Dionysus or Bacchus called the Bacchanalia in 186 B.C.[27] Because the practices of this group were considered extreme and "un-Roman," they were termed a superstition (Latin, *superstitio*) rather than a government-sanctioned religion (Latin, *religio*).[28] The increasingly political nature of some clubs led to their selective suppression in the late republic in legislation sponsored by Cicero and Julius Caesar, and finally, with the advent of the empire, Augustus required that every club receive sanction from the Senate or the empire.[29] Thus whereas Jewish synagogues, which were recognized

---

[26] Knight, *Pastoral Epistles*, 116, 331–34; Davids, *First Epistle of Peter*, 98–104.

[27] Livy 39.18. See the discussion of Wilken, *Christians As the Romans Saw Them*, 16–17.

[28] Mary Beard, John North, and Simon Price, *Religions of Rome, Volume 1: A History* (Cambridge: Cambridge University Press, 1998), 215–17.

[29] Stevenson and Lintott, "Clubs, Roman," in *Oxford Classical Dictionary*, 352; Beard, North, and Price, *Religions of Rome*, 230.

religious associations, and most trade and social clubs continued to be permitted, gatherings of unrecognized groups became illegal, which may have formed one of the bases for the sporadic persecution of Christians that seems to have begun about the time of the deaths of Paul and Peter. Although Christian congregations were in no way political, Christian rhetoric about the coming kingdom of God and Christ as king could easily have been misinterpreted by pagan neighbors and imperial officials.

In these circumstances, it must have become increasingly difficult for Christians to remain engaged in civic affairs and in local and imperial politics, further adding to their feelings of alienation from the society in which they lived. Whereas Jews, even those who had themselves or whose ancestors had obtained citizenship or civic rights, might not have felt as alienated because of their ethnic solidarity with the nation of Israel, Peter's transposition of Diaspora language to Christians—calling them exiles or visiting aliens (Greek, *parepidēmoi;* KJV, "strangers") scattered throughout the Roman provinces (1 Peter 1:1)—suggests that Christians found themselves as strangers in their own homelands.

Perhaps more important, the beliefs and practices of Christians were unfamiliar to Roman authorities, who viewed them as unauthorized *superstitio,* as opposed to legally recognized *religio.*[30] Significantly, Roman authors—including Pliny, Tacitus, and Suetonius—all characterized Christianity as an evil *superstitio* even though they were unaware of its doctrines or many details of its practice. For instance, Christians first came to the attention of the historian Tacitus and the biographer Suetonius in their accounts of the fire of Rome in A.D. 64. In their texts, Tacitus described Christians as a group "hated because of their crimes" (*per flagitia*

---

[30] Livy 39.18; see also Wilken, *Christians As the Romans Saw Them,* 16–17. Perhaps not surprisingly, many of the charges made against Christian practice seem to echo those made against the earlier proponents of Bacchic rituals.

invisos) and their religion as a "dangerous superstition" (*exitiabilis superstitio*), while Suetonius called them "a race of men holding a revolutionary and wicked superstition" (*genus hominum superstitionis novae ac maleficae*).[31] Roman historians generally note that the murder of Christians on the charge of incendiarism constituted an isolated and purely local affair, not a sustained, empire-wide persecution. Nevertheless, although the emperor Nero (A.D. 54–68) may have made the Christians scapegoats to deflect charges of his own culpability in the fire, the attitude reflected in the writings of Tacitus and Suetonius reveal that the emperor clearly exploited misunderstanding of and negative feelings about Christians.

The sufferings of their fellow Christians in Rome no doubt sent shockwaves throughout congregations of believers elsewhere, causing them to expect such persecution themselves. Nevertheless, evidence of any formal imperial policy is lacking before the reign of Trajan (A.D. 98–117), when he effectively established a "don't ask, don't tell" policy whereby governors such as his correspondent Pliny were directed not to actively seek out Christians. However, if any were delivered to Roman authorities, their beliefs should be tested by having them offer basic sacrifices before the statues of the state gods and Roman emperors.[32] Despite the lack of secure evidence for any kind of systematic persecution before Trajan, the fourth-century Christian historian Eusebius nevertheless described the reigns of Nero and Domitian (A.D. 81–96) as periods of persecution, placing the deaths of Peter and Paul in the first reign and the imprisonment of John in the second.[33] Given the memory of persecution from these periods and the lack of any clear imperial policy directing it, the possibility arises that the withdrawal of

---

[31] Tacitus, *Annales*, 15.44; Suetonius, *Nero*, 16. See Wilken, *Christians As the Romans Saw Them*, 48–50, 66–67.

[32] Pliny, *Epistles*, 10. See Wilken, *Christians As the Romans Saw Them*, 15–30.

[33] Eusebius, *Ecclesiastical History*, 2.25; 3.17–18, 32.

Christians from public and social life led to suspicion, which led to misunderstandings and anti-Christian feelings on the part of their neighbors and former friends. This, in turn, might have led to neighbors reporting Christians to local authorities on charges such as belonging to an illegal association or a lack of loyalty to the empire and emperor.

A Holy Nation and Peculiar People

As a result, conversion to Christianity made a considerable impact on the Gentiles who left their previous lifestyles. Not only did they leave the mainstream of Greek and Roman society, becoming a Christian often adversely affected their family, socioeconomic, and civic life. As Christians increasingly found themselves strangers in their own homes and local communities, they suffered alienation and social rejection. In extreme cases they may have realized that their neighbors held them suspect, viewing them as enemies of their society and established order. Then, because their beliefs and the nature of their new community were misunderstood, increasing demands of political loyalty led to sporadic persecution and Christians began to be seen as potential enemies to the Roman state.

In this context, Paul and Peter's use of the rhetoric of citizenship and nationhood takes on particular importance as Christians literally found themselves aliens in their own homes and lands. In the face of this alienation, the Apostles wanted them to remember that they were members of the body of Christ, giving them new citizenship and a new family: "Now therefore ye are no more strangers and foreigners, but fellowcitizens with the saints, and of the household of God" (Ephesians 2:19). Together with calls to live honorably among the Gentiles and make a positive difference in the communities in which they lived, Peter also sought to reinforce Christian dignity by stressing their new identity: "But ye are a chosen generation, a royal priesthood, an holy nation, a peculiar people; that ye should shew forth the praises of him who hath called you out of darkness into his marvellous light: which in time past were not a people, but are now the people of God: which had not obtained mercy, but now have obtained mercy" (1 Peter 2:9–10).

V.

THE ROMAN WORLD OUTSIDE JUDEA

ERIC D. HUNTSMAN

The kings of the Gentiles exercise lordship over them; and they that exercise authority upon them are called benefactors.

LUKE 22:25

Students of the New Testament Gospels quickly realize the need to understand the political conditions surrounding the life and ministry of Jesus. He was born at the end of the reign of Herod the Great (37–4 B.C.), who ruled all of greater Judea as a client-king closely allied with the Roman Empire. Most of Jesus' life and His entire ministry took place in a divided country. Herodian princes continued to rule tetrarchies, or portions, of Herod's former kingdom, in Galilee and the northeastern territories in subordinate roles to Rome. The remainder of the Holy Land remained essentially under the direct rule of a Roman governor, who governed largely through the priestly aristocracy in Jerusalem. This Jewish leadership was intent on doing whatever was necessary to maintain a measure of Jewish autonomy and have its own power and prerogatives. Discerning readers of the Gospels can see how the socioeconomic environment, and especially the political realities of this system, at times influenced the movements of Jesus, colored some of His teachings, and decisively affected the events surrounding His trial and crucifixion.[1]

Likewise the Roman provincial system *outside* of Judea subsequently affected the missionary labors of the Apostles and the growth of the early Christian movement as it spread throughout the Mediterranean basin. The system in place in the areas visited by Paul and Peter is often less familiar than the system in Judea, thus making a review of the genesis, development, and spread of the Roman provincial system helpful. This system, as reformed and finally established by Augustus (official rule, 27 B.C.–A.D. 14), not only provided the setting for the early Christian Church outside of Judea but also in many ways fostered its growth. Furthermore, readers of the second half of the New Testament are often less aware of the considerable diversity of communities and administration in these provinces, a diversity that becomes apparent in the varying experiences that Paul had in his three missionary journeys recorded in Acts.

The Development of the Roman Provincial System

The idea of directly governing conquered territories, usually at the expense of the original inhabitants, was actually a relatively late development in Roman history. During the Roman Monarchy (c. 753–509 B.C.), Rome was a comparatively small city-state in

---

[1] For some overviews of Rome's indirect and direct control of Judea, see F. F. Bruce, "Palestine, Administration of (Roman)," in Freedman, *ABD,* 5:96–99; John F. Hall, "Procurator," in Freedman, *ABD,* 5:473–74; Peter Richardson, *Herod: King of the Jews and Friend of the Romans* (Columbia: University of South Carolina Press, 1999), 295–314; E. Mary Smallwood, *The Jews under Roman Rule: from Pompey to Diocletian: a Study in Political Relations* (Boston: Brill, 2001), 144–200; Dana M. Pike, "Before the Jewish Authorities," in Richard Neitzel Holzapfel and Thomas A. Wayment, eds., *From the Last Supper through the Resurrection: The Savior's Final Hours* (Salt Lake City: Deseret Book, 2003), 210–68; Eric D. Huntsman, "Before the Romans," *From the Last Supper through the Resurrection,* 269–317; Richard Neitzel Holzapfel, Eric D. Huntsman, and Thomas A. Wayment, *Jesus Christ and the World of the New Testament* (Salt Lake City: Deseret Book, 2006), 26–27, 35–41.

central Italy that only gradually expanded its territory in the region of Latium. With the advent of the aristocratic government known as the Early Republic (509–264 B.C.), Rome engaged in a series of wars throughout the peninsula that eventually led to its control of the bulk of Italy.[2] In this period Rome began the practice of annexing some territory and sending colonies of Roman citizens and their Latin allies to settle strategic locations throughout the peninsula, but most of the land that came under Roman control was allowed to remain self-governing, with some areas receiving varying degrees of Roman citizenship and others being recognized with the status of *socii,* or dependent allies. The *socii* were obligated to fight under Roman command—thus augmenting the manpower of Rome's armies—but they maintained their own local governments and were not compelled to pay tribute.[3] In a later period, after the so-called "Social War" (91–88 B.C.) in which these allies fought for the full rights of Roman citizenship, all of Italy became coterminous with the Roman body politic.

Only with the Middle Republic (264–133 B.C.) and Rome's expansion overseas did Rome stop incorporating conquered peoples into its citizen body and institute a new form of government for territories that came under its control. After the First Punic War (264–241 B.C.)—fought against the city of Carthage in North Africa—Rome gained control of the island of Sicily. This new territory was not, as a whole, integrated into the Italian confederacy. Instead, the Romans used an annually elected official called a *praetor* to serve as its governor. Praetors were originally officials at Rome who served primarily as judges but who also had military authority. Consequently, when the first governor was given all of Sicily as his *provincia,* or sphere of military and civil authority,

---

[2] H. H. Scullard, *A History of the Roman World: 753–146* B.C., 4th ed. (New York: Methuen, 1980), 92–114, 131–46.

[3] Scullard, *History of the Roman World,* 146–53.

his role was judicial as much as military. This first provincial governor did not govern a tightly controlled, centrally administered province, and neither did his successors at the time of Peter and Paul. Rather, the praetor oversaw a diverse set of communities and primarily concerned himself with maintaining public order, defending the borders of the provinces, looking out for the interests of visiting Roman citizens, seeing that stipulated taxes and tribute were collected, and hearing court cases.[4]

This rather loosely organized province consisted of three kinds of city-states: allied cities, such as Syracuse, that had a treaty relationship with Rome (*civitates foederatae*); states that were self-governing and largely tax-free but whose liberty was held at the pleasure of Rome (*civitates liberae et immunes*); and a larger number of tributary states (*civitates stipendariae*). Only the last had a heavy tribute burden on property (*tributum soli*) and later a poll tax on persons (*tributum capitis*). In Sicily this latter property tax was generally collected as a tithe or proportion (*decuma*) of agricultural produce, although in many subsequently organized provinces the tribute was a fixed sum (*stipendium*) that the various communities were obligated to render to the governor. On the other hand, all city-states within a province, both tributary and relatively free, had to pay tariffs and tolls (*portoria*) to Rome on goods moving in and out of the province. It was these taxes, along with the tithe, that were often leased, or "farmed out," to private companies of *publicani*, or privately contracted tax collectors, for collection.[5]

---

[4] Scullard, *History of the Roman World*, 179–83; Frank Frost Abbott, *A History and Description of Roman Political Institutions* (Boston: Athenaeum Press, 1901), 186–88. Also Andrew Lintott, *The Constitution of the Roman Republic* (Oxford: Oxford University Press, 1999), 107–9. T. Corey Brennan, "*praetor*," in Simon Hornblower and Antony Spawforth, eds., *The Oxford Classical Dictionary* (Oxford: Oxford University Press, 1996), 1240–41, and Ernst Badian, "*provincia*," *Oxford Classical Dictionary*, 1265–67.

[5] A. N. Sherwin-White, *The Roman Citizenship* (Oxford: Oxford University Press, 1973), 174–89; Ernst Badian, *Publicans and Sinners: Private Enterprise in the Service*

Each state within the province had its own local government and judicial system, with the governor intervening or assuming jurisdiction of cases only when they involved plaintiffs from different cities or when a Roman citizen was involved. Since the governor commanded a relatively small garrison and directed a surprisingly small staff of Roman officials, most of the administrative work was handled by slave and freedmen members of his own household.[6]

By the end of the Second Punic War, 218–201 B.C., Rome acquired three more provinces, one in Sardinia and Corsica and two in what is now Spain. They, too, were governed by elected praetors and were organized under the same loose system as Sicily. With the final conquest of Macedonia in 147 B.C. and Carthage in 146 B.C., two more provinces were organized and the system began to change somewhat. Rather than electing praetors who would serve as governors of these provinces each year, current or former officials from Rome (consuls or former magistrates called *propraetors,* or proconsuls) were sent out as governors, and their term of office was often extended beyond the normal year term. With longer tenures, less and less oversight from Rome, and more opportunities to make money through corruption and extortion, Roman governors toward the end of the Middle Republic became increasingly guilty of administrative abuses and arbitrary behavior.[7] Infamous case studies of this can be found in the careers of Ser. Sulpicius Galba, governor of Further Spain from 151 to 150 B.C., who escaped punishment for his perfidious slaughter of provincials, and C. Verres,

---

of the Roman Republic (Ithaca: Cornell University Press, 1983), and "*Publicani,*" in *Oxford Classical Dictionary,* 1275–76; Graham P. Burton, "*tributum,*" *Oxford Classical Dictionary,* 1551.

[6] Scullard, *History of the Roman World,* 182–83. Judea, for instance, was occupied by a garrison of only twenty-five hundred infantry and five hundred cavalry, which was hardly enough to maintain basic order let alone brutally oppress the population. See Huntsman, "Before the Romans," 277–78.

[7] Scullard, *History of the Roman World,* 324–29.

governor of Sicily from 73 to 71 B.C., who was successfully tried for extortion in 70 B.C.[8]

By the Late Republic (133–27 B.C.), provincial maladministration and financial exploitation led to considerable anti-Roman feeling, particularly in the province of Asia (modern western Turkey), where in 123 B.C. the rights to collect property taxes and tariffs were sold at a spectacular rate to corporations of *publicani,* who recouped their outlay by extracting exorbitant sums from the provincials.[9] Consequently, when the region was invaded by Mithridates of Pontus in 88 B.C. and thousands of Romans and Italians residing in the province were reportedly massacred, Mithridates was welcomed as a liberator there and later in the provinces of Macedonia and Greece across the Aegean in Europe. These provinces were retaken by the Roman general Sulla in 87 and 86 B.C., and all opposition to Rome was so brutally suppressed that these areas never rose in revolt again.

Other threats to Roman rule in the eastern Mediterranean—such as a widespread movement of pirates—were suppressed by another general, Pompey, who also added considerable eastern territories between the years 67–63 B.C., when he extended the infamous system of Asian tax farming to the new provinces.[10] His settlement of the East, which brought Rome into the first direct and lasting contact with Judea in 63 B.C., led to the formation of a large number of provinces spread throughout the Mediterranean. These were interspersed, especially in the East, by client-kingdoms such as those of the Maccabees and later Herod the Great. In order to provide an outlet for the Roman population and to help

---

[8] Appian, *Roman History,* 6.10.59–90, and Cicero, *In Verrem.*

[9] The company that won the tax contract had to furnish the amount of their winning bid to the state treasury at the outset. The company would then make a profit by collecting more from provincials than they had paid into the treasury. This system obviously was unpopular and susceptible to large-scale corruption.

[10] Badian, "*Publicani,*" 1275.

better control strategic points, Rome periodically settled colonies of Roman citizens in the provinces, adding a fourth category of communities—and one with special rights and privileges—to the provincial mix.[11]

This phase of Roman history, while often negative for the provinces, was also a period of great social and political upheaval in Rome itself: the rich grew richer, the poor became poorer, and the powerful governing class increasingly fought within itself for political dominance. This turmoil was quickly exported to the provinces, which were frequently drawn into the civil wars of the Late Republic, especially since the governors of large provinces often commanded large armies compared to the small garrisons of the earlier provinces. Communities who chose the winning side in a war were often rewarded with privileges, including individual or corporate grants of citizenship, while those who chose the wrong side could be penalized or even destroyed.

The System Established by Augustus

As a result of the upheavals and insecurities of the Late Republic, the rise of Octavian, later known as the emperor Augustus, had a great impact on Rome and the provincial communities. Indeed, the system that he established was essentially the one in force at the time of the great Apostolic missions recorded in the New Testament. After he defeated his last enemies at the Battle of Actium in 31 B.C., Octavian brought an end to the wars that had raged across the empire by taking control of all the provinces and the armies stationed in them. Then, with a series of reforms beginning in 27 B.C., he changed the structure and particularly the complexion of his regime. After receiving the honorific name *Augustus,* he established a "disguised monarchy" by adopting

---

[11] Peter Garnsey and Richard Saller, *The Roman Empire: Economy, Society and Culture* (Berkeley: University of California Press, 1987), 26–28.

various republican constitutional titles and powers and restoring the formal function of the Roman republic while surrendering any seemingly dictatorial powers. Under this arrangement, he maintained overall political control of the government and absolute control of the military. While he ruled as *princeps,* or "first citizen," in Rome, he was seen as an absolute ruler throughout the rest of the empire, especially in the East, where his rule was seen in the same guise of the previous Hellenistic kings. He further established the so-called *Pax Augusti,* or "Peace of Augustus," which, in fact, did usher in a period of peace and prosperity that had not been seen in the Mediterranean for centuries.[12]

Augustus also turned his attention to reforming how the Roman provinces were governed. In 27 B.C. he gained control of half of the Roman provinces, which were invariably the most important ones that hosted the largest armies. Under this system, he appointed reliable deputies to govern the so-called imperial provinces, and he took responsibility for supervising them. In a series of provincial tours (Spain and Gaul in 27–25 B.C. and Greece and Asia Minor 22–19 B.C.), he personally regulated relations between provincial communities, their governors, and Rome. While the remaining provinces were returned to the jurisdiction of the Senate, which continued to appoint governors from among the number of former magistrates, Augustus increasingly exerted influence and oversight of these provinces as well by asserting his *imperium maius,* or "superior authority."[13]

In the imperial provinces, Augustus and his successors worked to appoint, as far as possible, men of experience with proven skill as governors. In the most important provinces, these were, in fact, senators who had held the position of praetors or consuls but who

---

[12] Edward Togo Salmon, *A History of the Roman World: From 30 B.C. to A.D. 138* (London: Routledge, 1990), 1–26.

[13] Salmon, *History of the Roman World,* 74–94.

now served at the discretion of the emperor as *legati*, or "deputies," and exercised authority delegated from Augustus. In smaller and less important provinces, such as Judea, governors called *praefecti*, or "prefects," were drawn from the equestrian class, the Roman social class that ranked next after the senatorial order. Like earlier Republican governors, they were responsible for maintaining law and order, seeing that taxes were collected, and sometimes raising supplementary military forces called auxiliaries. Because they were responsible to the emperor and their future appointment was largely dependent upon their performance, imperial governors, as opposed to senatorial ones, were more efficient. They also served longer than the usual annual term of a senatorial governor, and they gained more familiarity and experience with the provinces they were governing.[14] Longer tenures were a particular hallmark of the reign of Tiberius, who left governors such as Pontius Pilate in place for unusually long periods.

Interestingly, the Augustan reforms did not substantially increase the administrative bureaucracy of the provinces. The governors, while generally better, still had disproportionately small staffs and were dependent upon local political entities for governance. Nevertheless, Augustus tried to eliminate or at least reduce certain abuses by providing imperial financial officials, called *procuratores*, or agents, and eliminating imperial use of publicani. (Only after Claudius, who ruled A.D. 41–54, was the term *procurator* used for minor governors.) The burden of collecting taxes was shifted back to the cities, and publicans were employed only locally, as in the case of Matthew in the gospels. The publicans probably collected customs and tariffs for Herod Antipas and not the Romans.[15]

---

[14] This practice may also have made governors less likely to bleed a province dry if they were going to be there for more than a single year and have to deal with the potential consequences of their rapacity.

[15] Paul Barnett, *Jesus and the Rise of Early Christianity* (Downers Grove, Ill.: Intervarsity Press, 1999), 116.

Because of the continued autonomy and the increased responsibilities of cities of all types in the Roman provinces, by the second century the Roman Empire could almost be described as a "federation of city-states" rather than a strongly centralized empire.[16] In peaceful provinces the imperial government and its provincial representatives were only nominally involved in the day-to-day affairs of most provincials, although the continued presence of the empire and the emperors continued to be advertised through imperial propaganda on coins, art, public buildings, and increasingly in the religious system that was becoming the imperial cult. Prominent citizens of most cities competed for local offices and honors, and cities competed among themselves for status within a province, seeking to display loyalty to and gain recognition from Rome. Foremost among those cities were the number of Roman colonies that Augustus and his successors sprinkled through the provinces. Some of these, like earlier Republican colonies, were settlements of discharged veterans or even commoners from the capital itself, but increasingly, provincial cities were honored by receiving this coveted status and the prize of Roman citizenship that came along with it.[17] In addition to these block grants of citizenships, individual provincials could earn, be granted, or sometimes even purchase citizenship with its corresponding rights and privileges (see Acts 22:27–28).

Whereas the situation in Judea was almost constantly unsettled—particularly after a province was reestablished there following the brief rule of Herod Agrippa I (A.D. 41–44), most of the provinces visited or addressed by Paul and Peter enjoyed

---

[16] The ancient characterization comes from the sophist Aelius Aristides in his oration *To Rome* (*Orationes* 26), 63–69, 93–102. See Michael Ivanovitch Rostovtzeff, *The Social and Economic History of the Roman Empire* (Oxford: Clarendon Press, 1926), 130.

[17] S. R. F. Price, *Rituals and Power: The Roman Imperial Cult in Asia Minor* (New York: Cambridge University Press, 1984), 101–32. An example was the competition in and between cities for special treatments vis-à-vis the imperial cult.

considerable stability and prosperity, which did much to reconcile many local communities to Roman rule. For instance, the large cities of Asia province, which had risen against the Romans during the Mithridatic War during the Late Republic, began to prosper and, in the period immediately following Peter and Paul, began the transformation into "Roman" cities. While still of predominately Greek culture, the local elites attained Roman citizenship and strove for Roman honors and recognition, and Rome, in turn, supported and sustained their local preeminence.[18]

Despite continued tensions on the frontiers and occasional Roman civil wars that at times accompanied the change of imperial dynasties, most interior, populated provinces enjoyed peace and prosperity and the *Pax Augusti* became a more generalized *Pax Romana* ("peace of Rome"). This peace afforded freedom of movement and the cultivation of ideas previously unknown, and the relative religious tolerance of Rome toward local religions encouraged the spread of new cults from one region to another. This was particularly widespread in the eastern Mediterranean area, where Greek was the common language of the educated classes.[19] Communities of Hellenized Jews were also familiar features in many cities in the East; they were both the target of early missionary activities and provided an introduction of their basic ideas and practices to their Gentile neighbors. In fact, since Judaism was an officially recognized religion of the empire, early Christianity benefited from this protection and only came under increasing scrutiny, and eventually became the subject of opposition, when the Christians began to differ more distinctly from Jews.

---

[18] See, for example, L. Michael White, "Urban Development and Social Change in Imperial Ephesos," in Helmut Koester, ed., *Ephesos: Metropolis of Asia* (Cambridge: Harvard University Press, 1995), 30–35, 49–65.

[19] Holzapfel, Huntsman, and Wayment, *Jesus Christ and the World of the New Testament,* 39; Richard Lloyd Anderson, *Understanding Paul,* rev. ed. (Salt Lake City: Deseret Book, 2007), 13–16.

Paul's Varied Experiences with Provincial Officials and Communities

All of these factors played a role in the experiences of Paul since his missionary labors largely took place in the provincial system reorganized by Augustus and continued by his successors. Peter's vision and the baptism of Cornelius had already opened the door to preaching to Gentiles (Acts 10:1–48), and Paul and others were to start that initial work. The cosmopolitan nature of the cities of the eastern part of the empire provided considerable interaction between different peoples—Greeks, Romans, Jews, and local groups of various kinds—and this tended to foster a fair amount of openness to new ideas. Greek language and culture provided a common means of communication, at least in these urban areas, and the Roman political structure provided for freedom of movement and basic legal protections that generally allowed Paul to travel and preach. Still, the narrative of Acts reveals that he had varying experiences at the hands of the local officials whom he encountered and that his possession of Roman citizenship generally worked in his favor, especially in those cities that had the status of Roman colonies. Paul's activities also reveal the considerable autonomy exercised by even non-citizen communities such as Thessalonica, Athens, and Ephesus.

The first mission of Paul documented in detail in Acts began and ended in Syrian Antioch (Acts 12:25–14:28), the large Hellenistic metropolis which served as the capital of Roman Syria and the center of the Gentile mission. It was here that Jewish-Christians who had left Jerusalem after the death of Stephen appear to have preached to Greeks (Acts 11:19–21), which made sense given the long history of Jews and Gentiles living together in the city.[20] As the work progressed in Antioch, Barnabas brought Paul, who was uniquely qualified for preaching and ministering to Gentiles, to the city, where the disciples were first called Christians, perhaps by their pagan neighbors who needed a way of differentiating them from other Jewish groups (Acts 11:26).

When the Spirit moved local Christian leaders to set Barnabas and Paul apart for a new Gentile mission (Acts 13:1–3), their first destination was the neighboring island of Cyprus, the home of Barnabas, where he presumably had contacts and where he would later minister (Acts 4:36; 15:39). Luke gives no details of this mission except to document the interview that the missionaries had with Sergius Paulus, the governor of the province.[21] Cyprus was a senatorial province, whose governor was a high-ranking senator chosen by lot from the Senate rather than appointed by the emperor, and this distinction is made by Luke through his use of the term *anthypotos* (Acts 13:7, 8, 12; KJV, "deputy"), which was the standard Greek translation of the Latin title *proconsul*.[22] This same title is used for the governors of Achaea and Asia (Acts 18:12, 19:38), also senatorial provinces, whereas the leading Roman official of Judea, a minor imperial province, is described with the more generic term *hēgemōn* (Acts 23:24, 26, 33; 24:1, 10; 26:30; KJV "governor").[23]

---

[20] The term here, *Hellēnistas* (KJV, "Grecians"), is used two other times in Acts, where it actually refers to Hellenized Jews rather than ethnic Greeks. While that may be the case again here, the context makes it likely that it actually refers to Gentile Greeks. See F. F. Bruce, *The Acts of the Apostles,* 3d ed. (Grand Rapids, Mich.: Eerdmans, 1990), 272; Ben Witherington III, *The Acts of the Apostles: A Socio-Rhetorical Commentary* (Grand Rapids, Mich.: Eerdmans, 1998), 369. Some manuscript witnesses, in fact, read *Hellēnas* rather than *Hellēnistas;* see Bruce M. Metzger, *A Textual Commentary on the Greek New Testament,* corrected ed. (New York: United Bible Societies, 1975), 386–89.

[21] Bruce, *Acts,* 297.

[22] Henry George Liddell and Robert Scott, "*anthytopos,*" *A Greek-English Lexicon* (Oxford: Clarendon Press, 1996), 142.

[23] Liddell and Scott, "*hēgemōn,*" 763.

Barnabas and Paul may have obtained an audience with Sergius Paulus for the simple reason that he was interested in religious matters, as evidenced by the fact that he was already entertaining the sorcerer Elymus Bar-jesus (Acts 13:6–8). However, it is from this point that Luke begins to consistently refer to Paul by *Paulos,* the Greek form of his Roman name, whereas up to this point Luke had used Paul's Jewish name, *Saul.* This may, in fact, have reflected a conscious choice on Paul's part, since emphasizing his Roman citizenship had obvious advantages when moving increasingly into Gentile circles.[24]

The fact that both Paul and the proconsul Sergius Paulus had the same name was probably happenstance. However, Sergius Paulus's name does suggest a possible reason why the missionary tour took the turn that it did when Paul and Barnabas left Cyprus. After sailing to southern Asia Minor, they did not stay on the coast or take another ship to the more populous and important cities on the west coast. Instead they took the difficult overland journey through the mountains of south-central Asia Minor to the city of Antioch in Psidia (Acts 13:13–14). A collection of inscriptions from the site attests that several members of the family Sergii Pauli were there, where they may have held extensive property.[25] The possibility arises, although it cannot be conclusively confirmed, that Paul and Barnabas might have been pursuing important contacts they made through the governor of Cyprus. Another reason Paul may have traveled to Psidian Antioch—or why the Spirit led

---

[24] Bruce, *Acts,* 298; Witherington, *Acts,* 401–2.

[25] William Mitchell Ramsay, *The Bearing of Recent Discovery on the Trustworthiness of the New Testament* (London: Hodder and Stoughton, 1915), 150–72; C. J. Hemer, *The Book of Acts in the Setting of Hellenistic History* (Tübingen, Germany: Mohr, 1989), 109; Witherington, *Acts,* 399–400. Ramsay, writing soon after the inscriptions were discovered, suggests a rather different scenario from Witherington's, one that would have placed the two members of the family that he knew about in Psidian Antioch considerably after Paul's visit.

him there—was the status of the city as a Roman colony. Its remote location was the very reason that Augustus settled veterans there in 25 B.C.: to strengthen Rome's hold on the area. It became the leading city of the southern district of the Roman province of Galatia, and Paul's citizenship may have been a factor in his success, perhaps adding status to his position as a traveling teacher and gaining him access he might not otherwise have had.

His citizenship also played a role, albeit belatedly, in the first city he and Silas visited in Europe on the second missionary journey recounted in Acts. Forbidden by the Spirit to travel to the more obvious destinations of the great cities of Asia, he followed a vision to Macedonia. His first preaching destination there was Philippi, another Roman colony and the only one expressly identified as such by Luke, who uses the Greek transliteration *kolōnia* rather than the Greek term *apoikia* to emphasize its status.[26] Near Philippi, on the road across the Balkans known as the Via Egnatia, a Roman civil war battle had been fought in 42 B.C., when Mark Antony and Octavian defeated Brutus and Cassius, the assassins of Julius Caesar. Both Antony and Octavian, the future emperor Augustus, settled veterans there, and Philippi became very conscious of its Roman status (see Acts 16:20–21). Accordingly, the prominence and relative independence of Lydia, Paul's first convert in the city, might be reflective of the legal and social status of Roman women. When Paul and Silas were arrested there, Luke uses the term *stratēgoi* to refer to the city magistrates who examined them (Acts 16:35, 38; KJV, "magistrates"). *Stratēgos*, which means "general" in Greek, was the standard translation of the Roman office of *praetor*, the title earlier used for high officials in the capital and for the first provincial governors but which was also used for

---

[26] Bruce, *Acts*, 357; Witherington, *Acts*, 488–90, who also notes that one of the proposed places of origin was for Luke himself.

officials in colonies.²⁷ Upon discovery that both Paul and Silas were Roman citizens, the praetors in Philippi panicked because due process, the right of every Roman citizen, had been denied the captives (Acts 16:37–39).

Paul's experience in another Roman colony, Corinth, was considerably better. Although Corinth had been an important Greek city since the Archaic Period (750–500 B.C.), it had been destroyed by the Romans in 146 B.C. Julius Caesar refounded the city as *Colonia Laus Iulia Corinthiensis* and settled it with Roman citizens drawn from the freedmen class as well as discharged veterans.²⁸ Greeks were attracted to the new city in large numbers, as were people from throughout the eastern Mediterranean, making it a particularly cosmopolitan center in the first century A.D. The governor of the Roman province of Achaea had his seat in Corinth. Like Cyprus, Corinth was a senatorial province, so Luke correctly refers to L. Iunius Gallio Annaeus, the governor from A.D. 51 to A.D. 53 (see Acts 18:12–17),²⁹ as an *anthypotos,* or "deputy." Paul came before the governor as the result of a riot incited against him by local Jews who opposed his missionary efforts. He did not need to defend himself, however, because Gallio refused to be drawn into a religious dispute. Gallio probably viewed the situation as a disagreement between differing Jewish groups rather than as an actual disturbance of the peace. His reluctance to get involved against Paul here may signal that, in this period at least, he and other Roman officials were benignly disposed toward Christians when they individually came to their attention.

---

²⁷ Liddell and Scott, "*stratēgos,*" 1652.

²⁸ Appian, *Punica,* 136; Plutarch, *Caesar,* 57.5; Dio 43.50.3–5.

²⁹ J. H. Oliver, "The Epistle of Claudius Which Mentions the Proconsul Junius Gallio," *Hesperia* 40 (1971): 239–40; Holzapfel, Huntsman, Wayment, *Jesus Christ and the World of the New Testament,* 229.

This incident demonstrated that a Christian preacher could operate safely in a city such as Corinth, and, in fact, Paul stayed in that city for eighteen months, building a strong local church. Some of the early Christians here were known by name (Acts 18:7; 1 Corinthians 1:14, 16; 16:15–17; Romans 16:23), and some, such as Gaius and Justus, had Latin names, suggesting that they may have held Roman citizenship. Another, Erastus, may have held an important elective office in the city: Romans 16:23 calls him the *oikonomos,* or treasurer of the city (KJV, "chamberlain"), and there is a possible confirmation by a first-century Latin inscription from Corinth.[30] The fact that Erastus may have been holding this office later when Paul wrote to the Romans suggests that, at this period at least, Christians were able to serve in public office in their communities.

The position of women may also have been affected by Roman influence, since the social status, economic opportunities, and legal rights of Roman women were considerably greater than those of their Greek or Jewish counterparts. In the Roman colony of Philippi, one of Paul's first converts was Lydia, a "seller of purple," an independent businesswoman who was the head of her own household (Acts 16:14–15, 40).[31] The assertiveness of some Christian women, which Paul felt he needed to counter in Corinth (1 Corinthians 14:34–35) as well as in Ephesus (1 Timothy 2:11–

---

[30] John Harvey Kent, *Corinth: The Inscriptions, 1926–1950,* vol. 3, part 3 (Princeton: Princeton University Press, 1966), no. 232, 27, 99–100. Whether the Erastus commemorated in the inscription, who is identified as holding the Roman colonial office of *aedile,* should be identified with "Erastus the treasurer" is debated, since the *oikonomos* is the Greek translation of the lower office of *acarius,* not *aedilis,* see Holzapfel, Huntsman, and Wayment, *Jesus Christ and the World of the New Testament,* 227.

[31] Witherington, *Acts,* 491–93; *Jesus Christ and the World of the New Testament,* 167.

12), may reflect the privileged social status held by some elite Roman women.[32]

Other cities visited by Paul, although not colonies, still enjoyed the large degree of autonomy characteristic of communities in a Roman province. As was almost universally the case, they had locally elected officials, whose titles in Acts have been confirmed by external evidence. During the uproar against Paul in Thessalonica, he was brought "unto the rulers of the city" (Acts 17:6, 8). This is a direct translation of the Greek *epi tous politarchas,* and the office of *politarch* appears in a second-century inscription discovered in Thessalonica in 1835.[33]

In Athens, visited briefly by Paul on his way to Corinth, the archaic state council known as the Areopagus still functioned. Weakened during the Classical period, it enjoyed renewed prestige under the Romans and was responsible for the religious affairs of the city, among other things. The council took its name from its meeting place on the hill of Ares (Acts 17:22; KJV, "Mars' hill"), but in this period it may have, in fact, met in the Royal Stoa in the main marketplace.[34] Here Paul gave his famous speech "To the Unknown God" (Acts 17:23), although a division between its Stoic and Epicurean factions over the issue of resurrection seems to have kept the council from making any official decision on Paul's message (Acts 17:16–34).

---

[32] Paul's discussion of divorce in 1 Corinthians 7:10–11 presupposes the ability of women to initiate divorce, which makes sense only in a place where Roman civil law, unlike Jewish and Greek law, allowed a wife to divorce a husband. See Eric D. Huntsman, "Your Faith Should Not Stand in the Wisdom of Men: Greek Philosophy, Corinthian Behavior, and the Teachings of Paul," in Ray L. Huntington, Frank F. Judd, and David M. Whitchurch, eds., *Shedding Light on the New Testament: Acts–Revelation* (Provo, Utah: Religious Studies Center, 2009), 88 n. 46.

[33] T. C. Mitchell, *Biblical Archaeology: Documents from the British Museum* (Cambridge: Cambridge University Press, 1988), 98. See G. H. R. Horsely, "The Politarchs," in David W. J. Gill and Conrad Gempf, eds., *The Book of Acts in Its Graeco-Roman Setting* (Grand Rapids, Mich.: Eerdmans, 1994), 419–30.

[34] Bruce, *Acts,* 377–78; Witherington, *Acts,* 515–16.

Another city important in the missions of Paul was Ephesus, which was the largest city in the province of Asia. The cities of the province, although each individually self-governing, were also organized into a *koinon,* or league, the leaders of which were known as *Asiarchoi,* or "Asiarchs" (rulers of Asia).[35] While this league did not have any concrete political power, it helped foster loyalty to the regime and was an important point of contact between the Roman government and the local elites of the provinces. Many of the Asiarchs obtained Roman citizenship, and from their midst an honorary official was selected to serve as the high priest of the imperial cult in the province.[36] The fact that some of these Asiarchs are identified as friends of Paul and that they intervened to protect him during the anti-Christian demonstration that broke out in Ephesus (Acts 19:31, where the KJV calls them "the chief of Asia") suggests that there was no official opposition to Christianity at this point, even if there was a reaction against Paul among the common people who felt like their religious traditions (and in the case of the silversmiths, their livelihood) were threatened.[37] However, when the demonstration threatened to become a riot in the theater at Ephesus, it was a local city official, the *grammateus,* or "town clerk,"[38] who quieted the mob and dismissed their illegal assembly, noting that the city's precious autonomy was threatened by their behavior (Acts 19:35–41). Ephesus, although autonomous, enjoyed its liberty at the sufferance of the Roman government; the provincial governor, who was charged with maintaining law and

---

[35] Strabo, *Geography,* 14.1.42.

[36] See the discussion in Cecilia Peek and Eric D. Huntsman, "The Imperial Cult and the Beasts of Revelation," in this volume.

[37] Bruce, *Acts,* 418; R. A. Kearsley, "The Asiarchs," in Gill and Gempf, eds., *Book of Acts,* 363–76; Witherington, *Acts,* 595–96.

[38] A. N. Sherwin-White, *Roman Society and Roman Law in the New Testament* (Grand Rapids, Mich.: Baker, 1978), 86.

order in his province, could well intervene to the detriment of the city.

Early Christians in a Roman World

While Paul did run into considerable opposition during his missionary travels—often from unconvinced Jews and occasionally local officials—the narrative of Acts suggests that as far as official imperial policy, most Roman officials, and even some of the local elites were concerned, Paul and the Christian movement were not a threat. In fact, Paul seemed to have recognized the existing social and political order as established, or at least allowed, by God (1 Timothy 2:1–2). Other Apostles, notably Peter, even without holding Roman citizenship benefited from the *Pax Romana* and the general cultural unity that allowed them to travel and preach widely. In fact, Peter counseled that Christians "submit yourselves to every ordinance of man for the Lord's sake: whether it be to the king, as supreme; or unto governors, as unto them that are sent by him for the punishment of evildoers, and for the praise of them that do well . . . honour all men. Love the brotherhood. Fear God. Honour the king" (1 Peter 2:13–14, 17).

Here the "king," or *basileus,* was, in fact, the Roman emperor. Peter and Paul would both meet martyrdom in Rome, presumably at the hands of the same emperor's officials, and Christians after that period would increasingly find themselves marginalized and even persecuted in the Roman world in which they lived. Nevertheless, in these early decades of the Christian movement, it was still a relatively benign and beneficial, if not always friendly, world.

VI.

FROM TEMPLE AND SYNAGOGUE TO HOUSE-CHURCH

RICHARD NEITZEL HOLZAPFEL

For it hath been declared unto me of you, my brethren, by them which are of the house of Chloe, that there are contentions among you.

1 Corinthians 1:11

The "parting to the ways" is the story of how Christians, a group composed entirely of Jewish believers who attended the synagogue (Greek, *synagōgē*), eventually formed an independent church (Greek, *ekklēsia*) beyond Judaism. These early churches shared certain similarities with the synagogue but increasingly developed and adapted important and fundamental distinctive modes of worship, practice, and doctrine, separating themselves so completely from Second Temple Judaism that they were eventually viewed as a uniquely independent faith.

Jesus and Judaism

Jesus was not a Christian in the modern sense; He did not attend a Christian church, and He would never have thought that He had converted to Christianity from Judaism. The Gospels describe Jesus as thoroughly Jewish, practicing His faith in ways similar to those of other Jews of the first century and sharing certain assumptions, attitudes, beliefs, and scriptural interpretations with them. Nevertheless, Second Temple Judaism was not a monolithic block, and it is often described as Judaisms—emphasizing the "s"—because of the variety and creativity of the religion of the Jews during this period. The vast majority of Jews did not belong to one particular sect or group (Sadducees, Pharisees, Esseenes, priests, or scribes, for example). Religious Jews were generally united in their loyalty to God, the Torah, the temple, and the idea of a chosen people (Israel). Jesus clearly fits *within* Judaism in this milieu.

Jesus' ministry was performed in the framework of His Jewish faith, and His debates with Jewish officials were part of an intra-Jewish discussion on how one interprets the scripture and who had the right to do so. For example, Jesus assumed the scriptures were authoritative, and He claimed that He alone had the right to interpret them. Since He was the long-promised Jewish Messiah, as God's divine Son He knew God as His Father in a way no one else knew Him or even claimed to have known Him (see Matthew 11:27; compare Matthew 7:28–29).

Luke portrays Jesus' family as observant Jews throughout his narrative. For example, Jesus' parents made sure that He was circumcised on the eighth day as commanded by the Lord (Luke 2:21; Genesis 17:11–12); Mary performed the laws of purification according to the Torah (Luke 2:22–24; Leviticus 12:1–4); and Joseph and Mary "brought him to Jerusalem, to present him to the Lord" as the law required (Luke 2:22; Numbers 3:41–51). Additionally, Luke adds that Jesus' "parents went to Jerusalem every year at the feast of the passover," again faithfully observing the Lord's commandment regarding attendance of the pilgrimage feasts (Luke 2:41; Leviticus 23:1–21).

During a visit to Jerusalem when Jesus was twelve years old, His parents "found him in the temple," talking with the doctors of the law (Luke 2:46). Obviously, He had been reared in a home where traditional Jewish practices, such as almsgiving, prayer, fasting, and Torah study were taught and nurtured. Jesus respected the temple and the scriptures.

Luke informs his readers that Jesus could recite scriptures from memory (see Luke 4:1–13). This would not necessarily have been unusual in an oral culture, but His memorizing key passages from the scriptures suggests dedication to them. Additionally, Jesus learned to read the scriptures in Hebrew, and probably also in an Aramaic translation preserved in the Targums, and recited them in the synagogue (Luke 4:15–21). Jesus not only had learned key passages (Matthew 22:37–40) but also knew stories from the scriptures (Luke 4:25–27). He apparently accepted the traditional three-fold division of Jewish scripture—Torah, Prophets, and Writings—and assumed that they were authoritative (see Luke 24:27, 44). For Jesus, they provided the answers to life's important questions and provided insights on how God expected people to live: "Therefore all things whatsoever ye would that men should do to you, do ye even so to them: for this is the *law and the prophets*" (Matthew 7:12; emphasis added).

The Gospels highlight Jesus' personal religious experience. According to Luke, Jesus' custom was to go to the synagogue on the Sabbath day (see Luke 4:15–16), and He is often portrayed as teaching in the synagogue on the Sabbath day throughout His ministry (see Luke 4:31–32, 43–44). As an adult, Jesus continued attending the pilgrimage feasts at the temple in Jerusalem and at other times (see, for example, John 10:22, where He attended a *Hanukah* celebration). He is portrayed as praying often, especially at important and critical moments in His life (see Matthew 14:23). He sang religious hymns, most likely from the book of Psalms (see Matthew 26:30). As noted above, Jesus worshipped on the Sabbath, one of the quintessential boundary markers in first-century Judaism. Jesus is portrayed as accepting this Torah commandment, even though He disagreed with the narrow interpretation of the law as prescribed by some Pharisees (see Mark 2:23–28).

Along with His dedication and loyalty to God and the Torah, Jesus also recognized the temple as His Father's house (see Luke 2:49). The temple played a significant role throughout His ministry, especially during His last week when He "taught daily" (Luke 19:47). He loved Jerusalem, the Holy City, and He cried for the inhabitants, knowing beforehand that an enemy was gathering on the horizon (Matthew 23:37). He knew the magnificent temple would be destroyed, ending the daily sacrifices prescribed by the law (Matthew 24:2; John 4:21).

Even though Jesus respected the authority of the priests (Luke 17:12–14), He nevertheless stood above them, claiming authority and power to forgive sin (see Luke 5:18–25). During His own ministry, Jesus excused His disciples from certain Jewish practices, such as fasting (Luke 5:33–35), and announced that He was revealing something new (Luke 5:36–39). Finally, Jesus instituted the new covenant promised by God through Jeremiah (Matthew 26:26–28; compare Jeremiah 31:31).

Because of His unique claims, opposition against Jesus' mission began rather early and was sometimes centered in the main Jewish institutions of the day (see Luke 4:28–29). According to John, some synagogue leaders in Jerusalem began to "put out of the synagogue" anyone who confessed that Jesus was the Messiah (John 9:22; 12:42). Additionally, Jesus warned the disciples that troubling days lay ahead: "They shall put you out of the synagogues: yea, the time cometh, that whosoever killeth you will think that he doeth God service" (John 16:2). In other synagogues, however, Jesus was warmly and enthusiastically received, revealing the fractures in Second Temple Judaism (see Luke 4:14–15).

Jesus came into the world to save the world, not just covenant Israel. After the Resurrection, Jesus gave the disciples a commandment to preach the good news to all nations—to all people, both Jews and Gentiles (see Matthew 28:19). Nevertheless, He commanded the disciples to remain in Jerusalem until Pentecost because their mission would begin there among their fellow Jews (Luke 24:49).

Jewish-Christians

Although used by many scholars today, the terms Jewish-Christianity or Jewish-Christians are not found in the New Testament or used by the early disciples of Jesus to describe themselves. However, it may be helpful to adopt these modern designations as we describe what happened to those who accepted Jesus Christ as the Messiah after His death and Resurrection.

Eventually, how an individual interpreted scripture separated Jewish-Christians from other Jews, for "some found the answer [of authority] in the Torah as taught by rabbis, others found it in Jesus as fulfilment of the Torah."[1] Those who accepted Jesus have been described as Jewish-Christians.

The Establishment of House-Churches

At the beginning of His ministry, Jesus began teaching in home (see Mark 1:29–34), demonstrating that the temple, synagogue, and house were all appropriate places to heal, preach, and teach. Nevertheless, by the end of His ministry, Jesus had brought the house setting for worship to the forefront when He instituted the sacrament in an upper room on the night of His betrayal. This distinctive new ordinance, most likely rooted in the Passover Seder, became the focus of the weekly Christian worship meetings in the private homes and tenement apartments spread across the Mediterranean basin (see 1 Corinthians 10:16; compare

---

[1] Peter A. Petitt, "Hebrew Bible," in Edward Kessler and Neil Wenborn, eds., *A Dictionary of Jewish-Christian Relations* (New York: Cambridge University Press, 2005), 177.

11:26). Scholars identify private homes where the Church met as "house-churches," a term we will employ throughout this chapter. Eventually, with the destruction of the Jerusalem temple in A.D. 70 and the excommunication of believers from the synagogue by the end of the first century, the house-church became the center of Christian worship. The house-churches were not specific buildings dedicated solely to worship, but were the individual homes and apartments of members. Christians did not build special buildings designated for worship until the third century.

In the book of Acts we see this development rather clearly. At the very beginning of his story, Luke provides an important word-picture about early Christian worship: "The former treatise have I made, O Theophilus, of all that Jesus began both to do and teach, until the day in which he was taken up. . . . And, being assembled together with them, commanded them that they should not depart from Jerusalem. . . . And when they were come in, they went up into an upper room, where abode both Peter, and James, and John, and Andrew, Philip, and Thomas, Bartholomew, and Matthew, James the son of Alphaeus, and Simon Zelotes, and Judas the brother of James. These all continued with one accord in prayer and supplication, with the women, and Mary the mother of Jesus, and with his brethren" (Acts 1:1–2, 4, 13–14).

The upper room (Greek, *hyperōon*) was a rather large one, since it could accommodate some 120 people (Acts 1:15). Luke likely believed that it was the "same room" (Greek, *anagaion*) where the Last Supper was celebrated.[2]

Luke suggests that there was a network of house-churches in Jerusalem (Acts 2:46; 5:42). This would have been necessary given the number of people who had become followers of Jesus during this early period (see Acts 2:41; 4:4). Some commentators have

---

[2] James D. G. Dunn, *Beginning from Jerusalem: Christianity in the Making* (Grand Rapids, Mich.: Eerdmans, 2009), 2:151.

suggested that the Twelve presided over these individual congregations.[3] What is clear from Luke's account is that the house-church setting was becoming an integral part of early Christian worship. Even enemies of the Christians knew they could find them in various designated houses (Acts 8:3).

Nevertheless, the temple remained an important institution for the disciples: "And they, *continuing daily* with one accord *in the temple,* and breaking bread from house to house did eat . . . with gladness and singleness of heart, praising God, and having favour with all the people" (Acts 2:46–47; emphasis added). The temple was not only a place to announce the good news but also a place of worship.

Luke noted, "Peter and John went up together into the temple at the hour of prayer, being the ninth hour" (Acts 3:1). Later, Luke recorded, "And when they heard it, they glorified the Lord, and said unto him, Thou seest, brother, how many thousands of Jews there are which believe; and they are all zealous of the law. . . . Do therefore this that we say to thee: We have four men which have a vow on them; them take, and purify thyself with them, and be at charges with them, that they may shave their heads: and all may know that those things, whereof they were informed concerning thee, are nothing; but that thou thyself also walkest orderly, and keepest the law" (Acts 21:20, 23–24). However, the temple was primarily the place to teach (along with the developing house-churches): "And *daily in the temple,* and in *every house,* they ceased not to teach and preach Jesus Christ" (Acts 5:42; emphasis added).

Additionally, the early Christians did not immediately abandon the synagogue. Saul (Paul) understood he could find Jesus' followers there: "And Saul, yet breathing out threatenings and slaughter

---

[3] See ibid., 181.

against the disciples of the Lord, went unto the high priest, and desired of him letters to Damascus to the synagogues, that if he found any of this way, whether they were men or women, he might bring them bound unto Jerusalem" (Acts 9:1–2).

The house-church, found in the individual homes and apartments of disciples, became the primary place to worship outside the land of Israel. For example, crossing into Europe, Paul immediately looked for an opportunity to establish a house-church and did so through the conversion of Lydia, a "seller of purple, of the city of Thyatira, which worshipped God" (Acts 16:14). Apparently a God-fearer, she accepted the message and "was baptized, and her household" (Acts 16:15). Her larger-than-average home became the house-church in the city. Paul reflected in a meeting with the elders from Ephesus that he had "taught you publickly, and from house to house" (Acts 20:20).

Nevertheless, Paul's first missionary strategy always included attending the synagogue: "But when they departed from Perga, they came to Antioch in Pisidia, and went into the synagogue on the sabbath day, and sat down" (Acts 13:14). In fact, wherever he went, Paul taught in the synagogue before making any other effort (see Acts 9:20; 13:5, 14; 14:1; 17:1; 17:10, 17; 18:4; 19:8). We must assume that his purpose in attending was more than simply finding a place to worship.

Paul's letter to the Corinthian Saints reveals at least another house-church in the city, beyond the one originally established by Prisca and Aquila, when he refers to those "of the house of Chloe" (1 Corinthians 1:11). Luke also informs the reader that another home was a gathering place for worship: When Paul was denied the opportunity to continue preaching in the local synagogue in Corinth, he moved his work to another location—right next door! (Acts 18:7). Additionally, Paul baptized Crispus, the chief ruler of the synagogue, bringing into the fold an important Jewish leader (1 Corinthians 1:14; Acts 18:8).

The pattern of house-churches was not limited to the Pauline congregations. In Romans 16, Paul lists twenty-six individuals associated with at least five separate house-churches scattered throughout Rome. Three house-churches are specifically mentioned: (1) "the church that" meets at the house of Priscilla and Aquila (Romans 16:3, 5); (2) the house-church of Asyncritus, which included "Phlegon, Hermas, Patrobus, Hermes, and the brethren which are with them" (Romans 16:14); and (3) Philologus's house-church, which included "Julia, Nereus, and his sister, and Olympas, and all the saints which are with them" (Romans 16:15). Besides these three house-churches, two other pockets of Christians in the city of Rome are identified: (1) the Christians in "Aristobulus' household" (Romans 16:10), and (2) the Christians in the "household of Narcissus" (Romans 16:11). There may have been other house-churches in the city since fourteen people mentioned in this list were not specifically identified as belonging to the house-churches already noted. Dunn argues that in most cases, the "earliest house churches must have been fairly small, a dozen or twenty people in all."[4] Even in larger gatherings, when the "whole church" (see 1 Corinthians 14:23) met in a city, there may have been no more than forty or fifty people gathered.[5] Obviously, there were exceptions, as was the case in Jerusalem, where about "an hundred and twenty" people gathered (see Acts 1:15). By A.D. 67, one scholar estimates that there may have been about 40,000 Christians, with as many as 25,000 in Judea and Galilee, 5,000 in Asia, and 2,000 in Greece and Italy, gathering in various house-churches.[6]

---

[4] Ibid.

[5] Ibid.

[6] Bo Reicke, *New Testament Era: The World of the Bible from 500 B.C. to A.D. 100*, trans. David E. Green (London: A&C Black, 1969), 302–3. Jeffrey R. Chadwick of Brigham Young University believes the number of Christians in Jerusalem in A.D. 30

Worship in the House-Churches

The first day of the week (Sunday) became an important day for the early Christians. The disciples were gathered on the first Easter Sunday in an upper room when Jesus appeared to them (Luke 24:1, 36–48). John, who wrote the book of Revelation, may refer to Sunday as the "Lord's day" in the second half of the first century (Revelation 1:10). Nevertheless, when, where, and why Christians began celebrating exclusively the first day of the week as the "Lord's day" are difficult questions to answer because the sources are rather fragmentary. Craig Harline observes, "These difficulties are formidable, but they need not bog us down. For there is at least one basic point of agreement among almost all scholars that will move the story along: by at least A.D. 150, and perhaps sooner, most Christians were observing the first day as the Lord's Day by coming together to worship. This alone suggests the day's new importance for Christians."[7]

Interestingly, most Jewish-Christians continued observing the Jewish Sabbath on Saturday. They then added another day (Sunday) to celebrate Jesus' victory over death, providing them an opportunity to worship in both the synagogue and the house-church. As late as the fourth century, the Christian bishop Cyril seems to have attempted to force Christians to choose between synagogue worship and Sunday Christian services.[8]

When they gathered, the disciples worshipped in ways that shared important parallels to the rituals and practices of the synagogue but also highlighted unique features and specific

---

may have been even higher, perhaps as many as thirty thousand. Personal conversation, March 4, 2009.

[7] See Craig Harline, *Sunday: A History of the First Day from Babylonia to the Super Bowl* (New York: Doubleday, 2007), 6–9.

[8] John J. O'Keefe, "Christianizing Malachi: Fifth Century Insights from Cyril of Alexandria," *Vigiliae Christianae* 50 (1996): 143–44 n. 43.

practices informed by their belief that Jesus was both Messiah and Lord.

Although we have Luke's account of the early Church (found in the book of Acts) and Paul's letters directed to specific congregations (house-churches) or individuals who worshipped in house-churches, these writings are not a handbook of instruction outlining the who, what, when, and where of first-century Christian practice. In telling his story, Luke provides clues as to what it would have been like to attend a meeting with the followers of Jesus. Paul's letters were also not meant to be a history of the early house-churches, but, like Luke, he gives insight to the situations in the house-churches he addressed when he wrote to the Saints located throughout the Mediterranean basin giving them council, direction, and reproof. Additionally, Paul's letters are by and large addressed to Gentile-Christian congregations and offer very little in terms of describing how Jewish-Christians worshipped.

Luke describes the situation in the earliest meetings: "And they continued stedfastly in the apostles' doctrine and fellowship [Greek, *koinōnia*]" (Acts 2:42). The "apostles' doctrine" was based on scripture, the Old Testament in its various translations (Aramaic and Greek), and traditions about Jesus (see 1 Corinthians 11:23; 15:3). Jesus and His disciples accepted the Jewish scriptures (Torah, Prophets, and Writings) as authoritative. The first disciples from Galilee and Judea would have known the scriptures in Hebrew or in their Aramaic translations. When the good news spread to Greek-speaking Jews in Jerusalem (Acts 6:1), another translation of the scriptures would have been incorporated into use within the house-churches—a Greek translation of the scriptures known as the Septuagint (abbreviated as LXX). The authors of the Gospels and the authors of the second half of the New Testament show indications of having used the LXX and other Greek translations, including oral material. Jesus spoke Aramaic and quoted the scriptures in their Hebrew or in their Aramaic translation, so the Gospels preserve Jesus' words in translation.

Additional proverbs, along with other Jewish religious literature, were quoted and used by the early Church (see Jude 14–16). However, we cannot be certain who accepted the Book of Enoch as authoritative. Copies were found among the Dead Sea Scrolls. Those who gathered regularly in the house-churches to worship accepted the Apostles' doctrine, articulated on Pentecost. Peter said, "Whosoever shall call on the name of the Lord shall be saved" (Acts 2:21). Further he announced, "Therefore let all the house of Israel know assuredly, that God hath made that same Jesus, whom ye have crucified, both Lord and Christ" (Acts 2:36). The basic points—Jesus had died, was raised from the dead, and was exalted on the right hand of God—formed the basic message (see Acts 2:23–24, 32–33).

Those touched by his message asked, "Men and brethren, what shall we do?" (Acts 2:37). Peter responded, "Repent, and be baptized every one of you in the name of Jesus Christ for the remission of sins, and ye shall receive the gift of the Holy Ghost" (Acts 2:38). Baptism was the gate into the Church (see Acts 2:41), a gathering or assembly of disciples independent of the synagogue and the temple. In their meetings in the house-churches, the disciples broke bread (Acts 2:42, 46), prayed (Acts 2:42), sang "psalms and hymns and spiritual songs" (Ephesians 5:19; Colossians 3:16), preached and testified (Acts 20:7), enjoyed the gifts of the Spirit (1 Corinthians 14:23), and participated in the sacrament (see 1 Corinthians 11:26–34).

Although early Christians continued to use the book of Psalms as a hymnbook, like other Jews, they also incorporated new hymns that revealed their specific beliefs about Jesus Christ. Fragments of early Christian hymns are preserved in the New Testament (see John 1:1–18; Philippians 2:6–1; Colossians 1:15–20; Hebrews 1:1–4; 1 Timothy 3:16).

The focus of the gathering was the sacrament administered as part of a meal (see 1 Corinthians 11:20), as was the Last Supper (see Mark 14:22). The meal setting highlights another important reason the early Christians met in the homes of the early Saints. Bradley Blue argues, "The early believers met in houses *not by default alone* (i.e., there was nowhere else to meet) but deliberately because the house setting provided the facilities which were of paramount importance for the gathering. For example, the culinary [apparatus] necessary for the meal."[9]

Interestingly, Paul notes the presence of "them that believe not" (Greek, *apistoi*) and outsiders (Greek, *idiōtai;* KJV, "that believeth not") in attendance at the meetings (see 1 Corinthians 14:22–24).

Jewish Reaction

Because sources are fragmentary, it may be difficult to reconstruct the intra-Jewish debate between Jewish-Christians and other Jews. There is no scholarly consensus on the topic for the last half of the first century.

There seem to be some points that we can cautiously posit. First, it has been observed "after the Crucifixion, [Jesus'] followers regarded themselves as Jews who were committed to a belief in the messiahship of Jesus."[10] For a rather lengthy period, many Jewish-Christians "observed the Law while believing in Jesus."[11] Luke confirms this interpretation (see Acts 21:20). Additionally, Luke informs his reader that a large company of priests joined the Church (Acts 6:7). He also notes that members of the Pharisees sect believed (Acts 15:5). Paul likely reflected the feelings of many

---

[9] Bradley Blue, "Acts and the House-Church," in David W. J. Gill and Conrad Gempf, eds., *The Book of Acts in Its First-Century Setting* (Grand Rapids, Mich.: Eerdmans, 1994), 2:121.

[10] R. J. Zwi Werblowsky and Geoffrey Wigoder, "Christianity," *Oxford Dictionary of Jewish Religion* (New York: Oxford University Press, 1997), 158.

[11] Ibid., "Jewish Christians," 370.

Jewish-Christians when he declared, "For I also am an Israelite, of the seed of Abraham, of the tribe of Benjamin" (Romans 11:1).

Additionally, many commentators agree—and this is an important point—that "the early Church may have been perceived by other Jews as one among several sects."[12] Like the Sadducees, Pharisees, and the Essenes, other Jews most likely perceived the emerging Christian movement as being under the general umbrella of Judaism.

Eventually, between the destruction of the temple in A.D. 70 and the Bar Kochba Revolt in A.D. 135, many Jews came to believe that Jewish-Christians were apostates. Luke records at least one Jewish assessment of Paul: "And they are informed of thee, that thou teachest all the Jews which are among the Gentiles to forsake Moses, saying that they ought not to circumcise their children, neither to walk after the customs" (Acts 21:21). Although some argue this represents a false charge against Paul, it at least reveals what may have been a popular perception by some Jews living outside of Jerusalem. As more and more Jews began to see Jewish-Christians as being out of harmony with their point of view, Jewish followers of Jesus were stigmatized as apostates. "Judaism inevitably regarded apostasy as a despicable act of desertion, treason, and weakness."[13]

Apparently, many Jewish-Christians rejected the charge, believing they were faithful to God, the Torah, and the temple. An increasingly hostile attitude was formed by the end of the first century between Jews and Jewish-Christians.

According to one interpretation, "It was in order to drive the Jewish Christians from the Jewish religious communion that the patriarch Gamli'el II instructed R. Shemu'el ha-Qatan to compose the imprecation [a spoken curse] that became an additional paragraph to the existing *Amidah* [the main prayer in public and

---

[12] Ibid., "Christianity," 158.
[13] Ibid., "Apostasy," 57.

private worship]."[14] This curse, known as the *Birkat ha-minim,* has "undergone many changes and revisions, and the original wording cannot be reconstructed with certainty. *Genizah* texts [from Cairo, Egypt] of the benediction include a reference to *ntsrm,* commonly identified as Jewish-Christians."[15] One version, from the fifth century, reads, "For apostates who have rejected Your Torah let there be no hope, and may the Nazarenes and heretics perish in an instant. Let all the enemies of Your people, the House of Israel, be speedily cut down; and may You swiftly uproot, shatter, destroy, subdue, and humiliate the kingdom of arrogance, speedily in our days! Blessed are You, O Lord, who shatters His enemies and humbles the arrogant" (Talmud, *B'rakhot* 28b–29a).

Obviously, Jewish-Christians could not accept, let alone say "Amen" to such a public prayer, making it rather easy for others to detect their presence in a gathering.

Eventually identified as the *minim* in the Talmud and Midrash, which term may be derived "from *ma'amin Yeshu notseri* (believer in Jesus the Nazarene),"[16] the followers of Jesus were no longer considered Jews by other Jews. From a Jewish perspective, the break was final.

Gentile-Christianity

The transformation of the early house-churches dominated by Jewish-Christians was significant during the first century. At first, few Gentiles joined them in worship. Most likely the integration of a few Gentiles did not cause any concern initially. Jewish-Christians may well have accepted them in the same way that uncircumcised God-fearers had been accepted in the local

---

[14] Ibid., "Jewish Christian," 370.
[15] Ibid., "Birkat Ha-Minim," 131.
[16] Ibid., "Minim," 467.

synagogues—as a rather insignificant minority that may eventually become full-fledged Jews by submitting to circumcision.

Needless to say, as more and more Gentiles gathered in the house-churches for weekly worship without becoming Jewish, difficulties arose over table fellowship, a very practical issue given that Jews could not eat with Gentiles. When the situation finally became critical (see Galatians 2), Church leaders held a meeting, known as the Jerusalem Conference, in A.D. 49 (see Acts 15). This important council decided that Gentiles did not have to submit to circumcision—a rather far-reaching decision (see Acts 15:19).

That Judaism continued to require circumcision of Gentile converts separated them forever from Jewish-Christians, and Jews-as-Gentiles increasingly dominated the early house-church. With the death of the Apostles—in particular, Peter, Paul, and James (the Lord's brother)—the house-churches lost much of their Jewish connection. Between the first Jewish War, when the temple was destroyed, and the second Jewish War, when Rabbi Akiva announced that Bar Kochba was the Messiah, the ties between the synagogue and the church were finally broken once and for all.

Conclusion

The early Saints moved from worship in the temple and the synagogue to the house-church by the end of the first century. One scholar noted, "As the destruction of the Temple was nearing, the differences between Judaism and Christianity were widening. By the time the Temple was destroyed, the Jewish-Christians were a minority among the total number of Christians, and it was becoming clear that the future of the new religion would be dominated by Gentile Christians."[17]

As increasing numbers of Greek speakers were baptized into

---

[17] Lawrence H. Schiffmann, *Who Was a Jew? Rabbinic and Halakhic Perspectives on the Jewish Christian Schism* (Hoboken, N.J.: KTAV Publishing House, 1985), 53.

the Church, the language of worship became Greek—moving away from the original Aramaic of Jesus and the early disciples. The break between Christians and Jews was complete by A.D. 135 with the end of the Bar Kochba Revolt (the second Jewish War).

Later, when Christianity became the officially sanctioned religion in Rome, the Jewish minority living within the political boundaries of the empire suffered. A tradition of persecution and intolerance took root in the Roman Catholic and Greek Orthodox traditions, which was passed on to the Protestants and even exacerbated by them in some cases. Beginning in the fifteen century, this anti-Semitism eventually provided the religious context for traditionally Christian nations and people to murder six million Jews (half the worldwide population of Jews). During the long history of the New Testament from the second century until today, the insider debates between Jewish-Christians and Jews found within it were "exploited for [their] perceived anti-Jewish content" with devastating results.[18]

---

[18] James Carleton Paget, "*Adversus Judaeos* Literature," in Edward Kessler and Neil Wenborn, eds., *A Dictionary of Jewish-Christian Relations* (New York: Cambridge University Press, 2005), 6.

VII.

THE CONTINUING INFLUENCE OF THE FAMILY OF JESUS IN EARLY CHRISTIANITY

THOMAS A. WAYMENT

For neither did his brethren believe in him.

JOHN 7:5

Like so many documents that have survived long enough to shape history in a meaningful way, the New Testament is often much richer than the commentary that accompanies it. The text is filled with, among other things, unspoken implications, subtle suggestions, underlying rebukes, and undeclared true doctrines. One example of a story that is far richer than the accompanying commentary is that of Jesus' family, including His mother and father, and also His brothers and sisters. The story is by no means simple.

It would be rather straightforward to examine Jesus' family members, particularly His brothers, and what events they were involved in, and then draw conclusions from there. We could discuss the various meanings of the term *brother* and its implications for Jesus' immediate family. But like so many words, the word *brother,* for example, has a wider range of meanings beyond "sibling." From half-brother, stepbrother, to brother in the faith, the term has acquired many connotations. The same is true in the

New Testament when Mark first referred to the "brothers" of Jesus (Mark 6:3).[1]

Traditionally, as Latter-day Saints—who are not confined by the doctrine of the perpetual virginity of Mary—we have assumed that the brothers mentioned in Mark (6:3) and Matthew (13:55) were literal half-brothers of Jesus, siblings of the same mother but a different father.[2] That may be the case historically, but given the wealth of meaning of the simple term "brother" (Greek, *adelphos*), we should exercise some caution in assuming too little or even too much. We have also assumed a fairly easy transition from being a sibling of the Savior to becoming a follower of the Savior, but interestingly the Gospels do not tell the story that way. In their account of the events, there are twists and turns, difficulties and triumphs, and, in the end, belief.

It is the purpose of this chapter to consider the full impact of the family of Jesus and how they shaped the Church and its development during the first three decades after the death of Jesus Christ.[3] From the surviving evidence, it appears that the brothers of Jesus may have influenced the direction of the Church through their standing as brothers of Jesus rather than through a priesthood calling or position. Moreover, Paul assumed that a mischievous group of Judaizing Christians—Christians who sought to return to Judaism—had aligned themselves with the brothers of Jesus to try to change the hierarchy of the Church. Whether James endorsed their practices or refuted them will be a point of discussion in this chapter. In order to probe these questions fully, we must first seek clarification on the matter of whether the family of

---

[1] Arndt and Gingrich, *GEL*, "adelphos," 19.

[2] Rosemary R. Ruether, "Collision of History and Doctrine: The Brothers of Jesus and the Virginity of Mary," *Continuum* 7 (1969): 93–105.

[3] For a critical assessment of all the evidence, see John Painter, *Just James: The Brother of Jesus in History and Tradition,* 2d ed. (Columbia: University of South Carolina, 2004).

Jesus, particularly His brothers—James, Joses, Simon, and Judas—were His brothers, stepbrothers, or simply brothers in the gospel.[4] From that vantage point, we will then be able to determine with greater accuracy what influence they had on the first Apostles and missionaries.

Potential Relatives of Jesus

There are quite a large number of people who may be considered to be relatives of Jesus. Before Jesus' birth, His mother visited a "cousin" named Elisabeth: "And, behold, thy cousin Elisabeth, she hath also conceived a son in her old age: and this is the sixth month with her, who was called barren" (Luke 1:36). The word "cousin" (Greek, *syngenēs*) can mean anything from a distant relative to a fellow countryman to a first cousin.[5] Therefore, among the early experiences related in the Gospels is a story in which Jesus' mother found solace with a relative.

The Gospels end on a similar note by including a number of individuals who were relatives of Jesus on some level. According to the four evangelists, a number of women visited the empty tomb on Sunday immediately following the Jewish Sabbath. Those women included (1) Mary Magdalene, (2) Mary the mother of James the less and of Joses, (3) Salome, (4) Mary the mother of Joses (probably the same as [2]), (5) Mary the mother of James (probably the same as [2]), (6) the mother of the sons of Zebedee, (7) the other Mary, (8) Joanna, (9) Jesus' mother, (10) "his mother's sister," (11) and Mary the wife of Clopas (also spelled Cleophas; Matthew 27:56, 61; 28:1; Mark 15:40, 47; 16:1; Luke 24:10; John 19:25). Depending on how the evidence is interpreted, it is

---

[4] Note that Joses is a shortened form of Joseph, which Mark prefers, but Matthew does not. The King James Version uses Joses in Matthew 13:55, but older Greek manuscripts preserve the name as Joseph.

[5] Arndt and Gingrich, *GEL*, "*sungenēs*," 950.

possible that all of these women were somehow related to Jesus, thus making the Resurrection accounts, in part, a family affair.[6]

The evidence could be expanded to include Simon Zelotes, Mary the wife of Clopas, Judas Lebbaeus, and the sons of Zebedee (James and John) as cousins.[7] Although there are historic reasons for making such broad connections in the family of Jesus, it would be impossible to track down and assess the accuracy of each of the sources that preserve an account of these relationships in a single paper. Instead, while it is recognized that many individuals may have had close family ties with Jesus' parents, our earliest witnesses, the New Testament authors, did not appear to discuss these family relationships in any meaningful way, with the exception of the visitors to the cross and tomb of Jesus. Therefore, this chapter will look at the four brothers and unnamed and unnumbered sisters of Jesus because of the important role they played in the Gospels as well as their continued influence in the letters of Paul. At the same time, it is important to note that none of the New Testament authors appeared to have felt hesitant to name the relatives of Jesus in any way. They were comfortable with the idea that He had blood relatives, opening up the possibility that He had siblings as well.

The Brothers of Jesus in the Letters of Paul

The word *brother* (Greek, *adelphos*) was used broadly in Paul's epistles to describe both literal brothers, children of the same parents, and brothers in the sense of people who share the same faith. For example, in writing to a congregation that Paul had not visited and where he knew some of the Saints but not all of them, he

---

[6] See Bible Dictionary, "Mary"; Blair G. Van Dyke and Ray L. Huntington, "Sorting Out the Seven Marys in the New Testament," *Religious Educator* 5 (2003): 53–84; Richard Bauckham, *Jude and the Relatives of Jesus in the Early Church* (London and New York: T&T Clark, 2004), 5–44.

[7] Bruce R. McConkie, *The Mortal Messiah Book II: From Bethlehem to Calvary* (Salt Lake City: Deseret Book, 1980), 105 n 2, 113–14.

said, "Now I beseech you, brethren" (Romans 16:17). Elsewhere he drew a conclusion from their reported actions, saying, "I myself also am persuaded of you, my brethren, that ye are full of goodness" (Romans 15:14). At other times, however, Paul used the same Greek term to indicate a sibling: "Have we not power to lead about a sister, a wife, as well as other apostles, and as the brethren of the Lord, and Cephas?" (1 Corinthians 9:5). In this example, Paul referred to familial relationships, "a sister, a wife," and in that context mentions the "brothers" (KJV, "brethren") of Jesus. The brothers of Jesus envisioned in this verse cannot also be brothers of Cephas, which the comma in the English translation attempts to convey, while the Greek conveys the idea that they are only brothers of Jesus through a genitive construction (Greek, *hoi adelphoi tou kyriou*). Although they are unnamed in this instance, Paul was certainly aware that Jesus had mortal brothers.

With the recognition that Paul was aware of Jesus' mortal brothers, it becomes clear in other instances when he referred to Jesus' brothers that he was likewise speaking of mortal brothers and not simply brothers in the gospel. In an earlier epistle, Paul named one of Jesus' brothers: "But other of the apostles saw I none, save James the Lord's brother" (Galatians 1:19). Paul's emphasis on James and his silence regarding the other brothers is important because it demonstrates the pivotal position that James held in the three decades after Jesus' death and probably more specifically between A.D. 48 and his death in A.D. 62. Several other Pauline references indicate knowledge of James's position in the period leading up to and following the Jerusalem Council of c. A.D. 49. Paul noted that James was a witness of the resurrected Lord: "After that, he was seen of James; then of all the apostles" (1 Corinthians 15:7), and that James played a role in deciding matters in Jerusalem: "And when James, Cephas, and John, who seemed to be pillars, perceived the grace that was given unto me, they gave to me and Barnabas the right hands of fellowship; that we should go unto the heathen, and they unto the circumcision" (Galatians 2:9). In conjunction with this reference to James, Paul also noted a negative experience with some ill-intentioned followers of James who sought to make reforms in the branch of the Church in Antioch: "For before that certain came from James, he did eat with the Gentiles: but when they were come, he withdrew and separated himself, fearing them which were of the circumcision" (Galatians 2:12).

Paul's knowledge of the Lord's brothers was largely limited to James, although his use of the plural in 1 Corinthians 9:5 suggests that some of the other brothers had also accepted the gospel and worked as missionaries. These unnamed brothers were not nearly as influential as James in the Pauline writings. The importance of the Pauline references is immense because the information derives from the earliest period of Christianity, from a time before the Gospels were written; therefore, the Pauline letters may reveal a viewpoint different from how the brothers were viewed later when the Gospels were written.

Historically, from the Pauline letters, several conclusions can be drawn regarding James. First, James was called an apostle but was not included with the Twelve Apostles. Rather, there were three distinct groups who saw the risen Lord—the Twelve, the five hundred brethren, and the Apostles, which included James: "And that he was seen of *Cephas, then of the twelve:* After that, he was seen of above *five hundred brethren at once;* of whom the greater part remain unto this present, but some are fallen asleep. After that, *he was seen of James; then of all the apostles*" (1 Corinthians 15:5–7; emphasis added). The term *apostle* here in reference to James was being used in its nontechnical sense as one who served the Lord as a missionary (Greek, *apostellō,* "to send out"). This fits well with Paul's other reference in the same epistle that Jesus' brothers were also traveling and teaching the gospel as missionaries. Paul's intent in that verse (1 Corinthians 9:5) can be interpreted to mean that Paul was comparing his own experience to that of the Twelve

Apostles ("Have we not power to lead about a sister, a wife, as well as other apostles, and as the brethren of the Lord, and Cephas?"), but "apostle" in this verse may equally refer to the traveling missionaries and not negatively to the Twelve. This conclusion seems to be confirmed as Paul mentioned "Cephas" (Peter) by name, thus signaling that he did not intend the comparison to the Twelve Apostles but to the only member of that group who had visited Corinth. Thus, it is safe to say that Paul was not aware of James being ordained to the Apostleship, but only that he served as an apostle in the sense of being a missionary.

Second, from the letter to the Galatians, it was clear that James was influential in Jerusalem around A.D. 48, and that influence probably stretched back several years before the council was held c. A.D. 49. Paul, however, did not view James entirely as a positive influence in Jerusalem, and some of his language in the Galatians' letter hints that the Church in Jerusalem had fallen into disarray. It is important to note also that Galatians represents Paul's perspective on the matter and that the book of Acts records another view. In reporting from Antioch concerning a discussion in Jerusalem over the matter of circumcision and the collection for the poor Saints in that city, Paul noted that James stood alongside Peter and John, although his summary does not lend confidence that the Church was running smoothly: "And when James, Cephas, and John, *who seemed to be pillars*" (Galatians 2:9; emphasis added). That Paul could state that Peter, James, and John *seemed* to be in charge argues against equating the three names as equal in authority.[8]

Following a misunderstanding that resulted from Peter's actions in Antioch where he removed himself from eating in the

---

[8] The James mentioned in this verse is certainly the Lord's brother. James, the son of Zebedee, had been put to death by Herod Agrippa I in A.D. 44. References to James that occur after Acts 12:1–2 are to Jesus' brother of the same name.

company of Gentile-Christians, Paul offered a sharp rebuke, again suggesting a breakdown in communication with Jerusalem: "But when Peter was come to Antioch, *I withstood him to the face, because he was to be blamed*" (Galatians 2:11; emphasis added). This event was made worse because certain individuals who had traveled from Jerusalem claiming to represent James, caused Peter to remove himself: "For before that certain came from James, he did eat with the Gentiles: but when they were come, he withdrew and separated himself, fearing them which were of the circumcision" (Galatians 2:12). From Paul's perspective, the men from Jerusalem represented James, but it is unclear whether the evidence supports the conclusion that James actually sent the men to represent him (see Acts 15:13–21). It is a simple enough possibility that the men claimed James's endorsement when they did not have it. Barnabas, however, was convinced of their authority, a fact that would have made Paul more certain of their claim. In fact, Barnabas was so moved by the men from James that he removed himself from the dinner as well (Galatians 2:13).

Paul may have been largely unaware of events in Jerusalem because he spent most of his life after his conversion on the road visiting Christian communities in Asia and Greece. He traveled to Jerusalem on several occasions to attend the feasts of Passover and Pentecost but may have been unaware of the difficulties developing in that city while he was away. That he openly rebuked Peter is clear, but the Apostle likely had his own reasons for acting the way he did. Perhaps the most significant evidence from the Pauline letters is the idea that James's seeming endorsement was apparently reason enough to cause Barnabas and others to act differently from the way they had acted in the past. This mighty influence is not directly connected with a position in the Church in Paul's writings.

The Brothers of the Lord in the General Epistles

The letters of James and Jude are traditionally ascribed to the Lord's brothers of the same names (see Mark 6:3; Matthew 13:55). Interestingly, both authors identified themselves by name but did not hint at any filial relationship with Jesus. This is somewhat disconcerting because such a relationship would have been widely known and positively accepted. Perhaps the information was so widely known that both authors did not feel the need to mention it. James stated his name and his position in the Church in the opening lines of his only surviving letter: "James, a servant of God and of the Lord Jesus Christ, to the twelve tribes which are scattered abroad, greeting" (James 1:1). In a much later epistle, Jude likewise gave his name, but no mention is made of being a younger sibling of the Lord: "Jude, the servant of Jesus Christ, and brother of James, to them that are sanctified by God the Father, and preserved in Jesus Christ, and called" (Jude 1:1). Both authors used the term *servant* (Greek, *doulos,* "slave" or "servant") and not a priesthood title as Paul frequently did (2 Corinthians 1:1). Moreover, James and Jude intended their letters to be circulated widely "to the twelve tribes which are scattered abroad" and "to them that are sanctified . . . and called."[9]

Because both authors were in a position to write to the entire Church, it is possible that they did so by virtue of their ecclesiastical authority. Unfortunately, this evidence cannot be more forcefully asserted because other authors in the New Testament wrote without having been in a position of authority (Mark, Luke, and the anonymous author of Hebrews). Particularly, the author of Hebrews anonymously exhorted the Saints without reference to

---

[9] Many scholars have questioned the authenticity of these two letters. One of the reasons for doing so is that the authors fail to draw upon their filial relationship with Jesus. This piece of evidence has led some to wonder whether James and Jude mentioned in these letters are actually later individuals of the same name.

any ecclesiastical authority (see Hebrews 13:19–25).[10] But what is perhaps more telling in these two epistles is that Jude drew upon James's authority and nothing more. In his short introduction, he referred to himself as "the brother of James" without any further explanation, thus making it obvious that he was less widely known than James. The only two individuals with that name who could also have had such widespread recognition were James the Lord's brother and James the son of Zebedee.[11] This evidence fits squarely with the Pauline evidence that James was widely influential and recognized in Christian circles; and, ironically, the epistle of Jude, which may have been written as late as the last decade of the first century, could draw upon the name recognition of his brother who had passed away nearly thirty years before.

The Brothers of Jesus in the Book of Acts

The picture presented in Acts is much more complicated than that presented in Paul's letters or in the general epistles. The brothers of Jesus figured prominently in three separate events of the early Church. First, they were gathered with the eleven remaining disciples in Jerusalem shortly after the death of Jesus: "These all continued with one accord in prayer and supplication, with the women, and Mary the mother of Jesus, and with his brethren" (Acts 1:14). The possessive pronoun "his" indicates that they were Jesus' brothers and not a brother of a member of the Twelve Apostles. Second, James figured prominently in the Jerusalem Council (c. A.D. 49), at which he declared the council's decision (Acts 15:13–21). And finally, James attempted to help Paul avoid

---

[10] For an excellent discussion of whether Paul was the author of Hebrews, see Terrence L. Szink, "Authorship of the Epistle to the Hebrews," in Kent P. Jackson and Frank F. Judd, Jr., eds., *How the New Testament Came to Be* (Salt Lake City and Provo: Deseret Book and Religious Studies Center, 2006), 243–59.

[11] Bauckham, *Jude and the Relatives of Jesus,* 134–48.

arrest in Jerusalem at the end of Paul's final visit to the city (Acts 21:18–25).

Because the Gospel authors depicted the brothers (and possibly sisters) as unaccepting of Jesus' teaching, a tradition that was also conveyed in Luke's Gospel (see Luke 8:21; compare John 7:1–5), it was important for Luke to give an account of when the brothers of Jesus accepted the gospel. In Acts 1:14, the brothers are, for the first time, sympathetic to the gospel, and thus Luke preserved the only mention of their conversion, which he seemed to imply as having already occurred by the close of the forty-day ministry.

Like Paul, Luke largely relied on traditions, whereas James was already in a position of authority in the early Church. Without any hint or explanation of how he came into that position, Luke reintroduced James into the story some twenty years later at the Jerusalem Council. In that account, there was a subtle hint that the branch of the Church in Jerusalem was in disarray, much like Paul implied in his letters. Luke carefully reported that Peter declared openly his decision on the matter of circumcision being required of Gentile converts (Acts 15:7–11) but then also added that James offered a "sentence" (Acts 15:19). The word *sentence* in English carries negative connotations, but the Greek verb *krinō* implies a decision, perhaps even a summary in this context. In other words, after Peter had spoken, drawing upon the revelation he had received in Acts 10:9–16, James offered an application or summary judgment on the matter. As recorded in Acts 15, Peter and James worked in tandem on a troubling issue, on which they offered a decision together.

If the account ended at that point, the matter would be much simpler. James, following Peter's counsel, recommended that circumcision be done away with for Gentile members, but James also added that Gentile members should keep kosher and stop fornicating: "But that we write unto them, that they abstain from pollutions of idols, and from fornication, and from things strangled, and from blood" (Acts 15:20). Whether this summary judgment was part of Peter's declaration is not mentioned in Luke's account, but a subtle hint suggests that James had become the mediator between the Jerusalem hard-liners and the Gentile Christian missionaries. Luke introduced the chapter, relating that there were Christians who maintained their identity as former Pharisees: *"But there rose up certain of the sect of the Pharisees which believed"* (Acts 15:5; emphasis added). These Pharisee converts had sought to manipulate the proceedings by mandating circumcision for all male members. At the end of James's concluding thoughts, Luke added again a reference to those who sought for the brethren to make concessions in Church practice. He added, "And they wrote letters by them after this manner; The apostles and elders and brethren send greeting unto the brethren which are of the Gentiles in Antioch and Syria and Cilicia: forasmuch as we have heard, that certain which went out from us have troubled you with words, subverting your souls, saying, Ye must be circumcised, and keep the law: to whom we gave no such commandment" (Acts 15:23–24). Subtly, Luke raised the troubling thought that some in the Church "which went out from us" declared things contrary to what the Church leaders had taught. Interestingly, James's decision was given to clarify the confusion and may confirm in part that James took a position to moderate the dispute.

What is implied in Acts 15 is made explicit in Acts 21, where James attempted to broker Paul's freedom through a demonstration of faith. Paul, before sailing to Jerusalem at the conclusion of his third missionary journey, had taken a vow—probably a Nazarite vow—which he would have been required to fulfill in the Jerusalem temple.[12] When he arrived in Jerusalem, an event depicted in Acts 21, the brethren and James received him warmly:

---

[12] Numbers 6:13–21; Josephus, *AJ*, 19.294.

"And when we were come to Jerusalem, the brethren received us gladly. And the day following Paul went in with us unto James; and all the elders were present" (Acts 21:17–18). Because certain members of the Jerusalem branch were suspicious of Paul's mission, James proposed that Paul take four men into the temple with him and pay for the sacrifice that would signal the completion of their Nazarite vow: "Thou seest, brother, how many thousands of Jews there are which believe; and they are all zealous of the law: And they are informed of thee, that thou teachest all the Jews which are among the Gentiles to forsake Moses, saying that they ought not to circumcise their children, neither to walk after the customs. What is it therefore? the multitude must needs come together: for they will hear that thou art come. Do therefore this that we say to thee: We have four men which have a vow on them; them take, and purify thyself with them, and be at charges with them" (Acts 21:20–24).

Luke's account signals several underlying tensions, namely the suggestion that Paul's missionary work had been misrepresented in Jerusalem, that Paul was given a test to prove his faith, and that James may have been manipulated into setting Paul up for the persecution that followed. As the story proceeds, Paul did as James had requested and was arrested for taking a Gentile (Trophimus) into the temple (Acts 21:29). Because Paul had paid for the sacrifices of the four men, including Trophimus, he was also liable for bringing a Gentile into the temple. Ironically, James, or the zealous brethren of Jerusalem, identified the four men in the first place, thus effectively setting Paul up without his prior knowledge. It is likely, following Luke's overall portrait of James, that he was likewise manipulated by the Jerusalem hard-liners, a position that he appeared to be in, both in the letters of Paul and in Acts.

This complicated portrait of James, the only named brother of Jesus in Acts, presents him as an influential moderate in the Jerusalem branch of the Church who sought to carefully mediate between Christians who followed Peter's counsel and those who sought to follow the law of Moses while at the same time following the gospel. This conclusion fits nicely with the information found in Galatians where the men from James came to Antioch and sought to persuade Peter to stop eating with Gentiles. In all probability those men aspired to represent James but did not have his direct approval. The final scene with James in Acts 21 seems to suggest that he was manipulated by those very hard-liners that misrepresented him. That Agrippa I would kill him for being a Christian in A.D. 62 confirms his loyalty to the doctrine of the Apostles despite what others may have sought to say about him. Josephus preserved the only account of his death: "Festus was now dead, and Albinus was but upon the road; so he assembled the sanhedrin of judges, and brought before them the brother of Jesus, who was called Christ, whose name was James, and some others, [or, some of his companions]; and when he had formed an accusation against them as breakers of the law, he delivered them to be stoned."[13]

The Brothers of Jesus in the Gospels

Having established that the earliest New Testament authors knew of the brothers of Jesus, it is now easy to see that Matthew's and Mark's references to them by name is based on the Gospel authors' understanding that they were actual siblings of Jesus and not simply brothers of the same faith. Mark names them: "James, and Joses, and . . . Juda, and Simon . . . and are not his sisters here with us?" (6:3). Matthew knew their names from another source and his slight change in the order of names suggests that Judas was the youngest brother: "James, and Joses, and Simon, and Judas

---

[13] Josephus, *AJ*, 20.200.

... And his sisters, are they not all with us?" (13:55–56).[14] Both Matthew and Mark introduce the brothers and sisters in a scene where outsiders question Jesus, particularly because they know Him and His family, which seems to imply to the unbelievers that Jesus cannot be the Anointed One, or the Christ. The brothers and sisters here are entirely neutral, and are simply used as a foil by the unbelieving as a way to discredit the truthfulness of Jesus' teachings.

Two other events indicate that Jesus' siblings as a group did not believe in Him, although it is impossible to distinguish how they felt individually. In an event that is described in Matthew, Mark, and Luke, Jesus was accused of healing by the power of Beelzebub. At the conclusion of that story, and indeed appended to it, Jesus' family came to Him. In Matthew and Mark, the family of Jesus seemed to want to offer help in a difficult situation, but Jesus responded with what some scholars have interpreted to be a rebuke of His family.[15] In Mark the story is told in this way: "There came then his brethren and his mother, and, standing without, sent unto him, calling him. And the multitude sat about him, and they said unto him, Behold, thy mother and thy brethren without seek for thee. And he answered them, saying, Who is my mother, or my brethren? And he looked round about on them which sat about him, and said, Behold my mother and my brethren! For whosoever shall do the will of God, the same is my brother, and my sister, and mother" (Mark 3:31–35). The event can easily be interpreted as a social rebuke of His family, but it is unclear whether the rebuke

---

[14] The naming of the brothers in order of age is usually assumed, and Matthew and Mark's changes to the order may simply represent a lack of knowledge concerning who was the youngest sibling of Jesus. It may also hint that the youngest brothers of Jesus were no longer known to the writers roughly thirty to forty years after the death of Jesus.

[15] W. D. Davies and Dale C. Allison Jr., *The Gospel according to Matthew*, 3 vols. (Edinburgh: T&T Clark, 1998), 2:322–44.

came because of some perceived disbelief on their part, or part of a larger rebuke of those who had rejected His miracles (see Matthew 12:46–50). In Matthew and Mark, it is not clear that the intent was to chastise the brothers (and sisters?) for unbelief, although the social stigma of such a public rebuke was significant.

Luke's account of the saying "My mother and my brethren are these which hear the word of God, and do it" (Luke 8:21) came in a very different context and with very different inferences. In Luke, Jesus had just finished teaching about hiding one's testimony and works when He spoke about His family: "No man, when he hath lighted a candle, covereth it with a vessel, or putteth it under a bed; but setteth it on a candlestick, that they which enter in may see the light" (Luke 8:16). That teaching was followed by a saying that may imply that Jesus' siblings did not fully accept what they had: "Take heed therefore how ye hear: for whosoever hath, to him shall be given; *and whosoever hath not, from him shall be taken even that which he seemeth to have*" (Luke 8:18; emphasis added).[16] Indeed, it may even be a veiled reference to the crucifixion, hinting that the opportunity to know Jesus and the depth of His mission was missed by Jesus' siblings and that Jesus would soon be taken away from them. At the end of this interchange, Jesus' "mother and his brethren" came to see Him to which He responded, "*My mother and my brethren are these which hear the word of God, and do it*" (8:21; emphasis added), thus connecting the two stories closely. Perhaps it was Luke's intent to indicate that the family of Jesus did not wholly endorse His teachings, but again the family is treated as a unit, and there is no differentiation of feelings toward Jesus among the siblings.

This idea of rejection is stated explicitly in the Gospel of John,

---

[16] A similar conclusion is reached by Khiok-Khng Yeo, "The Mother and Brothers of Jesus (Lk 8:19–21, Mk 3:31–35, Mt 12:46–50)," *Asia Journal of Theology* 6 (1992): 311–14.

which is also the only source to openly address the issue of sibling rivalry between Jesus and His brothers. John set up the story with a contradiction: Jesus wished to attend the Feast of Tabernacles in Jerusalem, but He could not do so because the Jews in Jerusalem wished to kill Him (John 7:1–2). This paradox underlines the story of Jesus' brothers rejecting Him in the Gospel of John. This rejection was highlighted in Jesus' brothers' two taunts of the mortal ministry: "Depart hence, and go into Judaea, that thy disciples also may see the works that thou doest" (John 7:3) and "For there is no man that doeth any thing in secret, and he himself seeketh to be known openly. If thou do these things, shew thyself to the world" (John 7:4). Ironically, these challenges were the same as those implied in Luke's account where the siblings apparently did not realize Jesus was the Light of the World. This rejection of Jesus by His brothers was part of the oldest sources available to the Gospel authors, and tells us that their disbelief in Jesus was a result of their inability to accept Him as someone who could save the world. They appear to have thought His message and ministry too rural and private, at least according to the Gospel of John and implications in Matthew, Mark, and Luke. They wanted a major Judean ministry and for Jesus to take on the Jerusalem elite. Perhaps this is the reason that Luke related their conversion in Acts 1:14.

To summarize the issue thus far, it is important to note that the Gospels imply a common theme, namely that the family of Jesus, and probably more specifically His brothers and sisters, had difficulty accepting Jesus as anything other than a local Galilean upstart. That relationship punctuated all interaction between Jesus and His brothers as reported in the Gospels. Even if there were positive experiences between Jesus and His siblings, the Gospel authors did not report it. Paul, who wrote earlier than the Gospels but described a time later than that depicted in the Gospels, felt that James represented Jewish-Christian interests in Judea and that some of his positions contradicted the Gentile mission he was engaged in. Luke largely followed Paul's description but made more allowance for the possibility that James was a mediator between the Jewish-Christians in Jerusalem and the Gentile-Christians living in Antioch and elsewhere. By the time Paul and Luke wrote, only one brother of Jesus was influential, but during Jesus' lifetime it is apparent that several of His brothers were known to His disciples.

The Family of Jesus and the Crucifixion/Resurrection

All three synoptic Gospels mention the presence of Mary Magdalene at the tomb of Jesus as well as another woman named Mary. In the Gospel of Matthew she is referred to as the "other" Mary (28:1), and she may be the same person as "Mary the mother of James" (Luke 24:10) and "Mary the mother of James the less and of Joses" (Mark 15:40). The challenge with the identification comes because Jesus' mother was also named "Mary" and He had siblings named James and Joses as well. Logically, the natural assumption would be to associate the two Marys, but the immediate question arises whether an author would identify Jesus' mother without reference to her most famous son.

In Mark's Gospel, it appears that he gave the most complete reference first: "Mary the mother of James the less and of Joses" and then gave an abbreviated reference in the following verses: "Mary the mother of Joses" followed by "Mary the mother of James" (Mark 15:40, 47; 16:1). James the less (Greek, *tou mikrou*) in these references could refer to James the son of Alphaeus (Matthew 10:3; Mark 3:18; Luke 6:15; Acts 1:13) or to James the brother of Jesus.[17] The epithet "the less" is certainly comparative to another James, and the only person named James who could be considered

---

[17] There is no hint in the New Testament that James the son of Zebedee was ever referred to as "the less." Indeed, it appears that the term "the less" or "the smaller" is comparing another James to James the son of Zebedee. who was more well-known and, comparatively speaking, would have been "the greater."

greater than this one would be James the son of Zebedee, who died in A.D. 44 (Acts 12:1–2), which leaves Jesus' brother James, James the son of Alphaeus, and perhaps an otherwise unknown James as possible candidates for James the less. The son of Alphaeus can be ruled out by the sheer unlikelihood that the New Testament could preserve two stories of women named Mary who also had sons named James and Joses in the same order of Jesus' siblings and who were also close followers of Jesus. It is also unlikely that James the son of Alphaeus is intended here because he is nowhere else identified through his mother's name or by identifying his younger brother. Moreover, Matthew, Mark, and Luke all mentioned James the son of Alphaeus specifically and then also referred to Mary the mother of James without indicating any relationship between the two (Matthew 10:3; Mark 2:13; 3:18; Luke 6:15; Acts 1:13).[18]

This leaves the most likely candidate for James the less as Jesus' younger brother, who is referred to in association with His mother, Mary, and His younger brother Joses. Scholars who are also influenced by the doctrine of the perpetual virginity of Mary see this as a problematic identification, and therefore they argue that Mary wife of Cleopas is meant and her two sons.[19] Without any doctrinal constraints imposed upon the historical situation, it is possible to see this Mary as the mother of Jesus along with His two younger siblings.

Following this hypothesis, several intriguing possibilities emerge from the evidence. First, why would the synoptic evangelists refer to Jesus' mother through reference to His siblings? Second, does the reference indicate anything of the historical situation from the time when the Gospels were written or from the

---

[18] John P. Meier sees the evidence similarly, *A Marginal Jew*, 3 vols. (New York: Doubleday, 1991), 3:201.

[19] J. McHugh, *The Mother of Jesus in the New Testament* (London: Darton, Longman & Todd, 1975), 234–54.

time when the events occurred? And finally, if James and Joses are identified alongside Mary, is it possible to conclude that they had overcome their doubts expressed in John 7:1–5 and come to believe that their older brother was the Messiah while the other brothers (Judah/Simon) remained skeptical?

Certainly the simple fact that Matthew, Mark, and Luke referred to Mary the mother of Jesus through a reference to James and Joses is an interesting conundrum, and such a reference probably indicates two things. First, the reference may in fact be an expression of the brother's faith to counteract their previous demonstration of a lack of faith. This reference then may be included as a show of solidarity where there previously was none. Subtle hints in the Gospel accounts (see, for example, Mark 3:31–35), and the explicit reference in the Gospel of John, indeed beg the question of when the brothers of Jesus began to believe in the gospel message (see Acts 1:14). Second, the reference to the brothers of Jesus may show a certain degree of sensitivity to those who grappled with the implications of the physical birth of Jesus, an increasing problem in the latter half of the first century and well into the second century.[20] In other words, the Gospel authors nuanced the reference to avoid offending those whose faith was weak and who struggled over the mortal birth of Jesus. In fact, a similar problem arose from the reality of the crucifixion and the cross, which some Christians felt contradicted God's sovereignty and power: "But we preach Christ crucified, unto the Jews a stumblingblock, and unto the Greeks foolishness" (1 Corinthians 1:23). Interestingly, the source of the reference to "Mary the mother of James the less and of Joses" comes from the Gospel of Mark, in which there is no account of

---

[20] Interest in emphasizing Jesus' heavenly origins against his mortal beginnings is seen already in the *Gospel of Thomas* 28–29 and *Gospel of the Ebionites* 6, a Jewish-Christian source. Accessible translations for both of these references can be found in Bart D. Ehrman, *Lost Scriptures: Books That Did Not Make It into the New Testament* (New York: Oxford University Press, 2003), 14, 22–23.

the virgin birth or even any reference to it.[21] Matthew and Luke both took up Mark's reference and altered it slightly to reference James, the most influential sibling of Jesus at the time the Gospels were written, thus reflecting concerns from their day and age.

That the Gospel of Mark could refer to James as "the less" has been disconcerting to some when he played such a prominent role in the second half of the New Testament and where "the less" would certainly be an uncharacteristically negative description. Several historical factors weigh in against such a conclusion. James may have been less than the son of Zebedee in the sense that he was smaller than, or shorter than the other James. This interpretation would follow the meaning of the Greek. The epithet may also indicate the historical reality that James the brother of Jesus was indeed less faithful, less devoted, and less in stature in following Jesus during the mortal ministry and that only after James the son of Zebedee died in A.D. 44 did it no longer make sense to refer to him as the less. In fact, writings produced one to two generations after the canonical Gospels were written referred to this James as "the Just" because of his influence in the early Church, thus showing that his reputation grew over time.[22]

Because the Gospel authors referred to Mary the mother of Jesus in the crucifixion and resurrection accounts through her two son's names, it is probable that the situation represented historical fact in the years Jesus was alive and not exclusively the situation of the early Church in the period between A.D. 60–80 when the synoptic Gospels were written and where James appeared to have been

---

[21] The Gospel of John likewise omits any reference to the virgin birth, but the author shows knowledge of slander against Jesus because of the peculiarities of His birth, "Ye do the deeds of your father. Then said they to him, We be not born of fornication; we have one Father, even God" (John 8:41).

[22] The earliest of these references comes from the *Gospel of Thomas* 12. For a translation see John S. Kloppenborg et al., *Q Thomas Reader* (Sonoma: Polebridge, 1990), 132 .

the most influential brother. This conclusion is partly substantiated through the realization that during the last two or three decades of the first century, Jesus' brother Jude (Juda/Judah) was also active and influential and Joses and Simon were probably unknown and, as far as the historical sources permit one to say, relatively uninfluential. Thus one would expect a reference from the time when the Gospels were written to include a reference to Mary the mother of James and Jude, but not to the relatively unknown Joses. This is an important piece of evidence because it reveals Mark's interest to report the story as accurately as possible and not shape the story entirely by events taking place when he wrote, although certainly he considered the challenges of his day as well.

Conclusion

The New Testament tells two important stories of Jesus' brothers, one of faith and one of disbelief. The Gospels preserve a complex account of James, Juda, Joses, and Simon, who although not openly hostile to Jesus, had questions about Jesus' claim to be the Messiah. The questions are implied in the earliest Gospel accounts beginning with the Gospel of Mark, which was taken up and adapted by the Gospels of Matthew and Luke. Luke, like John, suggested that the questions among Jesus' siblings were more significant and divisive, creating a need at some point in their narratives to explain how the brothers came to accept Jesus—a fact demonstrated in the second half of the New Testament. Interestingly, it is the Gospel of Mark that shows the most concern for preserving an account of events in A.D. 30, whereas Matthew and Luke show some interest in relating the events of Jesus' family in a way that an audience struggling to find belief in the mortality and humanity of Jesus might find acceptable.

Paul wrote at a time when James the son of Zebedee had already passed away and when some of the brothers of Jesus had largely faded from the scene. For him, the only James of reputation was the brother of Jesus, although he did mention the brothers of Jesus on one occasion. For Paul, James represented those who wished to force full obedience to the law of Moses upon all Gentile-Christians, a position very popular with the Pharisaical faction within the Church but very unpopular with Paul. If the first-century Church functioned in A.D. 48–64 as a fully organized entity without difficulty, then this division might be disconcerting, but the belief that an apostasy affected events in the early Church helps us see that James may have simply been trying to hold the Jerusalem branch together.

That James could wield such power in the early Church, where he was strong enough to even attempt reconciliation between Pharisees who believed in Jesus Christ (Acts 15:5) and the prophet (Peter), speaks volumes of his influence and the respect that both sides felt for him. The synoptic Gospels show traces of shaping their message to reach out to those same Christians, thus helping the reader see how pervasive the division was in the early Church. That James stood solidly with Peter in the Church, but not necessarily representing a specific office, is confirmed in the fact that he suffered martyrdom by Agrippa I as a Christian representative of the Jerusalem branch of the Church in A.D. 62.

VIII.

THE EPISTLE OF JAMES: ANTI-PAULINE RHETORIC OR A NEW EMPHASIS?

BRIAN M. HAUGLID

Pure religion and undefiled before God and the Father is this, To visit the fatherless and widows in their affliction, and to keep himself unspotted from the world.

JAMES 1:27

Comparing James's "faith without works is dead" (James 2:26) with Paul's "a man is justified by faith without the deeds of the law" (Romans 3:28) can promote a lively debate. Some could conclude that it is impossible to reconcile or harmonize these two disparate statements. But the Epistle of James presents much more than merely a supposed rhetorical argument with Paul about faith and works. In fact, James's letter builds a unique and coherent case for Christian behavior rooted in faith, while Paul levels a very different argument for faith against the Jewish-Christians who tenaciously, albeit superficially, cling to the law of Moses. James does not appear to even engage the arguments of Paul in his epistle. On the contrary, the real or hypothetical opponent James addresses in his letter would, most assuredly, also be an opponent of Paul. Although Paul would likely agree with how faith is presented in the Epistle of James, his letter to the Romans takes a very different approach in terminology, background, and purpose. This helps to explain why both letters, while appearing irreconcilable, instead must be understood from their own points of view.

After a brief examination of the historical authenticity and authorship of the Epistle of James, an analysis of how James and Paul employ the terms *faith* and *works* from their separate backgrounds will demonstrate that James does not engage in anti-Pauline rhetoric. In fact, a textual study of the Epistle of James will show a developed and thematic presentation of James's primary injunction to his general Christian audience to focus on good Christian behavior, to be "doers of the word, and not hearers only" (1:22).

Historical Authenticity and Authorship

Surprisingly, the Epistle of James was not readily accepted as part of the New Testament canon. Even though it was considered one of the Catholic Epistles (that is, written to a general rather than a specific audience),[1] the Epistle of James was not included in such early Christian canons as those by Marcion (fl. 144),[2] Irenaeus (d. 202), Muratorian (ca. second century), and Eusebius (d. 340). It is not known for certain why this epistle was disputed; it may have been a question of authorship. Jerome (d. 420), speaking of James as the brother of the Lord, said: "He wrote only one Epistle, which is reckoned among the seven Catholic Epistles, and even this is claimed by some to have been published by some one else under his name, and gradually, as time went on, to have gained in authority."[3] However, from as early as the third century, both

---

[1] There are traditionally seven Catholic Epistles: James; 1 and 2 Peter; 1, 2, and 3 John; and Jude.

[2] Marcion rejected the entire Old Testament and accepted only the Gospel of Luke and ten epistles of Paul.

[3] As found in Bruce M. Metzger, *The Canon of the New Testament: Its Origin, Development, and Significance* (Oxford: Clarendon Press, 1987), 235.

Origen (d. 254) and Eusebius (d. 340) refer to James as the author of the epistle.[4]

Although specific reasoning and evidence concerning the question of authorship no longer exist, these divergent views do indicate that concerns arose over this issue. In any case, in A.D. 367, Athanasius included the Epistle of James in his authorized collection of the twenty-seven books of the New Testament, which became the officially accepted canon in 382. Inclusion of the Epistle of James was not questioned again until 1522 when Martin Luther, in his Preface to the New Testament, called it "an Epistle of straw."[5] "Because of what he saw to be James's rejection of the Pauline doctrine of justification by faith, Luther denied that the epistle had apostolic authority; and in his translation of the New Testament he relegated it from its canonical position to the end, together with his equally disliked Hebrews, Jude, and Revelation."[6] Despite the previous questions of authorship and Luther's concern with James's emphasis on works, James's teachings are generally highly valued by Christians.

Faith *(Pistis)* and Works *(Ergon)* for James and Paul

Among the most quoted verses in the Epistle of James is the declaration that "faith without works is dead" (2:26). Throughout his epistle James uses the Greek terms *pistis* for "faith" and *ergon* for "works." Identifying these Greek words and defining them helps us see that James's use of *pistis* and *ergon* focuses on a Christian

---

[4] Eusebius assumes he is the brother of Jesus. Cf. David Noel Freedman, ed., *The Anchor Bible Dictionary,* 6 vols. (New York: Doubleday, 1992), 3:622–23.

[5] Freedman, *ABD,* 3:622.

[6] Ibid. "It is sometimes suggested that James's argument is prior to Paul's and that Paul wrote in part to answer it, but while Paul's argument on justification does not require James's to explain it, the strongly polemical tone of James's language indicates that he knows a position which he is concerned to refute: 'and not by faith alone'" (ibid., 625). See "James, Epistle of," section 2, "James and Paul" for further study.

faith rooted in love and doing such good works as controlling the tongue, visiting widows, and praying over the sick. Paul, on the other hand, uses the same words but discusses them within the context of his Jewish-minded audience. He directs his arguments to Christian converts from Judaism, or Judaizers, who believe that the saving faith in Christ cannot be accessed without the works of circumcision and other works of the law of Moses.

In his epistle, James chastises a real or imaginary opponent who views faith quite differently than James does. James describes this faith as having no works and no power to save (2:14), a faith that is distinct and separate from works (2:18), a faith that is alone (2:24), a faith that is without works and is dead or useless (2:17, 20, 26). James also employs another cognate of *pistis* that translates to "believe," indicating the kind of faith his opponent adheres to, which James describes as a faith that God is one (2:19), a faith that even the devils possess (2:19), and a faith that contradicts the kind of faith Abraham possessed (2:23).[7] Thus James argues that faith and works go hand in hand and that "faith without works is dead" (2:17, 26), while his opponent views faith as entirely independent of works (2:14), making faith dead and works useless. However, when Paul uses the term *faith* he means that "salvation can be received as a gracious gift apart from any meritorious works because of the death and resurrection of his Son, Jesus Christ."[8]

Paul and James also view works quite differently. For James, good works include such behaviors as visiting "the fatherless and widows" (1:27), clothing the naked and feeding the hungry (2:15), and controlling the tongue (3:2–8; 4:11). Indeed, these works focus on mercy and loving-kindness toward fellow brothers and sisters. Paul, on the other hand, is opposed to such works as

---

[7] Robert H. Stein, "'Saved by Faith [Alone]' in Paul Versus 'Not Saved by Faith Alone' in James," *Southern Baptist Journal of Theology* 4, no. 3 (Fall 2000), 6.

[8] Ibid.

"circumcision (Rom 4:1–12; Gal 5:3; 6:15; 1 Cor 7:19; Acts 15:1, 5); ritualistically keeping certain days (Gal 4:10); abstaining from certain food and drink (Col 2:16); etc."[9] Paul makes it clear that one is saved apart from such works.

In other words, Paul and James address two separate audiences with different needs: Paul to certain Jewish-Christians concerned about the law of Moses, and James to inattentive Christians who do not see others' needs. These differing audiences make it necessary for them to use the same terms in different ways. Therefore, James does not engage in anti-Pauline rhetoric even to the least degree.

A brief word on two distinct ways faith is seen in the modern Christian context: (1) "It is objectively applied to the body of truth ('the Christian faith') to be found in the Creeds[,] Councils[,] teachings of doctors and saints, and, above all, in the revelation contained in the Bible." (2) Subjectively, "it is the human response to Divine truth, inculcated in the Gospels as the childlike and trusting acceptance of the kingdom and its demands."[10] Christians view the subjective part of faith as a supernatural event wherein the "Christian can make an act of faith only in virtue of God's action in his soul," and this is possible "only in the context of the Christian revelation."[11] Latter-day Saints also recognize faith as a spiritual gift (Moroni 10:11); however, an important difference emerges regarding the emphasis on obedient activity, which grows out of faith.

Christian faith, in its subjective sense as a "childlike and

---

[9] Ibid., 7. Cf. also Martin Dibelius, "James: A Commentary on the Epistle of James," in *Hermeneia—A Critical and Historical Commentary on the Bible,* ed. Helmut Koester (Philadelphia: Fortress Press, 1976), 174–80.

[10] F. L. Cross, ed., *The Oxford Dictionary of the Christian Church* (Oxford: Oxford University Press, 2005), 499.

[11] Ibid.

trusting acceptance,"[12] likely emerges from the Greek word *pistis,* which has both the sense of "trusting" and "worthy of trust."[13] However, "inasmuch as trust may be a duty, [*pistis*] can come to have the nuance 'obedient'."[14]

Textual Study of the Epistle of James

While James does not engage in a diatribe against Paul, he does give a new emphasis in his epistle for the need to exercise the kind of faith appropriate to works that grow out of true faith, such as prayer, visiting the sick and afflicted, controlling the tongue, and using the priesthood. He also shows that lack of faith is demonstrated through inappropriate works such as double-mindedness, deception, pride and riches, and sin in general. James wrote this epistle "to prevent the danger of a separation (*diastasis*) between faith and works.... It is this coherence of faith and deeds that gives a unifying theme to the entire document and makes it a genuinely Christian writing."[15] James identifies various activities that the follower of Christ should pursue. Faith is the element that holds these disparate subjects together. James illustrates the active faith of believers with his instruction to follow the path to perfection, seek wisdom, and avoid the sins of pride. His use of the imperative tense throughout the text further evidences James's concern that we put our discipleship into action.

Perfection

According to James, afflictions try faith, which then strengthens patience: "But let patience have her perfect work, that ye may

---

[12] Ibid.

[13] Gerhard Friedrich, ed., *Theological Dictionary of the New Testament,* 10 vols. (Grand Rapids, Mich.: Eerdmans, 1968), 6:175.

[14] Ibid.

[15] Ralph P. Martin, ed., *Word Biblical Commentary* (Waco, Tex.: Word Books, 1988), lxxix.

be perfect and entire, wanting nothing" (1:4).[16] The word for perfection in the Greek (*telos*) refers to "fulfillment" or "completion" and "denotes that which has reached its maturity or fulfilled the *end* contemplated."[17] Perfection, then, in the Epistle of James is more akin to spiritual maturity rather than absolute sinlessness.

James clearly teaches that to gain perfection one must perfect faith through good works: "Thou believest that there is one God; thou doest well: the devils also believe, and tremble. But wilt thou know, O vain man, that faith without works is dead? Was not Abraham our father justified by works, when he had offered Isaac his son upon the altar? Seest thou how faith wrought with his works, and by works was faith made perfect?" (2:19–22). "The devils also believe, and tremble" indicates that passive belief is not enough: faith must impel the disciple to acts of righteousness. Joseph F. Smith explains that the fatal flaw of Satan and his followers is a lack of pure intelligence:

"There is a difference between knowledge and pure intelligence. Satan possesses knowledge, far more than we have, but he has not intelligence or he would render obedience to the principles of truth and right. I know men who have knowledge, who understand the principles of the Gospel, perhaps as well as you do, who are brilliant, but who lack the essential qualification of pure intelligence. They will not accept and render obedience thereto. Pure intelligence comprises not only knowledge, but also the power to properly apply that knowledge."[18] President Smith, then, would agree with James that faith (pure intelligence) and obedience (works) are inseparably connected.

---

[16] "Note James' characteristic corroboration of a positive statement by a negative clause: *entire, lacking in nothing; God that giveth* and *upbraideth not; in faith, nothing doubting*" (Marvin R. Vincent, *Word Studies in the New Testament,* 4 vols. [Grand Rapids, Mich.: Eerdmans, 1975], 1:725).

[17] Ibid., 1:724.

[18] Joseph F. Smith, *Gospel Doctrine* (Salt Lake City: Deseret Book, 1977), 58.

Interestingly, a number of parallel verses can be identified between James's path of faith to perfection and the Savior's teachings in the Sermon on the Mount in Matthew. A comparison of the two shows that James's epistle reiterates the Savior's command that his disciples "let [their] light so shine before men, that they may see [their] good works, and glorify [their] Father which is in heaven" (Matthew 5:16).

As in the Sermon on the Mount, of which James likely was aware, James gives counsel on what the faithful should do to reach perfection or spiritual maturity. One powerful example James uses to illustrate the connection between spiritual maturity, or perfection and faith, is in the controlling of the tongue: "For in many things we offend all. If any man offend not in word, the same is a perfect man, and able also to bridle the whole body" (3:2). James characterizes the tongue as "a little member, and boasteth great things" (3:5); "a fire, a world of iniquity . . . and setteth on fire the course of nature; and it is set on fire of hell" (3:6); "but the tongue can no man tame; it is an unruly evil, full of deadly poison" (3:8). President N. Eldon Tanner was as blunt as James. He said:

"The tongue is the most dangerous, destructive, and deadly weapon available to man. A vicious tongue can ruin the reputation and even the future of the one attacked. Insidious attacks against one's reputation, loathsome innuendoes, half-lies about an individual are as deadly as those insect parasites that kill the heart and life of a mighty oak. They are so stealthy and cowardly that one cannot guard against them. As someone has said, 'It is easier to dodge an elephant than a microbe.'"[19] Learning to control the tongue, according to one commentator, is "overcoming the tendency of the mouth 'to stay open when it were more profitably closed.'"[20] To attain perfection, or completeness, according to the Epistle of

---

[19] N. Eldon Tanner, "Judge Not, That Ye Be Not Judged," *Ensign*, July 1972, 35.
[20] Martin, *Word Biblical Commentary*, 109.

Matthew	James
Rejoice in trials (5:12)	Count it all joy when ye fall into [JST] many afflictions (1:2)
Ask and it shall be given you (7:7)	Ask of God, that giveth . . . liberally (1:5)
Be ye therefore perfect (5:48)	Be perfect and entire, wanting nothing (1:4)
Judge not, that ye be not judged (7:1)	For he shall have judgment without mercy, That hath shewed no mercy (2:13)
Let your communication be Yea, yea; Nay, nay (5:37)	Let your yea be yea; and your nay, nay (5:12)
Blessed are the meek (5:5)	Shew . . . meekness of wisdom (3:13)
Lay not up for yourselves treasures upon the earth (6:19)	Your riches are corrupted (5:2)
Whosoever is angry with his brother . . . danger of judgment (5:22)	Wrath of man worketh not the righteousness of God (1:20)
Not every one that saith unto me Lord, Lord . . . but he that doeth (7:21)	What doth it profit . . . though a man say he hath faith, and have not works (2:14)

Source: Adapted from Martin, *Word Biblical Commentary,* lxxv-lxxvi. Note other parallels this commentary cites.

James, the believer is expected to exhibit a living, vitalized faith. This faith is manifest by good works such as patience and control of the tongue.

Wisdom

James discusses two kinds of wisdom—the wisdom of the world and the wisdom of God: "Who is a wise man and endued with knowledge among you? let him shew out of a good conversation his works with meekness of wisdom. But if ye have bitter envying and strife in your hearts, glory not, and lie not against the truth. This wisdom descendeth not from above, but is earthly, sensual, devilish. . . . But the wisdom that is from above is first pure, then peaceable, gentle, and easy to be intreated, full of mercy and good fruits" (3:13–15, 17).

James inextricably ties wisdom to good works. Like true faith that leads to righteous works, true knowledge, correctly applied, is wisdom that will lead to appropriate action. Nowhere is this more poignantly portrayed than in the account of the First Vision. After reading James 1:5, "If any of you lack wisdom, let him ask of God, that giveth to all men liberally, and upbraideth not; and it shall be given him," Joseph Smith recorded:

"Never did any passage of scripture come with more power to the heart of man than this did at this time to mine. It seemed to enter with great force into every feeling of my heart. I reflected on it again and again, knowing that if any person needed wisdom from God, I did; *for how to act I did not know,* and unless I could get more *wisdom* than I then had, I would never know; for the teachers of religion of the different sects understood the same passages of scripture so differently as to destroy all confidence in settling the question by an appeal to the Bible. At length I came to the conclusion that I must either remain in darkness and confusion, *or else I must do as James directs, that is, ask of God*" (Joseph Smith–History 1:12–13; emphasis added).

Joseph Smith's willingness to act on his faith, "as James directs," produced consequences beyond what even the Prophet himself could understand at that time. The effects of Joseph's decision to apply James's directive continues to unfold in both collective and individual ways and will likely do so until the work is done. Joseph may have read many other verses that taught about faith, but it was this verse in James that most profoundly compelled him to go into the grove and offer his prayer of faith. Elder Bruce R. McConkie expressed it well: "This single verse of scripture has had a greater impact and a more far reaching effect upon mankind than any other single sentence ever recorded by any prophet in any age. It might well be said that the crowning act of the ministry of James was not his martyrdom for the testimony of Jesus, but his recitation, as guided by the Holy Ghost, of these simple words which led to the opening of the heavens in modern times."[21]

Works of Pride

James exposes some common manifestations of pride that the spiritually alert should avoid. These sins of pride are opposite of the fruits or works that grow out of true faith. James identifies some of these vices as coveting and killing (4:2), adultery (4:3), and greed (5:1–5). James clearly ties these acts to pride with the question, "Know ye not that the friendship of the world is enmity with God?" (4:4). President Ezra Taft Benson observed that the meaning of pride is enmity or hostility towards God or our neighbor.[22] Well aware that pride is the source, James counsels, "God resisteth the proud, but giveth grace unto the humble. . . . Humble yourselves in the sight of the Lord, and he shall lift you up" (4:6, 10).

---

[21] Bruce R. McConkie, *Doctrinal New Testament Commentary*, 3 vols. (Salt Lake City: Bookcraft, 1973), 3:246–47.

[22] Ezra Taft Benson, "Beware of Pride," *Ensign*, May 1989, 4.

Whether encouraging one to attain perfection, to seek wisdom, or to abhor the sins of pride, the Epistle of James bases its approach on the application of faith. Its pragmatic themes build on the notion that "faith without works is dead."

James's Use of the Imperative Tense

The imperative command found throughout the letter displays James's desire for our dynamic discipleship. The following are some examples of James's imperatives:

Chapter 1
- Be perfect and entire (v. 4)
- Ask of God (v. 5)
- Ask in faith (v. 6)
- Rejoice in that he is exalted (v. 9)
- Be swift to hear, slow to speak, slow to wrath (v. 19)
- Lay apart all filthiness, etc. (v. 21)
- Receive with meekness (v. 21)
- Be ye doers of the word (v. 22)
- Visit the fatherless (v. 27)

Chapter 2
- Hearken, my beloved brethren (v. 5)
- Love thy neighbor (v. 8)
- Keep the whole law (v. 10)
- So speak ye (v. 12)
- Shew me thy faith (v. 18)

Chapter 3
- Shew out of a good conversation (v. 13)
- Lie not against the truth (v. 14)

Chapter 4
- Submit yourselves . . . to God (v. 7)
- Resist the devil (v. 7)
- Draw nigh to God (v. 8)

Cleanse your hands (v. 8)
Purify your hearts (v. 8)
Be afflicted, and mourn, and weep (v. 9)
Humble yourselves (v. 10)
Speak not evil (v. 11)

Chapter 5
Go to now (v. 1)
Be patient (v. 7)
Stablish your hearts (v. 8)
Grudge not (v. 9)
Swear not (v. 12)
Confess your faults (v. 16)
Pray one for another (v. 16)

Conclusion

James counseled: "Go to now, ye that say, To day or to morrow we will go into such a city, and continue there a year, and buy and sell, and get gain: Whereas ye know not what shall be on the morrow. For what is your life? It is even a vapour, that appeareth for a little time, and then vanisheth away. For that ye ought to say, If the Lord will, we shall live, and do this, or that" (4:13–15). This verse points out that the time we are given in this life will eventually pass like a vapor and that we should focus our attention on the things that are most worthy—things that bring us closer to God. In the same vein, the Nephite prophet Amulek said, "For behold, this life is the time for men to prepare to meet God; yea, behold the day of this life is the day for men to perform their labors" (Alma 34:32).

To some readers James's epistle may evidence anti-Pauline rhetoric. However, analysis of the words *faith* (*pistis*) and *works* (*ergon*) within the context of the epistles of Paul and James clearly shows that each of them defines the terms quite differently. James's argument, against a real or rhetorical opponent, characterizes that true faith must include good Christian works such as visiting the widows and blessing the sick. Paul, speaking to an audience made up primarily of Judaizers, contends that true faith is faith (like the faith of James that includes his definition of works) apart from the works of circumcision, rituals, and dietary restrictions related to the law of Moses. The concepts of faith and works throughout the epistle were then examined to show a new emphasis according to three of James's general themes: perfection, wisdom, and pride. Finally, James's use of the imperative tense was examined to demonstrate his desire to reinforce an active faith.

Like the instructions of James to couple our faith with good works, the Lord has given similar counsel today: "Wherefore, if ye believe me, ye will labor while it is called today" (D&C 64:25). The Epistle of James is an articulate expression of the interrelationship between faith and works for Christians of his day and ours. "For as the body without the spirit is dead, so faith without works is dead also" (2:26).

IX.

JAMES, FIRST AND SECOND PETER, AND JUDE: EPISTLES OF PERSECUTION

JOHN GEE

For there are certain men crept in unawares, who were before of old ordained to this condemnation, ungodly men, turning the grace of our God into lasciviousness, and denying the only Lord God, and our Lord Jesus Christ.

JUDE 1:4

The persistent theme of persecution strikes the student of early Christianity from the beginning, penetrating all aspects of the subject. By the second century, for example, the term *martyr* (Greek, *martys*) changed meaning in Christian contexts from a "witness," that is, "one who testifies in legal matters" or "one who affirms or attests,"[1] to "one who gives up his life for his beliefs."[2] The early Christian writers' obsession with persecution was rooted in historical reality. Although the early Christian churches enjoyed many seasons of relative peace and prosperity, they also suffered ongoing

---

[1] Arndt and Gingrich, *GEL*, "*martys*," 619–20.
[2] G. W. H. Lampe, *A Patristic Greek Lexicon* (Oxford: Clarendon Press, 1961), 831–33, with the earliest citations being *The Martyrdom of Polycarp,* (19.1), Irenaeus (*Against Heresies,* 5.9.2), and Clement of Alexandria (*Miscellanies* 4.4–5, 4.12).

discrimination and seasons of intense persecution. Persecution was usually local but on occasion became widespread, as it briefly did in the first century during the reigns of Nero (A.D. 54–68) and Domitian (A.D. 81–96).

From the beginning, Jesus had warned His followers to expect others to "criticize you and persecute you and say all manner of evil against you because of me" (Matthew 5:11; author's translation). It is one thing to say in the abstract that those who are persecuted are blessed or happy (Greek, *markarioi*) and that they should rejoice (Greek, *chairete kai agalliasthe;* Matthew 5:11–12); it is quite another thing to deal with the persecution when it actually arises.

Persecution, by design, is intended to coerce or intimidate individuals and groups into changing their attitudes, beliefs, and behaviors. Under persecution, an individual has to make a choice between seeking short-term relief from pain and unpleasantness or enduring the situation while anticipating that there will be something of value afterward. The leader of a covenantal group, entrusted with watching over and protecting those in his care, needs to focus his group's attention on the long-term benefits of the covenant over the short-term situation, however severe.

Just as Paul was sent out with letters allowing him to persecute the Saints (Acts 9:1–2), so the Church leaders wrote letters about how to deal with that persecution. It is in this light that we must view the epistles of persecution: James, 1 and 2 Peter, and Jude.

The Persecution of Saul

The first persecution of the early Church was the one with which Saul of Tarsus (later Paul) was associated.

The Church (Greek, *ekklēsia*, "assembly, congregation") was originally "a casual gathering of people"[3] in Jerusalem who attached

---

[3] Arndt and Gingrich, *GEL*, "*ekklēsia*"; compare the discussion in F. F. Bruce, *New Testament History* (New York: Doubleday, 1969), 206.

themselves to Jesus by baptism (Acts 2:38, 41). "They were adherents to the teaching of the apostles, the common way of life, the breaking of bread, and prayers" (Acts 2:42; author's translation). They held all their goods in common (Acts 2:44).

Lest this seem too idyllic a picture, it should be noted that the Church had a few minor problems. Not everyone, particularly those who had more than others, was willing to contribute to the common good (Acts 5:11). Some did not want to share or associate too closely with those of different ethnic backgrounds (Acts 6:1). The local rulers, who had been responsible for the death of Jesus just weeks before, were not enthusiastic about a group devoted to Him and spreading His teachings, and they spoke evil of His name (Acts 4:17–18; 5:28). Thus some murmuring existed in the ranks (Acts 6:1).

The calling of the seven to administer to the temporal needs of the members (Acts 6:1–7) was supposed to improve things for the Church, but one of the seven, Stephen, ran afoul of the local authorities and was spontaneously stoned to death when a riot erupted at his trial because he claimed to see God (Acts 6:8–7:60). Saul played a key role in this event (Acts 7:58; 8:1) and subsequently went throughout the city arresting those belonging to the Church and throwing them in prison (Acts 8:3). As a result of these events, "in that day there was a great persecution against the Church which was in Jerusalem and everyone scattered (Greek, *diesparēsan*) throughout the countryside of Judah and Samaria except for the apostles" (Acts 8:1; author's translation). Thus the Edenic existence of the earliest Church was shattered, and the Church went into its own diaspora, which is the term that Luke used to describe the situation.

James

The earliest Church dealt with such persecution by two means. One method was to send various leaders, such as Philip of the seven, to various places (Acts 8:5), and "the dispersed [Greek, *diesparentes*] went about spreading the word" (Acts 8:4; author's translation). The second method was to have those traveling individuals also carry letters with them to the congregations. That was the way the postal service for private individuals worked in the ancient world at that time. So Philip, going to Samaria (Acts 8:5), where those of the Church had gone (Acts 8:1), might have carried the letter of James with him.

The Epistle of James is usually credited to James the brother of Jesus[4] or to someone pretending to be him.[5] The epistle contains no polemic against Paul or even any reference to him.[6] Likewise, "no opposition to Gentile Christianity is discernible," and "circumcision is no problem at all."[7] So "either the epistle came into

---

[4] Richard L. Scheef Jr., "The Letter of James," in *The Interpreter's One-Volume Commentary on the Bible* (Nashville: Abingdon Press, 1971), 916; Luke T. Johnson, "James," in James L. Mays, ed., *Harper's Bible Commentary* (San Francisco: Harper and Row, 1988), 1272; Sophie Laws, "James, Epistle of," in Freedman, *ABD*, 3:622; D. Kelly Ogden and Andrew C. Skinner, *New Testament Apostles Testify of Christ: A Guide for Acts through Revelation* (Salt Lake City: Deseret Book, 1998), 264–65; Richard Lloyd Anderson, *Guide to Acts and the Apostles' Letters*, 3d ed. (Provo, Utah: FARMS, 1999), 95; Gerald Bray, *Ancient Christian Commentary on Scripture, New Testament XI: James, 1–2 Peter, 1–3 John, Jude* (Downers Grove, Ill.: InterVarsity Press, 2000), xix, 1; Craig D. Manscill, "'If Any of You Lack Wisdom': James's Imperative to Israel," in *Go Ye into All the World: Messages of the New Testament Apostles* (Salt Lake City: Deseret Book, 2002), 246; David M. Whitchurch, "Discipleship and the Epistle of James," in *Go Ye into All the World: Messages of the New Testament Apostles* (Salt Lake City: Deseret Book, 2002), 259; Brian M. Hauglid, "'As the Body without the Spirit': James's Epistle on Faith and Works," in *Go Ye into All the World: Messages of the New Testament Apostles* (Salt Lake City: Deseret Book, 2002), 277.

[5] A. E. Barnett, "James, Letter of," in *The Interpreter's Dictionary of the Bible* (Nashville: Abingdon, 1962), 2:795; Bo Reicke, *The Epistles of James, Peter, and Jude*, vol. 37 of The Anchor Bible (New York: Doubleday, 1964), 3–4; Scheef, "Letter of James," 916; Johnson, "James," 1272; Laws, *"James, Epistle of,"* 3:622–23; S. R. Llewelyn, "The Prescript of James," *Novum Testamentum* 39, no. 4 (1997): 385–86; Whitchurch, "Discipleship and the Epistle of James," 259–60.

[6] Reicke, *Epistles of James, Peter, and Jude*, 5.

[7] Ibid.

existence before Paul's ministry, or a considerable time after."[8] The assumption is that the letter is addressed to individuals "evidently thought of as living outside Palestine in various areas of the Roman empire,"[9] and the repeated mention of persecutions could not have occurred outside of Palestine "prior to Paul's time" because "none are known."[10] This assumption, however, is unnecessary. On the basis of these assumptions, scholars normally assert that the epistle is dated to the end of the first century (A.D. 90),[11] or the beginning of the second century (A.D. 100–125),[12] or even "the last three decades of the 1st century or the beginning of the 2d."[13] Under the earlier date, the persecution is thought to be the general persecution of the Church under Domitian when "the senators and the rich were involved in conspiracies against Domitian; in this they were supported by the Stoics and other philosophers, and probably also by certain prominent Jewish proselytes; the poorer classes, on the other hand, sided with the emperor."[14] This is thought to be a late enough date for the author to have "adopted the pseudonym of James of Jerusalem . . . when he had become a revered figure of the past."[15]

If the late date of the epistle is based on questionable assumptions, another alternative suggests itself: The letter might be early. Since this is not the usual interpretation of the epistle, the reasons for this view need to be set forth.

The address of the letter, "James, a servant of God and the Lord Jesus Christ, to the twelve tribes which are in the Diaspora,

---

[8] Ibid.

[9] Ibid., 4–5.

[10] Ibid., 5.

[11] Ibid., 6.

[12] Scheef, "Letter of James," 917.

[13] Laws, "James, Epistle of," in Freedman, *ABD*, 3:623.

[14] Reicke, *Epistles of James, Peter, and Jude*, 5–6.

[15] Laws, "James, Epistle of," in Freedman, *ABD*, 3:622.

greetings" (James 1:1; author's translation) identified the author as James and assumed that the addressees all knew who he was, as was typical for personal letters. The name *James* (Greek, *Iakōbos*) was common in that time and place.[16] So the person writing the letter had to have been sufficiently well-known to his audience to need no other identification than that he was a servant of God and Jesus. Words from the root *diaspora* (Greek, *diaspora*) occur only five times in the New Testament: (1) in the introduction to the Epistle of James 1:1 (Greek, *diaspora*), (2) in discussing the dispersal of the Church from Jerusalem (Greek, *diesparēsan;* Acts 8:1), (3) in identifying those who were thus scattered (Greek, *diesparentes;* Acts 8:4), (4) in identifying specifically "those who were scattered because of the affliction which happened because of Stephen" (Acts 11:19; author's translation), and (5) in what John called "the diaspora of the Greeks" (Greek, *tēn diasporan tōn Hellēnōn;* John 7:35; author's translation). For the New Testament writers, the diaspora referred to the scattering of the Church from Jerusalem and not the scattering of the Jews throughout the ancient world. Thus James's address of his epistle to those in the diaspora fit within the setting of the scattering of the Church after the death of Stephen.[17]

The themes of James also fit that setting. The Church that James addressed had problems favoring people because of who they were, and thus they were showing partiality to the rich (James 2:1–9) and speaking evil of one another (James 4:11). Rich men were oppressing the poor by defrauding the workers of their fair share (James 2:6; 5:1–5). The widows and the fatherless were neglected (James 1:27). Some of the people were naked and destitute (James 2:15–16). This caused bitter envying in their hearts (James

---

[16] "No fewer than six or seven persons known to the New Testament writers carry the name of James." Ralph P. Martin, *James,* vol. 48 of Word Biblical Commentary (Waco, Tex.: Word Books, 1988), xxxi. Josephus mentions another two.

[17] Thus Llewelyn, "The Prescript of James," 385, is incorrect when he asserts, "The identity of the recipients in the prescript is obscure."

3:14–16) and fighting among one another (James 4:1). It was a time when men were blaspheming the name of Christ (James 2:7). The term *blaspheme* (Greek, *blasphēmeō*) derives from a Greek term compounded of *blaptō,* "to harm," and *phēmi,* "to speak," and thus originally meant "to demean through speech" or "to speak in a disrespectful way that demeans, denigrates, maligns."[18]

The Church, having been driven out of Jerusalem, was decentralized and scattered. Central distribution of welfare was no longer efficient, and some seemed to have been suffering from it, which apparently created tensions. These issues had to be addressed, and the way that the Church administered to its members would have to adapt to the altered situation.

If the Epistle of James dates to the time immediately after the stoning of Stephen, the identification of James needs to be reassessed. The authoritative James, at that time, would have been not James, the brother of Jesus, but James, the brother of John and son of Zebedee. Herod put this James to death in A.D. 44 (Acts 12:1–2). James, the brother of Jesus, did not come into prominence until after that time, and he was the James who declared the verdict of the Jerusalem Council in A.D. 49 (Acts 15:13–21) and whom Paul consulted immediately before his imprisonment in A.D. 58 (Acts 21:18–26).[19] In time, the prominence of the later James as a Church leader with the same name in the same place eclipsed that of the earlier James, and thus by Eusebius's day, the epistle was assigned to the latter James.[20]

James's first piece of advice to those scattered and persecuted came because they could no longer listen to the Apostles directly (Acts 2:42). When new problems arose, the Apostles were

---

[18] Arndt and Gingrich, *GEL,* "*blasphēmeō.*"

[19] Dates are taken from Richard L. Anderson, *Understanding Paul* (Salt Lake City: Deseret Book, 1983).

[20] Eusebius, *Ecclesiastical History,* 2.23.25.

no longer at hand to answer them, and who would know when a leader would next visit the area? Apostolic wisdom was no longer readily available. Also, as the Church was scattered, it continued to grow in disparate places. New converts might not necessarily have ever met any of the Apostles or other leaders. When the Apostles did visit, how would individuals know that they were who they said that they were and not hucksters or false prophets? In later times, the Church had specific policies to deal with the situation.[21] So James's first instruction to the distant churches was that, in the absence of Apostles, if they needed wisdom, they should ask God for it (James 1:5–6).

In their persecution, James advised that the best thing for the Saints to do was to go about quietly doing good and keeping a low profile. They should be patient in their afflictions and temptations (James 1:12–15; 5:7–11). They should not strive to be popular with the world (James 4:4). They needed to put the things they heard into action (James 1:22–25; 2:12–26) and look after the helpless (James 1:27; 2:15–16). They should control their tongues (James 3:1–12), neither bragging nor boasting (James 1:9–10) nor accusing each other (James 4:11–12). "Let every man be quick to hearken, slow to speak, and slow to anger" (James 1:19; author's translation). In case of sickness, members should call on the elders of the Church (James 5:14–15).

James drew on two sources of authority for his teachings: the

---

[21] *Didache,* 11: "Whosoever comes to teach you the aforementioned things accept him. If when he teaches you he teaches you a different doctrine tending toward destruction, do not listen to him; but tending toward offering righteousness and the knowledge of the Lord, accept him as the Lord. Concerning apostles and prophets according to the doctrine of the gospel, do thus: Every apostle who comes to you, accept as the Lord; but he will only stay one day, or two days if necessary. If he stays three days, he is a false prophet. An apostle who comes will not accept anything except bread until he departs. If he asks for money, he is a false prophet."

Old Testament,[22] and the teachings of Jesus.[23] The Old Testament sources that James used were mainly from the Pentateuch (that is, Genesis through Deuteronomy) but ranged over the Old Testament, drawing mainly from the Septuagint.[24] James (2:8) quoted Leviticus 19:18 to love one's neighbor as oneself and used it the way that Jesus did (Matthew 22:39). He even termed it the law of the kingdom (Greek, *nomon basilkon*). He quoted two of the Ten Commandments (Exodus 20:13–14) as examples of laws that could be violated (James 2:11). He cited the example of Abraham (Genesis 15:6) to show how works perfect faith (James 2:22–23) and alluded to Rahab's example (Joshua 2) as being similar (James 2:25). James mentioned the Creation, specifically man's being created in the image of God (Genesis 1:27), as a reason not to curse one's fellowman (James 3:7–9). Proverbs (3:34) was quoted to show how the poor are given grace (James 2:6). James used a phrase from Isaiah (5:9) to express the notion of prayers for help being heard to the detriment of the oppressors (James 5:4). A phrase from Jeremiah (12:3), on the other hand, was used to show the ironic situation of those who indulge themselves at the expense of their neighbors (James 5:5). James also brought in the figure of Elijah as an example of an individual who did great things through the Lord's power (1 Kings 18:42–45), even though he was a weak mortal (James 5:17). He ended with a quotation of Proverbs (10:12) about how charity covers over sins (James 5:20). James also quoted unknown sources as scripture (James 4:5).[25]

---

[22] D. A. Carson, "James," in G. K. Beale and D. A. Carson, ed., *Commentary on the New Testament Use of the Old Testament* (Grand Rapids, Mich.: Baker Books, 2007), 997–1013.

[23] J. Ritchie Smith, "The Gospel in the Epistle of James," *Journal of Biblical Literature* 18, nos. 1–2 (1899): 145–46.

[24] Carson, "James," 997.

[25] The quotation is "the despair of commentators as to both its source and its meaning." Massey H. Shepherd Jr., "The Epistle of James and the Gospel of Matthew," *Journal of Biblical Literature* 75, no. 1 (1956): 40.

Although James used a number of Old Testament quotations, he also referred to the Sermon on the Mount. Thus James urged his brethren to take joy in temptations and persecutions (James 1:2; Matthew 5:10–12). He urged them to be doers of the word and not just hearers (James 1:22; Matthew 7:24–27). He proclaimed that the poor would inherit the kingdom (James 2:5; Matthew 5:3). He told them that faith needs works (James 2:14–26; Matthew 7:20–21) and that individuals would be judged for their actions (James 2:12; 5:9; Matthew 5:7; 6:15; 7:1–5). James (3:1), like Jesus (Matthew 6:24), warned against serving more than one master. He used Jesus' parable about not gathering the fruit of one tree from another (James 3:12; Matthew 7:16). He discussed how moth and rust corrupt (James 5:2–3; Matthew 6:19). And he urged them to avoid swearing oaths (James 5:12; Matthew 5:33–37).

James also used other teachings of Jesus. He stressed the need to ask in faith (James 1:6; Matthew 21:22). He used Jesus' interpretation of Leviticus 19:18 (James 2:5; Matthew 22:39). He warned of the accountability for one's speech (James 3:2–12; Matthew 12:36–37). He spoke of the need to humble oneself rather than to exalt oneself (James 4:10; Matthew 23:12).

These quotations and allusions show how James, soon after the death of Jesus, used the scriptures and the teachings of Jesus to instruct and comfort the Saints of his day in their tribulations. He set a pattern that would be followed in the Church afterward.

1 Peter

Though the epistles of Peter share the persecution situation with the epistle of James, they do not share the same setting. Modern scholars have "arbitrarily" tended to reject Peter as author of the epistle.[26] Historically though, 1 Peter was almost always seen as written by the chief Apostle, Peter.[27] The early Christian author Eusebius cited it as undoubtedly genuine.[28] The epistle was used extensively by Ignatius of Antioch,[29] Clement of Rome,[30] Polycarp of Smyrna,[31] Justin Martyr,[32] Irenaeus of Lyon,[33] and others.[34] Eusebius traced the influence back to Polycarp's use.[35] "Presumably Polycarp would not have done this if he had not believed that 1 Peter was authentic, and since he lived only a few years after the letter was written, he was in a good position to know what its origin was."[36]

The epistle is addressed to Pontus, Galatia, Cappadocia, Asia, and Bithynia (1 Peter 1:1), all Roman provinces in what is modern-day Turkey. Galatia seems to have been opened up by Paul about A.D. 49.[37] An early church tradition has Peter slain at the hands of

---

[26] Karl P. Donfried, "Peter," in Freedman, *ABD*, 5:262; John H. Elliot, "Peter, First Epistle of," in Freedman, *ABD*, 5:269–70.

[27] Bray, *James, 1–2 Peter, 1–3 John, Jude*, xvii, 65.

[28] Eusebius, *Ecclesiastical History*, 3.3.1.

[29] Ignatius, *Ephesians*, 5 (= 1 Peter 5:5), 9 (= 1 Peter 2:5, 9), 10 (= 1 Peter 2:23; 4:7); Ignatius, *Philadelphians*, 4 (= 1 Peter 2:9).

[30] Clement of Rome, *Corinthians* (=1 Clement), 2 (= 1 Peter 5:5, 17), 7 (= 1 Peter 3:20), 30 (= 1 Peter 5:5), 49 (= 1 Peter 4:8).

[31] Polycarp, *Philippians*, 1.3 (= 1 Peter 1:8), 2.1 (= 1 Peter 1:13, 21), 2.2 (= 1 Peter 3:9), 5.3 (= 1 Peter 2:11), 7.2 (= 1 Peter 4:7), 8.1 (= 1 Peter 2:22, 24), 10.2 (=1 Peter 2:12).

[32] Justin Martyr, *Dialogue*, 116 (= 1 Peter 2:9).

[33] Irenaeus, *Against Heresies*, 1.18.3 (1 Peter 3:20), 2.17.9 (= 1 Peter 1:12), 3.17.9 (1 Peter 2:23), 4.8.2 (= 1 Peter 2:5–9), 4.9.2 (= 1 Peter 1:8), 4.16.5 (= 1 Peter 2:16), 4.20.2 (= 1 Peter 2:23), 4.27.2 (1 Peter 3:19–20), 4.33.9 (= 1 Peter 4:14), 4.34.1 (= 1 Peter 1:12), 4.37.4 (= 1 Peter 2:16), 5.7.2 (= 1 Peter 1:8), 5.36.3 (= 1 Peter 1:12).

[34] *Epistle to Diognetus*, 6 (= 1 Peter 2:11); *Martyrdom of Polycarp*, 17 (1 Peter 3:18).

[35] Eusebius, *Ecclesiastical History*, 3.14.

[36] Bray, *James, 1–2 Peter, 1–3 John, Jude*, xviii.

[37] Anderson, *Understanding Paul*, 394.

Nero in Rome,[38] about A.D. 65. Thus there is about a fifteen-year time period in which the epistle could have been written.[39]

Every chapter of the epistle mentions suffering of some sort.[40] The first chapter mentions temptations that are a "trial of your faith" (1 Peter 1:7). The second chapter mentions suffering well (1 Peter 2:20) at the hands of "the ignorance of foolish men" (1 Peter 2:15) and holds up the suffering of Christ as an example (1 Peter 2:21–24). The third chapter enjoins not to return evil for evil (1 Peter 3:9) and says that one should be happy to suffer for righteousness' sake (1 Peter 3:14). Those who suffer for doing good are falsely accused (1 Peter 3:16–17). The fourth chapter notes that fiery trials are not strange because they enable one to partake of Christ's sufferings (1 Peter 4:12–13). Suffering for doing evil would be shameful, but suffering for being a Christian is no shame (1 Peter 4:15–16). The fifth chapter mentions that Peter was a witness to Jesus' sufferings (1 Peter 5:1).

Peter stressed that the Resurrection of Jesus provides an incorruptible inheritance (1 Peter 1:4), which is preferable to the wantonness, drunkenness, gluttony, graft, and idolatry of the world (1 Peter 2:11; 4:3; 5:2).

2 Peter

The second epistle of Peter has to have been written after the first epistle because it refers to it (2 Peter 3:1). It also refers to the letters of Paul (2 Peter 3:15–16), which appear already to have been circulating, having been written between A.D. 50 and A.D. 62.[41]

---

[38] Clement of Rome, *Corinthians* (= 1 Clement), 5; Eusebius, *Ecclesiastical History*, 3.1.

[39] For a discussion of the evidence for Christianity in Anatolia, see Gary J. Johnson, *Early Christian Epitaphs from Anatolia* (Atlanta: Scholars Press, 1995), 79.

[40] David Hill, "On Suffering and Baptism in 1 Peter," *Novum Testamentum* 18, no. 3 (1976): 181.

[41] Anderson, *Understanding Paul*, 395–96.

Clement of Rome perhaps had an allusion to it,[42] and a quotation from it.[43] The epistle of Barnabas also seemed to allude to it,[44] as did Ignatius[45] and Polycarp.[46] These, however, were allusions and not definite quotations. A number of the early Christian authors rejected the authenticity of the letter because its style differed from that of the first epistle.[47] Assuming that Clement meant to quote from 2 Peter, the letter would have to have been written about the second half of the first century. Closer is the explicit quotation of 2 Peter 3:3 attributed to the Apostle in Jude 1:18, which shows that Jude knew the text. The writer referred to his impending death (2 Peter 1:14). If the letter was genuinely Peter's, it would seem to date just before his death in A.D. 65.

As Peter went to his death (2 Peter 1:14), he took one more chance to stir up his readers to remembrance (2 Peter 1:12–13), so they could remember what they needed to do after he died (2 Peter 1:15). Peter told his audience that they could "become partakers of the divine nature having fled the corruption by lust that is in the world" (2 Peter 1:4; author's translation) by diligently adding to their faith, excellence, knowledge, self-control, patience, reverence, brotherhood, and love (2 Peter 1:5–7). He also admonished them to be careful about applying their own interpretations of prophetic scripture (2 Peter 1:20–21).

He warned that in the future there would be false teachers among the Christians who would lead individuals to immoral self-indulgences (Greek, *aselgeiais;* 2 Peter 2:1–3). Peter then referred to the story of the fallen angels from the book of Enoch, to the

---

[42] Compare Clement of Rome, *Corinthians* (= 1 Clement), 11, and 2 Peter 2:6–9.

[43] Clement of Rome, *Corinthians* (= 1 Clement), 23 (= 2 Peter 3:3–4).

[44] *Barnabas,* 15 (= 2 Peter 3:8).

[45] Ignatius, *Philadelphians,* 11 (= 2 Peter 3:9).

[46] Polycarp, *Philippians,* 3 (= 2 Peter 3:15).

[47] Bray, *James, 1–2 Peter, 1–3 John, Jude,* 129.

subsequent disobedience of the people in the time of Noah (2 Peter 2:4–5), and then to the destruction of Sodom and Gomorrah (2 Peter 2:6–7). These stories share themes of immoral conduct, subsequent divine destruction, and the escape of less than ten righteous individuals. Peter used these examples of the few tormented righteous people whom God saved in the midst of an immoral and wicked world as examples of what God could do for them.

Peter compared the men in his society to unthinking animals (2 Peter 2:12) and to spoiled brats who spent all their time seeking to steal and commit adultery with impunity (2 Peter 2:13–14). He also compared them to the Old Testament prophet Balaam (2 Peter 2:15), who sold the covenant people of God into immorality for a profit (Numbers 22–25; 31:7–18).

We should remember that Peter wrote at the same time that Petronius wrote his *Satyricon,* with its detailed descriptions of widespread immoral conduct, prostitution, and gluttony among the Romans.[48] About half a century before, Ovid had written detailed manuals about how men could seduce women and women could seduce men, describing how the games and the coliseums provided venues for hooking up with the opposite sex.[49] Within half a century, the Roman poet Martial described, with devastating wit, the decadent vices of Roman society.[50] Soon after, Juvenal wrote about the sodomy, adultery, and corruption endemic to his time.[51] Suetonius collected all the scandalous stories about the Roman emperors and wrote the reigning Nero's with relish.[52]

Writing during the great age of Roman rhetoricians, Peter warned that slick words about licentious conduct being conducive

---

[48] Petronius, *Satyricon.*
[49] Ovid, *The Art of Love.*
[50] Martial, *Epigrams.*
[51] Juvenal, *Satires.*
[52] Suetonius, *Nero.*

to liberty were illusory (2 Peter 2:18–21). Quintilian, who wrote the famous treatise on rhetoric,[53] was learning his trade at this time, as was the other student of rhetoric, Seneca.

The society that Peter addressed was more than just that of the quaint, small town in Galilee where he grew up; it was the rollicking and reeking Roman Empire in all its corruption.

Jude

Chronologically, the final epistle of persecution is that of Jude. Dating it is difficult, with opinions ranging between the suggestion that it "might be one of the earliest of the N[ew] T[estament] writings" to "the late 2d century."[54] Polycarp of Smyrna may have made a literary allusion to Jude (1:3),[55] but it also might be that they simply were expressing a similar thought, since only one word is shared between the two: two different forms of the passive participle (*paradothenta* in Polycarp vs. *paradotheisē* in Jude). Jude (1:7) was quoted with certainty by Irenaeus of Lyon,[56] so Jude was known to be in the standard repertoire of texts by the end of the second century. That still gives little indication of the date of writing.

The author of the Epistle of Jude claimed to be "Jude, the servant of Jesus Christ, brother of James" (Jude 1:1), who is usually equated with the Jude who was the brother of James and Jesus[57] and who is mentioned in the Gospels (Matthew 13:55; Mark 6:3). The second-century writer Hegesippus said that Jude's grandsons were denounced and brought before the emperor Domitian (A.D. 81–96) as politically dangerous, but the emperor considered them

---

[53] Quintilian, *Institutio Oratoria*.

[54] Richard Bauckham, "Jude, Epistle of," in Freedman, *ABD,* 3:1101.

[55] Polycarp, *Philippians,* 7.

[56] Irenaeus, *Against Heresies,* 4.36.4 (= Jude 1:7).

[57] Hegesippus, quoted in Eusebius, *Ecclesiastical History,* 3.19.1–20.6; Reicke, *Epistles of James, Peter and Jude,* 190; Bauckham, "Jude, Epistle of," 3:1101.

harmless farmers and released them; they survived as leaders of the Church until the reign of Trajan (A.D. 98–117).[58] Neither Jude nor his sons were mentioned in this account, so we can assume that they had died. The fact that Jude mentioned himself as the brother of James indicates that the letter had to have been written after James had become the leader in Jerusalem and after James the brother of John died in A.D. 44. The quotation of 2 Peter 3:3 in Jude 1:18 indicates that it must have been written after that date, and so probably after about A.D. 64. The reign of Domitian can be set as the date before which the letter must have been written, leaving a fifteen-year time period in which the epistle would have been written. Both whence and whither the letter was written are unknown.[59] If Jude was writing from the area of Judea, it seems likely that the letter would have been written before the destruction of Jerusalem in A.D. 70 and possibly before the arrival of the troops under Vespasian in A.D. 67 to quell the Jewish rebellion. Such a date narrows the time period between A.D. 64 and A.D. 70. Jude called himself merely a "servant" (Jude 1:1) and did not consider himself one of the Apostles (Jude 1:17).

The Epistle of Jude is a difficult text. Written in a more difficult Greek than the Gospel writers used, it did not address the subject directly, but rather addressed the subject through densely woven literary allusions with which it assumed the reader was intimately familiar. It was a manner of addressing the subject that was potently clear for the insider but utterly opaque to the outsider. For those who are not familiar with the literary palette with which Jude painted, the text needs to be closely examined.

Jude refers to a variety of stories, both inside and outside of

---

[58] Eusebius, *Ecclesiastical History*, 3.19.1–20.8.
[59] Bauckham, "Jude, Epistle of," 3:1101–2.

the canonical Old Testament.⁶⁰ While he sometimes used language from the Septuagint—that is, the Greek Old Testament—he also seemed to use the Hebrew one as well.⁶¹ Jude also used 2 Peter and was very familiar with that letter, quoting from it five times.⁶²

Jude used the book of Enoch as intensively as any other early Christian writer. He explicitly quoted from it (1:14),⁶³ and he also referred to it in reference to the erring stars (Jude 1:13).⁶⁴ His nature metaphors seem to have been taken from the book of Enoch, as well.⁶⁵ He mentioned the angels who kept not their first estate (Jude 1:6), which refers to the story of the children of God in Genesis (6:1–4) and is expanded in the book of Enoch.⁶⁶ According to the book of Enoch, God said: "O Enoch, the scribe of righteousness, go and say to the watchers from heaven who left the high heaven, the holiness of the eternal state, after defiling themselves with women, and, acting as though they were sons of earth, and did as they do, and took wives for themselves, you have caused a great abomination to appear in the earth."⁶⁷ "And in the great day of judgment they will be cast down into the fire."⁶⁸ So the story of the book of Enoch permeates the Epistle of Jude.⁶⁹ Jude also knew a

---

⁶⁰ Bauckham, "Jude, Epistle of," 3:1099–1100; D. A. Carson, "Jude," in *Commentary on the New Testament Use of the Old Testament*, 1069–79.

⁶¹ Carson, "Jude," 1069.

⁶² Jude 1:2 = 2 Peter 1:2; Jude 1:3 = 2 Peter 1:5; Jude 1:5 = 2 Peter 1:12; Jude 1:5–19 parallels 2 Peter 2:1–3:3; Jude 1:24 = 2 Peter 3:14.

⁶³ *1 Enoch*, 1:9.

⁶⁴ *1 Enoch*, 18:15–16.

⁶⁵ *1 Enoch*, 80; see Carson, "Jude," 1077–78.

⁶⁶ *1 Enoch*, 12:4.

⁶⁷ *1 Enoch*, 12:4.

⁶⁸ *1 Enoch*, 10:6; cf. *1 Enoch*, 22:11.

⁶⁹ This is asserted several times in the works of Margaret Barker; e.g. Margaret Barker, *The Older Testament* (London: SPCK, 1987), 6, 8–9; Margaret Barker, *The Lost Prophet: The Book of Enoch and Its Influence on Christianity* (London: SPCK, 1988), 5, 20; Margaret Barker, *The Great Angel: A Study of Israel's Second God* (London: SPCK, 1992), 29; Margaret Barker, *The Great High Priest: The Temple Roots of Christian Liturgy*

story about Michael and the devil disputing about whether Moses could be translated (Jude 1:9).

Jude was dealing with members of the Church who at one time had accepted the message of Jesus but who left the Church for immoral conduct (Jude 1:4, 8). He used the stories of the rebellion of the children of Israel after the Exodus from Egypt (Jude 1:5), of the fallen angels from the book of Enoch (Jude 1:6), and of Sodom and Gomorrah (Jude 1:7) as examples of the fate awaiting those who abandon their commitment to Jesus for the lusts of the flesh.

A related problem, with which Jude had to deal, was those who were speaking evil of their leaders (Jude 1:10). In the space of a single sentence (Jude 1:11), Jude refers to the Old Testament stories of Cain, Balaam, and Korah (Core). Cain had killed his brother for gain and was cursed and cast out of the presence of God (Genesis 4:1–16). For a price, Balaam had persuaded the Moabites to commit adultery with the Israelites as a way of cursing them and was later killed by the Israelites (Numbers 22–25; 31:7–18). Korah had disputed with Moses about who should lead the Israelites, and the earth swallowed him up (Numbers 16:1–50). Jude said that these people were after gain and would be destroyed (Jude 1:11). He said that these people fulfilled a prophecy of the Apostles (Jude 1:18).

Clearly the Church to which Jude wrote was having serious problems. The real question is why Jude wrote his letter. He did not identify himself as a Church leader but merely as the brother of one. He cited scripture and the Apostles as authority but claimed no presiding authority himself. If James, the brother of Jesus, had been around, why did he not write the letter himself? Perhaps James had already died. Josephus put the death of James during

---

(London: T&T Clark, 2003), 301. Barker is correct, but unfortunately she never explains to her audience why this is so.

the procuratorship of Albinus[70] and shortly before the destruction of Jerusalem. In that case, Jude would have been writing because there was no one else in the area with authority left to write.

Trajectories for the Early Church

Persecution was a fact of the early Church and remained so until Constantine turned the Christians into persecutors armed with the resources of a military state. Unfortunately, even that did not cause the persecution to cease, for the persecutors of Christians were often their fellow Christians. In the first century, it is clear that persecution from within the Church became greater than persecution from without.

In the time of James, the brother of John, Christians had recently lost a comparatively idyllic time when Church members were trying to live according to the teachings of Jesus. James showed that they still had some difficulty being fair to one another. Peter urged his listeners to live good lives as an example to those around them. In Jude's time, the Church no longer maintained any pretense of trying to live the teachings of Jesus; the Church had clear problems with immoral behavior and usurping of Church offices. The faithful were desperately trying to hold on to "the faith which was once handed down to the Saints" (Jude 1:3; author's translation).

As the curtain closes on the New Testament scene, we have no idea whether Jude's letter (or any of the other letters in the New Testament) did any good. As we view the end of the first century, the curtain parts ever so slightly, and we catch brief glimpses of what occurred: (1) Christians left the Church and renounced their faith in the seventies and eighties.[71] (2) Under Trajan, some Church members accused their leaders of being Christians so that

---

[70] Josephus, *AJ*, 20.200.
[71] Pliny, *Epistles*, 10.96.6.

the Romans would put them to death and the members could take over the leadership of the Church and teach what they wanted, thus corrupting the Church. They could do so, in part, because there were no general officers, such as Apostles, around to prevent it.[72] (3) Also in Trajan's day, the Church was in full "unholy sedition" (Greek, *anosiou staseōs*),[73] with "everyone abandoning the fear of God, and becoming blind to his faith, neither walking in the ordinances of his appointment, nor comporting according to Christian duty, but walking according to wicked lusts of his own heart."[74] Yet no one had the overall authority to straighten out the matter,[75] because, as everyone knew, a bishop was not an Apostle and could not set things in order (Greek, *diatassomai*) like one.[76]

As warnings for their day, the epistles of persecution have transcended time to provide a warning for our own. The most deadly combination for the Church in its first century was apostates within colluding with persecutors without. Judas Iscariot had used that combination to kill Jesus, and others found it equally effective in killing His Church.

---

[72] Hegesippus, quoted in Eusebius, *Ecclesiastical History*, 3.32.
[73] Clement of Rome, *Corinthians* (= 1 Clement), 1:1.
[74] Clement of Rome, *Corinthians* (= 1 Clement), 3.4.
[75] Clement of Rome, *Corinthians* (= 1 Clement), 42, 44.
[76] Ignatius, *Epistle to the Trallians*, 3.3.

X.

JOHN'S LATER MINISTRY AND HIS BANISHMENT TO PATMOS: THE BACKGROUND TO REVELATION

RICHARD D. DRAPER

John, who also am your brother, and companion in tribulation, and in the kingdom and patience of Jesus Christ, was in the isle that is called Patmos, for the word of God, and for the testimony of Jesus Christ.

Revelation 1:9

Crisis gripped the Christian Church in the Roman province of Asia (modern-day western Turkey). The heavy hands of the pagan officials were putting ever greater pressure on the Saints to leave their religion or suffer. Indeed, in some places, the civil government coupled with heathen religious institutions threatened them with deadly force. Some Jews joined in the persecution, throwing their weight against the Christians and causing increased distress and fear. Even in places where little outright persecution occurred, the pressure of threatened ostracism and the potential of maltreatment made the Saints' lives anxious and insecure. For example, in the rich city of Pergamum, the voice of the Jews had prompted city officials to move against the Church, resulting in the martyrdom of the faithful and stalwart Christian Antipas, likely a local leader (Revelation 2:12–13).

From the Lord's perspective, however, the social situation of the Saints, uncomfortable as it was, was not at the heart of the crisis. The Lord was well aware of the circumstances and the condition of His people. To them He said repeatedly, "I know thy works" (Revelation 2:2, 9, 13, 19; 3:1, 8, 15). In that statement, He revealed His close and intimate knowledge of current events and how the members of His Church were responding. No, divine concern did not center in the social condition of the Saints; the real threat lay elsewhere. The Lord's attention drew its strength from the Saints' increasing loss of religious devotion and commitment. He knew that many were not in a position, especially spiritually, to resist the ever-growing pressure to fall away from the truth. The fact was, if the majority of Saints yielded to the pressure, the fledgling Church would succumb to mutinous elements and lose its way and, thus, its spiritual life. The Lord knew what they needed if they were to get through this trying—even dangerous—time, and He had one ready to respond, one whom He had already foreordained for this mission: John, His beloved.

The Author of Revelation

Because the author of Revelation does not state clearly who he is and because the writing style of Revelation is quite different from that of the Gospel and the epistles of John, a number of scholars have argued that the author of Revelation is not the same as the author of the Gospel of John.[1] However, latter-day scripture

---

[1] Eusebius, *Ecclesiastical History*, 3.39, quotes Papias, who states there were two Johns. Eusebius suggests that John called "the presbyter" was the one who actually had the vision. To be fair, however, the historian also quotes Justin Martyr (*Ecclesiastical History*, 4.18.608) who insisted that the Apostle wrote Revelation. It is notable that most Christians ascribed the work to John the Apostle (see, for example, Justin Martyr, *Dialogue*, 81.4, and Irenaeus, *Against Heresies*, 5.30), but from the mid-second century,

confirms tradition, showing that the author of Revelation was, indeed, John the Apostle (see 1 Nephi 14:20–27).[2] He and his family made their livelihood from fishing. He was living in the village of Capernaum on the coast of the Sea of Galilee when the Lord called the young man into His service. Over the term of their ministry together, due to John's compassion and dedication to the work, he gained the wonderful sobriquet "the disciple whom Jesus loved" (John 21:7; see also D&C 7:1; John 19:26, and by inference, John 13:23; 20:2; 21:20).

Perhaps nothing better illustrates John's devotion to the Lord and his dedication to the ministry than the feelings he expressed in a confidential moment between him and the Savior. At that time the Lord asked him, "John my beloved, what desirest thou?" Without hesitation, John replied, "Lord, give unto me power over

---

according to Eusebius (*Ecclesiastical History*, 7.25), there were doubters. Among these was the influential Dionysus, Bishop of Alexandria. Today, many scholars subscribe to the view that the Apostle was not the author of Revelation. Some have even introduced a third John, one writing pseudonymously who was attached to the Johannine school. This view, however, has little going for it and has few followers today. On this, see R. H. Charles, *A Critical and Exegetical Commentary on the Revelation of St. John*, 2 vols. (Edinburgh: T&T Clark, 1920), 1:xxxviii–xxxix; he successfully refuted the idea. For discussion on the whole, see David E. Aune, *Revelation 17–22*, World Bible Series, ed. Bruce M. Metzger et al., 52 vols. (Nelson Reference and Electronic, 1997), 52a: xlvii—lvi.

[2] The difference in grammar and vocabulary between the Gospel and Revelation is rather obvious. R. H. Charles made a list of the differences concluding that these show two different authors. His view, however, has been countered by others who show that the differences are not as great as they appear and the number of similarities are striking and thus rule out the need for different authorship. The differences can be accounted for by such things as the work was originally written in Hebrew and then later translated into Greek, or that John did not have access to a scribe/editor on Patmos as he did during the writing of his other works, or that the change of genre demanded a change in style and vocabulary. For discussion on these issues see Charles, *Exegetical Commentary*, 2:lxxxvii–xci; V. S. Poythress, "Johannine Authorship and the Use of Intersentence Connections in the Book of Revelation," *Journal of the Evangelical Theological Society* 36 (1993): 41–54; and especially P. Whale, "The Lamb of God: Some Myths about the Vocabulary of the Johannine Literature," *Journal of Biblical Literature* 106 (1987): 289–95.

death, that I may live and bring souls unto thee." In response to this selfless request, the Lord said, "Because thou desirest this thou shalt tarry until I come in my glory, and shalt prophesy before nations, kindreds, tongues and people" (D&C 7:1–3).

John, as well as the other disciples, knew the road would not be easy. The Lord had made it abundantly clear on at least two occasions that the disciples, including John, faced a difficult and even deadly task. He had clearly warned them: "I sent you forth as sheep in the midst of wolves" and "Beware of men: for they will deliver you up to the councils, and they will scourge you in their synagogues; and ye shall be brought before governors and kings for my sake." Indeed, "brother shall deliver up brother to death," and further, "ye shall be hated of all men for my name's sake." Even so, they were to "fear not them which kill the body, but are able to kill the soul," for the Father, who knew the number of the very hairs of their heads, would look after them. Even so, "he that findeth his life shall lose it: and he that loseth his life for my sake shall find it" (Matthew 10:16–18, 21–22, 28, 39).

The words proved most prophetic. Over time, the Apostles were killed or grew old and died until, by the end of the first century A.D., it appears that only John was left. By that time, according to tradition, he had moved to Ephesus on the coast of Asia Minor and, from there, directed the affairs of the Church.[3]

Background to the Revelation

Some years before the persecutions began in earnest, John moved to the coastal city of Ephesus, the capital city of the Roman province of Asia.[4] It is little wonder the Apostle took up residence

---

[3] Hegesippus, as quoted by Eusebius, *Ecclesiastical History*, 3.20.10–11, states that the Apostle John, after returning from banishment, took up his residence at Ephesus and remained there into the reign of Nerva.

[4] For a discussion of the dating of the book of Revelation, see Eric D. Huntsman and Cecelia M. Peek, "The Imperial Cult and the Beasts of Revelation," in this volume.

there, for the area had seen many converts to Christianity. By the time John arrived, various Church leaders had been active all over Asia Minor for almost forty years. Men of stature such as Paul, Titus, Luke, Apollos, and Timothy labored there. Paul had sent letters to Ephesus and Colossae, cities of Asian Minor, and had written to Philemon, Titus, and Timothy who lived or worked in the area. Peter addressed one of his letters to the Saints in Asia as well as other places in the region (1 Peter 1:1). Ignatius, a Syrian Bishop, wrote to five branches in Asia about A.D. 107, and there were seven additional known congregations.[5] All these show that the Church had gained a strong presence there.[6]

In the final decade of the first century the Roman emperor Domitian developed a strong dislike for "atheism," that is, nontraditional religions, and moved against them. Early Church historians saw this as a direct move against the Christians and, thus, Eusebius, basing his words on a report from Irenaeus (c. A.D. 180), noted that in the fourteenth year of his reign (c. A.D. 96), Domitian began the persecution of the Christians, and under him the Apostle John was banished to Patmos, where he received the Apocalypse.[7] The forepart of the book of Revelation shows that the pagan population of Asia, already feeling threatened by the large number of Christian converts, responded to the emperor's antipathy toward Christians

---

[5] L. L. Thompson, *The Book of Revelation* (New York: Knopf Doubleday Publishing, 2000), 11–12.

[6] The writings of Pliny the Younger, the governor of Bithynia, a province bordering Asia, give a feel for the number of Christians that lived in the area just a decade or two after Revelation was written. He noted that Christians were found not only in the cities and in the villages but also in the countryside. Further, until Pliny shut down their meetings and began prosecuting them, the pagan temples were nearly abandoned, and few worshippers were buying animals for sacrifice. See Pliny, *Epistles,* 10.96. It is possible that he is exaggerating some for affect, but there is no doubt Christianity had really taken hold.

[7] See Eusebius, *Ecclesiastical History,* 3.18.1–2.

by persecuting and, in one documented instance (Revelation 2:13), killing a Christian.

It is not hard to see why the Saints had trouble in Asia. The province was very important to Rome. It was so rich in natural and human resources that many Roman nobles viewed it as a proconsular plum which guaranteed wealth to whomever the Roman Senate appointed as its overseer. Due to its excellent natural resources, good roads that connected it to both the East and the West, and excellent ports that gave it access to the broader Mediterranean world, its cities had become centers of manufacturing, especially textiles. By and large, many in Asia were rich, sophisticated, and cultured.

Making the province even more important was its position as a staging area for troops moving toward the eastern frontier of the empire. For over a century, being a part of the Roman domain had greatly benefited the Asians for, during that time, Roman attention and largesse kept the area well-assisted, strong, and pacified. Both Rome and Asia profited from their close ties, and loyalty on the part of the pagan populace was thus strong.

It is little wonder, therefore, that the area was the seat of emperor worship.[8] "No where else in the Roman empire," one scholar noted, "did the provincials practise so devotedly and earnestly the cult of *diva Roma* and especially of the divinely-honored emperor."[9] Few were willing to upset the status quo, and some among the prominent citizens were willing to force others to comply—even if it meant using ostracism, harassment, and when necessary, outright persecution to keep them in line.

The Christians at Ephesus had, up to this time, escaped much

---

[8] Thompson, *Book of Revelation*, 12.

[9] Johannes Weiss, *Earliest Christianity: A History of the Period A.D. 30–150*, trans. F. C. Grant, 2 vols. (New York: Harper & Row, 1937), 1:803. See also Ethelbert Stauffer, *Christ and the Caesars: Historical Sketches I*, trans. K and R. Gregor Smith, (Philadelphia: Westminster Press, 1955), 174–77.

of the persecution their fellow believers in other cities experienced. Therefore, it is not surprising that John would operate from a base in that region. Ephesus was, indeed, a good choice.[10] With Pergamum and Smyrna, Ephesus stood as one of the three great cities of Asia Minor. Of the three, it had the largest commercial center due to its excellent harbor. Adding to its status was its position as the chief administrative headquarters of the area whose governor directed all the affairs of the province.[11] The city was a center for the imperial cult, but its citizens were most proud of the large and beautiful temple dedicated to the Anatolian goddess Artemis, or Diana, as the Romans named her. The city also held the status of "temple warden" (Greek, *neōkoros*) of both the goddess Diana and the imperial cult.

Ephesus was also a center for the practice of the supernatural. Magicians (Greek, *magoi*) and sorcerers (Greek, *pharmakoi*) thrived there, as did a brisk publishing business dedicated to satisfying those eager to learn how to use mystic power. It was here that certain apostate Jews, the sons of one Sceva and practitioners of magic, tried to cast out demons in the name of Christ and learned a hard lesson in the process (see Acts 19:13–18). Amulets, books of spells, and other occult objects could be found in abundance.[12]

In spite of the solid pagan base that supported the religious system of the city, as noted, the Christian movement had, a generation earlier, made solid headway there. Luke provides us with two excellent examples that show the effectiveness of the missionary

---

[10] Just when John moved to Ephesus is unknown. It seems, however, to have been late in the century. For a summary of his ministry there, see Eusebius, *Ecclesiastical History*, 3.18.1; 3.23.3–4; 3.39.3–4; 4.18.6–8; 5.8.4; 5.18.14.

[11] Dio Chrysostom, *Orations*, 34.48, stated that Ephesus and Smyrna were bitter rivals. The geographer Strabo noted that Ephesus surpassed all other cities as an *emporion*, that is, as a commercial center. See his *Geography*, 14.1.24.

[12] For background on Ephesus, see Richard E. Ostler Jr., "Ephesus," in Freedman, *ABD*, 2:542–549.

work. The first was the number of people who had ceased to practice magic and had burned the scrolls containing the knowledge of the dark arts (Acts 19:19). The worth of the scrolls destroyed was about 50,000 drachmas, the equivalent of "a worker's wage for 137 years with no days off."[13] The staggering amount suggests that those converted away from practicing magic would have numbered in the thousands. The second was the number of people who no longer purchased images of the Greek goddess Diana, patron deity of the city, or attended pagan temple services (Acts 19:26–27). The decline of devotion threatened the livelihood of the idol makers and priests, who nearly started a riot to protest Christian inroads (see Acts 19:24–41). This event, again, suggests that a huge number of people were following the Lord Jesus Christ. Thus, the place was an ideal location as a Church center for the Apostle. John continued his ministry through the reign of Trajan, which ended about A.D. 117.[14] Though tradition states that John died and was buried in that city, the truth is that he was translated and carried on the Lord's work from another sphere (D&C 7:3).

Emperor Worship in Asia

Though one might think that the large numbers of Christians throughout all Asia would bode well for the movement, such was not the case. Indeed, their numbers threatened to bring down one of the mainstays of the region, the cult of the emperor. That the whole of the eastern empire readily adopted emperor worship is not surprising. From the days of Egypt's Pharaohs through the Greek Seleucids, the idea of mortals having divine status saturated the area. By the second century A.D. a number of leaders were given deific honors, which enhanced their prestige. From the time of Julius Caesar, the Senate had flattered various emperors'

---

[13] Arndt and Gingrich, *GEL*, "*argyrion*."
[14] Irenaeus, *Against Heresies*, 2.22.5; 3.3.4.

followers and family by bequeathing divine titles on the deceased. Domitian played on this. He was a staunch champion of Roman orthodoxy and an apostle of conformity. High on his agenda was sustaining and upbuilding the established cult and particularly the promotion of emperor worship which he pushed with every device at his command. He took a page out of Caligula's book (ruling between A.D. 33 and 41)[15] and demanded deification *before* his death. He especially enjoyed the title of "our lord and god." He also tied himself directly to the worship of the goddess Roma, thus equating loyalty to the state with loyalty to the emperor.[16] Though his divine aspirations sat poorly with some and even contributed to his eventual assassination, for a time the Senate acquiesced.

It took the people of Asia Minor little time to realize that monetary success was tied to emperor worship and joining the Roman imperial religious bureaucracy. One advantage was that a powerful, though mortal, god, being both tangible and immediate, could directly hear and respond to appeals for assistance. One did not have to rely on the mediation of priests to know how to worship this god or to receive blessings from him. Therefore, many in the East were very willing to accept the divine aspirations of this Caesar.

City magistrates felt honored when the emperor allowed them to build temples to the goddess Roma or to himself. Such acts of sycophancy gave them not only status but also access to imperial largesse.[17] Thereby, both civil and religious feeling promoted and defended the cult. In Asia proper, all the major cities but Philadelphia and Laodicea harbored imperial altars with their

---

[15] See Anthony Barrett, *Caligula—The Corruption of Power* (New Haven: Yale University Press, 1990).

[16] See Elmer T. Merrill, *Essays in Early Christian History* (London: Macmillan, 1924), 148, 155.

[17] For discussion, see S. R. F. Price, *Rituals and Power: The Roman Imperial Cult in Asia Minor* (Cambridge and New York: Cambridge University Press), 1984.

attendant priests, and all but Thyatira boasted imperial temples.[18] Thus the area was a hotbed of imperial worship. Though the temples were the centers of such worship, a good deal of devotion went on in other formal venues, especially among the trade guilds.

The Role of Guilds and Trade Unions

There is little wonder that guilds and trade unions were both ubiquitous and strong in this region. Wool and flax production abounded, and there were numerous carding and weaving facilities in such places as Laodicea and Colossae. Sardis and Lydia cooperated to produce the red-dyed cloth and embroidered garments that were in high demand over much of the empire. The area also abounded in silver- and goldsmiths, leather workers, and tanners. Most of these tradesmen combined to form guilds or trade unions to protect their jobs and promote their products.[19]

A practice at many guild meetings was to offer up incense or libations to the union's patron deity and to the emperor.[20] The act showed not only religious faith but also proper civic duty. As one scholar noted, "If the citizen refused such a test of loyalty, especially if it was demanded of him by competent legal authority (and it was for the magistrate himself to decide that point), or if he notoriously absented himself from such popular loyal demonstrations as involved this ceremonial, he appears to have been theoretically exposed to a charge of constructive treason, disloyal irreverence, 'atheism.'"[21] For the pagans, anyone who refused these simple,

---

[18] Price, *Rituals and Power*, xxii–xxv.

[19] See T. R. S. Broughton, "Roman Asia Minor," in Frank Tenney, ed., *An Economic Survey of Ancient Rome*, 5 vols. (Paterson, N.J.: Pageant Books, 1938), 2:841–846.

[20] For discussion of Christian harassment and Roman *collegia*, see Merrill, *Essays*, 183–85, and Samuel Dill, *Roman Society from Nero to Marcus Aurelius* (New York: Meridian Books, 1962), 264–67.

[21] Merrill, *Essays*, 154.

holy, and honorific acts not only dishonored the state but could also bring down divine disfavor, not something the locals wanted to chance. Therefore, it is little wonder the citizens strongly pressed the Saints to accommodate certain pagan practices, and some were yielding.[22]

The Position of the Christians

While John labored in the province of Asia, conditions worsened for the Church. As it moved into the last decade of the first century and its membership continued to grow, anti-Christian sentiment grew ever stronger. The emperor Nero, decades before, had laid the groundwork for the awful position in which the Saints continually found themselves. He had decreed that the Christians were the arsonists who had started the fire that burnt much of Rome and, therefore, ordered their arrest and execution.[23] His action came from and gave force to the rumors that Christians were haters of humankind, practiced cannibalism, and were guilty of other crimes against society. Believing such tales, many Romans could see Christians easily starting a horrendous fire that killed hundreds of Romans.

Nero's move did not, however, result in an empire-wide pogrom. One reason was that Roman magistrates all over the empire were, by and large, tolerant of religious systems and social clubs as long as they were viewed as benign and supportive of the state. Because the Christians were, for the most part, quiet, law-abiding, and hard-working, few magistrates saw them or their congregations as posing a threat to the government. Thus, for much of the first century of the Christian era, the higher class of Romans both in the capital and its provinces paid little attention to them. That is

---

[22] G. K. Beale, *The Book of Revelation: A Commentary on the Greek Text,* a vol. in The International Greek Testament Commentary (Grand Rapids, Mich.: Eerdmans, 1999), 233–34.

[23] See Eusebius, *Ecclesiastical History,* 2.25; 3.17.1.

not to say conditions were always peaceful for the Saints, but persecutions were, for the most part, sporadic, localized, and of short duration. Seldom did anything reach the ear of the emperor. As a result, specific legislation against Christians was slow to develop. Therefore, when charges were brought against the Christians, provincial governors had to deal with them on a case-by-case basis.[24]

Then came Domitian and his push for emperor worship. As noted, his move was not directed explicitly at the Christians, but it did result in their increased troubles in Asia. In this seedbed of emperor worship, some magistrates seemed to have felt Domitian's propensities and thus became ever more concerned with "atheism" and those who held and particularly promoted it. Some citizens, even those of high rank, who were connected with Judaism or Christianity, came under censure for this crime, and some even suffered death.[25]

The Church was clearly viewed as promoting atheism, and members who never broke a single civil law could still be condemned and thus disenfranchised, banished, tortured, or executed.[26] From the Roman point of view, such was understandable and even necessary. The Roman cult was the center of both civic and religious life. Though individuals privately worshipped whatever gods their ancestors did (the Jews were free to worship Jehovah, for example), they were also expected to show public piety toward the gods of Rome. Thus participation in an *externa religio* was considered an affront to the national gods and the greatness of Rome, and Roman lawyers could link sacrilege with atheism.[27]

---

[24] Merrill, *Essays*, 56–57.

[25] W. H. C. Frend, *Martyrdom and Persecution in the Early Church: A Study of Conflict from the Maccabees to Donatus* (New York: New York University Press, 1965), 212–16.

[26] For discussion, see Beale, *Revelation*, 5–10.

[27] *Maiestas* and *sacreligium* were seen as one and the same. See Marcian, *Digest*, 48.4.1.

In short, no one had to prove a Christian guilty of any immoral or illegal behavior; one had only to prove the person was a Christian and thereby an atheist by Roman standards. Given this fact, some modern scholars have concluded that just being a Christian was against the law. Such, however, is not the case. Evidence suggests that governors condemned not simply because the person confessed the name of Christ and would not recant but because Christians were automatically assumed to be guilty of the rumored crimes that circulated against them.[28] In short, the Christians were guilty by association.

Some tried to escape by hiding behind a Jewish façade. Long-standing Roman law recognized ancient religions and protected such groups, Jews among them. Since many provincials viewed the Christians as a subset of Judaism,[29] it was easy, if a Saint chose to do so, to play on this. In some cities, however, the Jews not only denied any relationship but also exposed Christians to the authorities (see Revelation 2:19; 3:9). This move greatly increased the amount of harassment the Saints had to endure. Their quasi-illegal status also made them victims of malcontents, bigots, or the spiteful. Any who harbored ill feelings toward a Christian could simply let the magistrate know who it was and let the law take its course.

Those Christians who belonged to the guilds or trade unions would have found themselves in a particularly perilous situation.

---

[28] The best material comes from Tertullian, a Roman Christian lawyer who labored in the beginning of the third century A.D. but whose arguments may have had a foundation even during John's time. In his *Apology,* 1.2, he shows that it was not simply being a Christian that was the problem but rather the bias of the magistrates who felt that any and all Christians were actually guilty of disloyalty to the state along with various heinous crimes. He goes on to say that if the governors would simply investigate, they would find the Christians innocent of such crimes and thereby let them off. His defense shows that there was no previous legislative act or edict against the Christians, but only a general and somewhat hazy summary of procedure that the magistrates were not under command to follow.

[29] See, for example, Suetonius, *Claudius,* 25.4; *Dio Cassius,* 60.6.6.

Unlike some of their brethren, who could simply avoid places where they might have to participate in some kind of pagan rite, the Christian trade workers had no way to dodge the accusation. During guild meetings, where members regularly paid obeisance to their patron deity or the emperor, Christians came face to face with the problem.[30] For them, there was only one Lord and God. To give that honor to another was to betray the very foundation of their religion. But to abstain from the common practice could mean expulsion from the union, loss of employment, and legal action.[31] Looking at John's letters to the seven churches, it seems clear that some Christians either could not find or had been forced out of jobs and were suffering in poverty (see, for example, Revelation 2:9).

All Christians, however, were living under the cloud of ever greater danger. Because pagan worship was so intimately tied with the state, Christians simply could not continually evade services of one kind or another. Increasingly, committed Christians came into conflict with the pagan state and its religious and civil leaders. Thus, it was not hard for a provincial governor, in order to win favor with the state and secure the blessings of the gods, to strike out against the Church and its leaders. John himself seemed to have been caught in this web of legal and religious entanglements, which may have led to his banishment.

John on the Isle of Patmos

Patmos, one of the Sporades Islands, lies about forty miles southwest of Ephesus. In ancient times, it was part of the territory of the city of Miletus. It is a small volcanic island, roughly

---

[30] Dill, *Roman Society*, 264–67.

[31] Merrill, *Essays*, 174–201, looks at the *collegium* and Christian associations during the reign of Trajan. Though this was two decades after Domitian, the situation would likely have been much the same.

butterfly-shaped and about ten miles long by six miles wide. Contrary to what some have said, it was not a Roman penal colony, and there is no evidence that anyone other than John was banished there.[32] The Miletians used this island, along with two others, as a naval station housing a garrison to ward off pirates. That John was there offers an interesting possibility about how certain Roman officials viewed the social status of the Christian leadership at the time. This possibility is best understood in light of the Roman practice of banishment.

Roman Forms of Banishment

The ancient sources all agree that John was exiled to Patmos. However, the Latin word *exilium,* or *exsul,* referred to a person leaving an area either on a voluntary or an involuntary basis and, therefore, does not tell us if John was banished to Patmos or went there of his own accord. It is noteworthy that the Roman legal system had a dual-penalty system that depended more on the social status of the individual than on the actual crime he committed. Those with proper *dignitas,* that is, rank or station, received more lenient sentences than those of lesser station. For example, the same crime that would require the death penalty for a lower-class individual mandated mere banishment for a member of the upper class.[33] Those with sufficient *dignitas* could often escape the death penalty even for capital crimes. They did not, however, get off totally without punishment. If the crime were of sufficient severity, even nobles were banished.

The law allowed for two types of compulsory banishment:

---

[32] See Pliny, *Natural History* 4.12.69. A number of commentators misread the text, among them such notables as Charles, *Exegetical Commentary,* 1:21; J. P. M. Sweet, *Revelation* (Philadelphia: Westminster, 1979), 12.

[33] P. Garnsey, *Social Status and Legal Privilege in the Roman Empire* (Oxford: Clarendon Press, 1970), 103–80.

relegatio and *deportatio*.³⁴ The former was often temporary (perhaps lasting as little as three years) and did not necessarily include the forfeiture of citizenship or property. This took two forms: *relegatio ad* or *relegatio in* was banishment *to* a place, often to an island or penal colony; or *relegatio ab,* also referred to as *relegatio extra,* was restriction *from* a place, allowing a person to travel or live anywhere but in a certain province or area. The second type of banishment, *deportatio,* was much more onerous, designating a long-term banishment to a specific place along with loss of citizenship and property. Nobles often chose this sentence in lieu of death.³⁵

Taking the facts of banishment into account, there are six possibilities that may explain how John came to live on Patmos. First, he may have decided to go to the island to preach the gospel to members of the garrison stationed there. Second, he may have gone under inspiration to have time to meditate in the seclusion necessary for receiving the Revelation. Third, a magistrate may have relegated him from the province (*relegatio ab*), and John went to the island voluntarily for refuge. Fourth, a magistrate may have banished him specifically to that island (*relegatio ad*) for a specific duration of time. Fifth, a magistrate may have relegated him to the island as a permanent exile with all loss of citizenship and property (the extreme form of *relegatio ad*). Sixth, a magistrate may have condemned him to death and, to avoid execution, the seer chose exile to the island (*deportatio*).

John's own testimony is quite helpful in understanding why he was there. He states that he "was in the isle that is called Patmos, for the word of God, and for the testimony of Jesus" (Revelation 1:9). Some have suggested, on the basis of the clause *dia ton logon tou theou,* "for the word of God," that John expressed the purpose

---

[34] *Oxford Latin Dictionary* (New York: Oxford University Press, 1982), "*relegatio*" and "*deportatio*."

[35] See Marcian, *Digest,* 48.22, where this Roman lawyer treats this material.

of his visit. The word translated "for" is the Greek *dia*. Some have suggested the phrase could be interpreted in a subjective or objective sense, that is, he was there because of the word from or about God and the testimony by or of Jesus. They conclude that he was there "in order to preach the word of God."[36] The problem is that the noun, *logon,* is not in the genitive case, which would allow this interpretation. Instead it is in the accusative, which connotes "cause or consequences." Thus, he was at Patmos in consequence of his faithfulness in not denying his testimony of the Lord.[37] This interpretation rules out possibilities one and two—that is, that he had gone there for either meditative or proselyting purposes.

That opens the way for the third possibility, *relegatio ab*. This is because John clearly states that when he received the Revelation he "was in the isle called Patmos," suggesting he was no longer there but, at the time of writing, was free again. However, a close examination of the passage suggests that this is not the case either. The aorist verb *egenomōn,* translated "I was," does not necessarily mean that John was no longer on Patmos. This tense is John's choice as he presents background material setting up a current circumstance.[38] Thus, his use of the tense does not mean he was no longer on the island but, rather, he had been and still was residing there when the vision opened. If that is the case, and it is a big *if,* he most likely was not suffering under *relegatio ab* since he had not yet been released and does not seem to know if he would be—hence his need to write to the churches rather than visit them. Because his letters give no hint that he knows of a termination date, it is

---

[36] The study by H. D. Saffrey, "Relire l'Apocaplypse á Patmos," *Revue Biblique* 82 (1975): 384–417, explores the idea that John voluntarily withdrew to the island for meditation.

[37] That is exactly how John uses the word in Revelation 6:9 and 20:4, where he attaches the phrase to martyrdom. For discussion, see Beale, *Revelation,* 202.

[38] See Beale, *Revelation,* 202.

unlikely he was suffering under *relegatio ad* (reason four) in which a magistrate banished him for a specific duration of time.

John's words to the Saints that he was their "companion in tribulation, and in the kingdom and patience of Jesus Christ" (Revelation 1:9), suggests that he had come to the island under harsh circumstances—that he had actually been banished there.[39] That suggests reasons five and six. Some object to either of these possibilities because they believe that John, as a Galilean Jew, would not have held Roman citizenship. They also insist that his being a Christian would preclude him from membership in any upper class anywhere in the empire. Greco-Romans would simply not see him as having *dignitas* and, therefore, he would not qualify for the special justice that nobles merited.[40] The point is well-taken because it is unlikely, though not certain, that John held Roman citizenship and status. The records, however, do show that some Christians did indeed belong to the elite strata. One evidence is that a number of Christians were executed by beheading, a death reserved for upper-class citizens.[41] Further, many Christians

---

[39] Clement of Alexandria states that John left Patmos after the death of Domitian (see *Salvation of the Rich*, 42, and in Eusebius, *Ecclesiastical History*, 2.23.5–19), when the Roman Senate annulled many of the late emperor's laws. They also returned confiscated property and restored the banished. Eusebius states that Domitian was second to organize a persecution against the Christians; Nero was the first (*Ecclesiastical History*, 3.17.1). In *Ecclesiastical History*, 3.18.1–2, the historian notes that John was "sentenced to confinement" to Patmos at this time due his testimony. In *Ecclesiastical History*, 5.8.4, he also says that John produced his Gospel in Ephesus. According to Victorianus, *Commentary on Revelation*, 10.11, John was "condemned to the mines of Patmos by Domitian Caesar" and there had his vision, which he published after Domitian's death. Tertullian, *Prescription against Heresies*, 36.3, states that John was banished from Rome. For an overview of the whole, see Beale, *Revelation*, 202.

[40] See William M. Ramsey, *Letters to the Seven Churches of Asia* (London: Hodder & Stoughton, 1904), 84, and G. B. Caird, *The Revelation of St. John the Divine* (Peabody, Mass.: Hendrickson, 1987), 21. Their conclusions are, however, too hasty. Quite a number of upper-class Romans are known to have been Christian, and their belief did not hurt their status.

[41] Tertullian argued for the fourth possibility, that is, *relegatio ad*. See *Prescription against Heresies*, 36. For discussion, see Aune, *Revelation*, 52c: 1086.

honored their leaders, whom they recognized as possessing very high status. That some of those who did the honoring were themselves members of the upper class reinforced their religious leaders' social rank. Some Roman governors may have sensed this, but it is unlikely they would have so honored John. Thus, reasons five and six are possibly ruled out.

So what is left? It is of note that the rulers at Ephesus, even though it was the capital of the region, do not appear to have moved against the Christians as did those in neighboring Smyrna and Pergamum. It may be that the Roman governor did not view the Christians as a threat to the state and may even have held them in some favor. Thus, he would not have viewed John as any kind of real threat either. However, with many being sensitive to Domitian's proclivities, there was a need to placate the local pagans. Even so, he seemed to have decided not to pull down the full weight of the state on John but, rather, to put the pesky Christian out of the way until tempers cooled and conditions returned more nearly to normal. If such were the case, it suggests that, in spite of fear, intolerance, or prejudice, respect for Christians was growing among some Romans, which brought a softening on their part. Thus, though John possessed no *dignitas,* he did have a certain cachet, which allowed him to be banished rather than executed.[42]

But why would John be sent to Patmos if it was not a penal colony? Provincial governors did not have the right to banish individuals to an island unless the island lay within the geographical bounds of their area.[43] Patmos was within the geographical jurisdiction of the governor of Asia and, therefore, a place to which

---

[42] John uses the phrase "on account of the word of God" two other times (see Revelation 6:9 and 20:4), each in connection with martyrdom, suggesting that this is the context in which the phrase should be understood.

[43] Urban prefects did have the power to banish people to islands. See Marcian, *Digest,* 48.22.6 and 48.22.7.1.

a governor could exile an annoying Christian, given the dual standard of punishment the empire allowed.[44]

According to Eusebius, John was eventually released due to a Roman practice that allowed an emperor to give amnesty to the prisoners of his predecessor. Upon Domitian's death, the Roman Senate recalled all the deceased emperor's exiles, which freed John to return to Ephesus and continue his ministry.[45] Again, this allows for the interpretation that the local magistrate held John and the Christians in some esteem.

The Background to the Visions

John's visions, however, seem to have come years before his release. The question is, What prompted the Revelation? John states that he was "in the Spirit on the Lord's day" when he heard "a great voice, as a trumpet" (Revelation 1:10) commanding him to write what the Lord was about to tell him and to send it to the

---

[44] The testimony of the early Church Fathers was that John was, indeed, exiled by a Roman magistrate. See Origen, *Commentary on Matthew*, 7.51; 16.6; Jerome, *De viris illustribus*, 10; Clement, *Salvation of the Rich*, 42; and Eusebius, *Ecclesiastical History*, 3.18. See Aune, *Revelation*, 51a: 82, who states that John's "presence on Patmos was the result of a capital penalty inflicted on him by Roman authorities."

[45] Eusebius, *Ecclesiastical History*, 3.20.8–9. He also states in 3.23.1 that John returned from banishment on Patmos to Ephesus. He agrees with Pliny, who states that Nerva freed many of Domitian's exiles. He also quotes Irenaeus in *Ecclesiastical History*, 2.22.5; 3.3.4, stating that John's ministry lasted until the time of Trajan. Origen, *Commentary on Matthew*, 16.6, also states that a certain emperor of the Romans condemned John to Patmos. Clement of Alexandria stated that John was released from banishment upon the death of "the tyrant" (*Quis div.*, 42, quoted by Eusebius, *Ecclesiastical History*, 3.23.5–19). Victorinus of Petau (c. A.D. 300) preserved the tradition that John was banished by Domitian and served in the mines of Patmos. See his *Commentary on Revelation*, 10.3. Still, there is some ambiguity among the ancient sources. Neither Origen nor Clement names the emperor. Epiphanius, *Panarion*, 51.12.1–2, states that John was more than ninety years old when he left Patmos during Claudius Caesar's reign. His reference could be to Nero, who was Nero Claudius, but the emperor Claudius was Claudius Nero. According to the Syriac Apocryphal "History of the Son of Zebedee," as quoted in Aune, *Revelation*, 78, it was Nero who banished John. Eusebius mentions Peter being crucified in Rome, Paul beheaded, and John exiled to Patmos, suggesting the events occurred in close proximity and happened at Rome.

seven churches in the province of Asia. From the point of view of the text, it was God, not anything John was doing directly, who precipitated the prophecy. In other words, the seer was not seeking answers to which the revelation was a response. Rather, the vision was a result of his being in the Spirit and thus prepared for what the Lord was about to show him.

Even so, there must have been circumstances which were either threatening the Church or soon would be, which caused the Lord sufficient concern to send this forceful message. Certainly an impetus was the increasing persecutions which threatened the lives of members of some of the branches of the Church in Asia Minor. For example, in the letter to Smyrna, the Lord stated that He knew their "works, and tribulation, and poverty" (Revelation 2:9). Note that Christians there suffered not only from dire poverty but also from tribulation, the Greek *thlipsis* (from the word *thlibō*, translated as "tribulation") meaning "to rub, press, or squash." The Lord's word choice suggests a deliberate and malicious persecution of the Saints aimed at the eradication of the branch. As noted previously, however, persecution, even in Asia Minor, was spotty and, overall, not nearly as brutal as some early Christian sources have suggested.[46] Still, what was happening in Smyrna showed which way the wind was blowing, and within a generation, the devastation was widespread. Even so, the current and growing maltreatment cannot fully account for the Lord's concern. Something else was pushing the need for the revelation. The impetus, by and large, grew out of the position in which the Christians found themselves.

The Position of the Christians

On the surface, it seems that the Saints could have escaped tribulation easily. All they had to do was offer a pinch of incense

---

[46] For discussion, see John A. T. Robinson, *Redating the New Testament*, (Philadelphia: SCM Press, 1976), 228–53.

at the emperor's shrine and mutter the empty formula, "Caesar is Lord." But, as noted, the faithful could not do that because they had but one Lord and that was Christ. Those at Pergamum knew the cost of refusing to conform, for they had already lost the first co-religionist of many to martyrdom.[47] Antipas, a very visible Christian, appears to have been publicly executed. Nothing is known of his life, but his enduring faith and refusal to bow to pagan pressures earned him a title that the Lord also held: "the faithful witness" (compare Revelation 1:5 with 2:13).[48]

Even so, in John's letters to the seven churches, though persecution was mounting, the major problem does not seem to be with the imperial cult or those who administered it.[49] There were problems—increased Jewish harassment, local intolerance (especially on the guild level), and the influence of general pagan wantonness. But none of these was at an all-time high. Thus, there had to be something more at play. What was it?

A look at the text shows that the Church was foundering in a number of areas, only one of which was direct outside pressure aimed at destroying the movement. There was, however, a related one. It was a steadily growing willingness on the part of an ever-increasing number of Saints to compromise with paganism, including, on the part of some members, paying homage to the emperor. This was far more dangerous to the spiritual life of the Church than pagan and Jewish torments. There were four other factors, but these were more internal: the acceptance of unauthorized leaders, the approval of doctrine that pseudo-prophets and false apostles

---

[47] Eusebius preserves the names of the martyrs Carpus, Papylus, and Agathonike. See *Ecclesiastical History*, 4.15.

[48] A legend preserved by Simon Metaphrastes and the Bollandists tells that he was roasted alive, but there is no historical basis for the tale. See Henry Alford, *Alford's Greek Testament: An Exegetical and Critical Commentary*, 4 vols. (Grand Rapids, Mich.: Baker Book, 1980), 4:569.

[49] See Robinson, *Redating the New Testament*, 14–15.

promulgated, the members' half-heartedness and indifference, and the loss of love for the Church and its Master.[50] Here is where the real danger lay. Though outside pressure would sweep some from the ranks of the Church, it was the inside pressure that threatened the movement as a whole, namely, wresting the control and direction of the Church from its divinely appointed leaders.

The Lord's Message

Given these conditions, the Lord's messages of warning to the seven churches were necessary. In spite of the success of missionary work in the region, trouble brewed because the area had become a hotbed of heresy. During his three-year ministry there, Paul had continually warned the Saints that after he left, "grievous wolves [shall] enter in among you, not sparing the flock. Also of your own selves shall men arise, speaking perverse things, to draw away disciples after them" (Acts 20:29–31). His words show that danger would come from two sources: the first would be "the wolves," those who joined the Church as a means of taking advantage of the Christians; the second would be the insiders, Christian leaders who would speak "perverse things" and use their positions to persuade congregations to follow another gospel, leading many astray.[51]

Paul's dire predictions proved true. It took only a few years for apostasy to spread over the area like a destructive flood. Thus, he could say to Timothy in about A.D. 64, "All they which are in [the province of] Asia be turned away from me" (2 Timothy 1:15).

The Apostasy began as false apostles and pseudo-prophets

---

[50] Richard D. Draper, *Opening the Seven Seals: The Visions of John the Revelator* (Salt Lake City: Deseret Book, 1991), 37.

[51] A scriptural example would be Diotrephes, "who loveth to have the preeminence among them" and who forbade his people to have anything to do with the apostles or their followers (3 John 1:9–10). He was not alone; John notes that at the time of his writing there were many antichrists. See 1 John 2:18–19. Compare Kent P. Jackson, "Early Signs of the Apostasy," *Ensign,* December 1984, 8; Smith, *TPJS,* 67.

breached the doctrinal levees that the Lord's teachings and His appointed leaders had once secured.[52] Entire congregations were ignorantly or willfully in danger of being swept away in the flood of falsehood that the counterfeit prophets and others promulgated. The messages to the seven churches show that the Savior was well aware of what was happening and that He was reaching out to save those islands where hope still remained. He gave each congregation specific and clear warnings. The most important warning was that He would abandon the churches unless they returned to Him. He clearly told each congregation to stop the spread of heresy, repent, hold to the truth, and thereby gain salvation—or else He would remove the Church from the earth.

The Seat of the Christian Crisis

Thus, it is clear that the crisis that triggered the revelation to John was less the social situation in which the Christians found themselves and more in the conflict within the Christian faith itself.[53] There is no doubt that the social situation exacerbated the real problem, apostasy. Many may have wondered why they were under such duress. The kingdom of God was supposed to be on the earth and triumph over all its enemies, yet the reality was that Rome had the upper hand and seemed in position to destroy the divine kingdom. The revelation came to relieve the tension. Through the power of its symbolism, the various visions corrected the Christians' false expectations and gave them a clear vision of the present reality, a reality they would have to endure. Indeed, the Lord showed them that "all living beings are given a place in a dualistic structure. At the pinnacle of power on one side is God, the

---

[52] The text gives the names of some: Phygellus, Hermogenes, Alexander the coppersmith, and Diotrephes (2 Timothy 1:15, 20; 2 Timothy 4:14; 3 John 1:19–10).

[53] Adela Yarbro Collins, *Crisis & Catharsis: The Power of the Apocalypse* (Philadelphia: Westminster Press, 1984), 106.

Pantocrator, ruler of all (1:8). On the other is Satan, the Dragon, who has power, a throne, and great authority (13:2). Allied with God is the Lamb who was slain (5:6). . . . Allied with Satan is the beast from the sea (13:1–2). . . . All the people of the earth are divided into two groups; those who have the seal of God on their foreheads and whose name are in the book of life (3:5, 12; 7:3; 20:4; 21:27; 22:4) and those who bear the mark of the beast and worship it (9:4; 13:8, 17; 14:9–11; 16:2; 20:15). There is also a sharp contrast drawn between the luxurious and voluptuous harlot, who represents Babylon . . . (ch. 17) and the pure bride of the Lamb, who symbolizes Jerusalem, the heavenly city of salvation (19:7–8; 21:2, 9–11)."[54]

Again the real problem was apostasy, not just apostasy *from* the Church but the apostasy *of* the Church. The problem was exacerbated due to growing pagan pressures. These pressures both pushed and pulled on the leaders, would-be leaders, and members. The pull came from the enticement of ease, comfort, acceptance, and wealth. The push came from the threat of punishment, ostracism, and perhaps even death. Thus, tension grew between the lure of the kingdom of Caesar and the promise of the kingdom of Christ.[55] The problem centered on how to resolve the real-life tension. Some Christians wanted to do it by making compromises with Rome, symbolized as Babylon.

It appears that some Christians were not only giving in to this economic and social pressure but also promoting their strategy as an advantageous solution to the problem. In short, one could have place in both worlds and enjoy the rewards of both. One was a woman whom John calls by the epithet "Jezebel." It appears that she developed a theology that appealed to those who opted for the compromises that let them escape persecution and enjoy the

---

[54] Collins, *Crisis & Catharsis*, 141–42.
[55] Collins, *Crisis & Catharsis*, 141–42.

prosperity of the city. Her logic could even have cited Paul's writings. Did he not teach that an idol was nothing and, therefore, eating sacrificial meat really posed no problem for believers? (see 1 Corinthians 8:4–6). Could one not extrapolate from his teaching that even offering a bit of incense or a drop of wine to an image of Caesar also meant nothing? Forget that Paul counseled against such practices because it opened the door to apostasy (1 Corinthians 8:10–13). Jezebel seems to have held and openly advocated compromise for the good of the security and prosperity of the Church and its members.[56] Of course, in doing so, she really led the way to its spiritual death.

It is important, however, to resist the idea that Revelation reflects only the dual tension between John's Church and Rome and between the forces of apostasy active in his day and the ideals of the true Church. Such a view is far too short-sighted, for it limits Revelation and its message exclusively to the historical past; doing so dilutes the message of the visions. Though tension with Rome is evident in Revelation, its primary role simply exacerbates the real problem. Indeed, the empire was but one physical manifestation of Satan's kingdom on earth—the kingdom that poses the real threat to the Church in any age. In John's day, the pagan and uncompromising Roman magistrates were one of the executors of Satan's kingdom, but others were the Christian Nicolaitans and the followers of Jezebel. Thus, Revelation shows that a battle—or more precisely, a campaign, because the time was filled with many battles—was raging on two planes: the physical and the spiritual.

Through the message of Revelation, we see the Lord advising the Saints to see their day in a broader perspective. They should maintain the same attitude as Paul, who knew that the Christians "wrestle not against flesh and blood, but against principalities,

---

[56] Robert H. Mounce, *The Book of Revelation* (Grand Rapids, Mich.: Eerdmans, 1972), 103.

against powers, against the rulers of the darkness of this world, against spiritual wickedness in high places" (Ephesians 6:12). By keeping this perspective, they understood the cosmic proportions of their struggle, making their current distress more understandable and giving them direction in which they should put their efforts.

Summary

The real threat against which John wrote was neither the imperial cult nor the civil and religious might of Rome, although they were certainly on stage. The crisis the Church faced, and the impetus to the Revelation, was the apostasy being pushed forward not so much by Christians yielding to the threat of Roman persecution as by yielding to the enticements of spiritual Babylon.[57]

The situation was critical. A circle of false prophets arose in competition with the true prophets for ecclesiastical domination and theological acceptance. False apostles tried to infiltrate the Church at Ephesus (Revelation 2:2); at Pergamum a faction upheld what John called the "doctrine of Balaam" (Revelation 2:14), probably a move to incorporate into Church practice certain elements of the pagan religion, while at Thyatira, Jezebel, the false prophetess with a large number of followers, seduced many with her teachings

---

[57] This statement is based on conditions which clearly existed about a decade later. The letters of Ignatius, a Syrian bishop writing in A.D. 107, emphasize the need of a non-prophetic Church order based on the authority of bishops. Tellingly, he never claimed prophetic power for the bishops. He wrote to the Philadelphians telling them that he continually cried out with a loud voice, even one of inspiration, to follow the bishops, presbytery, and deacons. Indeed, the congregations were to do nothing apart from what the bishop ordered (*Philadelphians,* 7.1). Such a stand suggests that the office and function of the bishop had not yet replaced those of the prophet but were well on the way. Still, many recognized the prophetic gift as essential within the Christian community. Thus, it was necessary to legitimize the central authority of the bishop by claiming the power of prophecy. See Elizabeth Schüssler Fiorenza, *The Book of Revelation: Justice and Judgment* (Philadelphia: Fortress Press, 1985), 142–43.

(Revelation 2:20). Heresy was spreading everywhere.[58] At this critical juncture, the Lord, through John, reached out in warning to the seven churches. The letters show the Lord's mercy because, for whatever happened to the several branches, the Lord promised faithful individuals eternal life because they had ears to hear.

Moreover, the letters also warn Saints in every age that Babylon (whether the old city of the Euphrates, Rome of the Tiber, or any of its modern equivalents) is not the real enemy. It is compromise which John shows is a real and most deadly sin. The Saints must not worship the dragon and his beast. They must not worship the great whore with all her glittering, seductive immorality and materialism. The Saints must worship God and the Lamb. They must come under the sealing power of the priesthood and look to the promise of eternal life. Trying to serve mammon and God will turn one's efforts into dust. John himself remained faithful to his Lord and Master, willing to suffer deportation to Patmos rather than to compromise his testimony.

Though it is true that Patmos was not a formal penal colony, the right of a Roman magistrate to banish criminals to an island within his jurisdiction suggests John was, indeed, incarcerated there as a penalty for being a Christian leader. As one authority has noted, it is likely "that John's presence on Patmos was the result of a capital penalty inflicted on him by Roman authorities."[59] That a Roman official banished him, rather than ordering his execution, suggests, however, that the Christian leaders had gained a certain amount of status in some provinces, and, therefore, could qualify for banishment rather than death. Such a condition implies that the Christian movement, though many viewed it as a threat, was gaining a certain amount of cachet. Though the force of

---

[58] Andre Feuillet, *The Apocalypse,* trans. Thomas E. Crane (New York: Alba House, 1965), 75–76.

[59] Aune, *Revelation,* 82.

Rome stood against it, the Lord's kingdom was demanding—and gaining—more respect. Of course, that was a two-edged sword, for some would view a more powerful Christianity as an even greater threat and move more fiercely against it. Even so, no earthly power could stop the movement.

Though a Roman magistrate may have hoped that banishing John to Patmos would weaken his influence and perhaps destroy the Christian faith, such was not the case. The island, instead, provided John with time to meditate and reach out to God. As a result of his time spent on Patmos, visions came, and with them direction for the Church.

Some have claimed that John intended nothing more than keeping the Saints in line by holding out the promise of eternal reward.[60] But John's aim seems far nobler. It is true that the course of history he presented stressed the ultimate rather than the immediate triumph of goodness over evil, but he also urged the Saints to work out their salvation in the present and to place their trust in God, who was not yet ready to expose His mastery over history. Triumph was, indeed, not immediately at hand. The Saints had to exercise faith through a hope that made no demands upon the present. They could not escape history; the work of God would continue for a long period within its confines. Even today, a characteristic of faith is a willingness to allow God to operate in His own way in the present, to take what comes, and to continue strong. God, through His Saints, will achieve ultimate victory. John's readers had to accept the agony of the present as travail necessary to bring into being a glorious future.[61]

Even so, as one Latter-day Saint scholar has noted, "The Lord's message, which John delivers, is primarily one of grace and peace,

---

[60] John R. May, "The Judaeo Christian Apocalypse," in Harold Bloom, ed., *The Revelation of St. John the Divine* (New York: Chelsea House, 1988), 39.

[61] May, "Apocalypse," 39–41.

not of persecution and death—grace, which is made possible through the atoning sacrifice; and inner peace, which comes from a knowledge of one's relationship with God. It is through these that the Lord offers comfort and hope to his people."[62]

---

[62] Gaye Strathearn, "Revelation: John's Message of Comfort and Hope," in Daniel K Judd, Craig J. Ostler, and Richard D. Draper, eds., *The Testimony of John the Beloved,* 27th Annual Sidney B. Sperry Symposium (Salt Lake City: Deseret Book, 1998), 287.

XI.

IMPERIAL CULT AND THE BEASTS OF REVELATION

ERIC D. HUNTSMAN AND CECILIA M. PEEK

And I stood upon the sand of the sea, and saw a beast rise up out of the sea, having seven heads and ten horns, and upon his horns ten crowns, and upon his heads the name of blasphemy.

REVELATION 13:1

A common approach to the study of the book of Revelation is to divide it into two main sections. One part of the Revelation deals with "things which must shortly come to pass," particularly the conditions of the seven contemporary churches to which the book is ostensibly addressed (1:1–3:22; 22:6–21). Most of the Revelation, however, treats "things which must be hereafter" (4:1–22:5), and this has led many readers to assume that the realization of these visions contained in the body of Revelation awaits future fulfillment. While it is true that much of this material may indeed have its final or fullest application in the eschatological future, to provide comfort and assurance for the Saints of John's age, Revelation must have also had meaning to its original readers and hearers. Indeed, identifying how the symbolism would have been interpreted and applied to the original reader often helps modern students of this text better understand how to apply it both to their own immediate time and to a yet future fulfillment.

This approach is especially useful in approaching the imagery of the beasts in 13:1–18 and 17:1–18. These chapters are partially shaped by an important political and religious practice of John's time: the spread and increasing obligations of Roman imperial cult. In the second half of the first century A.D., Christians, and to a lesser extent Jews, faced increasing challenges to their devotion to one—and only one—God. As monotheists in a predominately polytheistic society, they were constantly confronted with the gods and religious practices of those among whom they lived. Not participating in traditional polytheistic religious practices certainly had social, and at times political, implications which alienated them from the larger society and perhaps disqualified them from political involvement in their local communities.[1] Generally, however, polytheists in this period were relatively, or at least grudgingly, tolerant of the nonconformists in their midst.[2] On the other hand, when religious practices were used to secure loyalty, obedience, and deference to political leaders—as seems to have been the case with imperial cult—religious nonconformism could be seen as treason and result in severe sanctions, even death, for those who did not participate.

This appears to have been the case in the eastern provinces of the Roman Empire in the late first century, particularly in the province of Asia, now western Turkey, which was where all seven of the churches of Revelation were located. The phenomenon of imperial cult thus helps explain the symbolism and rhetoric of these passages, and an interpretation of these images more clearly delineates the lasting message that these pericopes contain about the nature of all false worship and those who support it. Understanding

---

[1] See Eric D. Huntsman, "The Impact of Gentile Conversions," in this volume.

[2] The famous example of Socrates, who was tried and executed on the charge of, among other things, "atheism," or "not believing in the gods that the state believed in" (Plato, *Apology*, 26), reveals that religion could always be used as a mask for political enmity.

more clearly this message can then help shape modern readings of these sections of Revelation.

The Development of Ruler Cult

Modern scholarship refers to the pattern of using religious practices and devotion to honor and signal loyalty to the Roman emperors as "the imperial cult." The Roman practice did not arise in a vacuum; rather, it had precedents in both Greek and Roman history and religion. Also, contrary to the designation "imperial cult," the accordance of divine honors to Roman rulers was not a systematic, uniform practice throughout the empire, nor was involvement in it always compulsory. Its practice varied from province to province over time, with some provinces and regions being more involved in it than others. In the period in which Revelation was written, certain patterns were still developing, although by the end of the century participation seems to have become increasingly compulsory, with enforcement and practice becoming somewhat more uniform.

Greek and Hellenistic Ruler Cult

Readers of Revelation must always keep in mind the original audience for the book, which consisted of the membership of seven churches in Asia. These churches were in Greek cities that had long histories before their incorporation into a Roman province. While Archaic and Classical Greek culture provided little precedent for according divine honors to mortal men and women, the cities of this region were in the forefront of the movement to deify rulers in the Hellenistic and Roman periods. The earliest surviving Greek literature reveals that while extraordinary men could be honored as "heroes" (Greek, *hērōes*), they were seldom given the same recognition as gods. While it is true that some of the greatest of the Homeric heroes were ostensibly demigods (Greek, *hēmitheos*), the belief that they must have had a divine, as well as a human, parent was most likely an etiological myth that sought to explain why their abilities and deeds were so much greater than those of other men. What made a great man "godlike" (Greek, *theiois*), whether he supposedly had divine parentage or not, were his deeds and accomplishments. The most prominent Greek hero ever to actually become a god was the extraordinary figure of Herakles, and that only after his death.[3]

Heroes, on the other hand, received a lesser form of worship at the tombs traditionally associated with them.[4] Because heroes had been great in life, they were assumed to be great in the world of the dead, where they could intercede in the interest of those who honored them. Because legendary heroes were usually associated with a particular geographic region, the oldest Greek cities claimed particular heroes as their founders. The worship of heroes had political significance because heroes were reputed to continue, from the underworld, to look after their cities and descendants.[5] During periods of subsequent Greek colonization, however, the traditional practice of offering heroic honors to a legendary founder was transferred to the known and historical founder of a new city (Greek, *oikistēs*). After his death, the founder was buried in a public tomb in the center of the city, where he received heroic cult status patterned after that accorded to legendary heroes.[6]

These two practices—honoring legendary heroes as "godlike"

---

[3] Others include the Dioskuroi (the twins Kastor and Pollux) and Asklepios, the god of healing. See Walter Burkert, *Greek Religion,* trans. John Raffan (Cambridge: Harvard University Press, 1985), 208–15.

[4] In the Archaic Period (c. 750–500 B.C.), Greeks began to associate great Mycenean tombs built in the Bronze Age with these heroic figures, assuming that these massive structures, so much greater than contemporary tombs, must have been built to house and honor figures far greater than men of their own day.

[5] Burkert, *Greek Religion,* 203–8; Everett Ferguson, *Backgrounds of Early Christianity* (Grand Rapids, Mich.: Eerdmans, 1993), 148–49, 187–88.

[6] Lily Ross Taylor, *The Divinity of the Roman Emperor* (Middletown, Conn.: American Philological Association, 1931), 7–8.

because of their great deeds and conferring heroic cult status on a founder figure—gave rise to the earliest examples of ruler cult in the late Classical period. During the Peloponnesian War (411–404 B.C.), when the Spartan general Brasidas died having accomplished more than thought possible against the Athenians in northern Greece, the citizens of Amphipolis built a tomb for him in the center of their city, sacrificed to him as a hero from that point on, and constituted him as the "new founder" of their city, replacing the earlier Athenian founder.[7] After the war, the victorious general Lysander, while he yet lived, was honored "as a god" at Samos, a Greek island off the western coast of Asia Minor, for liberating the Samians from the tyranny of Athens.[8]

During the course of Alexander's reign (336–323 B.C.), a more systematic and developed form of ruler cult emerged as a result of the immense power that the young king exerted over such a large area. As the founder of numerous Greek cities in his new empire—notably his namesake Alexandria in Egypt—he could be expected to receive heroic and even divine honors at least after his death.[9] Also, having delivered the Greeks and Macedonians from the Persian threat, he was seen as a military savior. Additionally, existing patterns of Near Eastern and Egyptian ruler cult no doubt contributed to the readiness of his subjects in those areas to recognize him with honors otherwise due only to the gods.

Specifically, his meeting with the priest of the Egyptian god Ammon at Siwa in 331 B.C., with the priest called Alexander the son of Amon-Ra, seems to have played a very influential role in how Alexander saw himself and even how other Greeks viewed

---

[7] Thucydides, 5.11.1.

[8] Plutarch, *Lysander,* 18.

[9] Taylor, *Divinity of the Roman Emperor,* 17–18; Peter Green, *Alexander to Actium: The Historical Evolution of the Hellenistic Age* (Berkeley: University of California Press, 1990), 404.

Alexander's new status.[10] In the end, however, Alexander's ruler cult was primarily a Greek phenomenon: the divine honors accorded Alexander occasionally during his lifetime and then extensively after his death can largely be seen as a result of the fact that he was simply a larger-than-life figure who accomplished deeds on a seemingly divine scale.

Alexander's successors strove both to emulate him and unify their disparate kingdoms in loyalty to the dynasties they established by fostering ruler cult in the cities and provinces of their empires. As with Alexander, this Hellenistic practice derived partially from earlier Greek practice but was also influenced by other cultures in the Near East—especially Egypt and Persia—that the Hellenistic kings ruled over. In its best attested practice, reigning kings and their queens were worshipped as gods, usually in conjunction with Alexander and with their deceased predecessors. With the rare exception of the megalomaniac Antiochus IV Epiphanes (175–164 B.C.), whose surname meant "god made manifest," this practice does not seem to have been compulsory or even completely religious. Instead, it seems to have served as a political and social compact between the ruler and the Greek cities of his kingdom that were technically independent and self-governing but were, in fact, completely dependent upon him for protection and patronage.[11] In return for benefactions, and perhaps in anticipation of hoped-for favors, cities set up statues of the king, granted titles such as "Savior" (Greek, *Sōtēr*) and "Benefactor" (Greek, *Euregetēs*), established altars and festivals, and selected priests—all of which were intended to honor the king more with homage than

---

[10] Taylor, 15–17; S. R. F. Price, "ruler-cult," in *The Oxford Classical Dictionary*, edited by Simon Hornblower and Antony Spawforth (Oxford and New York: Oxford University Press, 1999), 1337–39; Ferguson, *Backgrounds of Early Christianity*, 190–91.

[11] S. R. F. Price, *Rituals and Power: The Roman Imperial Cult in Asia Minor* (Cambridge: Cambridge University Press, 1984), 29–32.

with worship.¹² Such religious honors were a visible sign of loyalty and acknowledged the ruler's accomplishments and actual power without compromising the cities' theoretical political freedom, although in many instances it could no doubt decline into base flattery. This predominately political function does not rule out the possibility that at the common, individual level, the ruler could be seen as "god manifest on the earth, incarnate as the reigning monarch, and physically accessible to his petitioners."¹³

Indigenous Roman Practices

In contrast to the Greeks, the Romans had little precedent for honoring dead men as individual heroes or living men as gods.¹⁴ While the memory of the great deeds was carefully preserved and dead ancestors were repeatedly honored at family funerals and through the preservation of special death masks called *imagines,* the only "religious" honors given to the dead were part of a collective worship of ancestors known as the *Di Manes.*¹⁵ Numerous public, secular honors recognized the military and political achievements of civic figures, but only in the extraordinary honor of the Roman triumph did one receive something approaching a divine honor. When a commander brought a declared war over a foreign enemy

---

[12] For example, the Rhodians first called Ptolemy I (305–282 B.C.) *Sotēr* when he came to their military aid, c. 304 (Diodorus, 20.100; Pausainias, 1.8.6.), a name likewise given, or taken, by Antiochus I (281–261 B.C.). Antiochus II (261–246 B.C.) was granted the title *Theos,* or "God," after reestablishing democracy in Miletus (Appian, *Syriaca,* 65). See the discussion of cult titles in Green, *Alexander to Actium,* 402–403. The contemporary political use of these terms makes Jesus' statement particularly striking: "The *kings* of the Gentiles exercise lordship over them; and they that exercise authority upon them are called *benefactors*" (Luke 22:25; emphasis added). See Ferguson, *Backgrounds of Early Christianity,* 191–93.

[13] See the discussion of Taylor, *Divinity of the Roman Emperor,* 27–34; Green, *Alexander to Actium,* 399–406.

[14] Ferguson, Backgrounds of Early Christianity, 186.

[15] Ernst Badian, *"Imagines,"* and C. Robert Phillips, *"Manes,"* in *Oxford Classical Dictionary,* 749, 916–17.

to an end with a decisive victory—and fulfilled certain other requirements—he could be awarded a military triumph which allowed him a victory procession into Rome, dressed as either an ancient king or even the god Jupiter.[16] Even so, the honor lasted only one day, and supposedly a slave in his triumphal chariot would constantly remind him: "Remember you are a mortal."

The Romans did have one native myth about a founding figure, their first king, Romulus, becoming the god Quirinus upon his death. Otherwise, divine honors for men, living or dead, were not a regular form of Roman state religion, with the possible exception of Julius Caesar (100–44 B.C.), who is reported to have claimed certain divine honors toward the end of his rule. The evidence is mixed, and the honors he sought might have been based on a proposed revival of Etruscan kingship or were perhaps connected to his standing as a perpetual *vir triumphalis* rather than on eastern Greek models.[17] Regardless of his intentions, his assassination on March 15, 44 B.C., ended the experiment, although he was posthumously deified as *Divus Iulius* by senatorial vote in 42 B.C., perhaps on the model of Quirinus. Technically he was a *divus,* or "deified man," rather than *deus,* a god, but the full state cult that he received from that point would have important implications for the imperial period.[18]

Perhaps the most common setting where a form of indirect religious veneration could be accorded to a living man was in the home. In a domestic setting, Roman practice honored the *pater familias,* or "head of the household," through ritual directed not at him but at his *genius,* or guardian spirit. The *genius* symbolized

---

[16] Ernst Badian, "*Imagines*," and C. Robert Phillips, "*Manes*," in *Oxford Classical Dictionary,* 749, 916–17.

[17] Taylor, *Divinity of the Roman Emperor,* 58–77; Stefan Weinstock, *Divus Iulius* (Oxford: Clarendon Press, 1971), 270–341; Ferguson, *Backgrounds of Early Christianity,* 194.

[18] Taylor, *Divinity of the Roman Emperor,* 78–99; Weinstock, *Divus Julius,* 385–98.

the father's procreative force and spiritual power, and its prosperity guaranteed the prosperity of the entire household. This domestic practice consisted of simple religious honors such as libations and small sacrifices of flowers, incense, and wine offered by members of the household to the father's *genius* on his birthday, anniversary, and other important days.[19] When a leading Roman figure became *pater patriae,* or "father of the state," this domestic practice could extend to others outside the home and become a public practice. This was exactly what happened in the case of the first emperor, Augustus, who linked the Roman citizenry more closely with himself by having his *genius* thus honored in private homes, at banquets, and at public crossroad shrines called *compita.*[20] While this raised Augustus's profile and set him apart through extraordinary honors, this was, in fact, the only official form of religious devotion required of Roman citizens in the first century, at least of those in Rome and Italy.

Rome and Eastern Ruler Cult

The Romans' first recorded encounter with the Greek flattery of a ruler was in Sicily in 212 B.C., when the general Marcellus captured Syracuse. There he was welcomed as a "savior" and received a festival in his honor.[21] However, as the Romans moved into the eastern Mediterranean region, beginning in earnest with the Second Macedonian War of 200–196 B.C., they encountered more established forms of Hellenistic ruler cult. Toward the end of that war, the victorious general T. Quinctius Flamininus, who drove the Macedonians out of Greece, made a declaration of Greek freedom at the Isthmian Games of 196 B.C. When he followed through with a Roman evacuation of Greece two years later, the

---

[19] Taylor, *Divinity of the Roman Emperor,* 151–53, 181–83.
[20] Ibid., 184–94.
[21] Ibid., 35.

Greeks showered Flamininus with honors in return for this benefaction, including typically Hellenistic divine honors.[22] Subsequent Roman generals were similarly flattered.[23] Notable among these was Pompey the Great, who was hailed as a savior for suppressing piracy throughout the Mediterranean and who was recognized for his conquests and reorganization of the East.[24] Taylor has observed that the habit of offering extreme honors to political and military figures *"belongs particularly to the Greek cities of Asia* where worship of the kings had been far more effectively organized than had the more or less incidental ruler worship of the cities of Greece proper."[25] This observation is significant in regard to understanding the portrayal of ruler cult in Revelation.

Roman generals and governors came and went, however, so Greek cities, particularly in the Aegean and western Asia Minor, quickly adjusted to the different political system.[26] What was a constant force from this point on was Rome itself, so, not surprisingly, a number of cults dedicated to Roma—a personification of the city of Rome—appear in the early second century B.C. Preferring to honor the city rather than its transitory commanders, Greek cities seem to have modeled their worship of Roma on the Hellenistic concept of the *tychē*, or "good fortune," of a Greek city.[27] The earliest documented cult of Roma was in 195 B.C., when Smyrna, one of the cities mentioned in Revelation, dedicated a

---

[22] Ibid., 35–36; Plutarch, *Titus Flaminius*, 16.

[23] Roman officials honored with cult status in the east include Manius Aquillius, at Pergamum; Lucullus and Mucious Scaevola with games and festivals named after them in the cities of Asia; and Servilius Isauricus with a shrine to him and Roma in Ephesus (Taylor, *Divinity of the Roman Emperor*, 37–38). See also Steven J. Friesen, *Imperial Cults and the Apocalypse of John* (Oxford: Oxford University Press, 2001), 28–29.

[24] Taylor, *Divinity of the Roman Emperor*, 39–40.

[25] Ibid., 38; emphasis added.

[26] Price, "ruler-cult," in *Oxford Classical Dictionary*, 47.

[27] Taylor, *Divinity of the Roman Emperor*, 36.

temple to Roma.[28] What is striking is that at the time Smyrna was under the rule of the Seleucid king Antiochus III (223–187 B.C.), so the dedication seems to have been in anticipation of Rome's intervention, which occurred in the First Syrian War of 192–189 B.C. After Antiochus's defeat and expulsion from the Aegean and Asia Minor, a number of cities likewise established cults to Roma.[29] Significantly, many of the places known to have established the worship of Roma and which also honored Roman officials in a way that was an outgrowth of earlier Hellenistic ruler cult happen to have been in what became the province of Asia, where imperial cult seems to have been so prevalent at the time of Revelation.

When Octavian—later Augustus—decisively defeated his civil war enemy Mark Antony at Actium in 31 B.C., the provinces and cities of the eastern Mediterranean region who had been supporting Antony scrambled to realign their loyalties and were eager to proclaim their support of the new ruler. One of the first and most prominent of these was Pergamum, seat of another of the seven churches of Asia. Pergamum had been the capital of an independent Hellenistic kingdom under the Attalid dynasty, which had deftly used its alliance with Rome to annex all of the former Seleucid territory in western Asia Minor. When Attalus III, the last Pergamene king, died, he left his kingdom to the Roman people. When it was transformed into the new Roman province of Asia, many of the previous aspects of Attalid ruler cult were transferred to the goddess Roma. In 29 B.C., the entire province of Asia, as represented by its local nobility, dedicated a new temple to Roma and Octavian, changed to Roma and Augustus after Octavian took

---

[28] Tacitus, *Annales*, 4.56.1; see Taylor, *Divinity of the Roman Emperor*, 36–37.

[29] The best documented case is the island of Chios, which voted in 195 B.C. to hold a procession, sacrifice, and games for Roma because Rome had restored her freedom. See Price, "ruler-cult," in *Oxford Classical Dictionary*, 41.

his new title in 27 B.C.[30] In a further honor, the province made Augustus' birthday, September 23, its official New Year.[31] Every indication suggests that there were, in fact, actions that arose locally and without any overt Roman orchestration as attempts to establish a compact or relationship with the new ruler. This example was followed throughout the East and, to a lesser and modified form, in some of the Western provinces. However, nowhere is the pattern of adapting the forms of Hellenistic ruler cult to the new Roman situation better attested than in Asia Minor.

Imperial Cult in Asia from the Time of Augustus to Revelation

The process of applying local patterns of divine honors to Augustus and his successors developed differently in various areas of the empire, suggesting that, in the first century A.D. at least, there were in fact numerous imperial cults rather than a uniform, monolithic imperial cult. In addition to the provincial temple of Roma and Augustus in Pergamum, other cities in the province became rivals to each other in attempts to curry imperial favor. During the reign of Tiberius (A.D. 14–37), the cities of Asia petitioned to build a second imperial temple in gratitude to Tiberius for his intervention on their behalf which saved them from an extortionate governor. He approved a temple dedicated to himself, his mother, Livia, and the Senate, which was eventually built in Smyrna, another of the cities mentioned in Revelation.[32] Slowly,

---

[30] Friesen, *Imperial Cults and the Apocalypse of John*, 25–32.

[31] Robert K. Sherk, ed., *Rome and the Greek East to the Death of Augustus* (Cambridge: Cambridge University Press, 1984), 124–27. See also the discussion of Taylor, *Divinity of the Roman Emperor*, 205, and Friesen, *Imperial Cults and the Apocalypse of John*, 32–36.

[32] Tacitus, *Annales*, 4.15; see also Friesen, *Imperial Cults and the Apocalypse of John*, 36–38. Once the temple was approved, eleven cities competed for the honor of building it, the contest finally narrowing to Smyrna, which eventually received the temple, and Sardis, which was the site of another one of the Revelation churches.

and with occasional imperial guidance, certain forms and orders developed. During his lifetime, Augustus allowed himself to be "worshipped" only in conjunction with Roma, and he made a distinction between the actions appropriate to citizens and to noncitizens. Citizens could worship *Divus Iulius,* a state-recognized and sponsored cult, whereas noncitizens could offer the living Augustus divine honors in forms similar to those of Hellenistic ruler cult.[33] Gradually an organization developed to administer the province-wide cult and the temple at Pergamum. Known as the *koinon,* or "league," of Asia, it consisted of an assembly of notables from the different cities of the province, and it selected annually one of its members to serve as the high priest of the imperial cult.[34]

Augustus died in A.D. 14; his widow, Livia, and his successor, Tiberius, quickly worked to deify him as he himself had deified his adopted father, Julius Caesar. This brought Roman practice more closely in line with Hellenistic practice, where kings had received divine honors while living but generally were not formally enrolled—by their successors—among the number of state-recognized gods until after their deaths. The legendary story of Romulus's apotheosis and the recent example of Julius Caesar provided Roman precedents. In Rome and most western provinces the strict distinction between honoring the emperor's *genius* during life but worshipping him only after his death was generally maintained. While local cults in the East did not always make this distinction, the growing roster of deified imperial figures led to more temples, festivals, and cults. By the end of the century, for instance, there were municipal temples (local, city-sponsored cult centers as opposed to province-wide cults) of the *Sebastoi* (Greek,

---

[33] Dio, 51.20.6–9. See also Tacitus, *Annales,* 4.37, and the discussion of Friesen, *Imperial Cults and the Apocalypse of John,* 25–27, and Ferguson, *Backgrounds of Early Christianity,* 194–95.

[34] Friesen, *Imperial Cults and the Apocalypse of John,* 41–43. Price, "ruler-cult," in *Oxford Classical Dictionary,* 62–63.

"the Augusti") in Ephesus, the largest city of the province, and of the Julio-Claudian family in Aphrodisias, a much smaller city.[35]

Details of how imperial sacrifice and other aspects of ruler cult were carried out in the first century are sparse. Surviving inscriptions suggest that more often than not sacrifices were performed *for* the emperor rather than *to* the emperor, and these were almost always done in conjunction with the worship of the established gods of the community in order to seek the health and safety of the emperor and his family. Libations were poured out in honor of the emperor and ritual cakes, incense, and sometimes even an animal sacrifice were burned, often in front of statues of the emperor and his deified predecessors.[36] More frequently attested, and perhaps more significant, were imperial festivals, which seem to have been well-attended and popular public celebrations, but once again these seem to be as much *in honor of* the emperor as performances *to* him. In addition to sacrifices, imperial festivals consisted of processions, games, and feasts that not only honored Rome and the emperor but were also manifestations of local community pride.[37] When these were held with a specific focus on an imperial event, such as a birthday or an anniversary, the gods that shared the emperor's honor were his deified predecessors, thereby making the focus on the living figure somewhat less blatant.

The Requirements of Imperial Cult

While evidence for the practice of imperial cult is somewhat sparse, little also survives to indicate to what extent participation in imperial cult was considered obligatory in the first century. With

---

[35] The evidence for these two cult centers is almost entirely epigraphical and in the form of surviving architecture. Neither is mentioned in the surviving literary sources. See Friesen, *Imperial Cults and the Apocalypse of John*, 43–52, 77–95.

[36] Price, "ruler-cult," in *Oxford Classical Dictionary*, 210–15.

[37] Ibid., 101–14.

the exception of the temple that the emperor Gaius (popularly known as Caligula, who ruled A.D. 37–41) instructed be built to him in Miletus, known imperial temples were constructed on the initiative of local communities.[38] When the emperor died, Miletus dropped the project, much as Jerusalem was spared the megalomaniacal and incendiary demand to install a statue of Gaius in the Jewish temple. Just as the building of imperial temples was voluntary, involvement in imperial cult at the temples or in imperial festivals in the various cities of the provinces also seems to have been largely voluntary.

Indeed, there is not clear evidence that imperial cult was *required* before the reign of Trajan (A.D. 96–117), when correspondence between Trajan and Pliny, the governor of Bithynia, which neighbored Asia, revealed that offering prayers, incense, and wine before a statue of the emperor could be used as a test to reveal whether a suspected Christian was, in fact, someone unwilling to participate in this basic act of imperial cult.[39] Significantly, Pliny's letter to Trajan reveals that the image of the emperor was set up with the statues of the other gods, suggesting that the test presented accorded to a general pattern of imperial cult known from the first century—that worship offered to an emperor was almost always done in connection with other, established gods.[40]

While not worshipping the gods of a community could be considered atheism, at times that act was viewed as a crime, even if it was not regularly prosecuted. Since the time of Julius Caesar, Roman law exempted Jews from many legal obligations, including compulsory involvement in state cults outside of their ancestral

---

[38] Dio, 59.28.1.

[39] Pliny, *Epistles*, 10.96–97. See G. K. Beale, *The Book of Revelation: A Commentary on the Greek Text*, The International Greek Testament Commentary (Grand Rapids, Mich.: Eerdmans, 1999), 5.

[40] Duncan Fishwick, "Pliny and the Christians: The Rites *ad imaginem principis*," *American Journal of Ancient History* 9 (1984): 124–26.

religion.⁴¹ Consequently, Jews would have been exempted from any requirements for participating in imperial cult directly. Instead, following a custom that began during Jerusalem's domination by successive Hellenistic dynasties, Jews sacrificed *for* the emperor in their temple according to their own rites.⁴² This practice ceased when the First Jewish Revolt began in A.D. 66. When the Romans destroyed the temple in A.D. 70, all Jewish sacrifice ceased. This left the Jewish community in an ambiguous position, but because Judaism remained a legal religion and the Jews' legal exemptions remained intact even after the end of the revolt, there is no evidence that Jews were ever required to participate in imperial cult.

As long as the Romans viewed the Christian movement as a sect or faction of Judaism, Christians benefited from legal protections accorded to the Jews. While it is unclear that anyone was required, at least by the imperial government, to participate in imperial cult and festivals, two factors made it increasingly difficult for Christians to evade the suspicion of their neighbors who chose to express their loyalty to Rome in this way. First was the Christian view that the sacrificial death of Jesus Christ ended the practice of animal sacrifice. While Christians claimed that they continued to *pray* for the emperor and the state (Romans 13:1–7; 1 Peter 2:13–14), unlike Jews they could not openly demonstrate this loyalty in the external and culturally expected form of sacrifice.⁴³ Second, at some point after the fall of Jerusalem, the early rabbinic movement in Judaism fostered a clear break between Judaism and Christianity with the so-called *birkhat ha-minim,* a confessional test that could

---

⁴¹ Josephus, *AJ,* 14.10.1–8.

⁴² Price, "ruler-cult," in *Oxford Classical Dictionary,* 220. The only emperor who seems to have questioned this alternative practice was the aforementioned Gaius, who demanded that Jews sacrifice *to* him and then almost incited a rebellion in Judea by planning to install his statue in the Jerusalem temple. His assassination in A.D. 41 forestalled the crisis. Josephus, *AJ,* 18.8.1–9. Philo, *Embassy to Gaius,* 114–19.

⁴³ Price, "ruler-cult," in *Oxford Classical Dictionary,* 221.

be used to force "heretics" like the Christians out of the synagogue, making it clear that Jewish exemptions in matters of religion did not apply to them.[44]

Still, while broad assumptions have often been made about the requirements of imperial cult—such as the assumption that it was a capital offense to not participate—this maximalist position is not yet clearly established by the first century evidence. Instead, it is more likely that growing local opposition to Christianity would sometimes exploit the reluctance of Christians to participate in civic festivals and cult—including but not limited to imperial cult—to find reasons to attack individual Christians.

Interpretative Approaches to Revelation

Although there are many ways of interpreting Revelation and its visions, four major schools of interpretation are useful. The first is the so-called *preterist* approach. Meaning "past" or "already having happened," the preterist school assumes that some or all of the events described had already happened at the time of composition, and the text is seeking to explain the significance of these events to those who had suffered or experienced them, revealing how they fit into God's plan. Another approach, the *historicist* school, also seeks to put the events into a historical context but seeks to understand them as future events for the author and his original audience. In other words, many of the prophesied events were in the future for John and the seven churches, but some of them have already been fulfilled one or more times in our past. The *futurist* school assumes that most of the events have yet to be experienced; that is, they are in the future of both the original and a modern audience. A fourth school, the *idealist,* does not see the visions and prophecies as necessarily referring to specific events in the past or future but rather

---

[44] Ferguson, *Backgrounds of Early Christianity,* 461–62.

as symbolic representations of the kind of things that happen to the people of God in every age.

Interestingly the dispensationalist approach of Doctrine and Covenants 77:7, which describes the meanings of the events seen in the seven seals (Revelation 6:1–11:19), assumes a preterist interpretation for some, a historicist for others, and a futurist for the last, suggesting that LDS interpretation takes an eclectic approach. Even for those events from earlier dispensations that may have already received their initial fulfillment at the time that John wrote, the symbolism of the prophecies can still be applied to subsequent events, making the idealist school still of value. Thus when examining passages of Revelation that seem to make allusion to imperial cult—notably the beasts of Revelation 13, the great harlot, and the beast upon which she rides in Revelation 17—readers should keep in mind that what they symbolize may have already taken place or was about to happen at the time John wrote. Nevertheless, these warnings can apply symbolically to every age and may yet find application in our own near future.

The Problem of Dating Revelation

While accurately dating John's Revelation might seem essential to understanding its message, particularly if taking a predominantly preterist approach to the text, significant difficulties arise in attempting to identify a precise timeframe. Because John gives no clear chronology in his text, scholars have made deductions based largely on internal references. Two possibilities traditionally present themselves: the dating of John's Revelation is either during the reign of the Roman emperor Nero (A.D. 54–68) or during that of Domitian (A.D. 81–96), with the more popular possibility being the Domitianic date.

Those who accept a Neronian date point primarily to intratextual evidence.⁴⁵ These pieces of evidence range from general to specific. In general terms, one may look to the various mentions of persecution—such as John's seeming exile to the island of Patmos, general references to martyrdom, and the particular reference to the death of a Christian named Antipas (see Revelation 1:9; 2:13; 6:9)—and try to associate Revelation with known incidents of Christian persecution within the Roman Empire under Nero.⁴⁶ The first known instance of any official mistreatment of Christians in the Roman Empire certainly occurred during Nero's reign. In 64 A.D. a fire swept through Rome, devastating vast sections of the city. According to Tacitus, Nero was rumored to have started the devastating fire. In order to deflect the blame, he singled out Christians residing in Rome. Some of them "confessed." With information provided by those who confessed, Nero arrested a larger group. As punishment, some were thrown to dogs, others were crucified, and still others were burned.⁴⁷ This is, however, the only known occasion of Christian abuse under Nero, and it appears to have been limited geographically to Rome and chronologically to the period immediately following the fire of A.D. 64. In other words, Nero's

---

⁴⁵ For the view that Revelation can be dated near the reign of Nero, see Albert A. Bell Jr., "The Date of John's Apocalypse: The Evidence of Some Roman Historians Reconsidered," *New Testament Studies* 25, no. 1 (October 1978): 93–102; J. Christian Wilson, "The Problem of the Domitianic Date of Revelation," *New Testament Studies* 39 Issue 4 (October 1993): 597–98; Thomas B. Slater, "Dating the Apocalypse to John," *Biblica* 84 (2003): 252–58.

⁴⁶ Early tradition held that John was exiled or relegated to Patmos as part of an official, anti-Christian action. See the discussion of Robert H. Mounce, *The Book of Revelation* (Grand Rapids, Mich.: Eerdmans, 1977), 54–55. Despite the probability of this position, it is interesting to note that the expression "for the word of God, and for the testimony of Jesus Christ" in Revelation 1:9 *could* be taken to mean that he was led there independently by God for the purpose of bearing witness.

⁴⁷ Tacitus, *Annales,* 15.44. It remains uncertain whether the Christians confessed to starting the fire or to being Christians; it is equally uncertain whether the confessions were extracted under torture or not. Compare Eusebius, *Ecclesiastical History,* 2.24–26; 3.17–20. Eusebius here describes what he considered to be the two periods of significant persecution: under Nero and Domitian, respectively.

mistreatment of Christians did not extend to the churches of Asia, and one wonders whether this event centered in Rome is likely to be the persecution referred to in Revelation.[48]

As to specific internal evidence, scholars look to the five fallen kings of Revelation 17:9–10 and interpret them as Nero's predecessors, thus dating Revelation to Nero's time.[49] This presents the difficulty of assuming that Julius Caesar is to be counted as the first of the emperors, a position that Julius never presumed for himself and one that more appropriately belongs to Caesar Augustus.[50] One particular piece of evidence, the identification of the number 666 with the name *Nerōn Kaisar,* favors and is perhaps the strongest argument for the early date. By this argument, 666, the number of the beast (Revelation 13:18), can, by the application of *gematria* (whereby letters may also function as numbers, as they do in Greek and Latin), apply to Nero. Brown notes that "the Hebrew consonants transliterating the Greek form of the name Nero Caesar total to 666."[51] While this piece of evidence seems indisputable, there was a myth of a possible miraculous return of Nero after his death—*Nero redivivus.*[52] Indeed, the Roman authors Juvenal and Pliny the Younger both regarded Domitian as a second Nero![53]

This leads us to consider the possibility that the text should be dated to the reign of Domitian. The arguments for the Domitianic

---

[48] It is even unclear whether the event ought to be interpreted as a religious persecution of Christians, since Nero seems to have singled them out because they were unpopular rather than because of their religious views or affiliation. Nero, it should be noted, seems not to have been as keen on imperial cult as some later emperors. See Raymond E. Brown, *An Introduction to the New Testament* (New York: Doubleday, 1997), 805.

[49] See Bell, "The Date of John's Apocalypse," 99–100.

[50] Brown, *Introduction to the New Testament,* 805.

[51] Ibid., 793. See also 793n41, where Brown mentions the ancient variant 616, which would yield the Hebrew transliteration of the *Latin* form of Nero Caesar.

[52] Beale, *Book of Revelation,* 17–18, 24.

[53] Juvenal, *Satires,* 4.38; Pliny the Younger, *Panegyric,* 53.3–4.

date are as follows: First, and perhaps most important, Domitian's is the time assigned by Irenaeus. Specifically, Irenaeus said that the Apocalypse was "seen not such a long time ago, but almost in our own generation, at the end of the reign of Domitian."[54] As Irenaeus had been a disciple of Polycarp, and Polycarp, according to tradition, had personally known the Apostle John, this makes Irenaeus the earliest Christian author whose opinion on the dating of Revelation has survived, and one who was only one generation removed from John himself.[55]

Second, there is the view that John was on Patmos, the presumed location of the Revelation's composition, during the reign of Domitian. Clement of Alexandria claims that John moved to Ephesus from Patmos *after* the death of Domitian.[56]

The condition of the churches in Asia, to which John addresses his comments, is another argument advanced for a Domitianic date; the view is that the congregations of Asia had undergone notable decline since the time that Asia had been the focus of Paul's missionary labors. If Paul died in the A.D. 60s, as is presumed, some believe that the churches under his guidance could not have deteriorated so quickly after his death and during Nero's reign.[57] Furthermore, some believe that Revelation hints at the physical destruction of the temple in Jerusalem (Revelation 11:2) by Rome (symbolized by Babylon), an event that postdates Nero but would have been realized by the time of Domitian.[58]

Finally, some scholars argue that imperial claims to divine

---

[54] *Against Heresies,* 5.30.3.

[55] Against this, Slater comments that Irenaeus, writing a century after Domitian, is perhaps *not* a reliable external witness; see Slater, "Dating the Apocalypse," 252–58.

[56] Clement of Alexandria, *Salvation of the Rich,* 42; compare Eusebius, *Ecclesiastical History,* 3.23.6.

[57] See, for example, Robert L. Thomas, *Revelation 1–7: An Exegetical Commentary* (Chicago: Moody, 1992), 107, 22.

[58] Beale, *Book of Revelation,* 16–27.

honors had become more frequent and insistent during Domitian's reign, producing pressure on nonadherents to conform to the requirements of imperial cult.[59] In addition, Domitian is the other emperor besides Nero who is said to have initiated persecution of Christians, and on a wider scale than Nero. While the assumption of *empire-wide* persecution is convincingly disputed, there is still good reason to believe that Domitian's investigations into what he regarded as dangerous deviations from the state religion were more widespread than Nero's and reached to Asia Minor and Palestine. Thus they likely attracted the attention of the author of the Apocalypse and warranted a recollection of Nero and his localized ferocity.[60] Indeed, Domitian may have reminded others of Nero, as he did Juvenal and Pliny, and John may have intentionally linked the two emperors in his symbolic representation.

Regardless of the dating of Revelation, its message and the circumstances it describes must have had meaning for its original audience, even if the fulfillment of its prophecies were yet to be realized. This is particularly true since one of the purposes of apocalyptic literature was to provide comfort and guidance to an audience that was experiencing or about to experience a crisis, as the seven churches clearly were.[61]

Accordingly, modern readers must keep in mind that many of the events described in Revelation may have several applications or interpretations, in which case the realization or fulfillment most

---

[59] Brown, *Introduction to the New Testament*, 805–6.

[60] Mounce, *Book of Revelation*, 15–21; Beale, *Book of Revelation*, 12–16, 27. For the argument against an empire-wide persecution inaugurated by Domitian, see Leonard L. Thompson, *The Book of Revelation: Apocalypse and Empire* (New York: Oxford University Press 1990) 95–115; compare Beale, *Book of Revelation*, 13–14. For a brief, but thoughtful, discussion of the persecution under Domitian and the likelihood that his actions may be referenced in Revelation, see Brown, *Introduction to the New Testament*, 805–9.

[61] See Lars Hartman, "The Functions of Some So-Called Apocalyptic Timetables," *New Testament Studies* 22, no. 1 (October 1975): 1–14.

closely contemporary to the text's composition can provide guidance, or a model, to how the message can be applied in subsequent periods.

Reading the Beasts of Revelation 13 and 17

As we look to the description of the beast in Revelation 13:1, it is readily evident that it is reminiscent of chapter 7 of Daniel's apocalyptic text. The beasts therein are described thus:

"The first was like a lion, and had eagle's wings . . . a second, like a bear . . . and lo another, like a leopard . . . and behold a fourth beast, dreadful and terrible, and strong exceedingly; and it had great iron teeth: it devoured and brake in pieces, and stamped the residue with the feet of it: and it was diverse from all the beasts that were before it; and it had ten horns" (Daniel 7:4–7).

Daniel sees the thrones of the final beast cast down, slain, and given to be burned with fire (Daniel 7:11). Traditionally these beasts are interpreted as successive earthly kingdoms, all eventually giving way to the kingdom of God.[62] More specifically, the fourth and culminating beast in Daniel is read as embodying either the rule of Alexander the Great (the beast itself) and the Hellenistic kings who succeeded him (the ten horns), or as Rome.[63] Whether Daniel's final beast symbolizes the Hellenistic rulers or Rome, it denotes an earthly kingdom greater than any that had preceded it.

Scholars agree that the beast in chapter 13 of Revelation is meant to recollect Daniel's fourth beast: "and [I] saw a beast rise up out of the sea, having seven heads and ten horns, and upon his horns ten crowns, and upon his heads the name of blasphemy

---

[62] Steve Gregg, ed., *Revelation, Four Views: A Parallel Commentary* (Nashville: Thomas Nelson, 1997), 276–77. Compare Brown, *Introduction to the New Testament*, 792.

[63] For the beast as Alexander, see "Daniel 7," *New Oxford Annotated Bible*. For the beast as Rome, see, among others, Gregg, *Revelation*, 276, and Brown, *Introduction to the New Testament*, 792.

(Revelation 13:1)."[64] The repetition of the ten horns can be no accident. John is evoking therewith the strongest of the Gentile powers described by Daniel. Hence, if the symbolism is to be decoded, John's referent must be among the most powerful of his own day. John's first beast comes from the sea. Brown notes that from the perspective of the Asian churches, to which the Revelation was addressed, Rome came from across the sea to the western coast of Asia. The interpretation is confirmed in Revelation 13:1, which describes the seven heads of the beast as seven mountains—or the famous seven hills of Rome.[65] But John's Rome is something even more fearful than the dominant creature in Daniel's vision: "And the beast which I saw was like unto a leopard, and his feet were as the feet of a bear, and his mouth as the mouth of a lion: and the dragon gave him his power, and his seat, and great authority (Revelation 13:2)." The beast of Revelation includes elements of all four of Daniel's beasts, symbolizing, as Brown notes, "that the Roman Empire . . . is as evil as all the others combined."[66] This image gains additional force if we assume that Daniel's final beast represents, in fact, not Rome but instead the Macedonian world conqueror, Alexander the Great, and his successors. Revelation may thereby assert that Rome exceeds in territory, power, and wickedness all other kingdoms of this earth previously prophesied, even the famous empire of Alexander.

One of the seven heads of the beast appears wounded "as it were wounded to death" (Revelation 13:3), but the deadly wound was healed. One wonders if this may refer to the suicide of Nero in June A.D. 68. While Nero did not recover, there may have been a presumption—or even hope—that the entire Roman imperial system would collapse with the death of the final Julio-Claudian

---

[64] Gregg, *Revelation*, 276–78.
[65] Brown, *Introduction to the New Testament*, 792.
[66] Ibid.

emperor. This, however, was not to be. In that sense, the deadly wound was healed, and Rome continued dominant for a time.

The beast is further described as being worshipped, speaking blasphemies, and having power "over all kindreds, and tongues, and nations" (Revelation 13:5–7). The worship and the blasphemies might refer to emperor worship and the local imposition of ruler cult in the territory of Asia to which John speaks. Certainly provincial cults to the emperors are attested in Pergamum, Smyrna, and arguably in Ephesus.[67]

The second beast of the text comes from the earth. He has "two horns like a lamb, and he spake as a dragon" (Revelation 13:11). The phrase "up out of the earth" suggests that this beast is native to the vicinity of the churches of Asia. This beast is dangerous, because it is not what it appears. While it appears innocent as "a lamb," it is, in fact, an agent of the devil ("spake as a dragon"). This second beast promotes the worship of the first and performs signs and wonders, all of which are indicative of the panoply of imperial cult (Revelation 13:12).[68] It is perhaps better described as the imposition of that worship, as is explicitly said in verse 15: "And he had power to give life unto the image of the beast, that the image of the beast should both speak, and cause that as many as would not worship the image of the beast should be killed." Interestingly, the task of guaranteeing the worship of the first beast is left to the seemingly innocent native beast. This may well describe local authorities and structures—such as the provincial assembly or *koinon*,

---

[67] For the temple in Ephesus, see S. Friesen, "Ephesus: Key to a Vision in Revelation," *Biblical Archaeology Review* 19 (1993): 24–37.

[68] See S. J. Scherrer, "Signs and Wonders in the Imperial Cult: A New Look at a Roman Religious Institution in Light of Rev 13:13–15," *Journal of Biblical Literature* 103, no. 4 (1984): 599–610, who reads the signs and wonders as part of the ceremonial array of emperor worship. Compare Larry Kreitzer, "Apotheosis of the Roman Emperor," *Biblical Archaeologist* 53, no. 4 (1990): 210–17; and J. Nelson Kraybill, *Imperial Cult and Commerce in John's Apocalypse* (London: Sheffield Academic Press, 1996); Brown, *Introduction to the New Testament*, 792.

its elected high priest of the imperial cult, and the Asiarchs—that not only tolerated but also promoted and enforced the practice of emperor worship.[69]

Finally, in chapter 13 of Revelation, the number of the beast is given. As specified above, this number has been interpreted as a reference to the emperor Nero Caesar. It might, however, signify Nero not merely as a specific Roman ruler but as a type of all Roman emperors and of all earthly kings.

Why would Nero be chosen as such a symbol? He was the first emperor known to have persecuted Christians, and, while his mistreatment of Christian scapegoats after the fire in Rome in A.D. 64 may have been brief and localized, it was also unusually violent.[70] As the first imperial figure to be guilty of such a crime, he became the representative evil ruler; the empire he once ruled was the representative earthly kingdom doomed to give way before the kingdom of God.

If the Apocalypse was meant to offer any consolation to the Saints to whom John addressed his remarks anciently, one must consider a preterist reading of the text, which yields a pronouncement of the doom against Babylon (Rome). It is to be thrown into the sea, causing great sorrow among those who have been intimately involved with the corruption of the harlot.[71] Likewise, it will cause joy among those anticipating the arrival of the true king (and bridegroom).[72] The collapse of Babylon/Rome is vividly detailed (Revelation 17:1–19:10), and if one adopts an exclusively

---

[69] Undoubtedly local support of the imperial cult was done in exchange for some reward, including the favor of the emperor and the associated political and material advancement.

[70] Tacitus, *Annales,* 15.44.

[71] In other words, those who have enthusiastically, or even tacitly, complied with the requirements of the imperial cult or any other idolatrous acts.

[72] The image of the marriage between the Lamb and his virtuous bride is in sharp contrast to the image of the harlot drunk on the blood of the Saints.

preterist interpretation, this eventual downfall of the Roman Empire and the elimination of emperor worship is the comforting promise to the Christians of John's own time.

Implications for a Modern Reading of Revelation

But how might the richly evocative images of the beasts and of their defeat become meaningful to a modern reader? Applying an idealist reading—which draws its basic elements and images from the preterist interpretation—to the images of the beasts and their actions provides a real-time way of interpreting current events. The preterist interpretation established the beast from the sea as the overwhelming force of the Roman Empire that sought to be "worshipped," literally through the forms of the imperial cult but more broadly in the sense of seeking to control the hearts and minds of the people. Likewise, the beast from the land represented those local aristocracies that collaborated with and supported Rome's efforts to cement her subjects' loyalty through imperial cult. By taking an idealist reading, however, one can interpret the first beast not only as a symbol of Rome and its rulers and the second beast not only as a symbol of consenting supporters of Rome's blasphemies and vices but as symbols of any earthly kingdom and of any earthly influences. Thus, an idealist approach allows a modern application that identifies the beasts as any political system, any social construct, any religion or philosophy, or any individual or influence that invites Christians to have any god before the one, true God.

The beast and the whore of Revelation 17 have a powerful resonance with the image of the great and abominable church spoken of in 1 Nephi 14:9–17, which is likewise overthrown by the wrath of God. While the mother of harlots in the Book of Mormon seems to be ultimately overthrown at a specific future moment, what she represents has received a useful idealist interpretation in Latter-day Saint commentary: "The titles *church of the devil* and *great and abominable church* are used to identify *all churches or organizations of whatever name or nature—whether political, philosophical, educational, economic, social, fraternal, civic, or religious—which are designed to take men on a course that leads away from God and his laws and thus from salvation in the kingdom of God.* . . . Any church or organization of any kind whatever which satisfies the innate religious longings of man and keeps him from coming to the saving truths of Christ and his gospel is therefore not of God."[73]

Accordingly, just as the two beasts of Revelation 14 represent the idolatrous powers of worldliness and those who support them, the harlot on the back of the great beast in Revelation 17 represents all organizations and philosophies that lead away from the true and living God.

If one considers the beasts of Revelation together with the satanic dragon, the text presents a trinity of beasts surely meant to be a perversion of the godly trinity. Just as the second beast with the horns like a lamb "is an evil parody of Christ," the beastly triad is an evil parody of the Godhead. The most serious threats to the fidelity of the Saints are those that have the appearance of innocence. But the Saints can and will overcome. The great message of Revelation is the promise of the victory of Christ and His followers over those animal counterfeits.

In the concluding chapters, Christ is depicted as a great warrior and, significantly, as "KING OF KINGS, AND LORD OF LORDS" (Revelation 19:16), recalling the many allusions to earthly kings and kingdoms, none of which can stand against the true King. He shall conquer the beasts and the forces they represent and finally their master. The harlot is cast down into the sea, but the faithful have a better fate: "I Jesus have sent mine angel to testify unto you these things in the churches. I am the root and the

---

[73] Bruce R. McConkie, *Mormon Doctrine,* 2d ed. (Salt Lake City: Bookcraft, 1966), 137–38; emphasis added.

offspring of David, and the bright and morning star. And the Spirit and the bride say, Come. And let him that heareth say, Come. And let him that is athirst come. And whosoever will, let him take the water of life freely" (Revelation 22:16–17).

XII.

THE END OF THE EARLY CHURCH

KENT P. JACKSON

Now the Spirit speaketh expressly, that in the latter times some shall depart from the faith, giving heed to seducing spirits, and doctrines of devils

1 Timothy 4:1

Latter-day Saints believe that the Early Christian Church, established by Jesus and led after His Resurrection by Apostles, did not last long. We believe that an apostasy took place within the Church to the extent that Jesus withdrew His acknowledgment from it, and it wandered from then on without Apostles to guide it in His name. Apostasy is a conscious choice, not an accident or something that happens to someone. It is a decision by a member of a group to withdraw from that group and oppose it. "The Apostasy" was not a time period but an event. We sometimes use the term to represent the era from the days of the Apostles to the days of Joseph Smith. But in doing so, we are blaming victims for what was done by others who lived very early in the Church's history. As the New Testament demonstrates and as Latter-day Saints understand well, the Church of Jesus Christ is led by Apostles. Without Apostles, there is no Church of Jesus Christ. This is important as we consider the fact that by the end of the first century—fewer than seven decades after the life of

Jesus—there were no more Apostles. In fact, we have no evidence of new Apostles being called after A.D. 50, just twenty years after Jesus' time. Something must have happened—very quickly and very dramatically—that resulted in the end of the early Church.

In speaking of the events that led to the fall of the early Church, Latter-day Saints sometimes cite 2 Thessalonians 2:3. In that passage, Paul foretells that "a falling away" would take place. Unfortunately, the translation in the King James Version, "a falling away," is flawed on more than one level, and the choice of words has influenced how many Latter-day Saints have understood the way the Apostasy worked. The Greek word used by Paul is *apostasia,* of which the English word *apostasy* is an obvious derivative. The word means "rebellion," "mutiny," "revolt," or "revolution." It is used in ancient contexts with reference to uprisings against established authority.[1] In contrast, the words "a falling away" suggest a gentle drifting, not a revolution, distorting the true nature of the process that Paul foretold. The Apostasy was a conscious rebellion of members of the early Church against the teachings and authority of the Apostles. An additional problem with the King James translation is the translators' use of the indefinite article *a* before "falling away." Paul's Greek original has the definite article, *the,* suggesting strongly that *the* Apostasy already was a point of reference in the minds of Paul's readers and he was mentioning something they had heard about before.[2] If we envision the Apostasy as something akin to a mutiny on the high seas, we will have a good image of the nature of *apostasia.* In the process of commandeering a ship, mutineers first remove the leaders and replace them with others of their own choosing. But instead of traveling under new

---

[1] William F. Arndt, F. Wilbur Gingrich, and Walter Bauer, *A Greek-English Lexicon of the New Testament and Other Early Christian Literature,* 2d ed. (Chicago: University of Chicago Press, 1979).

[2] Other translations render *apostasia* in 2 Thessalonians 2:3 as follows: "the rebellion" (ESV, NIV, NRSV) and "the Great Revolt" (NJB).

management to the original port of call, they change direction and head to a new destination. This image is how the New Testament attests to the Apostasy.

Restoring the Fulness

The Restoration of the fulness of the gospel through the Prophet Joseph Smith proves the Apostasy. John the Baptist and Peter, James, and John—men known from the New Testament—came to Joseph Smith and conferred on him the priesthoods they once held, which would have been unnecessary had those priesthoods already been on earth. They were followed by other biblical characters, each in turn giving the latter-day Prophet powers and authorities entrusted to them anciently and now placed in the care of The Church of Jesus Christ of Latter-day Saints. God gave Joseph Smith new scriptures because truths known in ancient times had become lost. A new Church was organized, identified by the word of God as "the only true and living church upon the face of the whole earth" (D&C 1:30). And whole volumes of revelation came to Joseph Smith to enlighten God's people for the latter days. All these revelations of truths and powers attest to the fact that they had been lost anciently. The Apostasy is the reason why The Church of Jesus Christ of Latter-day Saints exists.

When Jesus appeared to Joseph Smith in the First Vision in 1820, He told him that "all religious denominations were believing in incorrect doctrines, and that none of them was acknowledged of God as His church and kingdom." Joseph Smith said, "I was expressly commanded to 'go not after them,' at the same time receiving a promise that the fulness of the gospel should at some future time be made known unto me."[3] We must be careful to distinguish what these words say from what they do not

---

[3] Joseph Smith, "Church History," *Times and Seasons* 3, no. 9 (March 1, 1842): 707.

say. Jesus told Joseph Smith that all denominations taught incorrect doctrine, but He did not say that all the doctrine they taught was incorrect. Indeed, through the Apostasy, the Christian Church was lost, but Christianity survived. Many Christians already had the gospel before the First Vision, but they did not have what the Book of Mormon calls the *fulness* of the gospel (e.g., 1 Nephi 10:14; 15:13). People all over the world were Christians because they had faith in Jesus Christ, repented of their sins through faith in His atoning sacrifice, were baptized, and sought spiritual rebirth through the reception of the Holy Ghost. They followed these first principles and ordinances because of the greatest legacy of the ancient Apostles—the New Testament—which the Book of Mormon calls "the records of the twelve apostles of the Lamb" (1 Nephi 13:41). The New Testament preserved the fundamental messages of Christianity, so that all who put trust in its words were blessed and influenced for righteousness, despite the absence of Jesus' authorized Church.

But the *fulness* of the gospel, the real "power of God unto salvation" (Romans 1:16), could only be made available through the Restoration. New scriptures needed to be revealed so the gospel could be taught in purity and plainness. Jesus' Church needed to be restored because it alone is the vehicle in which God's priesthood resides through which ordinances can be performed validly. Honorable Christians today are Christians by intent and belief, but they need Jesus' restored Church so their righteous desires can be further empowered. The priesthood is necessary for revelation to exist in the Church. Joseph Smith taught that the Melchizedek Priesthood "is the channel through which all knowledge, doctrine, the plan of salvation and every important matter is revealed from heaven. . . . It is the channel through which the Almighty commenced revealing his glory at the beginning . . . and through which he will make known his purposes to the end of time."[4] Thus the keys of the priesthood are the keys of revelation, and the restored Church is necessary because in it, revelation continues to God's people, and the doctrines are maintained and taught in purity by those He has called—prophets, seers, revelators, Apostles—and in turn by those whom they have called, taught, and sent forth.

New Testament Prophecies of Apostasy

Perhaps the most remarkable witness of the apostasy of New Testament Christianity is the New Testament itself. Its writers prophesied that apostasy would take place and have a grave effect on their work. Those prophecies are the best place to start as we endeavor to understand what happened to the early Church. They are important not only because they show that Christ and the Apostles anticipated the Apostasy but especially because they shed light on the nature of it and the process that brought it about. Space allows for only a brief outline of some relevant verses.[5]

Matthew 24:5, 9–11 (c. A.D. 34). "Many" false Christs "shall deceive many" (24:5), and "many false prophets shall rise, and shall deceive many" (24:11). The repetition of the word *many,* modifying both the perpetrators and the victims in each of these prophecies, illustrates the seriousness of Jesus' words. Further, in the phrase "then shall many be offended" (24:10), "offended" translates the Greek verb *skandalizō,* which means to "trip,"

---

[4] Andrew F. Ehat and Lyndon W. Cook, eds., *The Words of Joseph Smith: The Contemporary Accounts of the Nauvoo Discourses of the Prophet Joseph* (Provo: Religious Studies Center, Brigham Young University, 1980), 38–39.

[5] The following is based on a longer discussion in my "'Watch and Remember': The New Testament and the Great Apostasy," in *By Study and Also by Faith: Essays in Honor of Hugh W. Nibley on the Occasion of His Eightieth Birthday,* ed. John M. Lundquist and Stephen D. Ricks, 2 vols. (Salt Lake City: Deseret Book and Provo: The Foundation for Ancient Research and Mormon Studies), 1:81–95. Unless otherwise noted, all biblical quotations are from the KJV. In addition to the KJV, I have included some passages from the following good English translations: NIV, NJB, and NRSV.

expressing, in a religious context, the idea of giving up the faith: "Many will turn away from the faith" (NIV, 24:10).

2 Thessalonians 2:1–12 (c. A.D. 51). To the Thessalonian Saints, Paul wrote that before the day of the Lord, the *apostasia* would take place (2:3)—"the rebellion" (NIV, NRSV), "the Great Revolt" (NJB). Satan—the "man of sin," "the son of perdition"—would come to the fore (2:3) and would sit in God's place as though he were God (2:4). That "mystery of iniquity" was being held back until God would withdraw the power that restrained it (2:6–8). Whether that protective power was the apostleship or some other act of divine intervention, Paul's words seem to suggest that not much time would elapse before that restraint would be withdrawn. Paul asked, "Remember ye not, that, when I was yet with you, I told you these things?" (2:5). These words make it clear that they had already been warned.

Acts 20:29–31 (c. A.D. 58). When Paul met with the priesthood leaders of Asia for the last time, he foretold that "grievous wolves" would "enter in among" the Church, and they would not spare the flock (20:29). "Of your own selves," he said, men would arise, teaching "perverse things" in order to "draw away disciples after them" (20:30). Paul concluded by reminding them that they had been warned before: "Therefore watch, and remember, that by the space of three years I ceased not to warn every one night and day with tears" (20:31).

1 Timothy 4:1–3 (c. A.D. 63). "In the latter times some shall depart from the faith, giving heed to seducing spirits, and doctrines of devils" (4:1). The language makes it clear that what Paul saw was not an abandonment of religion but a shifting of loyalties—from "the faith" to a false faith. He gave as examples of false teachings a prohibition against marriage and unauthorized dietary restrictions (4:3). Paul asked Timothy to remind "the brethren" of these warnings (4:6).

2 Timothy 4:3–4 (c. A.D. 67). In his final letter, Paul wrote of the time in which Church members would reject "sound doctrine" (4:3). They would still have "itching ears" for religion; they just would not want *true* religion. Instead, they would seek out teachers after their own liking (4:3). They would "turn away their ears from the truth" and turn to "fables" (4:4). "To suit their own desires, they will gather around them a great number of teachers to say what their itching ears want to hear. They will turn their ears away from the truth and turn aside to myths" (NIV, 4:3–4).

2 Peter 2:1–3 (c. A.D. 67). Peter wrote to members of the Church that "there shall be false teachers among you" (2:1). Those teachers would "secretly introduce" (NIV) "damnable heresies" (2:1). "Many" would follow them (2:2), and as a result, "the way of truth" would be blasphemed (2:2). Thus, he wrote, they would "make merchandise of you" with false doctrine (2:3)—"feigned words," "stories they have made up" (NIV, 2:3).

Jude 1:4, 17–19 (c. A.D. 80). Jude wrote that there had been warnings long before about people infiltrating and perverting the faith (1:4). The Apostles warned, he said, of "mockers in the last time" (1: 18), which time had come.

Revelation 13:1–9 (c. A.D. 96). In the Apocalypse, John saw and recorded that Satan's beast would blaspheme against God and His work. He would make war against the Saints and would overcome them. He would have power over all the world, "over all kindreds, and tongues, and nations" (Revelation 13: 8).

1 John 2:18 (c. A.D. 98). John, perhaps in the last decade of the first century, wrote to remind his readers of prophecies they had heard before. In the "last time," "antichrist" would come in among them. He told them that they were then living in the time of fulfillment.

These prophecies were not the core message of the New Testament, and some of them are mentioned tangentially to make other points. Yet there are enough of them to make it clear that both Jesus and His Apostles knew that apostate influences would have a powerful effect on the Church, and some of them inform us that Church members had already been warned. The verses cited show the pattern of how the Apostasy would work: Church members would reject true doctrine, self-appointed teachers would come to the fore, and man-made religion would be introduced to replace what the Apostles had taught. Subsequent history shows that the Church did not survive the process intact.

Witnessing the Apostasy

Paul's prophecy in 1 Timothy 4:1–3 foretells apostasy in the "latter times" (Greek, *hysterois kairois*). Jude reminded his readers of prophecies that would take place in the "last time" (Greek, *eschatou chronou*), prophecies that were already coming to pass (Jude 1:17–18). Similarly, John wrote that he and his readers were then in the "last time"—or, more accurately, "last hour" (Greek, *eschatē hōra*), because a prophecy for that time was already being fulfilled—"whereby we know that it is the last time" (1 John 2:18). Jude and John knew that they were not living in the last days of the world's history, but it is clear that they knew they were living in the last days of the early Church. It is to those days that the New Testament prophecies above refer.

In the last generation of the early Church, the generation in which Jude and John wrote, it is obvious that things were not right in Christianity. But even in earlier decades, we see problems that were digging at the foundations of the Church. All of the New Testament letters, at least in part, were written to correct ideas and behaviors that if left unchecked would lead to greater problems in the future. By reading the letters in chronological order and in context, we see that in the earliest letters, the Apostles addressed issues that perhaps could be remedied by sound apostolic teaching. But very soon the doctrinal and behavioral aberrations they dealt with became very serious, showing that corrosive forces within the Church worked fast and were succeeding in damaging it severely. The latest letters show the greatest influence of apostasy in the Church. The New Testament recorded the Apostasy while it happened.

1 and 2 Thessalonians (c. A.D. 50–51). Paul's two letters to the Thessalonians reveal misunderstandings regarding the Second Coming of Jesus. In the first letter, we have a seemingly benign belief that those who are alive when that event takes place will have an advantage over those who have died (1 Thessalonians 4:13–17). But in the second letter, we see a belief that the "day of Christ" was "at hand" (2 Thessalonians 2:2–4), a notion the Thessalonian Saints had apparently acquired either by "spirit" or "word" or by a letter purporting to be from Paul. Paul identified the idea as a deception. His comments seem to suggest that already there were deliberate attempts to spread false doctrine.

Galatians (c. late 40s/mid-50s). Galatians presents evidence that some Church members were transforming their faith into a "Judaized" Christianity. They were bringing into the Church Jewish holidays (4:10), mandating circumcision (5:2–4; 6:12–13), and looking to the law of Moses for salvation (3:1–5; 4:21). Paul characterized these efforts as turning to "another gospel" under the influence of those who would "pervert the gospel of Christ" (1:6–7). He emphasized the authority of his calling and the doctrine he received by revelation (1:1, 8–9, 11–12), arguing against a circumcision faction (2:12) that endeavored to bewitch and trouble the Galatian Saints (3:1; 5:10, 12). These are clear indicators that there was serious trouble in the Church.

As in 2 Corinthians, these references from Galatians seem to suggest an organized effort among some Jewish Church members to counter the work of Paul and his teachings. We cannot tell to what degree Paul's letters and other exertions solved the problems, but we can be certain that without apostolic intervention, efforts like these would be disastrous for the Church.

James (c. A.D. mid-50s). Evident in James's letter is confusion regarding the relationship between faith and works (2:14–17, 26). It appears that some Church members, perhaps influenced by other teachers, had come to misunderstand the nature of works in the context of the gospel. As with all such matters addressed in the New Testament epistles, we have no way of knowing the response to the Apostles' corrective writings.

1 Corinthians (c. A.D. 56). Aberrant practices are readily apparent in 1 Corinthians. Paul contended against those who formed factions in the Church by playing favorites with leaders (1:10–16; 3:3–10; 11:18). The Corinthian Saints allowed a case of incest to go uncorrected (5:1–13), and they engaged in inappropriate observance of the sacrament (11:23–34). Each of these cases evoked pointed correction from Paul. Doctrinal problems apparent in the letter include distorted ideas concerning the gifts of the Spirit, which distorted ideas led the Corinthians to distorted behavior (14:1–14, 33), as well as to the teaching that Jesus did not rise from the dead and that there is no resurrection (15:1–58). In the simplest terms, a Christian was one who believed that Jesus had risen from the dead. Thus the idea that such had not taken place must be viewed as extremely serious and as existentially detrimental to the Church.

2 Corinthians (c. A.D. 57). Opposition to Paul himself was a major cause for the writing of 2 Corinthians (see especially chapters 11–12). It is apparent in this letter and in Galatians that there were outspoken critics of Paul within the Church who opposed his vision of the Christian faith and his efforts to promulgate it. Paul's letter is in part an *apologia* for himself and his message. He invoked his authority with strong language: "It is God who establishes us with you in Christ and has anointed us" (NRSV, 1:21), and "We are ambassadors for Christ, since God is making his appeal through us; we entreat you on behalf of Christ" (NRSV, 5:20). These assertions of authority were necessary, given the opposition Paul received from those who viewed themselves as superapostles

(11:5, 22–23; 12:11). He believed that his readers were in jeopardy, having been taught "another Jesus, whom we have not preached" (11:4) under the influence of "false apostles, deceitful workers, transforming themselves into the apostles of Christ" (11:13). Opposition to Paul, false apostles, another Jesus—all this within a quarter of a century of Jesus' ministry.

Colossians (c. A.D. 61). In Colossians we may be seeing the first evidences of a phenomenon that later blossomed into a movement called Gnosticism. Most of what we know of Gnosticism comes from sources a century or more after the days of the Apostles, so we understand it best in its fully developed form of later years. Gnosticism, an idea that had its roots in Platonic philosophy with its distinction between the material and spiritual worlds, was an aberrant Christian doctrine that taught that physical matter and everything associated with it was evil. Because God could not consist of matter or even be the creator of matter (matter being inherently evil), all material creation had to be looked upon as perverse. Some Gnostics believed in a chain of lower deities, each less holy than the one above. The lowest of these, the evil Jehovah of the Old Testament, created the material world.

In his letter to the Colossians, Paul contended with a doctrinal heresy that he neither named nor described. But the words he used to warn the Colossian Saints suggest that it shared similarities with what later became Gnosticism. Paul's emphasis on Christ's supremacy in the universe (1:16–19; 2:9–10) and his warning against the worship of "angels" (2:18; see also 1:15–2:23) seem to respond to a belief in lower deities and may reflect questions as to where Jesus fit in among the heavenly hierarchies. Paul gave a stern warning against accepting any doctrine that was different from the apostolic message that he had taught: "As ye have therefore received Christ Jesus the Lord, so walk ye in him: rooted and built up in him, and stablished in the faith, as ye have been taught, abounding therein with thanksgiving. Beware lest any man spoil you through philosophy and vain deceit, after the tradition of men, after the rudiments of the world, and not after Christ" (2:6–8). "Let no man beguile you" (2:18).

1 Timothy, Titus (c. A.D. 63). The Pastoral Epistles also show further evidence of something akin to Gnosticism. Paul's warnings against "genealogies" perhaps had reference to the descending chain of Gnostic deities. He wrote of "fables and endless genealogies" (1 Timothy 1:4), "vain babblings" (1 Timothy 6:20), and "foolish questions, and genealogies" (Titus 3:9). He also warned against "what is falsely called *knowledge*" (NIV and NRSV, 1 Timothy 6:20; emphasis added). "Knowledge" (KJV, "science") is the Greek *gnōsis,* from which the word *Gnosticism* comes. The Gnostics believed that they had a special revealed *gnōsis,* or knowledge, by which they alone understood scripture, knew God, and were saved. This knowledge, they believed, was not available to the uninitiated mainstream of Christianity.

2 Timothy (c. A.D. 67). In Paul's last known letter, the Apostle spoke of "profane and vain babblings," which "will increase unto more ungodliness. And their word will eat as doth a canker" (2:16–17). Two men guilty of spreading false doctrine had ruined the faith of some by teaching that the final resurrection had already taken place (2:17–18). Paul and his teachings were being rejected: "This thou knowest, that all they which are in Asia be turned away from me" (1:15). Paul had taught the gospel in the Roman province of Asia over a decade earlier, and his message had been accepted by tremendous numbers (Acts 19:8–22). Now they were "all" turning from him and his message.

Jude (c. A.D. 80).[6] Jude lamented the rejection of "the faith which was once delivered unto the saints" (1:3). He spoke of those

---

[6] We do not know if Jude was an Apostle. He calls himself "the servant of God, called of Jesus Christ" (JST, Jude 1:1), and he refers to the Apostles in the third person and in the past tense (Jude 1:17–18).

who "reject authority" (NRSV, 1:8). He reminded his readers that they had been warned previously about people infiltrating and perverting the faith. Now they are here, Jude said (1:4). The Apostles had warned of "mockers" in the last days of the Church (1:17–18). They are here now, he wrote. They do not have the Spirit, and they are dividing the Saints (1:19).

Revelation (c. A.D. 96). John's letters to the seven churches of Asia provide additional evidence of the growth of apostasy. He wrote of the existence of false apostles (2:2) and false prophecy (2:20), and he wrote extensively of apostate doctrine and behavior (2:4–6, 14–16, 20–24; 3:2–4, 15–17). If John's words paint a fair picture of the overall status of early Christianity near the end of the first century, one cannot avoid the conclusion that the prophecies of apostasy were then being fulfilled. Of the seven churches addressed in the book of Revelation, only two were not condemned. One was ready to die because of its sins; another was to be spit out of God's mouth. Of the rest, all were guilty of serious error, and each was told in strong terms that if it did not repent, it would be rejected.

1 John, 2 John (c. A.D. 98). John's letters, perhaps the latest writings in the New Testament, show additional evidence for Christian disdain for the idea of divine materiality and even the incarnation of Jesus Christ. The immediate apostate doctrine was called *Docetism*—the belief that Jesus did not really come in the flesh (see 1 John 4:2–3; 2 John 1:7). Docetism was a product of the fundamental philosophy that all matter is evil. Because a holy Jesus could not have actually had a material body (matter being inherently evil), He only *seemed,* or *appeared,* to come in the flesh.

We can readily see the consequences of this kind of belief. Like John, we can see that this doctrine denies the reality of Christ's mortal experiences, His suffering and death in the Atonement, His physical Resurrection, and ours, as well. John pointed out that the Saints had been warned that "antichrist" would come in the last days of the Church (1 John 2:18). They are here now, he wrote, and they came from among the Saints (1 John 2:18–19). Many false prophets have arisen (1 John 4:1). For John, the test of antichrist was whether one believed that Jesus actually came in the flesh (1 John 4:2–3). As an eyewitness of the Savior's ministry, he reminded his readers: "We have heard," "we have seen with our eyes," "we have looked upon, and our hands have handled, of the Word of life" (1 John 1:1). He pleaded with the Saints to hold on to true doctrine: "Let that therefore abide in you, which ye have heard from the beginning. If that which ye have heard from the beginning shall remain in you, ye also shall continue in the Son, and in the Father. . . . These things have I written unto you concerning them that seduce you" (1 John 2:24, 26).

3 John (c. A.D. 98). In what we assume is the last-written document of the New Testament, we have an example of direct rejection of the Lord's anointed leader. Diotrephes, a local Church leader who "loveth to have the preeminence" among the Saints (1:9), rejected John, the senior Apostle and probably the only remaining Apostle at the time. John had written to him, but Diotrephes would not receive him and excommunicated those who would (1:10). This was apostasy by any definition. John promised to deal with the offending leader when he could, but if Diotrephes did not recognize John's authority, no doubt he would not have responded to his discipline, either. At that point in the third generation of Christian history, we see not only doctrinal apostasy taking place but also an act of open rebellion against priesthood authority. This was not without significant consequences: those who rejected John severed the final legitimate link of doctrine and priesthood between Christ and the church that bore His name.

The Great and Abominable Church

After the Ascension of Jesus, it was not long before the Apostles selected a man to take the place of Judas Iscariot among the Twelve

(Acts 1:21–26). This action establishes the principle, which is confirmed by the practice of the Church today, that apostolic succession was to be continued. A new member of the Twelve would be called each time one died. We are aware of three others who became Apostles after Jesus' ascension: James the brother of Jesus (Acts 12:17; Galatians 1:19), Barnabas (Acts 14:14), and Paul (Acts 14:14). They were called early in the Church's history—before A.D. 50—but neither scripture nor other historical evidence gives us any indication that others were called after them. It appears that near the middle of the first century, the calling of Apostles came to an end, and the apostleship was allowed to die out. As far as we know, by the 90s only John remained. When he left his public ministry around A.D. 100, apostleship ceased, and the keys of the kingdom were taken from the earth.

As we saw in the passages cited above, in the decades after Jesus' ministry, Christianity gradually lost its doctrinal anchor. To me, this suggests that in time, the cumulative effect of false beliefs was more successful than the apostolic efforts to correct them. But once the keys of the kingdom—which include the keys of revelation—were gone, the true Church of Jesus Christ was no longer in existence. Thus John's departure was the end of the Church. Had it been God's will, He would have chosen others to hold the keys and to continue the succession of the Twelve. But it appears that the rejection of true doctrine and authority was so widespread that the Church could not continue, and it was allowed to die.

In the Book of Mormon, Nephi wrote regarding the time of the early Apostles. An angel taught him of a "great and abominable church" whose founder would be the devil (1 Nephi 13:6). That church would oppose the Saints and bring them "down into captivity" (1 Nephi 13:5). In part, it would do this by removing things "which are plain and most precious" (1 Nephi 13:26) both from the scriptures and from Christian teachings. The Bible would not go forth to the nations until it had been corrupted "through the hands of the great and abominable church" (1 Nephi 13:28), leaving it less pure and reliable than it had been when it was first written (1 Nephi 13:4–6, 20–29). The consequence would be significant: "Because of the many plain and precious things which have been taken out of the book, which were plain unto the understanding of the children of men, according to the plainness which is in the Lamb of God—because of these things which are taken away out of the gospel of the Lamb, an exceedingly great many do stumble" (1 Nephi 13:29). Joseph Smith spoke about the resulting biblical text: "Many important points, touching the salvation of man, had been taken from the Bible, or lost before it was compiled."[7] He also said, "We believe the Bible to be the word of God as far as it is translated correctly" (Articles of Faith 1:8), or "as it ought to be, as it came from the pen of the original writers."[8] Because the Prophet appears to have been speaking of more than translating from one language to another, the word *translated* in the eighth article of faith appears to include the entire process of transmission from original manuscripts to modern-language printings. On another occasion he pointed out that there are "many things in the Bible which do not, as they now stand, accord with the revelation of the Holy Ghost to me."[9]

Some Latter-day Saints, when reading Nephi's descriptions in 1 Nephi 13, envision medieval monks tampering with the Bible to change it according to their own desires, and they see the church of Rome as the great and abominable church of which Nephi wrote in that chapter. Neither of these interpretations can be reconciled with the scriptural evidence. Setting aside the fact that the Roman Catholic Church did not even exist until hundreds of years

---

[7] Dean C. Jessee, ed., *The Papers of Joseph Smith*, 2 vols. (Salt Lake City: Deseret Book, 1989), 1:372.

[8] Ehat and Cook, *Words of Joseph Smith,* 256.

[9] Ibid., 211; spelling and capitalization modernized.

after the time of which Nephi wrote, the Book of Mormon gives other evidence that helps us understand the prophecy correctly.[10] According to Nephi, the corruption of the biblical text and the removal of plain and precious things from Christianity would take place *before* the Bible would go to the world (1 Nephi 13:29). That happened very early, clearly in the first century A.D., because we have evidence that the dissemination of the writings of the New Testament was well under way early in the second century, when New Testament passages were already being quoted in Christian writings.[11]

The early dissemination of the New Testament, the appearance of aberrant beliefs very early in the Church, the prophecies about the Apostasy, and the descriptions of Nephi and his angelic instructor identify the great and abominable church of 1 Nephi 13 with the Christian church itself, now dominated by the beliefs and behavioral patterns of people who rejected, and then supplanted, the Apostles and the pure gospel they taught. Christ and the Twelve foretold, and the Apostles later witnessed, that Church members would look beyond the simple doctrines of the gospel and bring new ideas into the Christian faith. Though persecution sometimes caused difficulties for early Christians, from the historical record there is no reason to believe that it had anything to do with the Apostasy. Nor do the sources suggest that the Apostasy was the

---

[10] There is no convenient point in history when we can locate the beginning of what we now call the Roman Catholic Church, which evolved over the centuries. The reign of Constantine (A.D. 306–37) is the earliest point which we could call the beginning, but many characteristics of the church come from centuries later. Although the term "Catholic" is attested earlier, the "Roman" and the "Catholic" character of the church developed over the course of many centuries.

[11] See the references in the notes in Michael W. Holmes, ed., *The Apostolic Fathers: Greek Texts and English Translations* (Grand Rapids, Mich.: Baker Books, 1999); also Richard D. Draper, "The Earliest 'New Testament,'" in *How the New Testament Came to Be*, Kent P. Jackson and Frank F. Judd Jr., eds. (Provo: Religious Studies Center, Brigham Young University and Salt Lake City: Deseret Book, 2006), 260–91.

result of Christians becoming apathetic. Instead, we see zealous Church members who were not content with "sound doctrine" but still had "itching ears" for religion (2 Timothy 4:3). And they did what their counterparts do in our own day. They sought out what a modern Apostle has called "alternate voices,"[12] teachers whose words they found to be more "pleasing unto the carnal mind" (Alma 30:53)—more intellectually stimulating, more in style with contemporary ideas, or more spiritually titillating—than were the teachings of the Lord's authorized servants.

The perpetrators were members of the Lord's Church, converted by Apostles and missionaries sent by Apostles. They included both Jewish and Gentile converts. They reshaped Christ's Church in their own image, a reshaping that was already taking place while the New Testament was being written, that flourished while the Apostles were yet alive, and that continued after their deaths. Within just a few decades, it resulted in the spiritual transformation of Christianity. The divinely revealed authority of Apostles was replaced by the self-appointed authority of innovators whose names we don't even know.

As for the records of the Apostles that we now call the New Testament, the angel taught Nephi that changes would be made deliberately in the text: "All this have they done that they might pervert the right ways of the Lord, that they might blind the eyes and harden the hearts of the children of men" (1 Nephi 13:27). We do not know what those changes were, and because they were made prior to the time when copies of manuscripts began spreading throughout the world, we likely will not learn the content of the original texts from the thousands of ancient fragments that have been discovered so far, all of which appear to be copies of

---

[12] Dallin H. Oaks, "Alternate Voices," *Ensign,* May 1989, 27–30.

copies of copies of texts that had already been altered "through the hands of the great and abominable church" (1 Nephi 13:28).

As we have seen, the word *apostasia* does not mean attack from outside but revolution from within. Thus the Apostasy had to be an "inside job," the result of internal, self-inflicted wounds that eventually led to the death of the Church.[13]

The Next Generation of Christianity

Jesus' ministry took place in the early thirties of the first century A.D., and the synoptic Gospels were probably written within a generation of that time, and John's Gospel not long thereafter. The book of Acts continues Church history until about A.D. 63, and the letters of James, Peter, and Paul were all written in the fifties and sixties. Jude's letter was perhaps written a decade or two later, and John's writings likely come in the 90s. As we have seen, both Jude and John identified their own day as the last days of the Church when the warning prophecies were being fulfilled (Jude 1:17–19; 1 John 2:18).

Because of the paucity of records, we know very little about Christian history from the mid-60s until midway into the next century. It seems that John remained active in his public ministry long enough to be a witness that the prophecies were fulfilled, when there were too few in the Church who would "endure sound doctrine" (2 Timothy 4:3) to allow the Church to continue. At some point he had to abandon the church to its fate, going "underground," as it were, to fill other aspects of his life's calling (see D&C 7). Stephen E. Robinson describes what happened next: "We have good sources for New Testament Christianity; then the

---

[13] The description of the "great and abominable church" in 1 Nephi 13 is in concrete historical terms and pertains to the demise of the early Church. In 1 Nephi 14 the term is used very differently. There it is discussed in universal, apocalyptic language, and it refers to the conflict between good and evil primarily with respect to the latter days.

lights go out, so to speak, and we hear the muffled sounds of a great struggle. When the lights come on again a hundred or so years later, we find that someone has rearranged all the furniture and Christianity has become something very different from what it was in the beginning."[14] Christian literature begins again in earnest in the second half of the second century, but there are some documents that date near the end of the first century and in the first half of the second. They give us a view of what life was like after the days of the Apostles, and they show that a dramatic transformation had indeed taken place.

The earliest writers of the post–New Testament era are traditionally called the Apostolic Fathers, because it was believed that they knew, or knew people who knew, the Apostles themselves. Because of this connection with the generation of the Twelve, the words of these early writers became authoritative among Christians of later generations.[15] For us, they provide clear evidence that the Church of the Apostles had already passed away, and Christianity was in a new era.

The earliest document in the writings of the Apostolic Fathers is by a man named Clement, who was the bishop of Rome shortly before the end of the first century.[16] Clement wrote to the church in Corinth in about 95 to 97 to urge the Christians there to reject overt acts of rebellion that had occurred there recently. In what could be described as a *coup d'état,* the Corinthians had removed from office their leaders who had been appointed by Apostles, installing others in their places. Clement emphasized, on doctrinal grounds, the importance of sustaining those who had been called

---

[14] Stephen E. Robinson, "Nephi's 'Great and Abominable Church,'" *Journal of Book of Mormon Studies* 7, no. 1 (1998): 39.

[15] See Holmes, *Apostolic Fathers.*

[16] The document is anonymous, but since antiquity it has been attributed to Clement, the bishop of Rome. See Holmes, *Apostolic Fathers,* 22–25.

by authority. "The apostles received the gospel . . . from the Lord Jesus Christ; Jesus the Christ was sent forth from God. So then Christ is from God, and the apostles are from Christ. Both, therefore, came of the will of God in good order."[17] The Apostles, in turn, set apart bishops and others to preside in the congregations. "Those, therefore, who were appointed by them or, later on, by other reputable men with the consent of the whole church, and who have ministered to the flock of Christ . . . these men we consider to be unjustly removed from their ministry."[18] Clement pointed out the consequences of the Corinthians' rejection of their priesthood leaders: "Each one has abandoned the fear of God and become nearly blind with respect to faith in Him, neither walking according to the laws of His commandments nor living in accordance with his duty toward Christ. Instead, each follows the lusts of his evil heart."[19]

Clement spoke of the Apostles in the past tense and gave no indication that there were any still in the church. Similarly, a document called *The Shepherd of Hermas,* written perhaps in part quite early in the second century, also acknowledges that the Apostles were gone.[20]

Ignatius of Antioch wrote around A.D. 107[21] and knew that he was in the postapostolic era.[22] In his preserved writings, which consist of seven short letters, additional evidence for the Apostasy is apparent. Ignatius saw that apostate influences were working hard

---

[17] *1 Clement,* 42.1–2; Holmes, *Apostolic Fathers,* 75.

[18] *1 Clement,* 44.3; Holmes, *Apostolic Fathers,* 77, 79. See also *1 Clement,* 42.4–5.

[19] *1 Clement,* 3.4; Holmes, *Apostolic Fathers,* 33.

[20] See *The Shepherd of Hermas,* 13.1 (*Vision,* 3.5.1); 94.1 (*Parable,* 9.17.1); 102.2 (*Parable,* 9.25.2). Nostalgia for the days when Apostles were on earth is also found in Justin Martyr (A.D. 110–65), *Hortatory Address to the Greeks,* 8; and Hegessipus, in Eusebius, *Ecclesiastical History,* 3.32.7–8.

[21] See Holmes, *Apostolic Fathers,* 128–33.

[22] As implied in *Magnesians,* 13.2; *Trallians,* 2.2; *Smyrnaeans,* 8.1.

in the church.[23] He was especially concerned about the spread of Docetism, the doctrine that denied the physical reality of Jesus and His work.[24] He pleaded with his readers to stand firmly behind those who had been chosen to lead them—the bishops and the elders. They had been called by the Apostles or by others after the time of the Apostles. He believed that this link of authority would tie the Christians as closely as they could be tied to the apostolic age and that it would be a safeguard against the false beliefs that were circulating in the church.[25]

Polycarp, the bishop of Smyrna early in the second century,[26] was believed in antiquity to have known John, the last of the Twelve.[27] In his only extant work, an epistle to the church in Philippi from about A.D. 107, he warned against Docetism and other evils.[28] He urged the Philippians, "Let us return to the word delivered to us from the beginning."[29] A somewhat later document, *The Epistle of Barnabas* (probably written before 135[30]), identifies its time as the "last days" (Greek, *eschatai hēmerai*), "the age of lawlessness."[31]

Christian writers of the early second century knew that they were living in dark times for the church. Yet the Christianity evidenced in their words seems in many ways alien to readers of the New Testament. Ignatius's warnings show that he was well aware of changes taking place in the church, of threatening doctrines and self-appointed teachers, and of the need to hold fast to the last

---

[23] For example, *Ephesians*, 9.1; *Trallians*, 6.1; *Smyrnaeans*, 4.1.

[24] For example, *Magnesians*, 11.1; *Trallians*, 9.1–10.1; *Smyrnaeans*, 1.1–4.2; 5.2.

[25] See *Ephesians*, 3.2; 6.1; *Trallians*, 2.1–2.

[26] Holmes, *Apostolic Fathers*, 202–4.

[27] Ireneus, *Against Heresies*, 3.3.4; Tertullian, *Prescription against Heresies*, 32.

[28] *Philippians*, 7.1.

[29] *Philippians*, 7.2; Holmes, *Apostolic Fathers*, 215.

[30] Holmes, *Apostolic Fathers*, 270–72.

[31] *The Epistle of Barnabas*, 4.9, Holmes, *Apostolic Fathers*, 283.

remaining links to the Apostles. But without even knowing it, he himself was an example that the church had already passed into the new age. While Ignatius saw himself as a defender of apostolic tradition and orthodoxy, Latter-day Saints will recognize in his words some troubling signs that the orthodoxy that remained was no longer that of the pristine Church. The widespread celebrity status that Ignatius enjoyed, though a local bishop, seems out of harmony with the scriptures. The way he, Polycarp, and Clement confidently took it upon themselves to write letters instructing other congregations also seems irregular and points to a day in which there was no longer a central authority in the church.[32] Most noteworthy, however, was Ignatius's craving for martyrdom, a desire that has no precedent or justification in the scriptures.[33]

The Epistle of Barnabas uses an extreme interpretive method that allegorizes passage after passage from the Old Testament, reducing history to metaphor.[34] This mode of interpretation, employed extensively by the Jewish writer Philo in the first century, would become very popular in Christianity over the next two hundred years and would flourish in the writings of Origen and Clement of Alexandria.

By the middle of the second century, Bishop Polycarp of Smyrna was an old man. A document called *The Martyrdom of Polycarp* was written shortly after his death around 155–60.[35] It

---

[32] See *Philadelphians*, 7.1–2; 10.1–2; *Polycarp*, 7.2.

[33] "I want to fight with wild beasts" (*Trallians*, 10.1; Holmes, *Apostolic Fathers*, 165). "May I have the pleasure of the wild beasts that have been prepared for me; and I pray that they prove to be prompt with me. I will even coax them to devour me promptly. . . . Fire and cross and battles with wild beasts, mutilation, mangling, wrenching of bones, the hacking of limbs, the crushing of my whole body, cruel tortures of the devil—let these come upon me. . . . I am passionately in love with death" (*Romans*, 5.2–3; 7.2; Holmes, *Apostolic Fathers*, 173, 175).

[34] See, for example, the imaginative interpretations of Old Testament dietary laws in *The Epistle of Barnabas*, 10.1–9.

[35] Holmes, *Apostolic Fathers*, 222–23.

records that he was so revered by his disciples that he never had to unfasten his shoes, "not previously in the habit of doing this, because all the faithful were always eager to be the first to touch his flesh."[36] This extreme level of veneration for a mortal is further shown in the account of his burial. After his execution, an eyewitness disciple recorded, "We took up his bones, which are more valuable than precious stones and finer than refined gold, and deposited them in a suitable place."[37]

A book called the *Didache*, or *Teaching of the Twelve Apostles*, is believed to have been written before 150, with some of its content coming perhaps even before the end of the first century.[38] Thus it could reflect some of the earliest ideas of the postapostolic age. Latter-day Saints will find in the *Didache* a number of beliefs and practices that are manifestly out of harmony with revelation—notably so, given the early date of the book's composition. The *Didache* gives us history's first reference to baptism by sprinkling. Although it identifies immersion in running water as the preferred method, it allows for sprinkling if immersion is not practical.[39] This unscriptural innovation destroys the purpose of baptism by removing the doctrinal symbolism of death, burial, and new life that is taught so well by Paul in the New Testament (Romans 6:3–4; Colossians 2:12; 3:1). Similarly, the *Didache*'s sacramental prayers show nothing in common with Jesus' biblical words concerning the ordinance (see Matthew 26:26–28; 1 Corinthians 11:23–26), nor with the prayers that have been revealed in modern times (Moroni 4:3; 5:2; D&C 20:77, 79).[40] The *Didache* versions lack entirely the ordinance's doctrinal foundation: there is no reference

---

[36] *The Martyrdom of Polycarp*, 13.2; Holmes, *Apostolic Fathers*, 237.

[37] *The Martyrdom of Polycarp*, 18.2; Holmes, *Apostolic Fathers*, 241.

[38] Holmes, *Apostolic Fathers*, 246–48.

[39] *Didache*, 7.1–3.

[40] *Didache*, 9.1–4.

to witnessing or making a covenant, and there is no mention of the bread and wine being emblematic representations of Christ.

A final innovation of the *Didache* that is worth noting is a brief administrative instruction: "Therefore appoint for yourselves bishops and deacons."[41] While this, on the surface, may not seem like a major issue, it illustrates a fundamental redefinition of the Christian Church that had already taken place before the *Didache* was written. The New Testament pattern was not that the congregations would choose their own leaders but that divinely called Apostles, or those specifically assigned by Apostles, were to choose and appoint those who would preside, even in local congregations (e.g., Acts 14:23; Titus 1:5).

The Triumph of the Apostles

As time progressed, so also did the transformation of Christian practices and teachings: "Behold, verily I say, the field was the world, and the apostles were the sowers of the seed; and after they have fallen asleep, . . . [Satan] soweth the tares; wherefore, the tares choke the wheat and drive the church into the wilderness" (D&C 86:2–3). The "seed" in Jesus' parable was the word of the Lord, the gospel in its purity that was sown in fertile soil by the Apostles. The "tares" are the false word, false doctrines that choked out the true doctrines and supplanted them in the Lord's field. In the decades and centuries after the departure of the Twelve, the simple teachings of Jesus were replaced by complex theological speculations, all without apostolic guidance. Into the vacuum created by the Apostles' absence came the intellectuals, whose credentials were loud voices and fast pens but not divine callings. Under their guidance, new doctrines emerged, new ways to understand God, new ways to understand Jesus, and new ways to read scripture. Through

---

[41] *Didache*, 15.1; Holmes, *Apostolic Fathers*, 267.

the process of the councils, the creeds, and the writings of philosophers, a Christian theology developed that would have been almost unrecognizable to the converts of Jesus, Peter, and Paul.[42]

Despite all this, the Apostles did not fail in the mission for which they were sent forth. In fact, their work was a triumph. In a few short decades, they took Christianity into the world and planted it deeply enough that it still flourishes today, with more adherents on earth than any other religion. In spite of the unscriptural ideas that were codified in such places as Constantine's palace and Augustine's writing room, the fundamental Christian message has remained intact: God lives, and Jesus saves. This message has been one of the most powerful forces in human history, and it is the legacy of the early Apostles. Christianity survived because the apostles bequeathed to the world the scriptural record of their day, the New Testament. It, too, is a triumph. Even now, two thousand years after it was written, it still stands as the unparalleled eyewitness testament of Jesus Christ, blessing untold millions.

But the early Church was not destined to last forever, or even for more than a few decades. In light of the growing apostasy that was spreading, and having accomplished the mission for which the Twelve were sent forth, the Lord called His Apostles home when the time was right. Jesus had given them instructions on how to continue His work after His departure (e.g., Matthew 28:19–20; Acts 1:2–3), but nowhere in the New Testament are there instructions for how to administer the Church after the departure of the Twelve. The reason is clear: without Apostles, there is no Church of Jesus Christ.

---

[42] See Kent P. Jackson, *From Apostasy to Restoration* (Salt Lake City: Deseret Book, 1996), 31–56.

XIII.

SŌMA SĒMA: THE INFLUENCE OF "THE BODY IS A TOMB" IN EARLY CHRISTIAN DEBATES AND THE NEW TESTAMENT

GAYE STRATHEARN

We have this treasure in earthen vessels, that the excellency of the power may be of God, and not of us.

2 Corinthians 4:7

As we study the second half of the New Testament, it becomes evident very quickly that the early Church struggled with doctrinal drift. One of the central responsibilities of having a Church with apostles and prophets, we learn in Ephesians, is so "that we henceforth be no more children, tossed to and fro, and carried about with every wind of doctrine, by the sleight of men, and cunning craftiness, whereby they lie in wait to deceive" (Ephesians 4:14). Therefore, most of Paul's epistles were written to combat this doctrinal drift. But what happens when the people no longer listen to the Apostles? Paul warned the Saints to avoid those who teach different doctrines. For example, he warned the Saints in Rome to avoid those who cause divisions in the Church with doctrines "contrary to the doctrine which ye have learned" (Romans 16:17). Likewise, he charged Timothy to make sure that the Saints in Macedonia did not teach any "other doctrine" (Greek, *heterodidaskalos;* 1 Timothy 1:3), but Paul realized that "the time will come when they [the members of the Church] will not endure sound doctrine. . . . And they shall turn away their ears from the truth" (2 Timothy 4:3–4). And what happens when there are no longer functioning Apostles and prophets on the earth?

While part of this doctrinal drift seems to have originated with some Jewish-Christians (see Acts 11:1–3; 15:1–11; Galatians 2:12–14), I will focus on two issues that seem to have been influenced by a particular strain of Greek philosophical thought: "The body is a tomb." Although the ancients' view of the body was complex and multidimensional, I will focus on just some of the ramifications of this particular philosophical idea in the debates over the nature of the mortal Christ and the nature of the Resurrection.[1] Although these debates reach their zenith in the second century and beyond, we find evidence of their infancy in the New Testament. For example, John warns of "many antichrists" in the Church "who confess not that Jesus Christ is come in the flesh" (1 John 2:18; 2 John 1:7), and Paul complains to the Corinthian Saints, "How say some among you there is no resurrection of the dead?" (1 Corinthians 15:12).

In order to better appreciate the nuances of these New Testament passages, I will briefly discuss the nature of heresy, the philosophical teaching of "the body is a tomb," and the Christian debates that raged in the second century and beyond.

---

[1] For some discussions on the multidimensional views of the body in the Greco-Roman and Christian worlds, see Dale B. Martin, *The Corinthian Body* (New Haven: Yale University Press, 1995), and Gregory J. Riley, *Resurrection Reconsidered: Thomas and John in Controversy* (Minneapolis, Minn.: Fortress Press, 1995).

Christianities in the Second Century and Beyond

In the second century, Christianity was not a monolithic Church; rather, it was a collection of groups who had different ideas on what it meant to be a Christian. At times these groups coexisted with different levels of acceptance, but this diversity ultimately led to strained relations as each group sought to legitimate their own position.[2] Wayne A. Meeks described the resulting situation as a "vector constituted by tensions in many directions."[3] His imagery conveys well the strained pull between groups who sought to disengage the ties of shared belief that connected them so they could highlight the differences that separated them. It is during this time period that we see the development in meaning of the Greek word *hairesis* from simply "choice" to the more pejorative sense of "heresy"—a group that is isolated from the parent body by some form of deviation from the "truth."

Alain Le Boulluec convincingly argues that it was Justin Martyr, a second-century church Father, who invented the concept of heresy.[4] In doing so, Justin made an analogy between his opponents and the Greek philosophical schools. While he admits that in its purest sense philosophy was divinely sanctioned, two developments arose that fostered the concept of heresy. First, with time,

---

[2] Diversity can exist within an organization or religion if high levels of tolerance exist. However, if for some reason that level drops dramatically then some form of separation inevitably follows. For discussions on this process in religious circles, see Ferdinand Dexinger, "Limits of Tolerance in Judaism: The Samaritan Example," in *Jewish and Christian Self-Definition: Aspects of Judaism in the Graeco-Roman Period*, ed. E. P. Sanders, A. I. Baumgarten, and Alan Mendelson (Philadelphia: Fortress Press, 1981), 2:88–114; L. Michael White, "Shifting Sectarian Boundaries in Early Christianity," *Bulletin of the John Rylands University Library of Manchester* 70, no. 3 (1988): 7–24; and Graham N. Stanton, *A Gospel for a New People: Studies in Matthew* (Louisville: Westminster/John Knox Press, 1993), 113–68.

[3] Wayne A. Meeks, ed., *The Writings of St. Paul* (New York: W. W. Norton, 1972), xiii.

[4] Alain Le Boulluec, *La notion d'hérésie dans la littérature grecque, IIe–IIIe siècles*, 2 vols. (Paris: Études Augustiniennes, 1985), 1:110.

philosophy changed from a search for truth to the exposition of particular doctrines; second, the disciples of philosophical schools depended on human masters for truth, rather than depending on God.[5] Justin thus understood philosophical teachings to be the fountain from which the concept of heresy sprang. It is not surprising, therefore, that the early church Fathers who followed in Justin's footsteps, such as Irenaeus and Hippolytus, attacked heretical groups on the grounds of their philosophical teachings.

Sōma Sēma

One philosophical concept that undergirded some of these doctrinal disputes was *sōma sēma:* "The body is a tomb." In one of Plato's dialogues, Socrates says that the Orphics were probably the inventors of this idea (*Cratylus,* 400c; see also *Phaedrus,* 250c, *Gorgias,* 493a). This belief stemmed from the Orphic theogonic myth, about which we learn from a number of fragmented sources, but particularly from the Christian Father, Clement of Alexandria. Although Clement's purpose in recounting the myth is to discredit it, we are indebted to him for the information he records.

"The mysteries of Dionysos are wholly inhuman; for while still a child, and the Curetes danced around [Dionysos's cradle] clashing their weapons, and the Titans having come upon them by stealth, and having beguiled him with childish toys, these very Titans tore him limb from limb when but a child, as the bard of this mystery, the Thracian Orpheus says:—

"'Come, and spinning-top, and limb-moving rattles, And fair golden apples from the clear-toned Hesperides.'

"And the useless symbols of this mystic rite it will not be useless to exhibit for condemnation. These are dice, ball, hoop, apples, top, looking-glass, tuft of wool. Athene (Minerva), to resume our

---

[5] Le Boulluec, *La notion d'hérésie,* 1:54.

account, having abstracted the heart of Dionysus, was called Pallas, from the vibrating of the heart; and the Titans who had torn him limb from limb, setting a caldron on a tripod, and throwing into it the members of Dionysus, first boiled them down, and then fixing them on spits, 'held them over the fire.' But Zeus having appeared, since he was a god, having speedily perceived the savour of the pieces of flesh that were being cooked,—that savour which your gods agree to have assigned to them as their perquisite,—assails the Titans with his thunderbolt, and consigns the members of Dionysus to his son Apollo to be interred."[6]

What Clement does not record is that Zeus, in retribution, sent down his thunderbolts on the Titans and reduced them to ashes. From these ashes Zeus then created the bodies of the mortal race.[7] Thus, according to the Orphics, mortals consist of both a "Titanic nature (the fleshly body) and a Dionysian nature (the immortal soul)."[8] However, Latter-day Saints should understand that the word "soul" in ancient texts has a very different meaning than the one given by the Prophet Joseph Smith in Doctrine and Covenants 88:15, e.g., "the spirit and the body are the soul of man." Rather, in antiquity, the soul is the immaterial part of a person and is often synonymous with the spirit or the mind.

It seems that Plato and others agreed with the Orphic view. In the *Republic* Plato writes that in order to understand the true

---

[6] Clement of Alexandria, *Exhortation to the Greeks,* 2.17–18, in *Ante-Nicene Fathers: Translations of The Writings of the Fathers Down to* A.D. *325,* ed. Alexander Roberts and James Donaldson, 10 vols. (Grand Rapids, Mich.: Eerdmans, 1951), 2:176. Firmicus Maternus also refers to a Latin version of this myth in his *The Error of the Pagan Religions,* 6.1–4 (New York: Newman Press, 1970), 54–55. Firmicus explicitly states that the Titans consumed Dionysus's limbs. To assuage his grief, Zeus erected a statue of Dionysus and erected a temple instead of a tomb.

[7] For a summary of the sources for this part of the myth, see Erwin Rohde, *Psyche: The Cult of Souls and Belief in Immortality among the Ancient Greeks* (Chicago: Ares Publishers, 1987), 341, 354n39.

[8] Marvin W. Meyer, ed., *The Ancient Mysteries: A Sourcebook* (San Francisco: Harper & Row, 1987), 65.

nature of the soul, "we must view it not marred by communion with the body and other miseries as we now contemplate it, but consider adequately in the light of reason what it is when it is purified, and then you will find it to be a far more beautiful thing and will more clearly distinguish justice and injustice and all the matters that we have now discussed. But though we have stated the truth of its present appearance, its condition as we have now contemplated it resembles that of the sea god Glaucus whose first nature can hardly be made out by those who catch glimpses of him, because the original members of his body are broken off and mutilated and crushed and in every way marred by the waves, and other parts have attached themselves to him, accretions of shells and seaweed and rocks, so that he is more like any wild creature than what he was by nature—even such, I say, is our vision of the soul marred by countless evils."[9]

Epictetus, a Greek Stoic philosopher from the first century A.D. who was influenced by Socrates, teaches that the body "is not thy own, but only a fine mixture of clay" (*Dialogue,* 1:1). Further, he taught, "You are a little soul carrying a dead body" (Fragments CLXXVI).[10] Seneca, a Roman Stoic philosopher from the same time period, wrote that the soul "is weighted down by a heavy burden and desires to be freed and to return to the eleme nts of which it was once a part. For this body of ours is a weight upon the soul and its penance; as the load presses down the soul is crushed and is in bondage. . . . I regard this body as nothing but a chain which manacles my freedom" (*Epistle,* 65:16, 22). For Seneca, only the study of philosophy allows the embodied soul an element of

---

[9] Plato, *Republic,* 611.b–d, in *The Collected Dialogues of Plato: Including the Letters,* ed. Edith Hamilton and Huntington Cairns (Princeton: Princeton University Press, 1989), 836.

[10] George Long, *The Discourses of Epictetus with the Encheiridion and Fragments* (Philadelphia: David McKay, 1920), 445.

freedom.[11] From these sources it becomes clear that, at least in some sections of Greco-Roman philosophy, there is a very strong anti-body sentiment circulating from an early time—at least by the fourth century B.C. with the writings of Plato and continuing into the Christian era.

But this view of the body was not unique to the Greco-Roman world. There is evidence that it was also being assimilated into some Jewish traditions. Although there is not a large corpus of material dealing with the status of the body in early Jewish tradition, it appears that initially the body was regarded positively. Genesis 1:26–27 records that "God said, Let us make man in our image, after our likeness. . . . So God created man in his own image, in the image of God created he him; male and female created he them."[12] Isaiah teaches that in the resurrection "thy dead men shall live, *together with* my dead body [Hebrew, *nĕbēlāh*] shall they arise. Awake

---

[11] Richard M. Gummere, *Seneca in Ten Volumes*, Loeb Classical Library 75 (Cambridge, Mass.: Harvard University Press, 2008), 4:453, 457.

[12] The Hebrew word translated as image is *ṣelem*, which refers to "something cut out" ("צלם or *ṣelem*," Francis Brown, S. R. Driver, Charles A. Briggs, *Hebrew and English Lexicon of the Old Testament* [Oxford: Clarendon Press, 1952]). Of the thirty-four uses of *ṣelem* in the Hebrew Bible, twenty-seven of them refer to some type of statue with a definite physical form—usually a pagan idol. Nevertheless, many modern exegetes interpret Genesis 1:26–27 in a nonphysical sense. The author of the footnotes in the *HarperCollins Study Bible,* while acknowledging that the "biblical narrative was not hesitant to depict divine manifestation in human form," nevertheless describes Genesis 1:26–27 in a manner which is consistent with many modern and ancient interpretations: "paradoxically, the human image resembles imageless divinity in some respect—perhaps speech, reason, or morality" (Wayne A. Meeks, ed., *The HarperCollins Study Bible: New Revised Standard Edition* [New York: HarperCollins, 1989], "Gen. 1:26–27"). For an opposing view, see Gerhard von Rad, *Genesis: A Commentary* in *The Old Testament Library,* ed. G. Ernest Wright (Philadelphia: Westminster Press, 1972), 55–59. From a different perspective, J. R. Porter writes that the phrase "image of God" "probably means that God makes beings with whom he can communicate and who can respond, because, in contrast to the rest of nature, they are like him" (*The Oxford Companion to the Bible,* ed. Bruce M. Metzger and Michael D. Coogan [New York: Oxford University Press, 1993], "creation").

and sing, ye that dwell in dust: for thy dew is as the dew of herbs, and the earth shall cast out the dead" (Isaiah 26:19).[13]

The Jewish texts that we have from the intertestamental period are more mixed in their references to the body. On the one hand, in the 2 Maccabees account of the torture and martyrdom of the seven Jewish brothers, the third brother seems to have an expectation of a physical resurrection. "He quickly put out his tongue and courageously stretched forth his hands, and said nobly, 'I got these from Heaven, and because of his laws I disdain them, and from him I hope to get them back again" (NRSV, 7:10). Likewise, 2 Baruch teaches that the resurrected body will be a reconstitution of the earthly body: "For the earth will surely give back the dead at that time; it receives them now in order to keep them, not changing anything in their form. But as it has received them so it will give them back" (50:2).[14]

On the other hand, however, some Jewish sources show that the concept of body was being influenced by the Orphic maxim. The Jewish philosopher Philo accepted the Orphic doctrine that the body is a tomb: "Now, when we are alive, we are so though our soul is dead and buried in our body, as if in a tomb" (*Legum allegoriae*, 1.108). He argued that "it is not possible that he whose abode is in the body should attain to being with God; this is possible only for him whom God rescues out of prison" (*Legum allegoriae*, 3.42)—the implication being that it is the body that constitutes

---

[13] Job 19:26 is sometimes referred to in order to establish the doctrine of the resurrection of the flesh, but this text is problematic. The King James version reads, "Yet in my flesh shall I see God." The Hebrew text, however, uses the preposition *min*, which can be translated as "apart from." Thus the New American Standard Bible reads, "Even after my skin is destroyed, yet from my flesh shall I see God." See also the Jewish Publication Society version and the footnotes in the ESV, NIV, and the New Living Translation.

[14] A. F. J. Klijn, "2 (Syriac Apocalypse of) BARUCH: A New Translation and Introduction," in *The Old Testament Pseudepigrapha*, ed. James H. Charlesworth, 2 vols. (New York: Doubleday, 1983), 1:638.

the prison. This is a far cry from the Genesis view of the body as being created in the image of God. In practical terms this negative understanding of the body is played out in the emergence of ascetic groups, such as the Essenes, who sought to control their bodily impulses. According to the writings of Josephus (*JW,* 2.119–22) and Pliny (*Natural History,* 5.15.73), the Essenes were a celibate community who held all things in common. The basis for their celibate practices once again seems to stem from the notion that the body is a prison for the soul. Josephus records that the doctrine of the Essenes was "that bodies are corruptible, and that the matter they are made of is not permanent; but that the souls are immortal, and continue for ever; and that they come out of the most subtile air, and are united to their bodies as in prisons, into which they are drawn by a certain natural enticement; but that when they are set free from the bonds of the flesh, they then, as released from a long bondage, rejoice and mount upward" (*JW,* 2.47).

Thus they believed that true life consists of suppressing the body's desires in order for the soul to live (*JW,* 2.155).

The Nature of the Mortal Christ

If a person believes that the body is a tomb, how does he or she understand the Christian message of the incarnation of God in Jesus Christ? This question became an important issue for the early Christian Church. Two important and related questions with which the early Christians struggled were whether a god could have a body and whether he could experience suffering. These were such important questions for the Church that they eventually became the subject of a number of Ecumenical Councils in the fourth and fifth centuries.[15]

---

[15] For example, three of the first four Ecumenical Councils dealt with the issue of the nature of Christ. The Council of Nicaea (A.D. 325) was convened by Constantine to address the teachings of Arius, who claimed that Christ was not divine. Over a

At the heart of this controversy are the Docetists. There is some debate about whether they were a distinct group or whether—more likely—they represent a philosophical outlook found in a number of groups. Unfortunately, we do not have a lot of information about them. At the end of the second century A.D., Serapion, bishop of Antioch, wrote a letter to the church at Rhossos where he mentions a group known as the *dokētai* (as quoted in Eusebius, *Ecclesiastical History*, 6.12). He does not tell us much about them, just that they used the apocryphal Gospel of Peter and that he suspected a connection with Marcion. Clement of Alexandria notes that their name comes from their "peculiar dogmas" (*Miscellanies*, 7:17). *Dokētai* comes from a Greek word which means "to seem" or "to appear." In its simplest manifestation, therefore, Docetism taught that Christ only *seemed* to have a body.[16] This basic belief gave rise to three main interpretations.

The first interpretation is most clearly noted in the letters of Ignatius, bishop of Antioch. After he was arrested and as he traveled to Rome to face a martyr's death, he wrote letters to a number of churches. The letters are a fascinating insight into his understanding of the purpose of Christian suffering. In writing these letters, he vehemently argues against those who taught that Jesus only *seemed* to suffer because that would make Ignatius's own suffering meaningless. In Ignatius's letter to the Trallian Saints, he warned, "Be deaf, then, to any talk that ignores Jesus Christ, of David's

---

century later the Council of Ephesus (A.D. 431) addressed the controversy developing from the Nestorian doctrine that Christ had two separate natures—one divine and one human. Twenty years later, at the Council of Chalcedon (A.D. 451), another controversy erupted when Eutyches taught that Christ had no human nature, only a divine one. For a discussion of these issues, see Richard A. Norris Jr., ed., *The Christological Controversy* (Philadelphia: Fortress Press, 1980).

[16] For a discussion of the definition of Docetism, see Michael Slusser, "Docetism: A Historical Definition," *The Second Century* 1 (1981): 163–72 and Simone Pétrement, *A Separate God: The Christian Origins of Gnosticism,* trans. Carol Harrison (San Francisco: HarperSanFrancisco, 1990), 144–56.

lineage, of Mary; who was really born, ate and drank; was really persecuted under Pontius Pilate; was really crucified and died, in the sight of heaven and earth and the underworld. He was really raised from the dead, for his Father raised him, just as his Father will raise us, who believe on him, through Christ Jesus, apart from whom we have no genuine life. And if, as some atheists (I mean unbelievers) say, his suffering was a sham (it's really *they* who are a sham!), why, then, am I a prisoner? Why do I want to fight with wild beasts? In that case I shall die to no purpose. Yes, and I am maligning the Lord too!" (*Trallians*, 9–10).[17] Likewise he wrote to the Smyrneans, cautioning them: "For it was for our sakes that he suffered all this, to save us. And he genuinely suffered, as even he genuinely raised himself. It is not as some unbelievers say, that his Passion was a sham. It's they who are a sham!" (*Smyrneans*, 2).

The second interpretation took the denial of Christ's suffering further to argue that Jesus only *seemed* to be human, and therefore they made a distinction between the divine Christ and the man Jesus. Jesus, they argued was a man, like all other humans. Christ, however, as Cerinthus taught, "descended upon him in the form of the dove from the Supreme Ruler. . . . But at last Christ departed from Jesus" before the crucifixion (Irenaeus, *Against Heresies*, 1.26.1).[18] From a slightly different perspective, the Gnostic teacher Basilides taught the same idea: "He [i.e., Christ] appeared, then, on earth as a man, to the nations of these powers, and wrought miracles. Wherefore he did not himself suffer death, but Simon, a certain man of Cyrene, being compelled, bore the cross in his stead; so that this latter being transfigured by him, that he might be thought to be Jesus, was crucified, through ignorance and error,

---

[17] All of Ignatius's quotations are from Cyril C. Richardson, ed., *Early Christian Fathers* (New York: Macmillan, 1970).

[18] All of Irenaeus's quotations are from Roberts and Donaldson, *Ante-Nicene Fathers*.

while Jesus Himself received the form of Simon, and standing by, laughed at them. For since he was an incorporeal power, and the Nous (mind) of the unborn father, he transfigured Himself as he pleased, and thus ascended to Him who had sent him, deriding them, inasmuch as he could not be laid hold of, and was invisible to all" (Irenaeus, *Against Heresies,* 1.24.4; see also 3.18.3). This distinction between the human and divine was integral to the later doctrinal disputes over the nature of Christ: Was He by nature divine, or was He by nature human, or some combination of these?

As a logical extension of these positions, we come to the third interpretation: As God, Jesus could not have been born as a mortal. Marcion apparently argued this position, although our only evidence comes from Tertullian's refutation of it (*Against Marcion,* 3.11). According to Tertullian, Marcion denied that Christ had flesh. He argued that Christ was a spirit (Greek, "*phantasma*"; *Against Marcion,* 3.8). He took this position because he "was apprehensive that a belief of the fleshly body would also involve a belief of birth," and Marcion "rejected the sham of a nativity." Tertullian says that Marcion's chief argument against Christ being born was the defilement of the process of birth. "Come then, wind up your cavils against the most sacred and reverend works of nature; inveigh against all that you are; destroy the origin of flesh and life; call the womb a sewer of the illustrious animal—in other words, the manufactory for the production of man; dilate on the impure and shameful tortures of parturition, and then on the filthy, troublesome, contemptible issues of the puerperal labour itself" (*Against Marcion,* 3.11). Likewise, one Valentinian fragment recorded by Clement of Alexandra suggests that Valentinus taught that Jesus was not subject to corruption: "Valentinus in his letter to Agathopus says, 'Jesus showed his self-control in all that he endured. He lived in the practice of godhead. He ate and drank in a way individual to himself without excreting his food. Such was his power of self-control that the food was not corrupted within him, since he was not subject to corruption'" (*Miscellanies,* 3.59.3 or 3.7).[19] Thus these authors rejected Jesus' mortality because it would mean that He existed in a state of corruption.

While these issues were strenuously debated in the second through the fourth centuries, there is evidence that they began in the texts of the New Testament. Sometimes these scriptural texts, particularly the Johannine writings (Gospel of John, 1–3 John, and Revelation), became part of the later debate.

In his first two epistles, John warns his readers against many antichrists: "Little children, it is the last time: and as ye have heard that antichrist shall come, even now are there many antichrists; whereby we know that it is the last time" (1 John 2:18). These antichrists were not outsiders, rather "they went out from us, but they were not of us" (1 John 2:19). John provides a general definition of an antichrist: "Who is a liar but he that denieth that Jesus is the Christ? He is antichrist, that denieth the Father and the Son" (1 John 2:22). More specifically, however, John goes on to define an antichrist as "every spirit that confesseth not that Jesus Christ is come in the flesh is not of God: and this is that spirit of antichrist" (1 John 4:3). Furthermore, in his second epistle he writes, "For many deceivers are entered into the world, who confess not that Jesus Christ is come in the flesh. This is a deceiver and an antichrist" (2 John 1:7).

It appears that John writes these epistles to counter the teachings of Christian Docetists who argue that Christ did not come in the flesh.[20] John counters such teachings by declaring at the beginning of his first epistle, "That which was from the beginning, which we have heard, which we have seen with our eyes, which

---

[19] John Ferguson, trans., *Clement of Alexandria: Stromateis, Books 1–3* (Washington, D.C.: Catholic University of America Press, 1991), 292–93.

[20] A similar Docetic audience seems to be behind the Logos Hymn in John's Gospel (John 1:1–14).

we have looked upon, and our hands have handled, of the Word of life; (for the life was manifested, and we have seen it, and bear witness, and shew unto you that eternal life, which was with the Father, and was manifested unto us;) that which we have seen and heard declare we unto you" (1 John 1:1–3). In this passage John emphasizes Jesus' divinity by identifying Jesus as the Word (Greek, *ho logos*). This is a direct reference to the Logos Hymn that introduces John's Gospel. "In the beginning was the Word, and the Word was with God, and *the Word was God*" (John 1:1; emphasis added). But in declaring His divinity he also acknowledges Jesus' humanity. In the Logos Hymn, John specifically teaches, "And the Word was made flesh, and dwelt among us" (John 1:14). The introduction to John's epistle draws on both of these aspects: Jesus is God, but He is also mortal. John's understanding of Christ's mortal nature, however, is informed not by philosophical maxims but by his personal experience of hearing, seeing, and handling.

Tertullian specifically turns to John's teachings on the antichrist in his writings against groups who "have great cause for besetting the flesh of Christ also with doubtful questions, as if it either had no existence at all, or possessed a nature altogether different from human flesh" (*On the Flesh of Christ*, 1).[21]

"Surely he is antichrist who denies that Christ has come in the flesh [1 John 4:3]. By declaring that His flesh is simply and absolutely true, and taken in the plain sense of its own nature, *the Scripture* aims a blow at all who make distinctions in it. In the same way, also, when it defines the very Christ to be but one, it shakes the fancies of those who exhibit a multiform Christ, who make Christ to be one being and Jesus another,—representing one

---

[21] Tertullian's treatise *On the Resurrection of the Flesh* refers to this text, *On the Flesh of Christ,* and identifies those against whom he is arguing. He says that he is "contending with Marcion and Basilides that it [Christ's flesh] possessed no reality; or else holding, after the heretical tenets of Valentinus, and according to Appelles, that it had qualities peculiar to itself" (*On the Resurrection of the Flesh,* 2).

as escaping out of the midst of the crowds, and the other as detained by them; one as appearing on a solitary mountain to three companions, clothed with glory in a cloud, the other as an ordinary man holding intercourse with all, one as magnanimous, but the other as timid; lastly, one as suffering death, the other as risen again, by means of which event they maintain a resurrection of their own also, only in another flesh. Happily, however, He who suffered 'will come again from heaven' [Acts 1:11], and by all shall He be seen, who rose again from the dead. They too who crucified Him shall see and acknowledge Him; that is to say, His very flesh, against which they spent their fury, and without which it would be impossible for Himself either to exist or to be seen; so that they must blush with shame who affirm that His flesh sits in heaven void of sensation, like a sheath only, Christ being withdrawn from it; as well as those who (maintain) that His flesh and soul are just the same thing, or else that His soul is all that exists, but that His flesh no longer lives" (*On the Flesh of Christ*, 24). For Tertullian it is important to reject the Docetic teachings on the nature of the mortal Jesus because of the implications it has for the doctrine of the Resurrection.

The Nature of the Resurrection

In addition to questions about the nature of Christ, how does a person who believes that the body is a tomb deal with the doctrine of the Resurrection? Did Christ's Resurrection mean that He rose with a physical body, or was the Resurrection something different? What implications does the answer to this question have for the rest of humanity? These questions also became a major debate in early Christianity.

In the second century, Celsus recorded the argument that many educated non-Christians made when they heard the Christian doctrine of the Resurrection: "Jesus could not have risen again with

His body" (*Against Celsus,* 6.72).[22] The hope of a resurrection, Celsus says, "is simply one which might be cherished by worms. For what sort of human soul is that which would still long for a body that had been subject to corruption?" (*Against Celsus,* 5.14). Thus he dismisses the biblical accounts of the Resurrection as either hallucinations or a desire to impress people (*Against Celsus,* 2.55). Later Augustine records the depth of controversy that the doctrine of a physical resurrection elicited: "Yet on no other point is the Christian faith contradicted so passionately, so persistently, so strenuously and obstinately, as on the resurrection of the flesh. Many philosophers, even among the pagans, have argued at length about the immortality of the soul, and in their numerous and various books have left it on record that the human soul is indeed immortal. But when it comes to the resurrection of the flesh they never falter, but openly and plainly deny it. So flatly do they contradict us on this that they declare it impossible for earthly flesh to ascend to heaven" (*Exposition 2 Psalms,* 88.5).[23] In the New Testament, this position seems to be portrayed when Paul teaches among the philosophers in Athens. While they apparently had no problem with him teaching about an "unknown god" (Acts 17:23) or that "we are the offspring of God" (Acts 17:29), there was a polarizing reaction from his audience when he taught of the Resurrection. "And when they heard of the resurrection of the dead, some mocked: and others said, We will hear thee again of this matter" (Acts 17:32).

This rejection of a physical resurrection, however, was not limited to non-Christians. Celsus claimed that not even all Christians believed in the Resurrection (*Against Celsus,* 5.14*)*. We see

---

[22] All of Origen's quotations are from Roberts and Donaldson, *Ante-Nicene Fathers.*

[23] *Expositions of the Psalms,* 73–98, trans. Maria Boulding; *The Works of Saint Augustine: A Translation for the 21st Century,* ed. John E. Rotelle (Hyde Park, N.Y.: New City Press, 2002), 293–94.

evidence of this claim in a number of texts. In the second century, Polycarp, a disciple of John, describes Christians who twist "the sayings of the Lord to suit his own sinful desires and claims that there is [no] resurrection." He describes them as "the first-born of Satan" (*To the Philippians* 7.1).[24] Apparently this group or groups who denied the Resurrection were not numerically insignificant because Polycarp describes them as being "many" (Greek, *pollōn*; 7.2).

But why would so many Christians reject the concept of a resurrection, and specifically a resurrection of the flesh? Justin Martyr argues that the justification comes from philosophical teachings rather than from the teachings of Christ: "The Saviour in the whole Gospel shows that there is salvation for the flesh, [then] why do we any longer endure those unbelieving and dangerous arguments, and fail to see that we are retrograding when we listen to such an argument as this: that the soul is immortal, but the body mortal, and incapable of being revived? For this we used to hear from Pythagoras and Plato, even before we learned the truth" (*Fragments of the Lost Work of Justin on the Resurrection,* 10).[25] Tertullian devotes an entire treatise to argue the case for a resurrection of the flesh (third century A.D.).

Who were these Christians who denied the resurrection of the flesh? Tertullian identifies them as followers of Marcion, Basilides, and Valentinus, who taught that there was a separate creator god (*On the Resurrection of the Flesh,* 2). This view originates in Plato's *Timaeus,* where the world was created by the demiurge, a divine artisan, rather than the high god (*Timaeus,* 28A, 29A, 40C, 41 A&C).[26] Later, some Christians identified the demiurge with the

---

[24] *The Apostolic Fathers: Greek Texts and English Translations,* ed. Michael W. Holmes (Grand Rapids, Mich.: Baker Books, 1999), 213–15.

[25] Roberts and Donaldson, *Ante-Nicene Fathers,* 1:298–99.

[26] For a Christian example, see Irenaeus, *Against Heresies,* 1.26.1.

god of the Old Testament. They interpreted him to be a fallen divine being who was cast out of the presence of the other gods. In ignorance he declared, "I am God and there is no other God beside me" (*Apocryphon of John,* 11.20–21). In some sources this demiurge is called Yaldabaoth, meaning "child of chaos." He was responsible for creating the material world and creating the physical bodies, which was "the tomb of the newly-formed body" (*Apocryphon of John,* 21.10; see also 31.3–4). In the *Apocryphon of John* both salvation and damnation come when the souls "come out of their flesh" (*Apocryphon of John,* 26.22–27.30). In such a belief system, the notion of a resurrection of the flesh would be untenable.

It is clear that even in the New Testament the concept of a resurrection was difficult for many of the early Christians to understand. The women did not go to the sepulcher on Easter Sunday expecting to find Jesus resurrected. Rather, it was a shock to them when they found the tomb empty: "they trembled and were amazed" (Mark 16:8). When Mary Magdalene told the disciples, Mark says that they did not believe her (Mark 16:11). Luke records that the women's report "seemed to them as idle tales, and they believed them not" (Luke 24:11). But the difficulty was not just about the general concept of resurrection; it also seems to be over the nature of that resurrection. Luke and John, in particular, seem to have crafted their Gospels, at least in part, to respond to people who did not understand the Resurrection to be a physical event. Both authors insist that Jesus' resurrected body is indeed physical. Luke records that Jesus proved to the disciples that He wasn't a ghost or spirit (Greek, *pneuma*) by inviting them to touch His hands and His feet: "for a spirit hath not flesh and bones, as ye see me have" (Luke 24:39). Then, lest there be any doubt, He also ate fish and honeycomb (v. 42). This account has many similarities with the 3 Nephi account of the resurrected Jesus' appearance. John makes the same point through the account of Thomas's unbelief: "Except I shall see in his hands the print of the nails, and put my finger into the print of the nails, and thrust my hand into his side, I will not believe" (John 20:25). When the resurrected Jesus returns the following week, He specifically insists that Thomas "reach hither thy finger, and behold my hands; and reach hither thy hand, and thrust it into my side: and be not faithless, but believing" (John 20:27).

The most detailed canonical discussion, however, on the nature of the Resurrection is found in Paul's letter to the Corinthians. Paul writes 1 Corinthians because he has learned that there is contention in Corinth (1 Corinthians 1:11). This contention seems to have developed because some in Corinth were promoting a philosophical approach to the Christian teachings. Paul specifically argues against those who use "enticing words of man's wisdom" (1 Corinthians 2:4).

One of the issues of contention was specifically about the Resurrection. Apparently some members of the Church in Corinth were teaching that there was no Resurrection. In his writing Paul seems to be using some of the slogans of his opponents. So Paul asks, "Now if Christ be preached that he rose from the dead, *how say some among you that there is no resurrection of the dead?*" (1 Corinthians 15:12; emphasis added). Later, he helps us see more specifically what their concerns were about the Resurrection: "But some man will say, *How are the dead raised up? and with what body do they come?*" (1 Corinthians 15:35; emphasis added). In response to these two questions, Paul reaffirms the centrality of the doctrine. The Resurrection and the Atonement were the most important things (Greek, *en prōtois*) that he had taught the Corinthians (15:3), and without Christ's Resurrection, "then is our preaching vain, and your faith is also vain" (15:14). Further, "If in this life only we have hope in Christ, we are of all men most miserable" (15:19). The issue over the Resurrection here does not seem to be denying the existence of an afterlife—both Greeks and Romans believed in an afterlife, and the Corinthians were performing baptisms for the dead (1 Corinthians 15:29).[27] So when Paul lists all those who had seen the post-mortal Jesus, he would not have been arguing that Jesus' spirit continued to exist. Rather, the Resurrection must have entailed more. The reality of the Resurrection was itself a refutation of the body as a tomb that ceased to exist after death.

Paul did not think the resurrected body was, as Celsus argued, cherished by worms. Rather Paul anticipated it to be a transformed, "spiritual" body (1 Corinthians 15:44), which bears "the image of the heavenly" (v. 49), is incorruptible (v. 53), and immortal (vv. 53–54), but does not consist of "flesh and blood" (v. 50). The difficult point here is the last characteristic: a spiritual body that does not consist of flesh and blood. What does Paul mean by a "spiritual body"? Is a spiritual body inconsistent with a physical body? Certainly some in antiquity argued that this was indeed Paul's intent. Irenaeus claims "all the heretics" used this passage to argue that the body is not part of the Resurrection (*Against Heresies,* 5.9.1)

To understand Paul's teachings, a number of things should be noted. First, it is clear that Paul's teachings on the Resurrection must be understood to come from a very different starting point than the Orphics. Earlier in his epistle he has taught, "What? know ye not that your body is the temple of the Holy Ghost which is in you, which ye have of God . . . ?" (1 Corinthians 6:19).[28] Thus Paul did not view the human body as inherently evil, something to be shunned or rejected. Far from viewing the body as a tomb, Paul understood the spiritual capacity that enabled the body to be a temple, or a place for the Holy Ghost to dwell. This position

---

[27] A. J. M. Wedderburn, "The Problem of the Denial of the Resurrection in 1 Corinthians XV," *Novum Testamentum* 23, no. 3 (1981): 229–30.

[28] The Pauline context of 1 Corinthians 3:16 uses the term *body* as a reference to the Church, not to the physical body.

is fundamentally different from the Orphic view of the body. Therefore he is not under the same constraints when thinking about the resurrected body.

Second, even though a spiritual body does not consist of flesh and blood, that does not automatically mean that it cannot consist of flesh and bone. As noted earlier, in Luke's account of the Resurrection, Jesus specifically invited His disciples to handle His body so that they could understand that resurrected bodies consist of flesh and bones (Luke 24:39). In the Book of Mormon, Amulek, in teaching Zeezrom, defined a spiritual body as one in which "the spirit and the body shall be reunited again in its perfect form . . . never to be divided" (Alma 11: 43, 45). President Joseph F. Smith said it this way: "Our bodies are designed to become eternal and spiritual. God is spiritual himself, although he has a body of flesh and bone as Christ has."[29] Both Amulek and President Smith make it clear that spiritual bodies include physical bodies. The most natural reading of Paul's argument concurs with Amulek and President Smith. In the Resurrection we, like Christ, have a body that, although it has lain in the grave, rises again (1 Corinthians 15:4). The literary balance of this verse requires that Christ's body rose with Him in the Resurrection, and because His Resurrection is the prototype for the rest of humanity, all of us shall also be raised with a physical body.

The major thrust of Paul's position in 1 Corinthians 15, however, is not that our resurrected bodies are merely the "reanimation of a corpse to continue bodily existence in its *present* form"[30]—a state which would have certainly horrified many of the Corinthian Saints. Rather, Paul's message is that as people become "in Christ,"

---

[29] Joseph F. Smith, *Gospel Doctrine* (Salt Lake City: Deseret Book, 1986), 70.

[30] Gordon D. Fee, *The First Epistle to the Corinthians,* in The New International Commentary on the New Testament, ed. Ned B. Stonehouse, F. F. Bruce, and Gordon D. Fee (Grand Rapids, Mich.: Eerdmans, 1987), 741.

not only are their spirits enlarged and transformed but so are their resurrected bodies. Notice how in verses 36 through 38 he teaches this principle through the imagery of planted seeds: we may plant "bare grain," but "God giveth it a body." But note verse 39: "All flesh is not the same flesh: but there is one kind of flesh of men, another flesh of beasts, another of fishes, and another of birds." Paul follows this verse with a description of heavenly and earthly bodies: "There are also celestial bodies, and bodies terrestrial: but the glory of the celestial is one, and the glory of the terrestrial is another. There is one glory of the sun, and another glory of the moon, and another glory of the stars: for one star differeth from another star in glory" (1 Corinthians 15:40–41; cf. JST, 1 Corinthians 15:40).

In the passage's context, the celestial and terrestrial bodies refer to the type of bodies that one may receive in the Resurrection. It would seem, therefore, that there are differing degrees of spiritual transformation that our bodies experience in the Resurrection. In a 1917 general conference address, Elder Melvin J. Ballard said that "those who live the laws and attain unto the glory of the celestial shall have a body" whose "fineness and texture" or "composition" shall be greater than those who inherit a lower degree of glory.[31] Just as there are degrees of glory that we can inherit depending upon our faithfulness, so we too will inherit resurrected bodies that are commensurate with our spirits.[32]

Paul further testifies that although our physical bodies are sown in corruption, dishonor, and weakness, eventually they will be raised in incorruption, glory, and power. In short, our bodies may have been sown as a natural body of flesh and blood, but because of Christ's Resurrection they are raised as spiritual bodies

---

[31] Melvin J. Ballard, Conference Report, October 1917, 110.

[32] Note the following from President Joseph F. Smith about the Resurrection: "Deformity will be removed; defects will be eliminated, and men and women shall attain to the *perfection of their spirits,* to the perfection that God designed in the beginning" (*Gospel Doctrine,* 23; emphasis added).

(1 Corinthians 15:42–44), transformed so as to "bear the image of the heavenly [Christ]" (1 Corinthians 15:49). Thus, rather than being a proof-text for those Christians who argued against the physical Resurrection, Paul's teachings, when taken in context, have an exalted view of the body and its place in the Resurrection.

Conclusion

Tertullian once famously asked, "What indeed has Athens to do with Jerusalem?" (*Prescription against Heresies,* 7). In other words, what has philosophy to do with the Church and its doctrine? Historically, the answer is that in many areas, Athens had a profound influence upon the early Christian church. When revelation ceased to come through authorized priesthood leaders, philosophy began to take on a very important role in the development of the church and its doctrines. We have examined just one philosophical concept and showed in a limited way some of the tensions that developed in the doctrinal discussions of the nature of Christ and of the Resurrection. These tensions came to full fruition in the second to fourth centuries, but even before that time we see evidence that they were already beginning to surface during the apostolic period.

XIV.

THE CREEDS AND COUNCILS

JENNIFER C. LANE

For where two or three are gathered together in my name, there am I in the midst of them.

MATTHEW 18:20

Latter-day Saints are noted for setting themselves apart from traditional Christianity, particularly in rejecting certain theological points established in the creeds by early church councils. While we are not unique in being non-creedal Christians, this rejection of certain theological premises of creedal Christianity can make it difficult for other Christians to understand our faith. Many have connected acceptance of the doctrines of the creeds to the acceptance of Christ as Savior and Redeemer; this has long been the source of mutual misunderstanding.[1] In addition, our rejection of some of

---

The most important creeds and councils for our purposes are *The Apostolic Tradition* (A.D. 215); the Council of Antioch (A.D. 268); the First Council of Nicaea (A.D. 325); the First Council of Constantinople (A.D. 381); the Council of Ephesus (A.D. 431); the Council of Chalcedon (A.D. 451); the Second Council of Constantinople (A.D. 553); the Third Council of Constantinople (A.D. 680); and the Second Council of Nicaea (A.D. 787).]

[1] This misunderstanding is usually manifest in statements by creedal Christians that Latter-day Saints are not Christian, met by Latter-day Saints' bewildered protestations that we belong to the Church of Jesus Christ, trust in Him as our Savior and Redeemer, and try to live as Christians. The source of the misunderstanding, to some degree, is the question of what the term *Christian* means and what it means to believe in Christ. Those affirming the authority of the creeds will argue that Latter-day Saints

the creeds' theological premises and of the authority of this tradition can also make it much more difficult for us to understand the foundations of traditional Christian doctrine and its development.

The Latter-day Saint perspective on creeds and councils has also been strongly shaped by the Lord's reply to Joseph Smith during the First Vision. In response to Joseph Smith's question as to which denomination of Christianity he should join, Joseph reports that the Lord "answered that I must join none of them, for they were all wrong; and the Personage who addressed me said that all their creeds were an abomination in his sight; that those professors were all corrupt; that: 'they draw near to me with their lips, but their hearts are far from me, they teach for doctrines the commandments of men, having a form of godliness, but they deny the power thereof'" (Joseph Smith–History 1:19). This association of the term *creeds* with the phrase "an abomination" has had a powerful influence in shaping Latter-day Saint thought in regard to the creeds of early Christianity. Many familiar with the Lord's statement have assumed that it comments directly on the historical creeds of the early Christian centuries.

The goal of this chapter is not to bolster the claim that it is the

---

believe in "a different Jesus" and suggest that we do not believe that Christ is divine or that we believe that we can be saved through personal righteousness and without Christ. In some ways these assertions have been a misunderstanding of LDS doctrines, but at the same time, there clearly are differences between the creeds and the doctrines of the Restoration in regard to understanding the role and nature of Christ.

We will discuss some of these concerns, particularly the question of what divinity means in the creeds. It may be difficult for those who believe in the creedal definition of the Trinity to see anyone who takes issue with that definition as truly believing that Jesus is fully God in the same sense. For a more thorough discussion of this topic see, for example, Robert L. Millet, *A Different Jesus? The Christ of the Latter-day Saints* (Grand Rapids, Mich.: Eerdmans, 2005), as well as other discussions among Millet, Robinson, and Evangelical Christians. See Craig L. Blomberg and Stephen E. Robinson, *How Wide the Divide? A Mormon and an Evangelical in Conversation* (Downers Grove, Ill.: InterVarsity Press, 1997) and Robert L. Millet and Gerald R. McDermott, *Claiming Christ: A Mormon–Evangelical Debate* (Grand Rapids, Mich.: Brazos Press, 2007).

early Christian creeds to which this statement refers, nor is the goal to elaborate on how the theologies of creedal Christianity might merit that condemnation. It is worth noting that this phrase has also been understood to refer to Joseph Smith's religious contemporaries and their professions of belief rather than historical creedal statements.[2] This is an important question to consider, but it will not be the topic addressed here.

With regard to the creeds, another topic that is equally worthy of full discussion in another context is the shift in modern Christianity away from faith in the basics of creedal claims. As Latter-day Saints we may not be aware of the degree to which theologians of post–Enlightenment Christianity have begun to question many of the basic elements of faith in the creedal statements.[3] Belief in the virgin birth, a vicarious Atonement, the Resurrection, and other miraculous elements of Christ's life have increasingly been seen as part of the thought-world of late antiquity and not fit for contemporary, educated society. While we may differ on some points with early creedal statements, recognizing the modern undermining of many foundational beliefs helps us appreciate the spiritual truths the creeds preserved.

I will provide some background to early Christianity to explain what led to the meeting of councils and the creation and use of creeds. I will examine both the historical factors and political pressures that influenced the role of councils and creeds and the ideological framework that would have given them meaning. The

---

[2] This interpretation is suggested by Roger Keller in "Christianity," in *Religions of the World: A Latter-day Saint View*, ed. Spencer J. Palmer, et al. (Provo: Brigham Young University, 1997), 199.

[3] For an introduction to shifting theological assumptions in the modern world, influenced by such writers as Immanuel Kant, Friedrich Schleiermacher, and David Friedrich Strauss, see Alister E. McGrath, *Historical Theology: An Introduction to the History of Christian Thought* (Oxford: Blackwell, 1998), and John Macquarrie, *Jesus Christ in Modern Thought* (London and Philadelphia: Trinity Press International and SCM Press, 1990).

questions driving this study will be: What did the creeds and councils mean for these Christians? What were the fundamental premises that early Christians accepted that made these meaningful and how do they differ from the way we now see the world?

Context

It is clear from the New Testament that even during the Savior's lifetime the question of who He was—and what His relationship to the Father was—became a matter of thoughtful discussion and reflection. It took time for His contemporaries to come to understand both His messianic role and His divinity. We can see illustrations of this process both among the people in general and also among the twelve Apostles. In John 7 we see that those impressed with His teaching at the temple are also trying to make sense of how the idea that He was "the Prophet" and "the Christ" fit together with prophecies that seemed to contradict His Galilean origins (see John 7:40–43). We also see the Savior Himself asking the twelve Apostles to reflect on who men said that He was and what they themselves believed (see Matthew 16:13–16).

Because the conclusions in the New Testament seem simple and clear, we can sometimes become frustrated with post–New Testament era developments of doctrine. These developments can seem distant from the truths that we see taught in the Bible, so distant that it becomes difficult to understand where these notions came from. Scholars who study this period also recognize the striking theological shifts that occurred during this era. They discuss the process that took the fundamentally Jewish doctrine of Jesus as the Messiah and adapted it to the questions of a philosophically educated Greek audience. This cultural and intellectual shift plays an important role in explaining many of the developments and clarifications we see in the creeds.

Another dimension to keep in mind is what we as Latter-day Saints believe is the role of living prophets and Apostles to interpret earlier scriptural texts for contemporary situations. If we think about the Christians in the second through fifth centuries not as villains but as victims of circumstance, we are in a better position to sympathetically understand the solutions to the theological problems with which they were wrestling. During these centuries, questions arose about the nature of God and Christ that were not answered in New Testament texts. Just as we saw in John 7, Christians of this era asked questions, trying to reconcile what scripture taught with what they believed. Because of the Apostasy they were without living prophets and Apostles and had to find solutions using the resources available to them. This deliberative process of maintaining faithfulness to scripture while also trying to find answers to new questions through discussion and debate helps us understand the role of creeds and councils. Let us first consider the early creeds that developed before the rise of the ecumenical councils, then the role of those councils, and finally, the seven ecumenical creeds that are accepted by most Western and Eastern Christians today[4] and that were developed under the councils.

Early Creeds

The term *creed* has its root in the Latin *credo,* "I believe." A creed is a shared statement of belief that is considered normative.

---

[4] For an in-depth overview of the creeds, the standard work is still J. N. D. Kelly, *Early Christian Creeds,* 3d ed. (New York: David McKay, 1972). A recent encyclopedic overview of all Christian creeds, including all the major primary sources, is Jaroslav Pelikan and Valerie Hotchkiss, eds., *Creeds and Confessions of Faith in the Christian Tradition,* 4 vols. (New Haven: Yale University Press, 2003). An accessible introduction to the creeds and early Christian history is John H. Leith, ed., *Creeds of the Churches: A Reader in Christian Doctrine from the Bible to the Present,* 3d ed. (Atlanta: John Knox Press, 1982). He includes both primary sources and bibliographies. Gerald Bray's *Creeds, Councils, and Christ* (Downers Grove, Ill.: InterVarsity Press, 1984) offers a very accessible study of the early Christian historical and intellectual world. While he clearly has a thesis he is seeking to support about continuity from scripture to the creeds, his explanations and background can be very helpful to the general reader. He also has excellent suggestions for further reading.

While the first statements that are called creeds appear in the second century, many look to statements of belief in both the Old and New Testaments as creed-like in the sense that they are declaring foundational points of faith. Summaries of these statements are also referred to as "rules of faith" and are considered to be the "deposit of the faith" that is to be safeguarded.[5] The earliest and most foundational of these is the Shema, the Old Testament declaration, "Hear, O Israel: The Lord our God is one Lord."[6]

This doctrine, foundational to Judaism, is also understood as an undergirding principle in the Christian monotheistic understanding of God. In seeking to articulate this early Christian rule of faith, scholars add to the Shema lists of New Testament statements about the nature of God that form the basis for the Christian faith.[7] These include statements about the divinity of Christ and of the Holy Ghost. Some of these statements primarily affirm Christ's divinity, as in the Ethiopian eunuch's confession of faith: "I believe that Jesus Christ is the Son of God" (Acts 8:37). Others include all three members of the Godhead, as in Christ's

---

[5] Leith dates the appearances of the Rules of Faith to the second half of the second century. He argues that they provided "a basis for catechetical instruction and a guide for the interpretation of Scripture. They also provided theological material for defense against the heretics" (*Creeds of the Churches*, 20). Pelikan and Hotchkiss use the term "rules of faith" more generally to describe understanding of doctrine in both the first and second centuries (*Creeds and Confessions*, 1:8).

[6] This statement directly prefaces the command: "And thou shalt love the Lord thy God with all thine heart, and with all thy soul, and with all thy might. And these words, which I command thee this day, shall be in thine heart: And thou shalt teach them diligently unto thy children, and shalt talk of them when thou sittest in thine house, and when thou walkest by the way, and when thou liest down, and when thou risest up. And thou shalt bind them for a sign upon thine hand, and they shall be as frontlets between thine eyes. And thou shalt write them upon the posts of thy house, and on thy gates" (Deuteronomy 6:4–9). Many people today are familiar with how important this doctrine is in Judaism and how this commandment is obeyed through the use of the mezuzah and phylacteries.

[7] An example of these efforts to categorize New Testament texts can be seen in Leith, *Creeds of the Churches*, 12–16.

apostolic commission: "Go ye therefore, and teach all nations, baptizing them in the name of the Father, and of the Son, and of the Holy Ghost" (Matthew 28:19).[8]

In the New Testament we see not only efforts to positively state the doctrine of Christ but also rejections of incorrect interpretations of Christ's nature and saving role. In 1 John 4:2–3 we read, "Hereby know ye the Spirit of God: Every spirit that confesseth that Jesus Christ is come in the flesh is of God: And every spirit that confesseth not that Jesus Christ is come in the flesh is not of God: and this is that spirit of antichrist, whereof ye have heard that it should come; and even now already is it in the world." We see here that aspects of Christ's nature were debated even during the age of the Apostles. John's defense of the doctrine that Christ was embodied rejected the claims of Docetism—the view that Christ, being divine, could not have had a physical body.[9]

Here we see that theological debates were happening even before the writing of the creeds by the church councils. Assumptions about the divine being unembodied, even among Christians, would have been widespread given the influence of Platonic thought among the educated. A Docetic view of Christ as incorporeal was an important aspect of Gnostic religious models; it appears in a number of second-century noncanonical texts, including many of the Nag Hammadi texts and also the recently famous Gospel of Judas.[10] Early Christian efforts to defend the doctrine of

---

[8] See Pelikan and Hotchkiss, *Creeds and Confessions,* 1:27, for a discussion of the role of these two statements.

[9] For a brief introduction to Docetism, see Stuart G. Hall, "Docetism," in *The Oxford Companion to Christian Thought,* ed. Adrian Hastings, Alistair Mason, and Hugh Pyper (Oxford: Oxford University Press, 2000), 173.

[10] The standard English translation of the texts from Nag Hammadi is James M. Robinson, ed., *The Nag Hammadi Library in English,* 3d ed. (San Francisco: HarperCollins, 1988, 1990). The text of the more recently discovered Gospel of Judas can be found in Rodolphe Kasser, Marvin Meyer, and Gregor Wurst, eds., *The Gospel of Judas: From Codex Tchacos* (Washington, D.C.: National Geographic, 2006). A

the Incarnation—belief in the literal humanity of Jesus Christ—are particularly visible in the writings of the second-century Church Father Ignatius of Antioch. After this epoch, the doctrine of the Incarnation was maintained as an orthodox Christian teaching and is affirmed in all the creeds. What we must appreciate, however, is that this and other doctrines that we accept in the creeds were at one time challenged through differing interpretations of scripture and could have been lost from Christian belief.

Statements in the New Testament concerning the mission and divinity of Christ and the Holy Ghost, combined with the principle of monotheism in the Shema, are seen as the basis on which the doctrine of the Trinity is founded.[11] The development of the creeds may have functioned to reconcile the theological problem of faith in one God and yet in the Father, the Son, and the Holy Ghost. Aspects of Their nature, role, and either equality or subordination developed into major points in the theological discussion surrounding the development of the creeds.

Because Christians in the New Testament era and the next few centuries found it necessary to distinguish their faith from that of Judaism and to explain it to others, statements about faith in Jesus Christ as Lord and Savior and other distinctive Christian doctrines

---

discussion of its context and contents from an LDS perspective can be found in various articles in *BYU Studies* 45, no. 2 (2006).

[11] Pelikan and Hotchkiss note: "The history of the primitive rules of faith during the first and second centuries (and, by extension, of most of the creeds and confessions that were to follow throughout Christian history) may without exaggeration be regarded as the developing effort of the Christian community to square this primal and untouchable affirmation of the ancient *Shema,* which no amount of theological speculation about the doctrine of the Trinity could ever be allowed to jeopardize, compromise, or modify, with the new realities of the history of salvation and with the new traditions of the revelation in Christ that were being celebrated in the liturgy and that had been recorded in the pages of the New Testament" (*Creeds and Confessions,* 1:8–9). Some, like Pelikan himself citing Athanasius, will suggest that the doctrine of the Trinity was already contained in the rule of faith, *kerygma,* and was passed down to the time when the creeds were formed (*Creeds and Confessions,* 1:10–11).

were developed for use in teaching, preaching, apologetics, and in the liturgy (the practices and recitations of Christian worship services).[12] The first recorded creeds appeared in conjunction with baptism in the second and third centuries, before debates in the councils of the early Church over the development of creeds became a part of the historical record. Just as the Ethiopian eunuch's confession, "I believe that Jesus Christ is the Son of God," was associated with his baptism, and the Great Commission (Matthew 28:19–20) explicitly required that baptism be done "in the name of the Father, and of the Son, and of the Holy Ghost," early records of baptisms are the first places in which creedal formulas are found.[13]

The idea of affirming a baptismal candidate's acceptance of basic doctrinal points is familiar to Latter-day Saints in the practice of baptismal interviews. A similar practice can be seen in this passage from *The Apostolic Tradition,* circa A.D. 215. In these basic creedal points we can recognize New Testament doctrines concerning the Father, Son, and Holy Ghost:

"When the person being baptized goes down into the water, he who baptizes him, putting his hand on him, shall say: 'Do you believe in God, the Father Almighty?' And the person being baptized

---

[12] Kelly articulates the contexts for early "semi-formal confessions of faith" as "baptism, worship, preaching, catechetical instruction, anti-heretical and anti-pagan polemics, exorcism" all of which "provided occasions for giving concrete expression, along lines determined by the needs of the moment, to the cardinal articles of Christian belief." (*Early Christian Creeds,* 30). Pelikan and Hotchkiss describe these settings for early development of the creeds as coming from both evangelizing and "apologetics . . . to meet the objections of the cultured among the despisers of the gospel," and that in these efforts "there developed standardized creedlike formularies, which manifested certain parallels to those that were at work in congregational preaching, baptism, and antiheretical polemics" (*Creeds and Confessions,* 1:17).

[13] The long-standing nature of this view can be seen in Hans Lietzmann's oft-repeated assertion that "It is indisputable that the root of all creeds is the formula of belief pronounced by the baptizand, or pronounced in his hearing and assented to by him, before his baptism" (*Die Anfänge des Glaubensbekenntnisses* [Tübingen, 1921], 226; cited in Kelly, *Early Christian Creeds,* 30).

shall say: 'I believe.' Then holding his hand on his head, he shall baptize him once.

"And then he shall say: 'Do you believe in Christ Jesus, the Son of God, who was born of the Holy Spirit and the Virgin Mary, and was crucified under Pontius Pilate, and was dead and buried, and rose again the third day, alive from the dead, and ascended into heaven, and sat down at the right hand of the Father, and will come to judge the living and the dead?' And when the person says: 'I believe,' he is baptized again.

"And again the deacon shall say: 'Do you believe in the Holy Spirit, in the holy church, and in the resurrection of the body?' Then the person being baptized shall say: 'I believe,' and he is baptized a third time."[14]

We see in this baptismal interrogatory all the elements of an early creed, the basic doctrines foundational to Christian faith. A subsequent development required an oral "giving" (Latin, *traditio*) of the creed to catechumens—those preparing for baptism—during Lent, the forty-day period of fasting that begins on Ash Wednesday and ends on Easter Sunday. They then would formally "give it back" (Latin, *redditio*) during Holy Week, the celebration of Jesus' last week, preparatory to their baptism on Easter Eve. This giving of the "symbol" or creed as a sacramental mystery or *disciplina arcani* seems to have been a later development, starting perhaps late in the third century.[15] Preparation for baptism and

---

[14] Pelikan and Hotchkiss, *Creeds and Confessions,* 1:61; *Apostolic Tradition,* 12–18.

[15] Kelly dates it to the "heyday of the fully mature catechumenate, that is, to the second generation of the third century at the earliest" (*Early Christian Creeds,* 49). Earlier scholarship often suggests an earlier start to the practice, giving another explanation for the lack of documentation. See, for example, Philip Schaff, *The Creeds of Christendom, with a History and Critical Notes,* 3 vols. (Grand Rapids, Mich.: Baker Book House, 1977). Schaff argues that this "summary of the apostolic doctrine, called 'the rule of faith,' was kept confidential among Christians, and withheld even from the catechumens till the last stage of the instruction; and hence we have only fragmentary accounts of it in the writings of the ante-Nicene fathers. When controversies

baptism itself gave places for both declaratory and interrogatory creeds.[16]

A declaratory creed often linked to these early baptismal creeds is the Apostles' Creed. It has had a prominent role in Western tradition, and though it did not receive its final formation until the sixth or seventh century, most see its basic beliefs as going back to second-century baptismal statements:[17]

"I believe in God the Father almighty, creator of heaven and earth; and in Jesus Christ, His only Son, our Lord, Who was conceived by the Holy Spirit, born from the Virgin Mary, suffered under Pontius Pilate, was crucified, dead and buried, descended to hell, on the third day rose again from the dead, ascended to heaven, sits at the right hand of God the Father almighty, thence He will come to judge the living and the dead; I believe in the Holy Spirit, the holy Catholic [universal] Church, the communion of saints, the remission of sins, the resurrection of the flesh, and eternal life. Amen."[18]

For Latter-day Saints, the doctrine in the Apostles' Creed sounds generally familiar and biblical. While we do not use creeds

---

arose concerning the true meaning of the Scriptures, it became necessary to give formal expression of their true sense, to regulate the public teaching of the Church, and to guard it against error. In this way the creeds were gradually enlarged and multiplied, even to the improper extent of theological treatises and systems of divinity" (*Creeds of Christendom,* 1:5–6).

[16] Kelly insists that "declaratory creeds of the ordinary type had no place in the baptismal ritual of the period [the first three centuries]. . . . An affirmation of the faith was, of course, indispensable, but it took the form of the candidate's response to the offiant's interrogations." Kelly seeks to separate the baptismal ritual from the preparation for baptism in which the "declaratory creeds, conceived in the setting of their original purpose, were compendious summaries of Christian doctrine compiled for the benefit of converts undergoing instruction" (*Early Christian Creeds,* 48, 50). This is an important distinction liturgically because declaratory creeds do later become part of the baptismal liturgy, and Kelly is seeking to clarify the origins of this practice.

[17] See, for example, Leith, *Creeds of the Churches,* 22–23.

[18] Kelly, *Early Christian Creeds,* 369.

in our worship services, this foundational text reflects biblical faith which we resonate to and affirm.

The Role of the Councils

While the idea of having a written creed may seem somewhat unfamiliar to Latter-day Saints, for whom the Articles of Faith provide a weak parallel, the notion that the doctrine in the creed would be the matter of vigorous debate within an ecclesiastical council can be truly startling. The thought that the process could become a serious governmental, even imperial, concern can be even more incomprehensible. But if we are to grasp the later development of the creeds, it is essential to understand the role of the councils and the bishops and how they were entwined in the larger imperial politics of the era.[19] Before exploring the political context that led to the development of the ecumenical councils, it will be helpful to consider an episode in the New Testament that set councils as a model for responding to questions about practice and belief.

This New Testament precedent for councils can be found in Acts 15, which describes what is known as the Jerusalem Council or sometimes the Apostolic Council.[20] In this meeting we see a pattern of Church leaders deliberating over a difficult problem in their

---

[19] For an outstanding recent study of the dynamics and inner workings of the councils, see Ramsay MacMullen, *Voting about God in Early Church Councils* (New Haven: Yale University Press, 2006).

[20] Joseph Fitzmyer comments on this title: "This meeting has often been referred to as the Apostolic Council. That is really a misnomer, because the meeting as described is not a solemn assembly of authorities from all over the church. Moreover, it is never counted as one of the councils in the history of Christianity. Yet when one reflects on the issue that is discussed and its doctrinal significance for the future of the church, one can see why it might be regarded as a sort of 'Council.' . . . It is, in effect, the episode in the early church that eventually leads to the convening of official councils of later date" (*The Acts of the Apostles: A New Translation with Introduction and Commentary*, in The Anchor Bible [New York: Doubleday, 1998], 31:543).

role as the leading council of the Church.[21] Whether the Gentile members of the Church should be bound by the law of Moses is in debate. We see Church leaders who have gathered together to share their experiences and scriptural insights in an effort to find God's will regarding the question. We see Peter sharing his previous experience with teaching and baptizing Cornelius; Barnabas and Paul sharing their experiences of seeing God's "miracles and wonders" among the Gentiles (Acts 15:12); and then James sharing his insights into Old Testament prophecies foretelling of this day. The council ends with James suggesting a resolution to the question that was accepted. This shared vision of God's will for the Gentiles was then written and sent out as a letter to the Saints in Antioch, Syria, and Cilicia (see Acts 15:23–30). In this account we see a pattern that was followed by Christian leaders in later centuries: ecclesiastical leaders meeting together to share perspectives and counsel together regarding contemporary questions of belief and practice. The decisions reached by the ecumenical councils of later centuries were likewise communicated to the churches by letter and became the new standard for belief and behavior, although by the time of the later councils, church leaders acted as political leaders as well. The fundamental difference seems to be a shift from relying upon the Holy Spirit and prophetic revelation to issuing edicts that had both political and theological implications.

It is widespread knowledge that a little over a decade following

---

[21] The question of how to fit this description in Acts 15 with similar descriptions in Galatians 2:1–10 and Acts 11:27–30 is a very complicated point. There are a number of different views among New Testament scholars on how these passages are to be reconciled. Helpful summaries of the different efforts to harmonize can be found in Richard N. Longenecker, *Galatians,* vol. 41 of Word Biblical Commentary, ed. Bruce M. Metzger, David A. Hubbard, Glenn W. Barker (Waco, Tex.: Thomas Nelson, 1990), lxxiii–lxxxiii, 1; and in Howard Marshall, *The Acts of the Apostles: An Introduction and Commentary* (Grand Rapids, Mich.: Eerdmans, 1980), 242–47. Marshall also provides a helpful reading of the texts of Acts 15 and a consideration of its consequences (*Acts of the Apostles,* 247–56).

Constantine "converting" to Christianity and issuing the Edict of Milan, which legalized Christianity, the emperor called the First Council of Nicaea in A.D. 325.[22] Just why the emperor of the Roman Empire would choose to call together a meeting of Christian bishops to resolve the question of the relationship of the Father and the Son requires explanation. It is necessary to briefly discuss the ecclesiastical and political situation in the Roman Empire during the third and fourth centuries.

First, it is essential to understand that Nicaea was not the first council of bishops, though it was the first—but not the last—called by an emperor. This kind of imperial support and concern was a radical departure from the Christians' experience earlier in the fourth century when widespread persecution of Christians flourished under the emperor Diocletian. The record of bishops meeting in councils (the Latin term) or synods (the Greek term) dates to A.D. 253.[23] After the apostolic era, bishops continued to lead large Christian communities and saw themselves as the successors of the

---

[22] Among scholars of the life of Constantine, the question is debated as to whether the reported events at the Battle of Milvian Bridge and the legalization of Christianity with the Edict of Milan signal a conversion to Christianity or a strategic decision to embrace Christianity. Many are aware that Constantine was baptized near the end of his life and use that to argue that he was converted later, but it was not uncommon during this era to delay baptism. For a variety of classic viewpoints on Constantine and Christianity, see Ramsey MacMullen, *Constantine* (New York: Dial Press, 1969), and A. H. M. Jones, *Constantine and the Conversion of Europe* (New York: Collier, 1962). More recent discussions include H. A. Drake, *Constantine and the Bishops: The Politics of Intolerance* (Baltimore: Johns Hopkins University Press, 2002).

[23] In time, the terms *council* and *synod* took on more specialized meaning, but initially they were simply the same thing said in different languages. See Pelikan and Hotchkiss, *Creeds and Confessions,* 1:6–7. Because these terms do continue to be used in the Christian tradition it is valuable to know how they came to be used in English practice. Pelikan and Hotchkiss define "*synodal* creeds as those originating in an assembly, whether orthodox or heretical, that was local and regional in provenance and that remained so in authority; but *conciliar* creeds are those that were decreed by an assembly that was—or that was 'received' after the fact as having been—*ecumenical,* although this category, too, is ambiguous because of the fundamental difference between the East and the West on the status of the fourteen so-called ecumenical church gatherings that have met in the West since 787" (*Creeds and Confessions,* 1:7; emphasis in original).

Apostles. Generally, however, they saw their authority to preside as limited to the "see" (the episcopal seat) to which they were ordained.[24] The bishops' role in a large city or region was more supervisory, overseeing priests and other clergy who worked more closely with the laity. As Christianity spread during the second and third centuries, bishops could be found leading local Christian groups in most cities in the Roman Empire. The bishops were organized into provinces, mimicking the structure of the Roman Empire, and collectively would have numbered in the hundreds by the time the councils or synods began to meet. Certain cities, because of prominence or historical importance, were regarded as metropolitan sees, and their bishops had a higher level of status and influence than others in their region. The councils of bishops generally met on the level of the province; after Nicaea they were legislated to meet twice a year within each province.[25]

Second, it is essential to recognize that just as there were many bishops during this era and no centralized church leader, so there were many different forms of Christianity competing for legitimacy. In some cases, this would mean that a city would have more than one bishop, each of whom represented a different viewpoint. The theological disagreements between these different forms of Christianity are precisely what councils like the Council of Nicaea were seeking to resolve. At the end of each of the ecumenical councils in which a decision was reached and a creed written, some bishops had won and some had lost. Some positions were then considered orthodox and others heretical. It is from this gradual process of defining creedal orthodox Christianity that

---

[24] See Kenneth Scott Latourette, *A History of Christianity* (New York: Harper, 1953), 116–17. On the distribution of episcopal sees and some background on who served as bishops in the fourth century, see MacMullen, *Voting about God,* 5–11.

[25] MacMullin, *Voting about God,* 7.

Christian groups such as Arians, Monophysites, and Nestorians became defined as heretical.[26]

Among those who were on the victorious side at the time and are part of the orthodox tradition to this day, this victory is understood as a defense of the "deposit of faith" and the preservation of apostolic doctrine. There are, however, others, albeit in much smaller numbers, who disagreed with the decisions of the councils and, while considered "heretical" by their contemporaries and future defenders of orthodoxy, continued to hold to their theological positions. Those who differ from some of the ecumenical creeds can be found in such Eastern Christian traditions as the Assyrian church of the East ("Nestorian Christians") or the Coptic, Ethiopian, Syrian, and Armenian Orthodox churches ("Monophysite Christians").[27]

The scholarly view of early Christian heresy changed quite dramatically during the twentieth century from a position of accepting the view of the orthodox to recognizing the existence of multiple Christianities in the early Christian world.[28] This more recent view embraces the spiritual claim of none of these positions but instead looks at the political struggles from which the "orthodox" position and imperially backed "Great Church" became dominant. For Latter-day Saints who look at this era from the perspective of the Apostasy, it can be easy to jump on this bandwagon, but it is

---

[26] Dennis Groh, "*Arius, Arianism,*" in Freedman, *ABD,* 1384–86; F. L. Cross, ed., *The Oxford Dictionary of the Christian Church,* rev. ed. (Oxford: Oxford University Press, 1984), s. vv. "*Monophysitism*" and "*Nestorianism.*"

[27] These groups are not particularly fond of such titles as "Nestorian" or "Monophysite" because they see these terms as labeling their beliefs as heretical, which is different from their own perspective on their position.

[28] The most important work in promoting this shift is Walter Bauer's *Orthodoxy and Heresy in Earliest Christianity* (Philadelphia: Fortress Press, 1971), which originally appeared in German in the 1930s. Almost all work on early Christian heresy today follows this approach. See also Bart D. Ehrman, *Lost Christianities: The Battles for Scripture and the Faiths We Never Knew* (London and New York: Oxford University Press, 2003).

essential to keep in mind that most of the theologies promoted in these competing forms of early Christianity are even further from what we understand as the gospel of Jesus Christ. In many ways, the orthodox position and the creeds preserved many basic New Testament doctrines, such as the Incarnation and the bodily Resurrection.

To understand the context in which the ecumenical councils deliberated between A.D. 325 and 787, it is important to remember that with time the Eastern and Western parts of the Roman Empire began to take different political courses; these differences can be seen in the shifting ecclesiastical structures in the East and the West. As the Roman Empire gradually disintegrated in the West, illustrated by the sack of Rome in A.D. 410 and Odoacer's deposing of the last emperor of the Western Roman Empire, Romulus Augustus, in A.D. 476, this region looked more and more to the authority of the bishop of Rome. In a vacuum of political power, ecclesiastical power increasingly took the lead. Here we see the beginning of the papacy.[29] The prominent social and political role of the bishop of Rome remained a central feature of the medieval West and characterized political struggles for centuries to come.

In the heavily urbanized East, on the other hand, the empire remained intact and the emperor retained control throughout the barbarian invasions in the West. The bishops in the Greek-speaking East were numerous and did not coalesce under the authority of a single spiritual father or "pope" (papa). In fact, following the lead of Constantine, the emperors of the Eastern Roman (or Byzantine) Empire continued to take a vocal role in ecclesiastical matters. Just as Constantine had been active enough to style himself the "thirteenth apostle," so later emperors did not hesitate to continue

---

[29] For an overview of the rise of the papacy, see Geoffrey Barraclough, *The Medieval Papacy* (New York: W. W. Norton & Co., 1978), and also Eamon Duffy, *Saints and Sinners: A History of the Popes,* 2d ed. (New Haven: Yale University Press, 2002).

to call councils and make declarations on theological topics that were seen as binding—such as Leo III declaring that religious images (icons) were not legitimate objects of veneration during the iconoclastic struggles of the eighth century.[30] The prominent role of the emperors in the affairs of the church in the East has been called "caesaropapism." These differences in ecclesiastical government along with later theological rifts gradually paved the way for the Roman Catholic Church and the Eastern Orthodox Church to exist as separate religious institutions. It is essential to remember, however, that through the eighth century, conditions were gradually forming that would bring these two institutions into being. During all seven of the ecumenical councils (from A.D. 325 to 787) these institutions did not exist as separate churches. The bishops who met together saw themselves as part of a holy catholic—meaning universal—church.

Councils Writing Creeds

As Constantine sought to use Christianity to bring greater political unity to his divided empire, he came to realize that the religion that he had recently backed was, in fact, quite splintered over various theological issues. This was not only a question of theological division but also of ecclesiastical government because, especially in the Western empire, there were cities in which rival bishops competed for followers. In response, he called together bishops from throughout the empire to meet at the city of Nicaea in modern-day Turkey. At the time of the First Council of Nicaea in A.D. 325, the major rift was over the division between the Arian and non-Arian positions on the relationship of the Father and the Son. It has been observed that the earlier creeds, often associated with baptism, were designed to determine the orthodoxy of those

---

[30] See Kenneth Scott Latourette, *A History of Christianity* (New York: Harper, 1953), 292–95.

who were becoming Christians, and the later creeds, those written by the councils, were designed to determine the orthodoxy of the bishops.[31]

The role of the First Council of Nicaea was monumental, both theologically and politically. Those who won the debate in the Council saw the issue as a matter of preserving the doctrine of Christ's divinity. Simply put, the Arian position stated that "there was a time when Christ was not."[32] This statement was intended to distinguish the Father and the Son. This commonsense idea that first there was a Father and then a Son was also easily embraced by many of the more recently converted Germanic peoples in the Western empire who were less theologically nuanced.

For Eastern, philosophically educated churchmen, the idea that "there was a time when Christ was not" was outrageous because to them it said that Christ was not really divine. The principle of Christ's eternal divinity had been defended earlier against the doctrine of Adoptionism, which claimed that Christ only became divine through the influence of the Holy Spirit at His baptism.[33] The doctrine of Arianism was seen by these theologians as having ultimately the same effect—the basic understanding of divinity in Greek thought required that it be an eternal principle. To say that there was a time "when Christ was not" was to say that He was a creation, not the Creator; it was to bring Christ to the side of humanity and away from divinity. For these philosophically informed early Christian theologians, humanity and divinity were ontologically different categories—different kinds of being. Thus

---

[31] See Robert McQueen Grant, *Gods and the One God,* in Library of Early Christianity, vol. 1 (Philadelphia, Penn.: Westminster Press, 1986), 169.

[32] The Arian position takes its name from Arius (A.D. 250–336) who taught in Alexandria.

[33] In A.D. 268 Paul of Samosata was deposed as bishop of Antioch by the Council of Antioch for advocating Adoptionism.

we can see the importance of their insisting that the Father and the Son shared the same kind of being, essence, or substance.

It is hard to overstate the importance of this fundamental premise in understanding the process of reasoning involved in the councils and their creeds. These early Christian leaders and theologians were seeking to understand the nature and relationship of Christ and the Father. Widely shared ideas about divinity as eternal and radically different from humanity were an essential factor in their development of Trinitarian and Christological definitions in the creeds. They had to preserve the doctrine that Christ, as the Son of God, was divine, but, as we shall see in the Council of Chalcedon, they would later also need to posit that He is also human in order for Him to act as the Savior.

Insisting that Christ, like the Father, had always existed did not fully resolve the theological problems; there remained the debate that Arius had tried to resolve—how to distinguish the Father and the Son. The orthodox sought to resolve this by declaring that Christ was "eternally begotten," seeking to preserve both His eternal nature and also His Sonship. It was in the context of trying to clarify the relationship of the Father and the Son while insisting on the divinity of Christ that the famous term *homoousios* was developed. There was actually a debate over whether to use this first expression or the related but different term meaning that the Father and the Son were *homoiousious* (of *like* substance or essence), but, despite contemporary concerns for the nonbiblical nature of the term, *homoousios* finally won acceptance and was included in the creed. The use of the term was debated for the next half-century and substitute formulas were tried, but this articulation of the relationship of the Father and the Son finally became normative.[34]

---

[34] Leith notes that "various alternatives were tried: 'Exact image of the Godhead' (Second Creed of Antioch, 341); 'Like the Father who begot Him according to the Scriptures' (Dated Creed, Fourth of Sirmium); 'Like the Father in all things' (Dated

While the Nicene Creed (the Creed of Nicaea) is globally famous today because of its prominent liturgical role, what most do not realize is that the creed which is now accepted and widely used in both Eastern and Western Christian traditions is actually the Niceno-Constantinopolitan Creed of A.D. 381, written by the First Council of Constantinople. This, the second ecumenical council, was called by the emperor Theodosius. He had recently gone beyond Constantine's legalization of Christianity earlier in the century to declare Christianity the official or only legal faith of the empire. This move followed a brief suppression of Christianity under the reign of Julian the Apostate from A.D. 360/61–363. The First Council of Constantinople reaffirmed the teachings and language of the creed of the First Council of Nicaea of A.D. 325 with some modifications. Added in the Niceno-Constantinopolitan Creed is a fuller statement regarding the Holy Spirit.[35] The original creed had an ending statement pronouncing an anathema (curse) on those who do not accept the doctrine which is now lost.

Here is the text of the Nicene, or Niceno-Constantinopolitan, Creed, of A.D. 381:

"We believe in one God, the Father, almighty, maker of heaven and earth, of all things visible and invisible;

"And in one Lord Jesus Christ, the only begotten Son of God, begotten from the Father before all ages, light from light, true God from true God, begotten not made, of one substance [*homoousios*] with the Father, through Whom all things came into existence, Who because of us men and because of our salvation came down from heaven, and was incarnate from the Holy Spirit and the Virgin Mary and became man, and was crucified for us under

---

Creed, Fourth of Sirmium); 'Of like essence with the Father' (Ancyra, 358); 'Unlike the Father' (the teaching of Aetius and Eunomius and, by implication, of the Second Creed of Sirmium, 357)" (*Creeds of the Churches*, 29).

[35] The creed of the First Council of Nicaea merely says, after articles of belief in the Father and the Son, "and in the Holy Spirit" (Kelly, *Early Christian Creeds*, 216).

Pontius Pilate, and suffered and was buried, and rose again on the third day according to the Scriptures and ascended to heaven, and sits on the right hand of the Father, and will come again with glory to judge living and dead, of Whose kingdom there will be no end;

"And in the Holy Spirit, the Lord and life-giver, Who proceeds from the Father, Who with the Father and the Son is together worshipped and together glorified, Who spoke through the prophets; in one holy Catholic and apostolic Church. We confess one baptism to the remission of sins; we look forward to the resurrection of the dead and the life of the world to come. Amen."[36]

This creed is the most universally accepted in the Christian world. To this day it is used in the liturgy of the Eastern Orthodox churches, the Roman Catholic church, as well as the Anglican and Lutheran churches.

There are, of course, some fundamental differences that developed after the era of the early creeds. The medieval Western inclusion of the Latin term *filioque* ["and the Son"] to the statement that the Holy Spirit "proceeds from the Father" was seen by Eastern Christians not only as theologically incorrect but also as rupturing the foundational role of this creed—having been agreed upon, no party was at liberty to change the doctrine. This, along with the increased role of the papacy, contributed significantly to the eventual break between the Eastern Orthodox and the Roman Catholic churches. While many in the modern world may find it difficult to understand how the question of who the Spirit proceeds from could be this important for either side, the weight these doctrines held—and their long-term consequences—says something about how important interpretations of the Trinity have been and are. This question of whether the Father and the Son are seen more as equals, as in the West, or if the Son is seen as more subordinate, as

---

[36] Kelly, *Early Christian Creeds*, 297–98.

in the East, were theological matters that continued to be discussed and debated.

After the First Council of Constantinople, in A.D. 381, the third and fourth councils, those of Ephesus, in western Turkey, and of Chalcedon, near Istanbul, both took place about a half-century later, in A.D. 431 and 451. Like the First Council of Nicaea in A.D. 325, these councils were both called by the emperor and required the clarification of theological divisions that were threatening to rupture now-intertwined religious and political stability. It is also important to realize that while the bishops from East and West all still met together, in the fifth century the Roman Empire underwent a period of dramatic transition with the rising power of the Germanic tribes in the West. Theological tensions, however, struck right in the heartland of the Eastern empire. At the end of this period of increased theological definition, many of the Christians in Egypt, Palestine, and Syria were, as Monophysites, considered heretical as the newly sanctioned creeds more narrowly defined orthodoxy, leaving this region alienated from the orthodox position of Constantinople. The long-term effect of their stigmatization and persecution under the imperial banner has been considered a contributing factor in the quick fall of these areas to the Muslim armies that burst out of the Arabian peninsula in the early seventh century. They believed they would receive better treatment as Christians under Islamic rule than as heretics under Byzantine rule.

The theological and political maneuvering that lay behind the Councils of Ephesus and Chalcedon are even more complex than the debates covered to this point. Simply put, while the first two ecumenical councils dealt with Trinitarian issues, both the Councils of Ephesus and Chalcedon needed to refine Christological doctrine. Rather than focusing on the relationship of the Father, Son, and Holy Ghost, they sought to answer new questions revolving around Christ's nature. What did it mean for Him to be both man and God? Could it be said that God was born and that Mary was the mother of God? Could it have been God that suffered and died on the cross? Did Christ have a human soul? Was Christ in two natures or of two natures? At the end of the Council of Ephesus the doctrine of Nestorianism was declared a heresy, and at the end of the Council of Chalcedon the doctrine of Monophysitism was declared a heresy.

The complex and fascinating stories of the individuals involved in these debates—as was also true for Nicaea and Constantinople—lie beyond the scope of this brief survey. It is important, however, to remember this personal dimension—that each of these ideas had been thought, taught, believed, and fought against by individuals. These doctrines may seem distant and abstract today, but they were vibrant and widely followed during the fifth century. It is reported that during the debates over whether Christ was in two natures or of two natures that "if you desire a man to change a piece of silver, he informs you wherein the Son differs from the Father; if you ask the price of a loaf, you are told by way of reply that the Son is inferior to the Father; and if you inquire whether the bath is ready, the answer is that the Son was made out of nothing."[37] The bishops may not have thought it fitting that commoners were discussing these things so widely, but clearly these theological topics mattered in fifth-century Byzantium.

Rather than attempt to summarize the important but complex stories leading the development of the debates over Nestorianism and Monophysitism in the third and fourth ecumenical councils, I will briefly explain some of the theological issues involved and how they grew out of the premises already developed in the process of creedal definition. All agreed that Christ was divine,

---

[37] This is Edward Gibbon's restatement of Bishop Gregory of Nyssa's concern that common people were discussing such matters. For the citation and a discussion of Gibbon's sources, see MacMullen, *Voting about God*, 37, 130n39.

but the Christological debates centered on questions of how His divinity and His humanity were related. Should they be seen as separate, as in a divine person (the second person of the Trinity, the Logos) dwelling in a human person (Jesus)? Nestorius argued that it was appropriate to say that Mary was the Christ-bearer, Mother of Christ (Greek, *Christotokos*) but not that she was the God-bearer, Mother of God (Greek, *Theotokos*). To the opponents of Nestorianism, this kind of effort to distinguish the divine and human in the person of the incarnate Christ lacked ontological unity and undermined the belief that Christ was fully God.[38] Nestorius refused to accept the declaration of the third ecumenical council, the Council of Ephesus (A.D. 431), on Mary as the *Theotokos* (Mother of God).

The issues of Nestorianism were also folded into the Definition of Chalcedon, the last major creedal statement of the early Christian era. Against the orthodox view that triumphed at the fourth ecumenical council, the Council of Chalcedon (A.D. 451), the opposing side of the debate consisted of viewpoints that sought to unify rather than distinguish the natures of Christ. The heterodox position that Christ's nature was more united than the Definition of Chalcedon's "two natures" is known as Monophysitism, and a branch of Monophysitism is known as Eutychianism. There is a sense where this position can be seen as a reaction to Nestorianism's effort to radically separate the human Jesus and the divine Christ. Here the opposite move is made, bringing the natures together in one.

---

[38] Additional resources to understand the early Christological debates are provided by recent surveys such as John McIntyre's *The Shape of Christology: Studies in the Doctrine of the Person of Christ*, 2d ed. (Edinburgh: T&T Clark, 1998), as well as Roch A. Kereszty's *Jesus Christ: Fundamentals of Christology*, ed. J. Stephen Maddux (New York: Alba House, 1991), and Gerald O'Collins, *Christology: A Biblical, Historical, and Systematic Study of Jesus* (Oxford: Oxford University Press, 1995). There is some discussion as to whether Nestorius was actually a Nestorian.

On the landmark status of the Definition of Chalcedon, the classic nineteenth-century scholar of the creeds, Philip Schaff, has written: "It substantially completes the orthodox Christology of the ancient Church. . . . As the Nicene doctrine of the Trinity stands midway between Tritheism and Sabellianism, so the Chalcedonian formula strikes the true mean between Nestorianism and Eutychianism."[39] In a close examination of the Definition of Chalcedon we can see how the initial premises of a fundamental ontological distinction between divine and human essence led to the need to resolve complex theological problems about distinguishing between nature and person, articulating the duality of the natures of Christ, while at the same time defending the unity of the person of Christ.[40]

The Definition of Chalcedon (A.D. 451), after restating the Nicene and Niceno-Constantinopolitan creeds, sets up this background, preparatory to declaring its resolution of the debates: "But since those who, taking in hand to set aside the preaching of the truth by heresies of their own, have uttered vain babblings, some daring to pervert the mystery of the dispensation, which for our sakes the Lord undertook, and denying the propriety of the name *Theotokos,* as applied to the Virgin [Nestorianism], and others bringing in a confusion and mixing of natures, and fondly feigning that there is but one nature of the flesh and Godhood, and by this confusion absurdly maintaining that the divine nature of the only begotten is passible [Monophysitism]—for this reason. . . ."; they then go on to condemn these positions as heretical and provide the orthodox definition of the person and natures of Christ.[41]

---

[39] Schaff, *Creeds of Christendom,* 1:30.

[40] This list comes from Schaff's enumeration of the "leading ideas of Chalcedonian Christology" (*Creeds of Christendom,* 1:30–31).

[41] Text from J. Stevenson, *Creeds, Councils, and Controversies: Documents Illustrating the History of the Church, A.D. 337–461,* 3d ed., ed. W. H. C. Frend (London: SPCK, 1989), 351–52.

Just as during the Trinitarian debates when the orthodox sought to stake out a middle position between belief in three Gods (Tritheism) and one God who simply put on different masks or personas (Sabellianism), during these Christological debates the orthodox saw themselves as defending an understanding of the person and nature of Christ that they believed would allow Him to act as Savior by suffering in the flesh but also preserve His divinity. As was noted in the creedal rejection of the Monophysite position that "there is but one nature of the flesh and Godhood, and by this confusion absurdly maintaining that the divine nature of the only begotten is passible," a fundamental working premise of the orthodox was that the divine was impassible—unable to suffer or be moved.

For the orthodox theologians, in order to insist that Christ was divine, this distinction had to be maintained. He had to be human in order to suffer but also divine in order to be God and to act as Savior. It was Christ's humanity that suffered, not His divinity. Thus we can see the importance of resolving the question of how the human and divine natures of Christ were combined, and why a proponent of orthodoxy such as Schaff would say that "the Chalcedonian formula strikes the true mean between Nestorianism [ontologically separated divine and human natures and persons in Christ] and Eutychianism [one commingled divine and human nature in Christ]."[42] The Definition of Chalcedon is sometimes called the Doctrine of the Hypostatic Union, since its central theological formulation is the statement that the two *hypostases* (Greek, "nature" or "fundamental essence"), divine and human, are united in the one person of Christ. The definition of that hypostatic union takes this form:

"Wherefore, following the holy Fathers, we all with one voice

---

[42] Schaff, *Creeds of Christendom*, 30.

confess our Lord Jesus Christ one and the same Son, the same perfect in Godhead, the same perfect in manhood, truly God and truly man, the same consisting of a reasonable [rational] soul and a body, of one substance [*homoousios*] with the Father as touching the Godhead, the same of one substance with us as touching the manhood, *like us in all things apart from sin;* begotten of the Father before the ages as touching the Godhead, the same in the last days, for us and for our salvation, born from the Virgin Mary, the *Theotokos,* as touching the manhood, one and the same Christ, Son, Lord, Only begotten, to be acknowledged in two natures, without confusion, without change, without division, without separation; the distinction of natures being in no way abolished because of the union, but rather the characteristic property of each nature being preserved, and concurring into one Person and one subsistence (ὑπόστασις [*hypostasis*]), not as if Christ were parted or divided into two persons, but one and the same Son and only begotten God, Word, Lord, Jesus Christ; even as the Prophets from the beginning spoke concerning him, and our Lord Jesus Christ instructed us, and the Creed of the Fathers has handed down to us."[43]

One of the most heavily contested questions was whether Christ was "in two natures" or "of two natures." Those of the Monophysite traditions believed that it should be said that He was "of two natures," but with the Chalcedon council, "in two natures" became the orthodox definition. As noted before, these theological divisions have hardened into splits within Christianity wherein a number of Eastern Christian churches consider themselves orthodox, but because they do not accept the Definition of Chalcedon, they are considered heretical by other Christians.

The last three of the ecumenical councils, the Second Council

---

[43] Stevenson, *Creeds, Councils, and Controversies,* 352–53; emphasis in original.

of Constantinople (A.D. 553), the Third Council of Constantinople (A.D. 680), and the Second Council of Nicaea (A.D. 787) were important but do not hold the same landmark positions as the first four councils. The Second and Third Councils of Constantinople featured efforts to negotiate some theological differences with the large bloc of Eastern Christians that had been labeled Monophysite heretics after the Council of Chalcedon (A.D. 451). These efforts ultimately were not successful and the Monophysite tradition continues in what are now known as the Oriental Orthodox churches. The final ecumenical council was an effort to resolve the raging iconoclastic controversy that had consumed the Byzantine Empire. It finally established the orthodoxy of the veneration of images, a practice that was violently rejected by the iconoclasts and was slow to be appreciated and adopted by Western Christians. This practice is noteworthy in its centrality to the religious life of Eastern Orthodox Christians to this day.

Conclusion

Early Christian creeds and councils can be seen from multiple perspectives. From the perspective of secular history we can see hard-fought political battles between bishops with imperial agendas looming large. From the perspective of non-creedal Christians still faithful to their tradition today, we can see those holding minority opinions suppressed and persecuted. From the perspective of those faithful to the orthodox position, we can see humans struggling to preserve divine truths as they understood them, and with their faith in the authority of these councils and creeds, the importance this tradition holds for them in indicating how scripture and doctrine are to be understood. Jarislov Pelikan has expressed the beliefs of those who trust in the creeds and councils in these terms:

"Underlying the creedal and conciliar definition of orthodoxy from the beginning have been three shared presuppositions: first, that there is a straight line . . . from the Gospels to the creed;

consequently, second, that the true doctrine being confessed by the councils and creeds of the church is identical with what the New Testament calls 'the faith which was once for all delivered to the saints'; and therefore, third, that continuity with that faith is the essence of orthodoxy, and discontinuity with it the essence of heresy."[44]

As Latter-day Saints seeking to be understood by our fellow Christians, it is also imperative that we seek to understand them. While we may not agree with the fundamental assumptions that they make about the continuity between scriptures and the creeds, it is essential that we understand why the creeds and their doctrine are taken so seriously by others. Our rejection of the truthfulness of some of these beliefs need not blind us from understanding them. We may disagree when other people call us heretical, but we can also understand why they hold that position.

By looking at the creeds and councils from the perspective of the Restoration, we can see the difference it makes to have additional truths about the nature of God and human nature revealed through modern-day prophets. Belief in an embodied God and an understanding of all human beings as "a beloved spirit son or daughter of heavenly parents" with "a divine nature and destiny" are not creedal doctrines.[45] They are, however, central to our faith as Latter-day Saints. While we appreciate the additional light and knowledge made available through the Restoration, we should, however, also look back in gratitude for early Christians who struggled to preserve the doctrine of Christ's redemption—the Incarnation, vicarious Atonement, and bodily Resurrection.

With all the creeds and councils, we rejoice to know that "He was arrested and condemned on spurious charges, convicted to

---

[44] Jaroslav Pelikan, *Credo: Historical and Theological Guide to Creeds and Confessions of Faith in the Christian Tradition* (New Haven: Yale University Press, 2003), 9.

[45] "The Family: A Proclamation to the World," *Ensign,* November 1995, 102.

satisfy a mob, and sentenced to die on Calvary's cross. He gave His life to atone for the sins of all mankind. His was a great vicarious gift in behalf of all who would ever live upon the earth."[46] Prophets and Apostles today also testify that "Jesus is the Living Christ, the immortal Son of God. He is the great King Immanuel, who stands today on the right hand of His Father. He is the light, the life, and the hope of the world. His way is the path that leads to happiness in this life and eternal life in the world to come."[47] Early Christians shared this hope and sought to defend their faith in salvation through Christ. Today we can look back with thoughtful recognition for what they passed on and appreciate the challenges they faced as they struggled to answer their questions about the nature of God without continuing revelation to help clarify essential doctrine.

---

[46] "The Living Christ: The Testimony of the Apostles, The Church of Jesus Christ of Latter-day Saints," *Ensign*, April 2000, 2.

[47] Ibid.

CONCLUSION

PROFOUND EFFECTS OF THE SECOND HALF OF THE NEW TESTAMENT ON THE GOSPEL

RICHARD NEITZEL HOLZAPFEL
AND THOMAS A. WAYMENT

Nephi saw in vision the coming forth of the Bible "by the hand of the twelve apostles of the Lamb" (1 Nephi 13:26). Generally, we focus our attention on Nephi's warning that "they have taken away from the gospel of the Lamb many parts which are plain and most precious; and also many covenants of the Lord have they taken away" (1 Nephi 13:26), forgetting an important earlier insight: "Nevertheless, they contain the covenants of the Lord, which he hath made unto the house of Israel; wherefore, *they are of great worth unto the Gentiles*" (1 Nephi 13:23; emphasis added).

Although the rebellion (Apostasy) in the first century ultimately brought about the end of the Church, the basic gospel message—"We preach Christ crucified . . . Christ the power of God, and the wisdom of God . . . for the preaching of the cross is to them that perish foolishness; but unto us which are saved it is the power of God" (1 Corinthians 1:23–24, 18)—remains embedded in the New Testament that survived to be read, copied, heard, and read again by generations of people.

Today, Christianity is the largest and most influential religious movement on earth. During its turbulent history, people have invoked its name in various causes, including conflicts and wars. However, Christianity has done much to make the world a better place. In western Europe it eliminated slavery for the very first time in human history. In the wake of the fall of the Roman Empire in the West, Christianity filled the vacuum by providing not only spiritual comfort to countless people but also offered social services, including care for the sick and needy, education, and judicial intervention. Christian monasteries were refuges during times of natural disasters and human conflict, inns for people on the move, schools, and hospitals. Monks and priests helped clear the land and performed other duties that lessened the burdens of the working poor. Nuns offered kindness and performed great service to countless people. Additionally, monasteries were libraries and book production facilities—countless manuscripts were preserved and copied by the clergy. Additionally, Christianity provided the working poor relief from a seven-day workweek with numerous religious holy days (holidays) that punctuated the yearly calendar—making their life sustainably better than it was in previous generations.

Of course, Christianity was the context of the Restoration. Joseph Smith lived in an environment where few people questioned the authority of the Bible. The Smith family, like other families living in nineteenth-century America, owned a Bible and taught their children from its pages. Moved by his trust in the New Testament promise found in James 1:5, Joseph Smith went into a grove of trees near his home to pray in the spring of 1820. This prayer resulted in the First Vision—in which Joseph saw the Father and the Son—and began a spiritual sunrise unexpected by men and women of Joseph's own day but anticipated by the prophets and Apostles of old (see, for example, Acts 3:21).

The power and influence of the New Testament would be difficult to measure. Elder Bruce R. McConkie reflected, "There are no words to describe the power of a single book. . . . During all this long period the Bible did more to mellow the souls of men, more to keep such light and truth alive as was then found on earth, more to prepare me for a day when new revelation would come, than any other book."[1]

For countless people the New Testament has kept alive the memory of Jesus of Nazareth, His amazing deeds and words. The story of His birth, ministry, death, and Resurrection has inspired individuals, families, and whole nations to accept Him as the Savior of the world (see John 20:31). The New Testament preserved His profound teachings from the Sermon on the Mount and the Bread of Life discourse (Matthew 5–7; John 6:35–59). Because the story was preserved in the New Testament, we know that He met with His disciples on the "same night in which he was betrayed" (1 Corinthians 11:23) to institute a new covenant with Israel. The story of His suffering, death, and Resurrection are preserved in the New Testament because the first Christians remembered, recalled, and recorded the story of the transcendent events in the upper room, Gethsemane, Golgotha, and the Garden Tomb as told by eyewitnesses. In addition, the New Testament provides the meaning of these events because the authors, particularly Paul, provided their insight in the second half of the New Testament.

Paul's Message of Salvation

Paul preached the gospel and often provided historical facts of what Jesus did (see 1 Corinthians 11:23–25; 15:1–4). However, his main purpose and message was to help the early Saints understand why Jesus did what He did and how the events of Jesus' suffering, death, and Resurrection changed the cosmos once and for all time.

The basis of Paul's understanding of what God did through His Son was the belief that all had sinned and fallen short of the glory of God. He emphasized the universality of sin in Romans: "[We]

---

[1] Bruce R. McConkie, *Doctrines of the Restoration: Sermons and Writings of Bruce R. McConkie,* comp. Mark L. McConkie (Salt Lake City: Bookcraft, 1989), 266–67.

are all under sin . . . there is none righteous . . . not one . . . none . . . seeketh after God" (3:9–11). Furthermore, Paul argued, "They are all gone out of the way, they are together become unprofitable. . . . For all have sinned, and come short of the glory of God" (3:12, 23). Worst of all, in a clearly intended climax, Paul says that humans are "ungodly" (5:6), "sinners" (5:8), and "enemies" of God (5:10; see also Ephesians 2:1–3). These observations confirm Paul's understanding that the effects of sin were irreversible without the Atonement. We are shocked but not surprised by the evening news when we hear about the evil that exists in the world. Something has fundamentally gone wrong—and more important, no person can save himself or herself.

Nevertheless, Paul preached the good news that God had provided a means of salvation, not just to individuals but also to all humanity—in fact, to all creation ("to reconcile *all things* unto himself" Colossians 1:20; emphasis added). He testified in what may be one of his most famous statements, "I am not ashamed of the gospel of Jesus Christ: for it is the power of God unto salvation *to every one that believeth*" (Romans 1:16; emphasis added).

Paul wrote, "For when we were yet without strength, in due time Christ died for the ungodly. For scarcely for a righteous man will one die: yet peradventure for a good man some would even dare to die. But God commendeth his love toward us, in that, while we were yet sinners, Christ died for us. Much more then, being now justified by his blood, we shall be saved from wrath through Him. For if, when we were enemies, we were reconciled to God by the death of his Son, much more, being reconciled, we shall be saved by his life" (Romans 5:6–10).

Throughout Paul's writings, the gospel, the good news of what God had done through His divine Son, consisted of the basic proclamation that Jesus "died for our sins according to the scriptures; and that he was buried, and that he rose again the third day according to the scriptures" (1 Corinthians 15:3–4). Note the three-fold

CONCLUSION: PROFOUND EFFECTS

assertion: Jesus died, was buried, and rose from the dead. However, between those historical facts (the first two are universally accepted as reliable and undeniable historical truths) are Paul's important insights. First, it was all part of God's will and foreordained plan, "according to the scriptures" (1 Corinthians 15:3). Second, and fundamentally crucial to the story—Jesus died "for our sins" (1 Corinthians 15:3).

It is important to remember that Paul did not believe that Jesus' death fully explained what God did to solve the problem of human sin. N. T. Wright observed, "For Paul the resurrection of Jesus was also significant in God's dealing with sins (e.g., 1 Corinthians 15:17). Had crucifixion been the end of Jesus' story, no one would ever have ascribed saving significance to the event. The resurrection casts a retrospective coloring over the crucifixion."[2] Another scholar concluded, "One should therefore be wary of restricting NT views about the atoning work of Christ to discussions of the meaning of Jesus' death alone."[3]

Paul believed that it was beyond human capacity to completely understand how the suffering, death, and Resurrection of Jesus Christ effected salvation; nevertheless, he had faith and trust in the saving or atoning gift of Christ Jesus. Paul also knew that for those who had no faith, salvation in Jesus was nonsense: "For the preaching of the cross is to them that perish foolishness; but unto us which are saved it is the power of God. . . . But we preach Christ crucified, unto the Jews a stumbling-block, and unto the Greeks foolishness" (1 Corinthians 1:18, 23).

As Paul attempted to explain the meaning and purpose of the Atonement, he "seems never to tire of adding new images to his

---

[2] N. T. Wright, "The Letter to the Romans: Introduction, Commentary, and Reflections," in *The New Interpreter's Bible: A Commentary in Twelve Volumes* (Nashville: Abingdon Press, 2002), 10:467.

[3] C. M. Tuckett, "Atonement in the NT," in Freedman, *ABD,* 1:518.

interpretive vocabulary by way of explicating its significance."[4] In so doing, he utilized a rich and varied range of metaphors or models in his attempt to spell out the significance of what Jesus did.[5] Paul would often blur categories in this attempt to understand the Atonement. As in so many other instances, Paul took ordinary Greek words and transformed them, adopted and adapted them, to help express the profound meaning that Jesus' life, death, and Resurrection had for him. As Ben Witherington has noted, "Paul was no ordinary wordsmith."[6]

One of the threads that runs through the various metaphors Paul uses to describe Jesus' loving and saving mission is His Father's activity—His initiative: "*God sent forth* his Son" (Galatians 4:4; emphasis added). None of these Pauline models of salvation illustrates independently or fully what Jesus has done, but each is useful in conveying an aspect of the saving, healing, and strengthening power of the Atonement.

Commentators often assert that Paul's most important model, given the ubiquitous nature of ancient sacrifice, is the expiation model.[7] Paul borrowed from the imagery of Israelite sacrifices to reveal a meaning, not the full meaning, of Jesus' suffering and death. He obviously, like Book of Mormon prophets, believed that the sacrifices in ancient Israel prefigured Jesus' death (2 Nephi 11:4; Mosiah 14:7; Alma 34:14; Ether 13:10).

Paul believed Jesus "covered" our sins with His blood,

---

[4] J. B. Green, "Death of Christ," in *Dictionary of Paul and His Letters*, ed. Gerald F. Hawthorne, Ralph P. Martin, Daniel G. Reid (Downers Grove, Ill.: InterVarsity Press, 1993), 203.

[5] Numerous commentators have highlighted the various models and metaphors. We have drawn extensively from James D. G. Dunn, *The Theology of Paul the Apostle* (Grand Rapids, Mich.: Eerdmans, 1998), 227–30.

[6] Ben Witherington III, *The Paul Quest: The Renewed Search for the Jew of Tarsus* (Downers Grove, Ill.: InterVarsity Press, 1998), 300.

[7] David M. Hay, "Expiation," in *Eerdmans Dictionary of the Bible*, ed. David Noel Freedman (Grand Rapids, Mich.: Eerdmans, 2000), 444–45.

removing the effect of sin that keeps unclean things out of the presence of God. Paul added, in what has been described as "dense and unusual language"[8] that God "set forth [His Son] *to be a propitiation through faith in his blood,* to declare his righteousness for the remission of sins that are past, through the forbearance of God" (Romans 3:25; emphasis added).

Note the unfortunate choice of the word "propitiation" in KJV Romans 3:25. The English word *propitiation* denotes an effort to appease God. The LDS Bible footnote in Romans 3:25, "GR mercy seat" (Greek, *hilastērion*), helps unpack the nuance of the Greek term. This is the same word used in the Septuagint (LXX) for the lid of the ark of the covenant, or the "mercy seat." It is the place where, on the Jewish holy day *Yom Kippur,* atonement was made for all the assembly of Israel (Leviticus 16:16–17). N. T. Wright notes, "The LXX verb for 'make atonement for' [Greek, *exilasketai*] is from the same root as *hilastērion.*"[9]

The ancient non-Israelite sacrificial model often entailed the need for humans to appease the angry gods by offering some type of sacrifice. In some ancient cultures, appeasing the gods required the death of someone—anyone. However, this may not be the best model to use in understanding what Paul intended here—at least from a Restoration perspective. Certainly, from time to time, ancient Israel adopted such an appeasing model from their neighbors instead of applying an appropriate understanding of the law of sacrifice. In Hebrew, the object of the atoning act is to remove sin—purifying the person by wiping out sin. Atonement is made "for" a person or "for sin." God is never the object of the *Atonement.* Note Paul's conclusion: God Himself provides the expiation (see Romans 3:25). Interestingly, some scholars even surmise that

---

[8] Wright, "Letter to the Romans," 466.
[9] Ibid., 474.

CONCLUSION: PROFOUND EFFECTS

Romans 3:23–26 was the conclusion to a homily delivered by Paul on the Day of Atonement in a synagogue in Ephesus.[10]

Another important model of salvation for Paul is often identified as the redemption model.[11] This is again deeply rooted in the Old Testament—especially in the story of the Exodus. The word *redeem* means literally "to buy back" and suggests that because we are slaves to death and sin, we need to be snatched from the effects of sin and death. In this model, Jesus purchased us through His blood (see Galatians 4:5; Titus 2:14). Peter had a similar idea in mind when he stated, "But ye are a chosen generation, a royal priesthood, an holy nation, *a peculiar people;* that ye should shew forth the praises of him who hath called you out of darkness into his marvellous light" (1 Peter 2:9; emphasis added). Here "peculiar" comes from the Greek word for *purchased* (Greek, *peripoiēsin*).

Another way Paul explained the Atonement is through the *substitution model*. Paul assumed that a punishment is affixed to every broken law. Given the fact that we are all sinners, we are condemned to be punished for breaking the law. In what may be the single most important shift in Paul's understanding, he believed that Jesus was punished in our place, becoming, in the words of Paul, "a curse for us" (Galatians 3:13; see also 2 Corinthians 5:21).

We may never know the root cause of Paul's persecution of the early Church: "And Saul, yet breathing out threatenings and slaughter against the disciples of the Lord, went unto the high priest, and desired of him letters to Damascus to the synagogues, that if he found any of this way, whether they were men or women, he might bring them bound unto Jerusalem" (Acts 9:1–2). However, he may have provided several clues in his letters that may reveal at least one of the issues involved. In 1 Corinthians

---

[10] A. J. Hultgren, *Paul's Gospel and Mission: The Outlook from His Letter to the Romans* (Philadelphia: Fortress Press, 1985), 55–60.

[11] John D. Harvey, "Redemption," in Freedman, *Eerdmans Dictionary of the Bible*, 1114.

he reflected, "For the Jews require a sign, and the Greeks seek after wisdom: *But we preach Christ crucified, unto the Jews a stumbling-block,* and unto the Greeks foolishness" (1 Corinthians 1:22–23; emphasis added). Here, Paul highlights the problematic nature of preaching a crucified Messiah from a first-century Jewish perspective. In reality, a crucified Messiah was an oxymoron. The two words *crucified* and *Messiah* did not go together. The reason first-century Jews did not think of the Messiah as one crucified is most likely rooted in a passage from the book of Deuteronomy, "And if a man have committed a sin worthy of death, and he be to be put to death, and thou hang him on a tree: His body shall not remain all night upon the tree, but thou shalt in any wise bury him that day; (*for he that is hanged is accursed of God;*) that thy land be not defiled, which the Lord thy God giveth thee for an inheritance" (Deuteronomy 21:22–23; emphasis added).

Apparently, many first-century Jews believed that the Lord would spare a righteous person from crucifixion. However, if he or she were executed, then it would be known that God had judged them—in fact, had cursed them. It is not hard to understand how first-century Jews may have reacted to the disciples' proclamation that Jesus, who had been crucified, was the Messiah of God, His special anointed servant. Such a reading may have led Paul to persecute the early Saints believing their message was nothing more than blasphemy. Following such an understanding, one might assume that Jesus was not even a good man, let alone the Messiah; He was in fact "accursed of God."

However, when Paul met the risen Jesus Christ on the road to Damascus, he removed his first-century Jewish lens and then reread the scriptures through the lens of the Resurrection. What had been problematic for him before, based on the passage in Deuteronomy, was now the key to understanding the life, suffering, and death of Jesus of Nazareth. He observed and interpreted the same passage in light of those transcendent events: "Christ hath redeemed us from the curse of the law, *being made a curse for us:* for it is written, Cursed is every one that hangeth on a tree" (Galatians 3:13; emphasis added).

In his next attempt to help explain the significance of Jesus' death, Paul offered another model, often referred to as the *reconciliation model*.[12] Developing further the Old Testament idea of atonement, which included reconciling an estranged people to God, Paul beautifully illustrated this concept when he wrote: "For if, when we were enemies, we were reconciled to God by the death of his Son, much more, being reconciled, we shall be saved by his life" (Romans 5:10). Indeed, the reconciliation model is the paramount explanation of the Atonement. While the word *atonement* appears only once in English in the King James Version (see Romans 5:11), it derives from the Greek words for *atone* and *atonement*. These words appear elsewhere in Paul's writings, where they are usually translated as "reconciling" and "reconciliation" (Romans 11:15; 2 Corinthians 5:18–19).

Again, it would be a fundamentally flawed assumption to imagine that Paul thought God was an angry tyrant who needs to be appeased, whose feelings must be soothed by some human offering. Rather, Paul believed that God was the injured partner who nevertheless seeks reconciliation with us. He does so by sending His Son.

In 2 Corinthians 5:18–20, Jesus is the representative of God in effecting the reconciliation, and therefore the Apostles are the representatives of God in proclaiming it. Paul says that God made His appeal through them (and by implication through us). Jesus reconciles not only individuals to God (Colossians 1:22) but also the very cosmos to God: "to reconcile *all things* unto himself" (Colossians 1:20; emphasis added).

---

[12] Barbara E. Bowe, "Reconciliation," in Freedman, *Eerdmans Dictionary of the Bible,* 1112–13.

CONCLUSION: PROFOUND EFFECTS

In what may be familiar from similar thought in the Book of Mormon, Paul taught that Jesus shares the pains and suffering of His people, who likewise are transformed by sharing in some way in what Jesus experienced: "If so be that we suffer with him, that we may be also glorified together" (Romans 8:17). This model is identified as the *participation model*. This is particularly important for explaining the role of ordinances such as baptism in conveying the grace of Christ (see Romans 6:3–11).

Again, Latter-day Saints are familiar with Paul's next model because of passages like Doctrine and Covenants 45:1–5. In this model, God, as judge, acquits individuals of their guilt, declaring him "justified" (in harmony with law) by imputing the righteousness of Jesus to the believer (see Romans 4:5; 8:30–33; Galatians 3:8). Commentators often identify this as the *judicial model*. However, it is important to remember that Paul does not portray God as a stern judge with the Advocate "pleading with him, against (as it were) his better judgment, to exercise clemency. Rather, what takes place in Jesus and supremely on the cross is all from God's side. As Paul will insist in [Romans] 5:6–10, the death of Jesus reveals the love of God. God does not, so to speak, have to be persuaded that Jesus' death makes a good enough case for sinners to be justified. It was God who initiated the movement in the first place."[13] This reminds us that no model completely or fully reveals what the Father has done through His Son. They are in fact, models that represent but do not fully explain the Atonement. For Paul, "the depths of the significance of the death of Christ can scarcely be plumbed."[14]

Another model familiar to countless Christians over two thousand years is the *rescue model*. In this, the Father sends a *savior*. Half of the usages of *savior* (Greek, *sōtēr*) in the New Testament are

---

[13] Wright, "Letter to the Romans," 471.
[14] Green, "Death of Christ," 205.

CONCLUSION: PROFOUND EFFECTS

found in Paul's letters. The word *savior* often means "one providing salvation." Its related meanings include "deliverer" or "protector." Interestingly, Luke preserves Paul's sermon in Acts where he uses the term to identify Jesus, "Of this [David's] seed hath God according to his promise raised unto Israel a Saviour, Jesus" (Acts 13:23). Further, Paul said, "Men and brethren, children of the stock of Abraham, and whosoever among you feareth God, to you is the *word of this salvation* sent" (Acts 13:26; emphasis added). The "word of this salvation" (Greek, *ho logo tēs sōtērias*) focuses on Jesus' loving gift to us. The Savior of the world rescues humans not only from sin but also from death (see Romans 5:9; 11:26; 1 Timothy 1:15; 2 Timothy 1:9). He is the Redeemer of sin and the Savior of souls as reflected in the angel's announcement to Joseph, "And she shall bring forth a son, and thou shalt call his name Jesus: for *he shall save* his people from their sins" (Matthew 1:21; emphasis added).

Paul did not arrive at his understanding of the Atonement as a university-trained theologian sitting in a room surrounded by books, paid to teach, think, and write. His attempt to explain Jesus' Atonement may have been enriched by his training at the feet of Gamaliel (see Acts 22:3). Nevertheless, Paul knew Jesus Christ by the real and personal benefits of the Atonement—it grew out of his personal experience. He said, "In the cross of our Lord Jesus Christ, by whom the world is crucified unto me, and I unto the world" (Galatians 6:14).

Just as the most brilliant diamond reflects light because of the way that each facet is cut, so each facet is important to the total effect of the diamond. The same is true of Paul's teachings regarding the meaning and purpose of the Atonement. One model or metaphor cannot explain adequately or completely what Jesus did in Gethsemane and at Golgotha. Each model may get at some reality, approximating some truth, but ultimately fails to provide an adequate understanding of the events. The primary message of the

CONCLUSION: PROFOUND EFFECTS

Atonement is enhanced as we draw deeply from all the models and metaphors. Each opens a door of understanding that allows us to appreciate what Jesus Christ did for us.

In the end, without the ability to fully comprehend the love of God as manifested in the coming of His Son (see John 3:16), we conclude with Paul's testimony and witness from the life and teachings of the Apostles:

"What shall we then say to these things? If God be for us, who can be against us? He that spared not his own Son, but delivered him up for us all, how shall he not with him also freely give us all things? Who shall lay any thing to the charge of God's elect? It is God that justifieth. Who is he that condemneth? It is Christ that died, yea rather, that is risen again, who is even at the right hand of God, who also maketh intercession for us. Who shall separate us from the love of Christ? shall tribulation, or distress, or persecution, or famine, or nakedness, or peril, or sword? As it is written, For thy sake we are killed all the day long; we are accounted as sheep for the slaughter. Nay, in all these things we are more than conquerors through him that loved us. For I am persuaded, that neither death, nor life, nor angels, nor principalities, nor powers, nor things present, nor things to come, nor height, nor depth, nor any other creature, shall be able to separate us from the love of God, which is in Christ Jesus our Lord" (Romans 8:31–39).

CONTRIBUTORS

Gaye Strathearn
Associate Professor of Ancient Scripture, Brigham Young University
Ph.D. from Claremont Graduate University in Religion (New Testament)
Richard Neitzel Holzapfel and Gaye Strathearn, *He Will Give You Rest: An Invitation and a Promise* (Salt Lake City: Deseret Book, 2010).

Jennifer C. Lane
Associate Professor of Religious Education, Brigham Young University–Hawaii
Ph.D. from Claremont Graduate University in Religion with an emphasis in history of Christianity
"The Whole Meaning of the Law: Vicarious Sacrifice Strengthening Our Faith in Christ," in D. Kelly Ogden, Jared W. Ludlow, and Kerry Muhlstein eds., *The Gospel of Jesus Christ in the Old Testament* (Salt Lake City: Deseret Book, 2009), 67–85.

John Gee
Senior Research Fellow, William (Bill) Gay Professor of Egyptology, Neal A. Maxwell Institute for Religious Scholarship, Brigham Young University
Ph.D. from Yale University in Egyptology
"Egyptologists' Fallacies: Fallacies Arising from Limited Evidence," *Journal of Egyptian History* 3, 1 (2010): 137–58.

Brian M. Hauglid
Associate Professor of Ancient Scripture, Brigham Young University
Ph.D. from the University of Utah in Arabic and Islamic Studies
A Textual History of the Book of Abraham (Provo, Utah: Maxwell Institute, Brigham Young University, forthcoming).

Richard Neitzel Holzapfel
Professor of Church History and Doctrine
Ph.D. from University of California–Irvine in Ancient History
Richard Neitzel Holzapfel, Eric D. Huntsman, and Thomas A. Wayment, *Jesus Christ and the World of the New Testament* (Salt Lake City: Deseret Book, 2006).

Thomas A. Wayment
Associate Professor of Ancient Scripture, Brigham Young University
Ph.D. from Claremont Graduate University in Religion (New Testament)
Richard Neitzel Holzapfel and Thomas A. Wayment, *Making Sense of the New Testament* (Salt Lake City: Deseret Book, 2010).

CONTRIBUTORS

Richard D. Draper
Professor of Ancient Scripture, Brigham Young University
Ph.D. from Brigham Young University in Ancient History
Richard D. Draper, Kent Brown, and Michael Rhodes, *The Pearl of Great Price: A Verse-by-Verse Commentary* (Salt Lake City: Deseret Book, 2005).

Eric D. Huntsman
Associate Professor of Ancient Scripture, Affiliated Faculty, Classics and Ancient Near Eastern Studies, Brigham Young University
Ph.D. from University of Pennsylvania in Ancient History
"Livia Before Octavian," *Ancient Society* 39 (2009): 121–69
"And the Word Was Made Flesh: An LDS Exegesis of the Blood and Water Imagery in John," *Studies in the Bible and Antiquity* 1 (2009): 51–65.

Cecilia M. Peek
Associate Professor of Classics and Comparative Literature, Brigham Young University
Ph.D. from University of California–Berkeley in Ancient History and Mediterranean Archaeology
"The Death of John the Baptist," in Richard Neitzel Holzapfel and Thomas A. Wayment, eds., *From the Transfiguration through the Triumphal Entry,* vol. 3 of The Life and Teachings of Jesus Christ (Salt Lake City: Deseret Book, 2006), 208–35.

Kent P. Jackson
Professor of Ancient Scripture, Brigham Young University
Ph.D. from University of Michigan in Old Testament and Ancient Near Eastern Studies
"Joseph Smith and the Bible," *Scottish Journal of Theology* 63, no. 1 (2010): 24–40
Richard Neitzel Holzapfel and Kent P. Jackson, eds., *Joseph Smith: The Prophet and Seer* (Provo, Utah: Religious Studies Center, Brigham Young University, 2010).

SCRIPTURE INDEX

Genesis
1:26–27, p. 282
1:27, p. 179
4:1–16, p. 188
9:4, p. 77
10, p. 41
15:6, p. 179
17:9–14, pp. 76, 77
17:11–12, p. 118

Exodus
15:20, p. 47
20:13–14, p. 179
22:31, p. 77
34:11–17, p. 77

Leviticus
12:1–4, p. 118
16:16–17, p. 336
17:8–9, 10–16, p. 77
18:6–29, p. 77
19:18, p. 180
21:18–21, p. 68
23:1–21, p. 118

Numbers
3:41–51, p. 118
6:13–21, p. 145
11:29, p. 46
16:1–50, p. 188
22–25, pp. 184, 188
24:17–19, p. 13
31:7–18, p. 184

Deuteronomy
6:4, p. 32
6:4–9, p. 304
23:1, p. 68

Joshua
2, p. 179

2 Samuel
7:12–13, p. 14

1 Kings
13:1–2, p. 13
18:42–45, p. 179

2 Kings
22:14, p. 47

2 Chronicles
34:22, p. 47

Job
19:26, p. 283

Psalms
16:8–11, p. 14
73–98, p. 291
110:1, p. 14

Proverbs
10:12, p. 179

Isaiah
26:19, p. 283
45:1, p. 13
61:1–2, p. 20

Jeremiah
12:15, p. 77
31:31, p. 120

Ezekiel
37:22–26, p. 13

Daniel
7, p. 243
7:4–7, 11, p. 243

Joel
2:28–32, p. 14

Matthew
1:21, p. 341
5:3, p. 180
5:5, p. 165
5:7, p. 180
5:10–12, p. 180
5:11–12, p. 172
5:12, 22, 37, 48, p. 165
5:16, p. 164
5–7, pp. 30, 332
6:15, 24, p. 180
6:19, pp. 165, 180
7:1, 7, p. 165
7:1–5, 16, 20–21, 24–27, p. 180
7:12, p. 119
7:21, p. 165
7:28–29, p. 118
8:23–27, p. 30
9:1–8, p. 30
9:9, p. 28
10, p. 43
10:1–5, 7–8, p. 38
10:3, p. 152
10:5–6, p. 64
10:16–18, 21–22, 28, 39, p. 194
10:17, p. 90
10:34–37, p. 83
11:27, p. 118
12:46–50, p. 149
13, p. 30
13:55, pp. 136, 142, 185
13:55–56, p. 148
14:3–5, p. 30
14:23, p. 119
16, p. 210

16:13–16, p. 302
16:18, pp. 36, 37, 39, 57
16:19, p. 39
16:21–22, p. 14
17:1–13, p. 39
18, p. 39
18:15–18, p. 40
18:17, pp. 37, 40
18:20, p. 299
18–19:1, p. 30
20:26, p. 51
21:22, p. 180
22:13, p. 51
22:37–40, p. 119
22:39, pp. 179, 180
23:12, p. 180
23:37, p. 120
24–25, p. 30
24:2, p. 120
24:5, p. 254
24:5, 9–11, p. 254
24:10, pp. 254, 255
24:11, p. 254
26:14–16, p. 3
26:26–28, p. 273
27:52, p. 59
27:56, 61, p. 136
28:1, pp. 136, 151
28:19, pp. 121, 305
28:19–20, pp. 275, 307

Mark
1:14–15, p. 9
1:29–34, p. 121
2:1–12, p. 30

345

SCRIPTURE INDEX

2:13, p. 152
2:23–28, p. 120
3:18, pp. 151, 152
3:31–35, pp. 148, 149, 153
4:35–41, p. 30
6:3, pp. 135, 142, 147, 185
6:7–13, p. 38
6:44, p. 25
8:9, p. 25
9:35, p. 51
10:43, p. 51
13:9, p. 90
14:22, p. 129
15:40, p. 151
15:40, 47, pp. 136, 151
16:1, pp. 136, 151
16:8, 11, p. 293

Luke
1:1–4, p. 5
1:2, pp. 22, 28
1:3, p. 31
1:36, p. 136
2:22–24, 41, 46–47, p. 118
2:36, p. 47
3:16, p. 65
4:1–13, 15–21, 25–27, 31–32, 43–44, p. 119
4:14–15, 28–29, p. 120
4:16–30, p. 20
5:18–25, 33–35, 36–39, p. 120
6:13–16, p. 38
6:15, pp. 151, 152
8:1–3, p. 6
8:16, 18, 19–21, p. 149
8:21, pp. 144, 149
9:1–6, p. 40
9:28–31, p. 6
9:51–18:14, p. 31
9:52–53, p. 40
10:1, 4, p. 40
10:17, 20, p. 41
11:49, p. 47
21:12, p. 90
22:14, p. 38

22:25, pp. 97, 227
23:49, 55, p. 6
24:1, 36–48, p. 126
24:1–4, p. 6
24:10, pp. 136, 151
24:11, p. 293
24:27, 44, p. 119
24:33–36, p. 63
24:39, pp. 293, 296
24:42, p. 293
24:44–46, p. 7
24:45–47, p. 63
24:47, p. 65
24:49, p. 121

John
1:1, pp. 17, 289
1:1–14, p. 288
1:1–18, p. 128
1:3, p. 17
1:14, p. 289
2:5, 9, p. 51
3:16, p. 342
4:1, p. 37
4:3–4 (JST), p. 37
4:21, p. 120
6:23, p. 8
6:35–59, p. 332
6:67–70, p. 38
7, pp. 302, 303
7:1–2, p. 150
7:1–5, pp. 144, 153
7:3–4, p. 150
7:5, p. 134
7:35, p. 176
7:40–43, p. 302
8:41, p. 154
9:22, pp. 90, 120
10:14, p. 48
10:22, p. 119
10:24, p. 14
11, p. 293
12:26, p. 51
12:42, p. 90
13:16, p. 38
13:23, p. 193
16:1–4, p. 120
16:2, p. 24
19:25, p. 136

20:2, p. 193
20:24, p. 38
20:25, 27, p. 294
20:31, pp. 11, 332
21, p. 293
21:15, p. 48
21:20, p. 193
26, p. 293

Acts
1, pp. 6, 38, 45
1:1–2, 4, 13–14, p. 122
1:1–3, p. 5
1:3, p. 41
1:5, p. 65
1:8, pp. 41, 65, 69, 78
1:9–10, p. 7
1:11, pp. 65, 290
1:13, pp. 55, 151, 152
1:14, pp. 143, 144, 150, 153
1:15, pp. 53, 122, 125
1:21–26, p. 264
1:22, p. 45
2:2–5, 7, 9–11, p. 65
2:16–18, p. 46
2:21, 23–24, 32–33, p. 128
2:32, p. 15
2:36, pp. 14, 15, 32, 128
2:37, p. 128
2:38, pp. 15, 128
2:38, 41, p. 173
2:41, pp. 26, 53, 65, 122, 128
2:42, pp. 127, 128, 173, 177
2:42, 46, p. 128
2:44, p. 173
2:46, pp. 55, 122
2:46–47, p. 123
3:1, p. 123
3:1–11, p. 43
3:6, pp. 15, 43
3:21, p. 331
4:4, pp. 65, 122
4:10, p. 15

4:17–18, p. 173
4:34–35, p. 43
4:34–37, p. 25
4:36, p. 109
4:37, p. 54
5:1–11, p. 54
5:11, p. 173
5:12, p. 43
5:12, 14, p. 53
5:28, p. 173
5:42, pp. 122, 123
6, p. 53
6:1, pp. 53, 65, 127, 173
6:1–4, p. 44
6:1–7, p. 173
6:2–4, p. 54
6:2–6, p. 66
6:3, p. 42
6:7, pp. 55, 129
6:8–7:60, pp. 54, 173
6:8–15, p. 66
7:54–60, p. 66
7:58, pp. 69, 173
8:1, pp. 69, 173, 174, 176
8:1–3, p. 3
8:1–4, p. 66
8:3, pp. 69, 123, 173
8:4, pp. 174, 176
8:5, p. 174
8:5–13, 26–40, p. 66
8:5–40, p. 54
8:14–25, p. 67
8:15, 17, p. 54
8:17, p. 43
8:27, p. 68
8:27–28, p. 67
8:35–38, p. 68
8:37, p. 304
9:1, p. 70
9:1–2, pp. 124, 172, 337
9:1–20, pp. 3, 69
9:2, pp. 58, 70
9:3–6, 10–16, p. 71
9:4–6, 11, 14, p. 70

346

9:13, p. 59
9:15–16, 22, p. 71
9:20, pp. 71, 124
10:1–2, p. 26
10:1–48, pp. 69, 108
10:3–6, 10–16, p. 71
10:9–16, p. 144
10:11–16, 22, 30–33, p. 72
10:24, p. 56
10:28, pp. 64, 71, 80
10:44, p. 71
11, p. 72
11:1–3, p. 277
11:1–18, p. 69
11:3, p. 72
11:11–12, 13–14, 15–17, 18, p. 73
11:19, p. 176
11:19–21, p. 108
11:26, pp. 60, 109
11:27–28, pp. 46, 60
11:27–30, p. 311
11:29–30, p. 50
11:30, p. 73
12:1–2, pp. 44, 140, 152
12:12, p. 55
12:17, pp. 57, 264
12:25–14:28, p. 108
13, p. 75
13:1, pp. 46, 49
13:1–3, 7, 8, 12, p. 109
13:5, 14, p. 124
13:6–8, 13–14, p. 110
13:14, p. 124
13:26, p. 341
14, p. 44
14:1, p. 124
14:4, 14, pp. 44, 45
14:14, p. 264
14:23, pp. 50, 274
14:27, p. 77
15, pp. 45, 73, 74, 79, 132, 144, 145, 310, 311
15:1, 5, p. 161
15:1–2, p. 75
15:1–11, pp. 26, 277
15:1–34, p. 69
15:2, pp. 26, 50, 63
15:2, 4, 6, 22–23, p. 50
15:4, p. 42
15:5, pp. 76, 77, 129, 145, 156
15:7, 11, p. 76
15:7–11, p. 144
15:12, pp. 77, 311
15:13–21, pp. 77, 141, 177
15:19, pp. 77, 132, 144
15:20, p. 145
15:22, p. 77
15:23–24, p. 145
15:23–30, p. 311
15:32, p. 46
15:39, p. 109
16:4, p. 50
16:10, p. 5
16:14, p. 124
16:14–15, p. 9
16:14–15, 40, p. 113
16:15, pp. 56, 124
16:18, p. 15
16:20–21, 35, 38, p. 111
16:37–39, p. 112
17:1, 10, 17, p. 124
17:6, 8, 16–34, p. 114
17:28–29, 32, p. 291
18:4, pp. 24, 124
18:7, pp. 113, 124
18:8, p. 124
18:12, p. 109
18:12–17, p. 112
18:26, p. 20
19:6, p. 46
19:8, p. 124
19:8–22, p. 261
19:13–18, p. 197
19:19, p. 198
19:23, p. 59
19:24–41, 26–27, p. 198
19:31, 35–41, p. 115
19:38, p. 109
20:7, p. 128
20:20, p. 124
20:25, 28, p. 50
20:29, p. 255
20:29–31, pp. 213, 255
20:30–31, p. 255
20:35, p. 3
21, pp. 145, 147
21:8, pp. 48, 66
21:9–10, p. 46
21:17–18, p. 146
21:17–25, p. 50
21:18–26, p. 177
21:20, pp. 60, 129
21:20, 23–24, p. 123
21:21, p. 130
21:29, p. 146
22:3, pp. 8, 341
22:4, p. 59
22:27–28, p. 106
23:24, 26, 33, p. 109
24:1, 10, p. 109
24:5, 14, 22, p. 59
26:28, p. 60
26:30, p. 109

Romans
1:1, pp. 9, 45, 59
1:16, pp. 253, 333
3:2, p. 61
3:9–12, 23, p. 333
3:23–26, p. 337
3:25, p. 336
3:28, p. 157
4:5, p. 340
5:6–10, pp. 333, 340
5:9, p. 341
5:10–11, p. 339
6:3–11, p. 340
8:17, 30–33, p. 340
8:31–39, p. 342
9:1–2, p. 51
11:1, p. 130
11:15, p. 339
11:26, p. 341
12:6, p. 46
13:1–7, p. 236
13:4, p. 51
15:8, p. 51
15:14, p. 138
16, p. 125
16:1, pp. 51, 52
16:3–5, pp. 56, 125
16:7, p. 44
16:10–11, 14–15, p. 125
16:14–15, p. 56
16:17, pp. 138, 277
16:23, pp. 56, 113

1 Corinthians
1:1, pp. 45, 47, 59
1:2, p. 59
1:10–16, pp. 57, 259
1:11, pp. 117, 124, 294
1:14, p. 124
1:14, 16, p. 113
1:16, p. 56
1:18, 23, p. 334
1:22–23, p. 338
1:23, pp. 9, 153
1:23–24, 18, p. 330
2:4, p. 294
3:3–10, p. 259
3:5, pp. 51, 52
3:16, p. 295
5:1–13, p. 259
5:9, p. 5
6:9–11, pp. 80, 81
6:19, p. 295
7:10–11, p. 114
7:12, p. 22
7:12–13, 15, p. 83
7:17–24, p. 69
8:1–13, p. 87
8:4, 10–13, p. 216

347

SCRIPTURE INDEX

9:1–5, p. 45
9:5, pp. 138, 139
10:16, p. 121
10:25, p. 87
10:27–29, p. 87
11:4–5, p. 46
11:5, p. 47
11:18, p. 259
11:20, p. 129
11:23, pp. 22, 332
11:23–25, pp. 3, 21, 332
11:23–34, p. 259
11:26, p. 122
11:26–34, p. 128
12:7–10, p. 47
12:10, p. 46
12:28, p. 35
14:39, p. 47
14:1–6, 22–26, 31–32, 37, 39, p. 46
14:1–14, 33, p. 259
14:22–24, p. 129
14:23, pp. 56, 125, 128
14:26, p. 19
14:26–40, p. 47
14:34–35, p. 113
15, pp. 21, 296
15:1, p. 22
15:1–4, pp. 20, 332
15:1–58, p. 259
15:3, pp. 15, 127, 294, 334
15:3–4, p. 333
15:4, p. 296
15:5, 7, p. 44
15:5–7, p. 139
15:5–8, p. 21
15:6, p. 26
15:7, p. 138
15:9, p. 46
15:12, pp. 277, 294
15:14, 19, p. 294
15:29, p. 295
15:35, p. 294
15:36–38, 39, p. 297

15:40–41, p. 297
15:42–44, p. 298
15:44, p. 295
15:49, pp. 295, 298
15:50, 53–54, p. 295
16:15–16, p. 57
16:15–17, p. 113
16:19, p. 56

2 Corinthians
1:1, p. 142
1:21, p. 259
3:6, p. 51
4:7, p. 276
5:18–20, p. 339
5:20, p. 259
5:21, p. 337
6:4, p. 51
6:14, p. 83
8:23, p. 44
11:4, p. 260
11:5, 22–23, p. 260
11:13, p. 260
11:15, 23, p. 51
11:22–28, p. 4
11–12, p. 259
12:11, p. 260
12:12, p. 43

Galatians
1:6, p. 258
1:6–7, p. 22
1:9, 11–12, 13–14, 15, p. 23
1:18–19, p. 24
1:19, pp. 138, 264
2, p. 132
2:1–3, p. 73
2:1–10, p. 311
2:4, p. 4
2:4–5, p. 74
2:9, pp. 26, 139, 140
2:10, p. 59
2:11, p. 141
2:11–12, p. 74
2:12, pp. 74, 139, 141, 258
2:15, p. 64
2:17, p. 51

3:1–5, p. 258
3:8, p. 340
3:13, pp. 337, 339
3:27–29, p. 9
4:4, p. 335
4:5, p. 337
4:10, 21, p. 258
5:2–4, p. 258
5:10, 12, p. 258
6:12–13, p. 258
6:14, p. 341

Ephesians
2:1–3, p. 333
2:19, p. 95
2:19–20, p. 42
2:20, p. 47
3:5, p. 47
3:7, p. 51
4, p. 48
4:11, p. 47
4:11–14, p. 42
4:12, p. 59
5:19, p. 128
5:21–6:9, p. 81
5:25, p. 83
6:4, p. 83
6:12, p. 217
6:21, p. 52

Philippians
1, p. 181
1:1, pp. 45, 51, 52
2:6–1, p. 128
2:6–11, p. 16
2:25, p. 44
3, p. 183
7, pp. 185, 271, 292

Colossians
1:7, 23, 25, p. 52
1:15–2:23, p. 260
1:15–20, pp. 17, 128
1:16–17, p. 17
1:16–19, p. 260
1:20, pp. 333, 339
1:22, p. 339
2:6–8, p. 261
2:9–10, p. 260
2:12, p. 273
2:18, p. 261
3:1, p. 273

3:16, p. 128
3:18–24, p. 81
4:7, p. 52
4:15, p. 56

1 Thessalonians
3:2, p. 52
4:13–17, p. 258
5:20, p. 46

2 Thessalonians
2:1–12, p. 255
2:2–4, p. 258
2:3, pp. 251, 255
2:4–8, p. 255

1 Timothy
1:3, p. 277
1:4, p. 261
1:7, p. 49
1:18, p. 46
2:1–2, pp. 92, 116
2:7, p. 49
2:11, p. 113
3:1, 10, p. 42
3:2, 5, p. 51
3:8–13, p. 52
3:16, p. 128
4:1, pp. 250, 255
4:1–3, pp. 255, 257
4:6, pp. 52, 255
4:14, pp. 46, 50
5:17, p. 50
6:20, p. 261

2 Timothy
1:9, p. 341
1:11, p. 49
1:15, pp. 213, 261
1:15, 20, p. 214
2:11–13, p. 17
2:16, p. 261
2:17–18, p. 261
4:3, pp. 256, 267, 268
4:3–4, pp. 255, 256, 277
4:5, p. 48
4:14, p. 214

Titus
1:1, p. 45
1:5, pp. 50, 54, 274

1:7, 9, p. 51
2:1–10, p. 81
2:3, p. 49
2:14, p. 337
3:1–2, p. 92
3:9, p. 261

Philemon
1:1, p. 45
1:1–2, 10, p. 57
1:2, p. 56

Hebrews
1:1–4, p. 17
5:1, p. 54
8:3, p. 54
13:19–25, p. 143

James
1:4, p. 163
1:1, pp. 142, 176
1:2, pp. 165, 180
1:4, pp. 165, 168
1:5, pp. 165, 166, 168, 331
1:5–6, p. 178
1:6, pp. 168, 180
1:9, p. 168
1:9–10, p. 178
1:12–15, p. 178
1:19, pp. 168, 178
1:20, p. 165
1:21, p. 168
1:22, pp. 158, 168, 180
1:22–25, p. 178
1:27, pp. 157, 160, 168, 176, 178
2:1–9, p. 176
2:5, pp. 168, 180
2:6, pp. 176, 179
2:7, p. 177
2:8, pp. 168, 179
2:10, p. 168
2:11, p. 179
2:12, pp. 168, 180
2:12–26, p. 178
2:13, p. 165
2:14, pp. 160, 165
2:14, pp. 180, 259
2:15, 17, 26, p. 160
2:15–16, p. 178
2:18, pp. 160, 168

2:19, p. 160
2:19–22, p. 163
2:22–23, p. 179
2:23–24, p. 160
2:26, pp. 157, 159, 170
3:1, p. 180
3:1–12, p. 178
3:2, p. 164
3:2–8, p. 160
3:2–12, p. 180
3:5–6, 8, p. 164
3:7–9, p. 179
3:12, p. 180
3:13, pp. 165, 168
3:14, p. 168
4:1–3, p. 167
4:4, pp. 167, 178
4:5, p. 179
4:6, p. 167
4:7, p. 168
4:8, pp. 168, 169
4:9, p. 169
4:10, pp. 169, 180
4:11, pp. 160, 169, 176
4:11–12, p. 178
4:13–15, p. 169
5:1, 7–8, p. 169
5:1–5, pp. 167, 176
5:2, p. 165
5:2–3, p. 180
5:4–5, p. 179
5:7–11, p. 178
5:9, pp. 169, 180
5:12, pp. 165, 169, 180
5:14–15, pp. 50, 178
5:16, p. 169
5:17, 20, p. 179

1 Peter
1:1, pp. 93, 181, 195
1:4, 6–7, p. 182
1:8, 12–13, 21, p. 181
2:5–9, p. 181
2:9, pp. 181, 337
2:9–10, p. 96
2:11, pp. 181, 182

2:11–3:12, p. 81
2:12, p. 83
2:13–14, p. 236
2:13–14, 17, p. 116
2:13–17, p. 92
2:15, 20–24, p. 182
2:16, 22–24, p. 181
2:25, p. 51
3:1, p. 83
3:9, 14, 16–17, p. 182
3:18–20, p. 181
4:3, 12–13, p. 182
4:7–8, 14, p. 181
4:12, p. 171
4:16, p. 60
5:1, pp. 50, 182
5:1–2, p. 49
5:1–3, p. 50
5:2, p. 182
5:3, p. 50
5:5, p. 181
5:5, 17, p. 181

2 Peter
1:2, 5, 12, p. 187
1:4–7, 12–14, 20–21, p. 183
1:19, p. 46
2:1, pp. 49, 256
2:1–3, pp. 183, 256
2:1–3:3, p. 187
2:2–3, p. 256
2:4–5, 6–7, 12–14, p. 184
2:6–9, p. 183
2:18–21, p. 185
3:1, 15–16, p. 182
3:3, pp. 183, 186
3:3–4, 8–9, 15, p. 183
3:14, p. 187

1 John
1:1, p. 263
1:1–3, p. 289
2:18, pp. 256, 257, 263, 268, 277, 288

2:18–19, pp. 213, 263
2:19, 22, p. 288
2:24, 26, p. 263
4:1, p. 263
4:2–3, pp. 262, 263, 305
4:3, pp. 288, 289

2 John
1:1, p. 29
1:7, pp. 262, 277, 288

3 John
1:1, p. 29
1:9–10, pp. 10, 57, 213–14, 263

Jude
1:18, p. 256
1:1 (JST), p. 262
1:1, pp. 142, 185, 186
1:2, p. 187
1:3, pp. 185, 187, 189, 261
1:4, pp. 256, 262
1:4, 8, p. 188
1:4, 17–19, p. 256
1:5–6, pp. 187, 188
1:7, pp. 185, 188
1:8, p. 262
1:10–11, p. 188
1:13, p. 187
1:17, p. 186
1:17–18, pp. 257, 262
1:18, pp. 183, 186, 188
1:19, p. 262
1:24, p. 187
14–16, p. 128

Revelation
1:3, p. 46
1:5, p. 212
1:8, p. 215
1:9, pp. 191, 208, 239
1:10, p. 210
1–7, p. 241
2:2, pp. 217, 262

SCRIPTURE INDEX

2:2, 9, 13, 19, p. 192
2:3, p. 239
2:3, 9, p. 91
2:4–6, 14–16, 20–24, p. 262
2:9, p. 211
2:12–13, p. 192
2:13, pp. 196, 212
2:14, p. 217
2:19, p. 203
2:20, pp. 217, 262
3:2–4, 15–17, p. 262
3:5, 12, p. 215
3:9, p. 203
4:1, p. 221
5:6, p. 215
6:1–17, p. 238
6:9, pp. 207, 209, 239
7, p. 243
7:3, p. 215
7:13–17, p. 10
8:1, p. 238
9:4, p. 215
10:11, p. 46
11:2, p. 241
13, pp. 238, 243, 246
13:8, p. 256
13:1, pp. 221, 243, 244
13:1–2, p. 215
13:1–9, p. 256
13:1–18, p. 222
13:2, pp. 215, 244
13:3, p. 244
13:5–7, p. 245
13:8, 17, p. 215
13:11–12, 15, p. 245
13:18, p. 240
14, p. 248
14:9–11, p. 215
16:2, p. 215
16:6, p. 46
17, pp. 215, 238, 247, 248
17:1–18, p. 222
17:1–19:10, p. 246
17:9–10, p. 240
18:20, 24, p. 46
19:7–8, p. 215
19:10, pp. 46, 48
20:4, pp. 207, 209
20:15, p. 215
21:2, 9–11, 27, p. 215
22:1–7, p. 10
22:4, p. 215
22:6–7, 9–10, 18–19, p. 46
22:6–21, p. 221
22:16–17, p. 249

1 Nephi
13, pp. 265, 266, 268
13:4–6, 20–29, p. 265
13:23, p. 330
13:26, pp. 265, 330
13:27, p. 267
13:28, pp. 265, 268
13:29, pp. 265, 266
14, p. 268
14:9–17, p. 247
14:20–27, p. 193
15:13, p. 253

2 Nephi
11:4, p. 335

Mosiah
14:7, p. 335

Alma
11:43, 45, p. 296
30:53, p. 267
34:14, p. 335
34:32, p. 169

3 Nephi
27:13–14, 20–21, p. 58
27:13–15, p. 20

Ether
13:10, p. 335

Moroni
4:3, p. 273
5:2, p. 273
10:11, p. 161

Doctrine and Covenants
1:30, p. 252
7, p. 268
7:1, p. 193
7:1–3, p. 194
7:3, p. 198
13–16, p. 39
20:77, 79, p. 273
45:1–5, p. 340
64:25, p. 170
77:7, p. 238
86:2–3, p. 274
88:15, p. 280
110:11, p. 39

Joseph Smith–History
1:19, p. 300

Articles of Faith
1:6, pp. 35, 62
1:8, p. 265

Apocrypha
2 Maccabees
7:10, p. 283
50:2, p. 283

SUBJECT INDEX

Acts: understanding, 1–3; Paul and, 3–4, 5; Gospel of Luke and, 5–7; brothers of Jesus in, 143–47; prophesies of Apostasy, 255
Adoptionism, 317
Afflictions, perfection and, 162–63
Agabus, 46
Agathē tychē, 84
Agathos daimōn, 84
Agrippa I: term *Christian* and, 60; rule of, 97, 106; James and, 140, 147, 156
Akiva, Rabbi, 132
Alexander the Great, 225–26, 243
Amidah, 130
Ananias, 70
Andronicus, 44
Antichrist, 288, 289–90
Antioch, 73–76, 108–9
Antiochus I, 227
Antiochus II, 227
Antiochus III, 231
Antiochus IV Epiphanes, 226
Antipas, 212
Antony, Mark, 111, 231
Apocalypse, 246–47
Apollo, 84
Apostasia, 251
Apostasy: beginning of, 9–10; persecution and, 189–92; Paul's warning and, 213–17; overview of, 250–52; restoration of gospel and, 252–54; New Testament prophesies of, 254–57; witnesses of, 257–63; "great and abominable church" and, 263–68; post-New Testament Christianity and, 268–74; Apostles and, 10, 250–51, 263–65, 274–75; *sōma sēma* and, 276–77
Apostle(s): Apostasy and, 10, 250–51, 263–65, 274–75; bear witness of Jesus Christ, 21–23; written testimonies of, 25–27; calling of, 38–40, 42–44, 63–64; in early Church, 42–46; Twelve, 44–45; prophets and, 47; Pentecost and, 64–65; Greek-speaking, 65–67; James as, 139–40; persecution of, 194; Clement on, 270; importance of, 274–75. *See also* Ministries of Apostles
"Apostolic Decree," 76–78
Apostolic Fathers, 269–74
Apostolos, 38
Aquila, 56, 124
Areopagus, 114
Arianism, 317
Ariston, 27
Arius, 284
Artemis, 84
Articles of Faith, 35, 61–62
Ascension, 7, 41–42
Asia: Roman Empire and, 102; Paul and, 115–16; persecution in, 191–92, 194–200, 201–4; guilds and trade unions in, 200–201; imperial cult in, 232–34
Asiarchs, 115
Athanasius, 159
Atheism, 202–3
Athens, 114
Atonement: in early Church meetings, 19–21; Paul's teachings on, 332–42
Attalus III, 231
Augustine, 291
Augustus, 92, 98, 103–7, 111, 231–33

Bacchanalia, 92
Balaam, 188
Ballard, Melvin J., 297
Banishment, 205–10, 218–19

SUBJECT INDEX

Baptism, 37–38, 128, 307–9
Bar Kochba, 132
Barnabas, 109–11
Basilides, 286–87, 292
Beasts of Revelation: introduction to, 221–23; description of, 243–47; modern reading of, 247–49
Benson, Ezra Taft, 167
Bible, 264–66, 330
Birkat ha-minim, 130–31, 236–37
Bishops, 50–53, 217, 312–13
Blaspheme, defined, 177
Blue, Bradley, 129
Bodies, 295–98. *See also Sōma sēma*
Book of Enoch, 187–88
Brasidas, 225
Brother, meaning of title, 134–35, 137–38
Brothers of Jesus: in letters of Paul, 137–41; in general epistles, 142–43; in Acts, 143–47; in Gospels, 147–51; conclusions on, 155–56
Brutus, 111
Burial societies, 89–90

Caesar, Julius, 92, 112, 228, 233, 240
Caesaropapism, 316
Cain, 188
Caligula. *See* Gaius
Candace, Queen, 67
Cassius, 111
Catholic Epistles, 158
Celestial bodies, 297
Celsus, 290–91
Chadwick, Jeffrey R., 125
Charles, R. H., 193
"Chrestus," 60
Christ, as title, 15
Christian hymns, 128–29
Christian(s): expelled from synagogues, 25; as title, 60–61; persecution of, 93–95, 171–72, 189–92, 201–4; alienation of, 95–96; Roman government and, 116; in Jerusalem, 125; threats to, 211–17, imperial cult and, 236–37; "Judaized," 258; in post–New Testament era, 268–74; in second century, 278–79; Latter-day Saints as, 299; effects of, 330–31
"Christus," 60
Church, defined, 37
"Church Discourse," 39–40

Church of Jesus Christ of Latter-day Saints, The, 35–36, 299
Cicero, 92
Circumcision, 74, 75, 76–78
City-states, 100–101, 106
Civic affairs, 91–95
Claudius, 105
Clement of Alexandria: on Apostles, 41; on banishment of John, 208, 241; *sōma sēma* and, 279–80, 287–88; on Docetists, 285
Clement of Rome, 181, 183, 269–70
Collegia, 88–89, 92–93
Colossians, 260–61
Constantine: persecution of Christians and, 189; Roman Catholic Church and, 266, 315; First Council of Nicaea and, 284, 311–12, 316
Conversion(s): of Ethiopian eunuch, 67–69; of Paul, 69–71; of Peter, 71–72; of Jerusalem Church leaders, 72–73. *See also* Gentile conversions
Corinth, 112–13
Cornelius, 56, 71–72, 108
Council of Chalcedon, 285, 321–26
Councils: role of, 310–16; creeds and, 316–27; conclusions on, 327–29
Councils of Ephesus, 285, 321–26
Court official, conversion of, 67–69
Creation, 17
Creeds: overview of, 299–303; early, 303–9; councils and, 316–27; conclusions on, 327–29
Crispus, 124
Crucifixion, 151–55, 338–39
Cyprus, 109–10
Cyril, 126
Cyrus, 13

Daniel, 243–44
Day of Pentecost, 13–15
Deacons, 51–53
Definition of Chalcedon, 323–26
Degrees of glory, 297
Demiurge, 292–93
Deportatio, 205–6
Diakonoi/Diakonos, 51–52
Diaspora, 176
Didache, 273–74
Di manes, 86
Dionysus, Bishop of Alexandria, 193
Diotrephes, 10, 263

Di penates, 85
Disciples. *See* Apostle(s)
Divorce, 114
Docetism, 262, 271, 285, 305
Doctrine of the Hypostatic Union, 325–26
Domitian: persecution under, 94, 172, 175, 195; Jude and, 185, 186; emperor worship and, 199, 202; John and, 210; dating Revelation and, 240–42
Dunn, James D. G., 77–78, 125

Early Christian hymns, 15–18, 32–33
Early Christian meetings, 18–24, 55–57, 89–90, 92–93. *See also* House churches
Early Church: decline of, 9–10; Jerusalem as center of, 25–26; introduction to, 35–36; during Jesus' ministry, 36–41; following Ascension, 41–42; Apostles in, 42–46; prophets in, 46–48; administration of, 53–57; as Jesus' church, 57–61; conclusions on, 61–62
Early Republic, 99
Eastern Orthodox Church, 316
Edict of Milan, 311–12
Ekklesia, 37, 89–90
Eldad, 46
Elders, in early Church, 49–50
Elias, 6–7
Elisabeth, 136
Elymus Bar-jesus, 110
Emperor worship, 198–200, 202. *See also* Imperial cult
Enoch, 187–88
Epaphroditus, 44
Ephesus, 115–16, 194–200
Epictetus, 281
Episkopoi, 50–51
Epistle of Barnabas, 272
Epistle of James: introduction to, 157–58; authenticity and authorship of, 158–59; faith and works in, 159–62; textual study of, 162; perfection in, 162–66; wisdom in, 166–67; pride in, 167–68; imperative tense in, 168–69; conclusions on, 169–70; persecution in, 173–80; prophesies of Apostasy, 258–59
Epistle of Jude, 185–89, 256, 261–62
Erastus, 113

Ergon, 159–60
Essenes, 284
Euangelistes, 48
Eunuch, conversion of, 67–69
Eusebius: on persecution of Christians, 26, 94, 195; on Gospels, 29–30; on Apostles, 41; on Epistle of James, 158, 159; on 1 Peter, 181; on John, 192, 210
Eutyches, 285
Eutychianism, 323–25
Evangelists, 48
Expiation model, 335

Faith: James and Paul on, 157–62, 169–70; James on, 162; perfection and, 162–66; works and, 258–59
False gospel, 22–23
Family, Gentile conversions and, 81–86
"The Family: A Proclamation to the World," 82
Family of Jesus: religious practices of, 118–19; overview of, 134–36; potential members of, 136–37; in letters of Paul, 137–43; in general epistles, 142–43; in Acts, 143–47; in Gospels, 147–51; crucifixion and, 151–55; conclusions on, 155–56
Fire of Rome (A.D. 64), 93–94
1 Corinthians, 259, 294–98
First Council of Constantinople, 319–21
First Council of Nicaea, 284, 311–12, 316–17
1 John, 256, 262–63
1 Peter, 180–82
1 Thessalonians, 258
1 Timothy, 255, 261
First Vision, 166–67, 252–53, 300, 331
Fitzmyer, Joseph, 310
Flamininus, T. Quinctius, 229–30
Funerals, 89–90
Futurist school, 237

Gaius, 113, 235, 236
Galatians, 22–24, 258
Galba, Ser. Sulpicius, 101
Gallio, 112
Gamli'el II, 130
Garden Tomb, 6–7
General Epistles, 142–43
Genius, 85
Gentile conversions: first, 67–69;

SUBJECT INDEX

introduction to, 80–81; impact on family life, 81–86; impact on social and economic life, 86–91; impact on civil and political life, 91–95; alienation following, 95–96; early Christian worship and, 131–32
Gentiles: table fellowship and, 64; Antioch conflict and, 73–76; Jerusalem Conference and, 76–78
Glory, degrees of, 297
Gnosticism, 260–61
God, nature of, 316–26
God-Fearers, 68, 75, 90–91
Gospel: sources of learning in, 21–24; defined, 58. *See also* Oral gospel
Gospels: oral gospel and, 27–32; brothers of Jesus in, 147–51
"Great and abominable church," 263–68
Greek society, 80–86
Greek-speaking disciples, 8, 65–67
Gregory of Nyssa, 322
Guilds, 200–201, 203–4

Ha-Qatan, R. Shemu'el, 130
Harline, Craig, 126
Hegesippus, 27, 185, 194
Helene of Adiabene, Queen, 67
Hellēnistas, 109
Hellenized Jews, 107
Hera, 84
Heracles, 224
Heresy, 278–79. *See also* Apostasy
Herod Agrippa I. *See* Agrippa I
Herod Antipas, 105
Herod the Great. *See* Agrippa I
Heroes, 223–25
Hestia, 84
Hetairiai, 88–89, 92–93
Historicist school, 237
Holy Ghost, 64–65, 320
Houlden, J. L., 69
House churches: worship in, 55–57, 126–29; functions of, 89–90; opposition to, 92–93; synagogues and, 117; establishment of, 121–25; Gentiles and, 131–32
Household codes, 81–83
Hymns, early Christian, 15–18, 32–33, 128–29
Hypostatic union, 325–26

Idealist school, 237–38

Ignatius of Antioch: on priesthood offices, 51, 52–53, 217; term "Christian" and, 61; 1 Peter and, 181; 2 Peter and, 183; Asian church and, 195; writings of, 270–71; Apostasy and, 271–72; on suffering of Christ, 285–86
Imperial cult: requirements of, 91–93, 234–37; overview of, 221–23; development of, 223; Greek and Hellenistic, 223–27; Roman, 227–32; in Asia, 232–34. *See also* Emperor worship
Incarnation, 306
Intelligence, 163
Irenaeus of Lyon: Epistle of James and, 158; 1 Peter and, 181; Jude and, 185; on persecution of Christians, 195; on Apocalypse, 241; on Resurrection, 295

James, 138–48, 155–56. *See also* Epistle of James
James the less, 151–55
James the son of Alphaeus, 151–52
James the son of Zebedee, 140, 143, 151, 152, 154, 177
Jehovah, 14–15
Jerome, 158
Jerusalem: fall of, 12, 25–27; Christians in, 125
Jerusalem Council, 76–78, 132, 144–45, 310–11
Jerusalem Temple, 12
Jesus Christ: in second half of New Testament, 2–3; as fulfillment of Law, 7; life and ministry of, 7–9; as Messiah, 13–14; written biography for, 33–34; early Church and, 36–41, 57–61; Judaism and, 117–21; authority of, 118, 120; as source of James' teachings, 180; nature of, 284–90, 316–26; creeds and, 304–6; salvation through, 332–42. *See also* Family of Jesus
Jewish-Christians, 121, 129–32
Jewish scriptures, 127–28
Jews: early Christian hymns and, 17–18; table fellowship and, 64; Antioch conflict and, 73–76; Jerusalem Conference and, 76–78; imperial cult and, 91–93; Hellenized, 107; Jewish-Christians and, 129–31; persecution

354

of, 133; Christian persecution and, 203. *See also* Judaism
Jezebel, 215–16, 217
John (Gospel): Logos Hymn and, 16–17; on expulsion of Christians from synagogues, 25; *apostolos* in, 38
John the Beloved: revelation on Apostasy and, 10; persecution of Christians and, 191–92; Revelation and, 192–94, 210–11; banishment of, 204–10, 218–19; Jesus Christ and, 288–89
John the elder, 29–30
Joseph (husband of Mary), 118–19
Josephus, 147, 188–89, 284
Joses, 147
Joshua, 46
Judaism: converts to, 67; Jesus Christ and, 117–21; imperial cult and, 235–36; Christianity and, 258; views on body, 282–84. *See also* Jews
Judaizers, 160
Judaizing Christians, 135
Judas, 147
Judas Lebbaeus, 137
Jude, 142–43, 155. *See also* Epistle of Jude
Judicial model, 340
Julian the Apostate, 319
Junia, 44
Justin Martyr, 18–19, 181, 192, 278–79, 292
Justus, 113
Juvenal, 184, 240

Keys, 39, 263–64
Knowledge, 163, 166
Koinon, 115
Korah, 188

Lar familiaris, 85
Law of Moses, 7
Le Boulluec, Alain, 278
Leo III, 315–16
Livia, 232, 233
Logos Hymn, 16–17, 289
Lucullus, 230
Luke (Gospel), 5–7, 27–32
Luke, Paul and, 4–5
Luther, Martin, 159
Lydia, 113, 124
Lysander, 225

Manius Aquillius, 230
Marcellus, 229
Marcion, 158, 287, 292
Mark (Gospel), 27–32
Marriage, Gentile conversion and, 83–84
Martial, 184
Martyr, defined, 171
The Martyrdom of Polycarp, 272
Mary (mother of James the less and Joses), 151–55
Mary (mother of Jesus), 118–19, 151–55, 323
Mary (wife of Cleopas), 137, 152
Matthew (Gospel), 27–32
Matthews, Robert J., 41
Matthias, 41
McConkie, Bruce R., 167, 331–32
Meat, sacrificial, 86–87
Medad, 46
Meeks, Wayne A., 278
Melchizedek Priesthood, 253–54
Messiah: expectations for, 13–14; Jesus Christ as, 118; crucifixion and, 338–39
Millet, Robert L., 41
Ministries of Apostles: calling to, 63–64; Pentecost and, 64–65; outside of Jerusalem, 65–67; first Gentile convert from, 67–69; conversion of Paul and, 69–71; conversion of Peter and, 71–72; ministries of Jerusalem Church leaders and, 72–73; Antioch conflict and, 73–76; Jerusalem Conference and, 76–78; conclusions on, 78–79
Mithridates of Pontus, 102
Monophysitism, 321, 322–26
Moses, 6–7, 46
Mount of Transfiguration, 6–7
Mucious Scaevola, 230
Muratorian, 158
Murphy-O'Connor, Jerome, 71, 74–75

Nazarite vow, 145–46
Nero: persecution of Christians and, 94, 172, 201; Suetonius and, 184; dating Revelation and, 238–40; beast of Revelation and, 244–45, 246
Nestorius/Nestorianism, 322–26
New Testament: understanding last half of, 1–3; Paul and, 3–4; prophesies of Apostasy, 254–57; power and influence of, 331–32

Nibley, Hugh, 41
Niceno-Constantinopolitan Creed, 319–21
Nymphas, 56

Octavian. *See* Augustus
Old Testament, 14–15, 19–21, 179
Onesimus, 57
Oral gospel: introduction to, 11–13; discourse on Day of Pentecost and, 13–15; early Christian hymns and, 15–18; early Church meetings and, 18–24; fall of Jerusalem and, 25–27; synoptic Gospels and, 27–32; conclusions on, 32–34
Origen, 159
Orphics, 279–80, 295–96
Ovid, 184

Paganism: in family life, 84–88; in civic and political life, 91–95, 204; guilds and, 200–201; as threat to Church, 212–13, 215
Papacy, beginnings of, 315
Papias, 192
Pastors, 48–49
Pater familias, 85, 228–29
Patmos, 204–10, 218–19
Patriarchs, 48
Patrōoi theoi, 84
Paul: influence of, 3–4; Luke and, 4–5; life and ministry of, 7–9; as Apostle, 45–46, 47; conversion of, 69–71; Roman officials and, 108–16; James and, 145–46; faith versus works and, 157–58, 159–62, 169–70; persecution of, 172–73; opposition to, 259–60; on salvation, 332–42
Pauline letters, 137–41
Pax Augusti, 104
Pax Romana, 107, 116
Pelikan, Jaroslav, 327–28
Pella prophecy, 26–27
Peloponnesian War, 225
Pentecost, 64–65
Perfection, 162–66
Persecution: of Christians, 93–95, 171–72, 189–92, 201–4; of Apostles, 120; of Jews, 133; of Paul, 172–73; in Epistle of James, 173–80; in 1 Peter, 180–82; in 2 Peter, 182–85; in Epistle of Jude, 185–89; in Asia, 194–200; guilds and, 200–201
Peter, 13–15, 71–72, 140–41
Petronius, 184
Phebe, 52
Philemon, 56, 57
Philip, 48, 54, 66–69, 173–74
Philippi, 111–12
Philippians hymn, 16
Philo, 283–84
Pilate, Pontius, 105
Pistis, 159–60
Plato, 280–81, 292–93
Pliny the Younger, 87, 93, 195, 235, 240
Polycarp of Smyrna: 1 Peter and, 181; 2 Peter and, 183; Jude and, 185; John and, 241, 271; veneration of, 272–73; on Resurrection, 292
Pompey the Great, 102, 230
Poor, 59–60
Praefecti, 105
Praetors, 99–100
Preterist school, 237, 246–47
Pride, 167–68
Priesthood: in early Church, 35–40, 42–53; promise of, 39; revelation and, 253–54; taken from earth, 263–64
Prisca/Priscilla, 56, 124
Prophets/prophecy, 46–48, 302–3
Ptolemy I, 227
Pure intelligence, 163

Quintilian, 185
Qumran, 59

Reconciliation model, 339–40
Redemption model, 337
Relegatio, 205–6
Rescue model, 340–41
Restoration, 252–54, 328, 331
Resurrection, 151–55, 290–98
Revelation: on Apostasy, 10; keys of, 263–64
Revelation (Book): understanding, 1–3; author of, 192–94; background of, 194–200, 210–11; apostasy and, 213–17; conclusions on, 217–20; interpretive approaches to, 237–38; dating, 238–43; modern reading of, 247–49; prophesies of Apostasy, 256, 262. *See also* Beasts of Revelation
Robinson, Stephen E., 268–69

Roma, 230–31
Roman Catholic Church, 265–66, 316
Rome: impact of Gentile conversions on, 80–81; family in, 81–86; political conditions in, 97–98; provincial system under, 98–103; Augustus and, 103–7; Paul's experiences with, 108–16; Christianity and, 116; house churches in, 125; immorality of, 184–85; forms of banishment under, 205–10, 218–19; imperial cult and, 222–23, 227–32; councils and, 315–16
Romulus, 228
Ruler cult. *See* Imperial cult
Rules of faith, 304

Sabbath, 119–20, 126
Sacra, 86
Sacrament, 18–19, 21, 121, 129
Sacrifice: meat offered as, 86–87; under imperial cult, 234
Sacrificial model, 336–37
Saints, 59
Salvation: through Jehovah, 14–15; taught in early Church meetings, 19–21; James and Paul on, 159–62; through faith and works, 258–59; Paul's message of, 332–42
Samaritans, 66–67
Satan, 163
Saul. *See* Paul
Savior, 340–41
Schiffmann, Lawrence H., 132
Scriptures, 118, 119, 127–28
Second Coming, 258
2 Corinthians, 259–60
Second Council of Constantinople, 326–27
Second Council of Nicaea, 327
2 John, 262–63
2 Peter, 182–85, 256
2 Thessalonians, 255, 258
2 Timothy, 255–56, 261
Selem, 282
Seneca, 185, 281–82
Sepphoris, 8
Septuagint, 127
Serapion, 285
Sergius Paulus, 109–10
Sermon on the Mount, 164, 180
Servilius Isauricus, 230

Seven, calling of, 54–55
Seventy, calling of, 40–41
Shaff, Philip, 324, 325
Shema, 32, 304
Sicily, 99–100
Silas, 111–12
Simon, 147
Simon Zelotes, 137
Smith, Joseph: Articles of Faith and, 35; on evangelists, 48; organization of Church and, 61–62; seeks wisdom, 166–67; Restoration and, 252–54, 331; on Bible, 265; on souls, 280; First Vision and, 300
Smith, Joseph F., 163, 296
Social networks, 88–89, 92–93
Socii, 99
Socrates, 222, 279
Sodales, 88–89, 92–93
Sōma sēma: introduction to, 276–77; heresy and, 278–79; views on, 279–84; nature of mortal Christ and, 284–90; nature of Resurrection and, 290–98; conclusions on, 298
Soul, 280–82
Spiritual body, 295–96
Stephen, 54, 66, 173
Strabo, 197
Strathearn, Gaye, 219–20
Substitution model, 337
Suetonius, 93–94, 184
Sulla, 102
Sunday, as Sabbath, 126
Synagogues: early Christian worship and, 24, 123–24; expulsion of Christians from, 25; house churches and, 117

Table fellowship, 64, 74–75, 132
Tacitus, 93–94, 239
Talmage, James E., 35–36
Tanner, N. Eldon, 164
Taxation, 100, 105
Teachers, in early Church, 49
Teaching of the Twelve Apostles, 273–74
Temple, 120, 123, 235
Terrestrial bodies, 297
Tertullian, 203, 287, 289–90, 292, 298
Thaddaeus, 41
Theodosius, 319
Thessalonica, 114
Third Council of Constantinople, 327
3 John, 263

357

Thomas, 41
Tiberius, 105, 232
Timothy, 48
Titus, 73
Titus (Book), 261
Tomb, women at, 136–37
Tongue, controlling, 164–66
Torah, 19
Trade unions, 200–201, 203–4
Trajan, 94, 186, 189–90, 235
Trials, perfection and, 162–63
Trophimus, 146

Upper room, 122

Valentinus, 287–88, 292
Verres, C., 101–2
Vespasian, 186
Vesta, 85

"The Way," 58–59
Welch, John W., 48
Widows, 53–54
Wisdom, 166–67
Witherington, Ben, 335
Witnesses, of Jesus Christ, 21
Women: as prophets, 47; rights of, 113–14; at tomb, 136–37
"The Word," 17, 289
Works: James and Paul on, 157–62, 169–70; perfection and, 162–66; wisdom and, 166–67; faith and, 258–59
Wright, N. T., 334
Written gospel, 33–34

Zeus, 84